PENGUIN BOOKS

ROANOKE

Lee Miller holds a master's degree in anthropology from Johns Hopkins University. She was head of research and a writer for the CBS-TV series *500 Nations* and a consultant for the BBC-TV series *Land of the Eagle*. She has also served as a consultant for various Indian nations, as well as for U.S. federal and state agencies, including the Library of Congress. Of Kaw heritage, she is the founder of the Native Learning Foundation and the author of *From the Heart: Voices of the American Indian*. She lives in upstate New York.

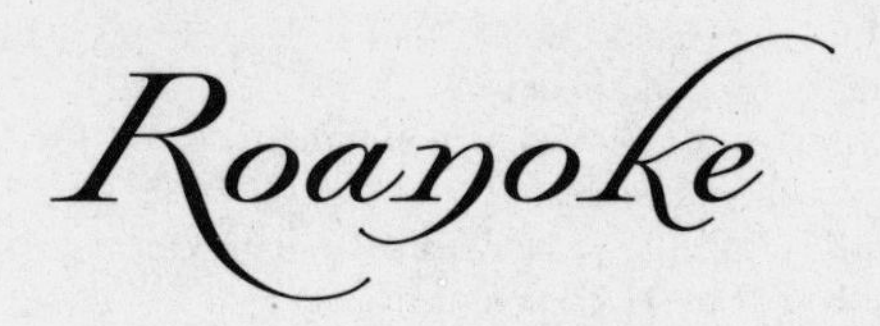

Solving the Mystery
of the Lost Colony

LEE MILLER

PENGUIN BOOKS

TO MY PARENTS
WITH LOVE

PENGUIN BOOKS
Published by the Penguin Group
Penguin Putnam Inc., 375 Hudson Street, New York, New York 10014, U.S.A.
Penguin Books Ltd, 80 Strand, London WC2R 0RL, England
Penguin Books Australia Ltd, 250 Camberwell Road,
Camberwell, Victoria 3124, Australia
Penguin Books Canada Ltd, 10 Alcorn Avenue, Toronto, Ontario, Canada M4V 3B2
Penguin Books India (P) Ltd, 11 Community Centre,
Panchsheel Park, New Delhi – 110 017, India
Penguin Books (N.Z.) Ltd, Cnr Rosedale and Airborne Roads,
Albany, Auckland, New Zealand
Penguin Books (South Africa) (Pty) Ltd, 24 Sturdee Avenue,
Rosebank, Johannesburg 2196, South Africa

Penguin Books Ltd, Registered Offices: Harmondsworth, Middlesex, England

First published in Great Britain by Jonathan Cape 2000
First published in the United States of America by Arcade Publishing, Inc. 2001
Reprinted by arrangement with Arcade Publishing
Published in Penguin Books 2002

10 9 8 7 6 5 4 3

THE LIBRARY OF CONGRESS HAS CATALOGED
THE AMERICAN HARDCOVER EDITION AS FOLLOWS:
Miller, Lee.
Roanoke : solving the mystery of the lost colony / Lee Miller. — 1st U.S. ed.
p. cm.
Includes bibliographical references and index.
ISBN 1-55970-584-1 (hc.)
ISBN 0 14 20.0228 3 (pbk.)
1. Roanoke Colony. 2. Roanoke Island (N.C.) — History — 16th century. I. Title.
F229 .M65 2001
975.6'175—dc21 20010224466

Printed in the United States of America
Set in Ehrhardt

CONTENTS

Preface vii
Acknowledgments x
Maps xii

PART ONE A CASE OF MISSING PERSONS

1 The Disappearance 3
2 A Case of Missing Persons 19
3 John White: Governor 21
4 Of London 30
5 Of Population 40
6 Of Religion 43
7 The Colonists 48
8 In Certain Danger 57

PART TWO A CASE OF MURDER

9 Sabotage 61
10 The Second Roanoke Expedition: Grenville and the Secotan (1585) 80
11 The Second Roanoke Expedition: Lane's Command (1585–1586) 97
12 Chaunis Temoatan and a Murder (1586) 110

PART THREE A CASE OF CONSPIRACY

13 The Lost Colonists (1587) 127
14 Raleigh's Rise to Power 135
15 Political Turmoil 145
16 The Players 162
17 The Motive 180
18 The Game 185
19 The Fall 192

PART FOUR WHO ARE THE MANDOAG?

20 Raleigh's Search 207
21 Jamestown 212

22 War on the Powhatan 218
23 Requiem 223
24 Deep in the Interior 227
25 Who Are the Mandoag? 238
26 Epilogue 261

Appendix A: Wingina and the Secotan 265
Appendix B: The Meaning of Mandoag and Nottoway 271
Notes and References 273
Bibliography 333
Index 353

LIST OF ILLUSTRATIONS

Sir Walter Raleigh, attributed to "H" (monogrammist), fl. 1588 *(courtesy of the National Portrait Gallery, London)*.

Detail of Whitehall stairs, from Visscher's view of London, 1616 *(copyright © The British Museum, London)*.

Elizabeth I, Armada Portrait, attributed to George Gower, from Woburn Abbey, Bedfordshire *(courtesy of W. Tyrwhitt-Drake/Bridgeman Art Library, London)*.

John White's map *(courtesy of Rare Book Division, Library of Congress, Washington, D.C.)*.

Detail from the Zúñiga map *(reproduced from* The Jamestown Voyages Under the First Charter, 1606–1609, Vol. I, *Works issued by The Hakluyt Society, second series, no. CXXXVI, London, 1969)*.

Indians fishing, by John White *(copyright © The British Museum, London)*.

Woman and child of Pomeioc, by John White *(copyright © The British Museum, London)*.

Sir Francis Walsingham, by John de Critz the Elder, c. 1555–1641 *(courtesy of the National Portrait Gallery, London)*.

William Cecil, Lord Burghley, attributed to Marcus Gheeraerts the Younger *(copyright © The Marquess of Salisbury)*.

Lord Robert Dudley, Earl of Leicester, attribute to Meulen *(copyright © The Wallace Collection; reproduced by permission of the Trustees of the Wallace Collection, London)*.

Sir Christopher Hatton, by an unknown artist, 1589 *(courtesy of the National Portrait Gallery, London)*.

PREFACE

When I first began work on this book, I intended to write a straightforward history, whose ending included a mysterious disappearance that I hoped to solve. However, I was wholly unprepared for what very rapidly emerged as three mysteries in one. It was apparent that I was dealing with a hugely complex sequence of events that did not all begin the moment 116 men, women, and children landed on Roanoke Island, subsequently to disappear without a trace. Their story was vastly more than that.

Sir Walter Raleigh said that although a prince's business is *seldom hidden from some of those many eyes which pry both into them, and into such as live about them, they yet sometimes . . . conceal the truth from all reports.* What is true of princes is also true of others, and such concealment was certainly the case with the Lost Colony tragedy. Evidence indicates that the truth about the colonists' fate was known, although misleading official statements were passed off in its place.

One great flaw in the writing of history is that we often tend to accept easy explanations of events. The job of an historian, said Raleigh, being full of *so many things to weary it, may well be excused, when finding apparent cause enough of things done, it forbeareth to make further search. . . . So comes it many times to pass, that great fires, which consume whole houses or towns, begin with a few straws that are wasted or not seen.*

This was true here. There was something wrong with the Lost Colony story as it had been told. It went like this: Sir Walter Raleigh obtained a royal patent from Queen Elizabeth I for rights to settle North America. In the spring of 1584, he launched an exploratory expedition under Captains Philip Amadas and Arthur Barlowe which located Roanoke Island before returning home that autumn. The following year, he raised a military expedition headed by Sir Richard Grenville which reached Roanoke Island in the summer, built a fort there, and remained in it until the spring of 1586. Finally, in 1587, Raleigh sent a colony of men, women, and children to the Chesapeake Bay with their governor, John White, with instructions to call at Roanoke on the way. For some reason — White's ineptitude as a leader, his preference for Roanoke Island, or unruly mariners — they went no farther than Roanoke and settled there in the abandoned military fort. Already short of supplies, White reluctantly returned to England with the transport ships. Unfortunately, his arrival in London coincided with the coming of the Spanish Armada. With England at war, he was unable to relieve the colony until 1590. When he finally did return to Roanoke, the colonists had vanished. Years later, Jamestown officials reported that the "Lost Colonists" had been murdered by the Powhatan Indians of Virginia.

This story is solidly backed by four hundred years of retelling. It is a myth created to explain glaring inconsistencies, to smooth out the rough edges of unanswered questions. Without the myth, none of the circumstances make sense. Why did John White take his colonists to Roanoke, and not to the Chesapeake Bay as planned? Why did he return to England? If not to fetch supplies, then why did he leave his colony? If not the war, then why didn't he come back? And if the Powhatan didn't kill them, then where were the Lost Colonists? The moment the accepted story is pulled away, the questions leap out, demanding answers. The moment the questions are asked, the accepted story no longer fits.

There is something unsettling about a mystery. When it involves tragedy, it is doubly so. When that tragedy is the loss of 116 people and their inexplicable disappearance, the need to find answers is compelling. When history said there was nothing left to tell, we had only scratched the surface of the puzzle. It is still possible, at this late date, to wring out the facts, to squeeze out more information, to uncover that which it was never intended we should uncover. To learn the truth. To solve a mystery.

Some will find it jarring. Raleigh himself did not write his own side of the story, though perhaps he gave us his reasons when he wrote, *I know that it will be said by many, that I might have been more pleasing to the reader if I had written the story of mine own times. . . . To this I answer that whosoever . . . shall follow truth too near the heels, it may happily strike out his teeth.*

A note about methodology is in order. The quotes used in this book date from the sixteenth and seventeenth centuries. They are interspersed within the text in a way that was intended to be as seamless as possible, but are distinguished from it by being rendered in italics. For ease in reading and to maintain a consistent style, spellings and punctuation have been modernized with the exception of personal names — which have been modernized or not according to context — and Indian names, which I left as they appeared in the original.

The story of the Lost Colony is America's oldest mystery. To tell it properly, I felt that it had to be told as a mystery, not simply as a chronological history. This allows the reader to approach the material as a series of questions, each one leading to the next, in order to preserve both a sense of discovery and a sense of the complexity of the data, which at first sight seems baffling, inexplicable, and contradictory.

Contrary to the impression generally given, clues to the Lost Colonists' whereabouts abound, although they have never been given equal value in any previous treatment of the subject. As a consequence, the mystery has not been solved. The single most important question surrounding the Lost Colonists is: Why were they left on Roanoke Island? From this question all else follows: Who was responsible for this, and why? What were the initial reports filtering into London? If the colony was in trouble, why did its governor, John White, abandon it and return to England? Do we know something about his background, or about the colonists themselves, that could explain what was happening? What does John White's own account reveal of the problem? What were the conditions on Roanoke that would explain the colonists' disappearance? What of the conflicting reports from Jamestown of Lost Colony sightings?

Question after question drives us back in time from effect to cause until we finally reach the first plateau: Why were the colonists lost? Only when we understand this, and the danger posed by Roanoke Island and its environs, can we move forward to trace what happened after their disappearance. I chose to tell this story, then, as a series of discoveries generated by key questions. The result is not a traditional history format. If it conveys, as I hope, anything of the tension and drama of the story itself, then I have succeeded.

ACKNOWLEDGMENTS

I wish to express my most sincere thanks to all those who helped to bring *Roanoke: Solving the Mystery of the Lost Colony* to fruition. A very special and heartfelt thanks to my editor Cal Barksdale and to Jeannette and Dick Seaver of Arcade. Their enthusiasm and support is unrivaled, and it is with a profound sense of gratitude and pleasure that I extend to them my warmest thanks.

At Random House, UK, I am grateful, as always, to my editor Will Sulkin and to Jörg Hensgen for their constant support and untiring efforts on my behalf. Thank you also to the rest of the team: to Sue Amaradivakara, Jenny Chapman, and Catherine Graham.

As always, Dave Kelly's patience and skill as a research librarian at the Library of Congress is indispensable, as is that of Thomas Mann. I value their efforts highly, and greatly appreciate their interest and encouragement. Many thanks also for the generous assistance of Daniel DeSimone, head of the LOC Rare Book Division, Tracy Arcaro, and Cynthia Earman.

My deepest gratitude to Kathleen Parkhurst and Larrie Bishop-Stevens of the Finger Lakes Library System Interlibrary Loan Department, without whom I could never have completed this book; to Julie Widger and Suzanne Searle of the Lamont Memorial Free Library; the staff of the Cornell University Law Library and the Carl A. Kroch Library Division of Rare and Manuscript Collections; and Syracuse University's E. S. Bird Library Special Collections and the microfilm collections of the Department of Media Services.

I would also like to extend my thanks to Vincent Brooks of the Virginia State Library in Richmond, and to Steven Case of the North Carolina State Library in Raleigh, for their valuable and willing assistance.

In Britain, I am indebted to Steve Nichols and Victoria Coules, who made it possible for me to travel to England, and whose generous offering of their time and, indeed, their home, enabled me to see sights connected with the Roanoke ventures firsthand. Thank you also to the people of Roanoke Island and the neighboring Banks — the friendships I have formed there over the years are among my very best. And to Danielle Sioui of Wendaki and Whapmagoostui, my sister and friend, who helped me sort out difficult words with great enthusiasm and care; and to many others, whom space prevents me from naming individually — university linguists in both Canada and the United States; Algonquian speakers from Big Cove, Maliotenam, Whapmagoostui, Abitibi, and Maniwaki; Audrey Shenandoah, and the multilingual translators at the Freedom School at Akwesasne.

And finally — a thank you to the Secotan, for it was you — across four hundred years of history — who lent me the insight to accomplish this work, and upon your land that I respectfully and humbly began it.

Grateful acknowledgment is made to the following for permission to reproduce copyright material: Ayer Company Publishers for extracts from David Beers Quinn, Alison M. Quinn, and Susan Hillier (ed.), *New American World: A Documentary History of North America to 1612*, New York: Arno Press and Hector Bye, 1979, reproduced by permission of Ayer Company Publishers; Folger Shakespeare Library for extracts from William Harrison, *The Description of England, Scotland and Ireland*, ed. Georges Edelen, Ithaca: Cornell University Press, 1968, reproduced by permission of the Folger Shakespeare Library; The Hakluyt Society for extracts from *The Jamestown Voyages Under the First Charter, 1606–1609* by Philip Barbour (1969), *The Original Writings and Correspondence of the Two Richard Hakluyts*, edited by Eva G. R. Taylor (1935), *The Troublesome Voyage of Captain Edward Fenton, 1582–1583* by Eva G. R. Taylor (1959), and *Further English Voyages to Spanish America, 1583–1594*, edited by Irene A. Wright (1951), all published by The Hakluyt Society; University of North Carolina Press for extracts from David Beers Quinn, *Set Fair for Roanoke: Voyages and Colonies, 1584–1606*, Chapel Hill: University of North Carolina Press, 1985, © University of North Carolina Press, used by permission of the publisher; University of Toronto Press for extracts from David Beers Quinn and Neil M. Cheshire, *The New Found Land of Stephen Parmenius*, Toronto: University of Toronto Press, 1972, reprinted with the permission of the publisher.

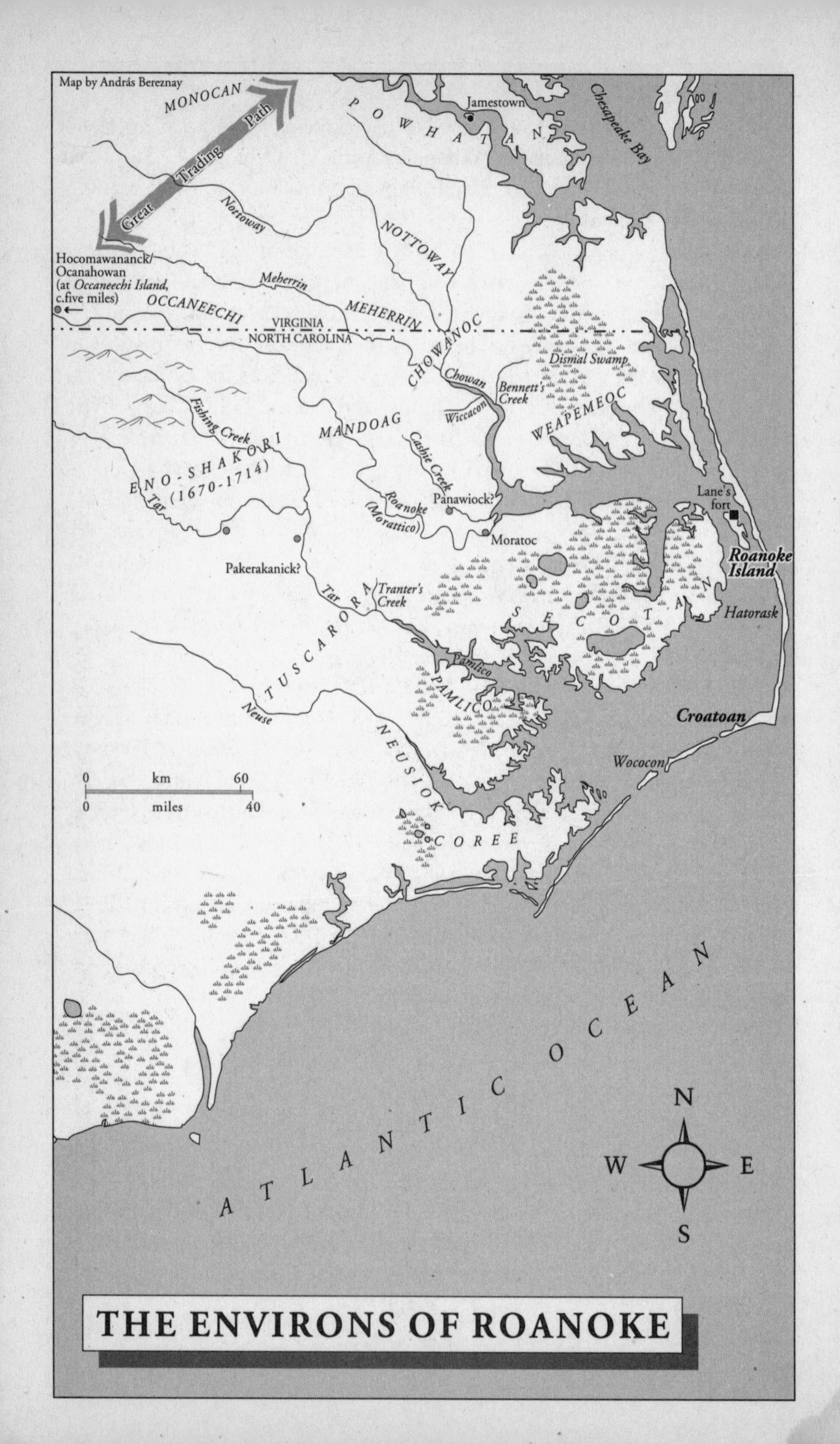

THE ENVIRONS OF ROANOKE

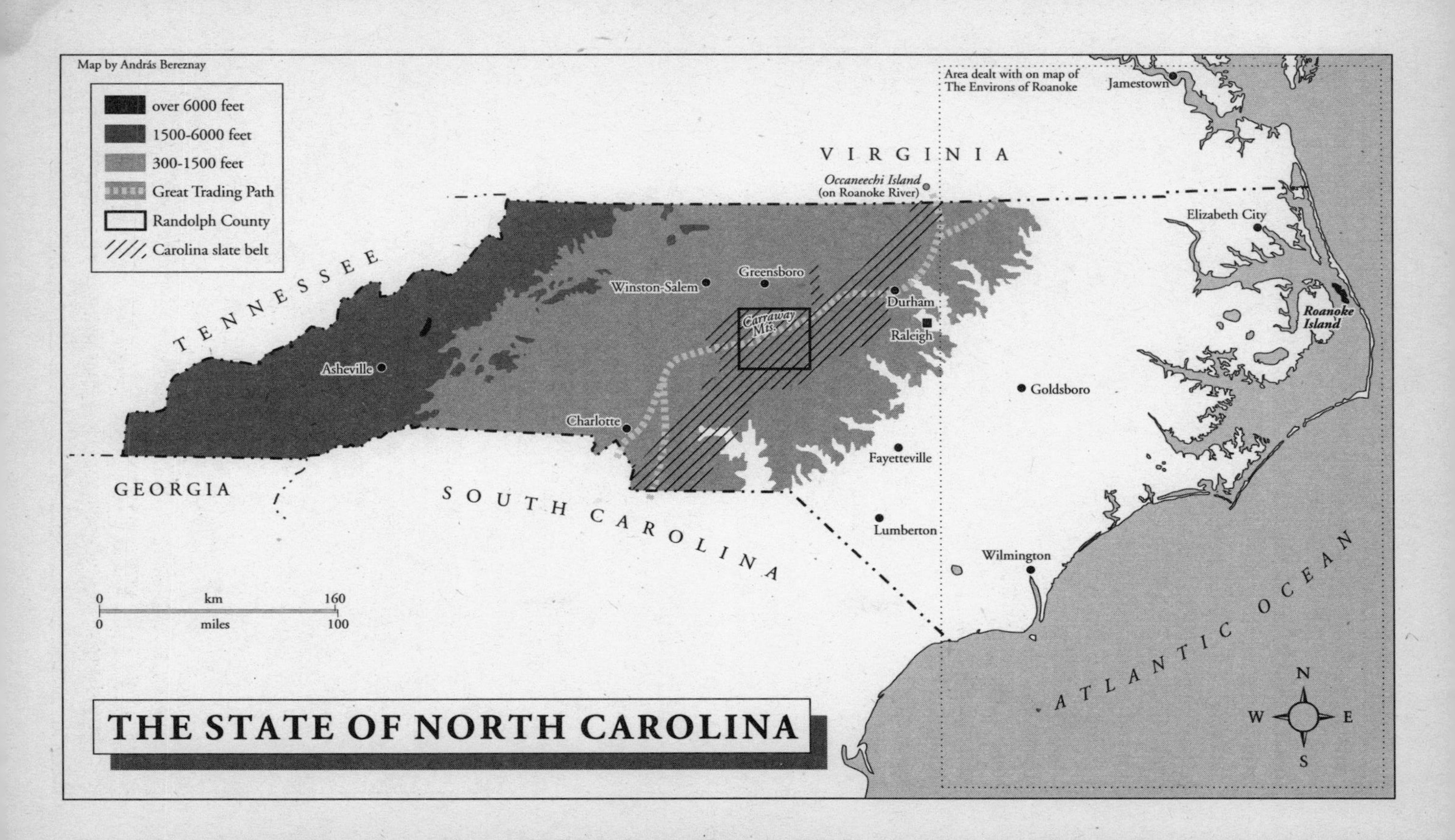
Map by András Bereznay
over 6000 feet
1500-6000 feet
300-1500 feet
Great Trading Path
Randolph County
Carolina slate belt
TENNESSEE
VIRGINIA
GEORGIA
SOUTH CAROLINA
ATLANTIC OCEAN
Area dealt with on map of The Environs of Roanoke
Jamestown
Occaneechi Island (on Roanoke River)
Elizabeth City
Roanoke Island
Winston-Salem
Greensboro
Carraway Mts.
Durham
Raleigh
Asheville
Goldsboro
Charlotte
Fayetteville
Lumberton
Wilmington
0 km 160
0 miles 100
N
W
E
S
THE STATE OF NORTH CAROLINA

PART ONE

A CASE OF MISSING PERSONS

1 THE DISAPPEARANCE

Roanoke Island, North America—July 1587. A mystery is unfolding. One hundred and seventeen people have landed on a remote island off the North American coast. The men, women, and children, sent out by Sir Walter Raleigh, are the first English colonists in America. Despite the care taken for their safety, the explicit instructions, the plans for provisions, all will vanish. The only known survivor will be their Governor, John White—an artist and veteran of Raleigh's previous Roanoke expeditions. He had known, from the moment they landed, that they could not survive on Roanoke Island.

The commander of the ship that brought them there reported nothing amiss. In the weeks before he left them, the colonists had begun to repair the houses of an abandoned English fort. New cottages were constructed of brick and tile,[1] and on August 18, White's daughter Eleanor and husband Ananias Dare became the parents of a baby girl. Christened Virginia, she was the first English child born in North America. Several days later, another celebration. A boy was delivered to Dyonis and Margery Harvie.[2]

And yet the ship's captain was mistaken, for something *was* wrong. Terrible events had been set in motion from which there would be no escape. No one on the island knew what form it would take or when it would strike. Defenseless and impotent, they could only wait. In one of the last glimpses we have of them, it has already begun: colonist George Howe has been found dead, floating facedown among the reeds along the shore. With time running out, an envoy is urgently dispatched for help to the neighboring Secotan nation through an Indian liaison named Manteo. There is no response.

August 27. At the height of the turmoil John White abruptly abandons the island. He leaves behind his daughter Eleanor, her baby Virginia, relatives and close friends, and sails back to England, pledging to return within three months. It is a promise he fails to keep.

A Four-Hundred-Year-Old Mystery

From the moment John White left Roanoke, no European laid eyes on the colonists again. He had vowed to rescue them within three months. Yet it was 1590, *three years later,* and after the opportunity to save them had been lost, before White finally returned . . . and found no one. The colonists were gone and the island deserted. The fort, partially dismantled, lay empty. Everything marking where people had been: houses — boards, nails and all; belongings; supplies; weapons — had vanished without trace.

Years after the tragedy, when the English were permanently settled in North America, tantalizing signs of the colony surfaced. Strange sightings were reported in Virginia and again in North Carolina, in areas widely separated. Search parties dispatched from Jamestown combed swamps and unexplored rivers, offering only hints and incomplete fragments. There were rumors and clues. Some genuine, others hoaxes.[3]

For four hundred years the disappearance of the Lost Colony has remained a mystery. There is a reason why: it has never been examined as a crime. If it had, it would have been apparent from the beginning that much more was involved than a simple case of missing persons. It is still possible to solve the crime — if only we unravel the clues.

John White's Letter

In the beginning few people in England were told that the colony was missing. Although White's failed rescue mission was disclosed to Raleigh in the autumn of 1590, it was not until the winter of 1593 — three years after his attempt to rejoin his family — that White composed a letter to geographer and historian Richard Hakluyt, detailing the sad events.[4] It appeared to be a farewell letter; afterward, White seemingly vanished. Seven years later it was published:

4 *February* 1593

To the worshipful and my very friend Master Richard Hakluyt, much happiness in the Lord.

Sir, as well for the satisfying of your earnest request, as the performance of my promise made unto you at my last being with you in England, I have sent you . . . the true discourse of my last voyage into the

West Indies, and parts of America called Virginia, taken in hand about the end of February, in the year of our redemption 1590. And what events happened unto us in this our journey, you shall plainly perceive by the sequel of my discourse. . . .

The Discourse

March 20, 1590. Three ships put to sea from Plymouth harbor in Devon: the flagship *Hopewell,* Captain Abraham Cocke, commander, the *Little John* under the direction of Captain Christopher Newport, and the consort *John Evangelist.* In tow are two shallops, small shallow-water boats, vitally important to John White aboard the flagship. In fact, they are the only hope he has of ever seeing his family again.

It has been three years since he left them on Roanoke Island, alone and without supplies. The moment of departure still painful: the memory of parting sorrows, of Eleanor, trembling between hope and despair, clinging to Ananias and their baby, Virginia. White's eyes lingering upon them, huddled on shore, blurring out of range. Angry at the tiny island receding in the distance, a speck against the wilds of a vast, unknown land.

Raleigh had selected Roanoke for its inaccessibility. A jagged sliver of island, caressed by a sheet of water thin as tissue paper.[5] The sound is so shallow, in fact, that only light craft, buoyant as eggshells, can float upon it. Not warships. Beyond it, the Atlantic rages against miles of unyielding barrier islands. Sand-dune sentinels pressing hard against the sea. Hiding the coast. Its unforgiving shoals and bars forcing shipping into the safety of the open road beyond this Skeleton Coast.[6] Impatiently rolling with the waves.

The only way to reach Roanoke is by coaxing small vessels through the treacherous channels to skitter, butterfly-like, into the protected sounds. White eyes the shallops anxiously as they trail behind the *Hopewell* on his heart's lifeline, too little attention paid them *by the boatswaine's negligence.* Five days out they sink.

John White must wonder what he is doing here. After *daily and continual petitions,* he at last has secured passage on these privateering vessels bound for the West Indies and *absolutely determined* for Spanish riches. In point of fact, they are pirate ships, but for the legal distinction of bearing a license from the Queen. All three vessels are outfitted under the *special charge* of the celebrated John Watts of London. *Master* John

Watts, *merchant.* The Spaniards know him differently. They will tell you he is the notorious John Watts, *greatest pirate* on the high seas.[7] It is the best ride that White can get if he wishes to reach Roanoke.

Twelve days out the *Hopewell* encounters a London merchantman, and two *shipboats* are purchased to replace the *loss of our shallops.* The convoy must intend them to pull double duty in prizetaking; otherwise White might not have expected such good treatment. His relief must be tempered by that fact.

The West Indies

By April's end, after a skirmish off the Canary Islands, the expedition reaches the Caribbean. The *Hopewell* and *John Evangelist* strike out alone, leaving the *Little John* plying off Dominica *hoping to take some Spaniard outward bound to the Indies.* Without her, they glide past Guadeloupe and St. Kitts. The Spaniards report *many corsairs* about, who *are bold.*[8] The voyage, which has made good time crossing the Atlantic, now slows down, and down again. Tracing serpentine paths through the islands. Searching for plunder.

Past *the Virgines,* through the milky blue water of *the Passage,* the *Hopewell* and *John Evangelist* approach Puerto Rico. The Spaniards see them, and know what they see. *They discerned us to be men of war.* Fires glimmer across the darkened, wave-lapped shoreline as the ships pick their way along, *for so their custom is,* notes White, whenever warships are observed *on their coasts.* He is no closer to Roanoke.

Patrolling the northern end of the island, the *Hopewell* captures a Spanish frigate hailing from Guantanamo, Cuba, *laden with hides and ginger.*[9] While they unload her, a man escapes. He is *Pedro,* a *Mulatto.* An evil turn. He carries with him knowledge of *all our state.* Whether or not he talks to the Spanish authorities hardly matters: on the southern tip of Puerto Rico the *John Evangelist* does.

From his headquarters, Governor Diego Menendez de Valdés composes a hurried letter to the Spanish Crown. Reporting, in blotched ink, the English ship's presence, armament, and munitions. More importantly, he relays crucial information gathered from an unguarded word spoken by the crew. The English ship *was going,* the Governor noted pointedly, *to Florida to take off 200 English cast away there.*[10]

Here, at last, is tangible evidence of a permanent English settlement which the Spaniards have long suspected, and dreaded. Search parties had combed the coast for it, sending alarming reports across the Atlantic. Yet its location remained elusive. Roanoke was too well hidden. In 1588, Captain Vicente Gonzalez was dispatched to scour the eastern seaboard of North America and, though he came up empty-handed, he made a significant discovery: on the Carolina Outer Banks, he spotted a slipway for vessels, English casks sunk into the sand, debris.[11] The Spaniards did not find the colony, but Gonzalez narrowed the field considerably. And now the English Governor rides off the Puerto Rican coast, a passenger in a pirate ship that shows little sign of leaving. Valdés sinks pen into ink and hurriedly notifies Spain.

As far as John White is concerned, circumstances are completely altered. If he had been anxious to reach Roanoke before, he is doubly so now. Spain will swiftly mount an investigation. With frantic urgency, he realizes they must reach the Carolina coast before the Spaniards beat them to it. Spain, aware of *all our state.* But Watts's ships are in no hurry, and the futility of White's situation is made painfully clear. If only, he said, *my daily and continual petitions* to keep their promise had *taken any place.*

Sea Fight

Days slip into weeks. The ships *lay off and on* the islands, *hoping to take some of the Domingo Fleet:* the treasure-carrying galleons. There is sporadic action, small skirmishes. Nothing lost, nothing gained. Reports stream in to Spanish officials from all quarters of the Caribbean. English corsairs are about. *The shamelessness of these English ships* soon reaches the powerful Audiencia of the Council of the Indies. From Havana, it is reported that the *Hopewell* and her consorts have *seized or chased every vessel entering or leaving the harbour.*[12] And then word of depredations arrives from Jamaica: the long-awaited Santo Domingo fleet was sighted and attacked.

The English are jubilant. But who could have predicted the awful irony? The commander of the Santo Domingo fleet is none other than Vicente Gonzalez. Intelligence gathered from his crews, captured and released by the *Hopewell,* enables the Spanish authorities to renew the search for Roanoke with vigor. In Havana, depositions are taken. Antonio de la Mata reports the English colony to be *in Florida, in a certain harbour.* The *Hopewell* carries a civilian passenger bound for this place. Deponent Blas Lopez confirms this, testifying that *they had a governor* aboard, and he is *to be left in the settlement they have made in Florida, whither they will go for that purpose.*[13]

But will they? The days are fast dwindling. July fades into August. John White must be aware of the calculations. In order to recross the Atlantic for England before winter, the *Hopewell* must depart from the Outer Banks by August's end. It is now almost too late to reach Roanoke. Reluctantly the *Hopewell* heads north as the year enters the peak hurricane season.[14] The crew *too wholly disposed themselves,* White bitterly writes, *to seek after purchase & spoils, spending so much time therein, that summer was spent before we arrived at Virginia.*

The Outer Banks

August 1. Foul weather amid *much rain, thundering, and great spouts.* The ships are buffeted by gales that last for days. Sails are hauled in and the slick, water-choked decks roll with every pitch and heave. At nightfall on the third day, the *Hopewell* lies north of Cape Fear approaching the southern Banks. But still *the weather continued so exceeding foul that we could not come to an anchor.* A week slides by.

August 10. Finally, *Monday, the storm ceased.* A welcome relief, but small progress is made. On the evening of the twelfth, they are forced to anchor at the northeast end of Croatoan Island on account of a *breach which we perceived to lie out two or three leagues into the sea.*[15] The following morning, the shallops are sent out to *sound over this breach.* Lead casts slice through ocean swells, sinking heavily through the water; White waiting anxiously as the readings come back *deepening and shallowing for the space of two miles.* There is no map of the shoals to guide them; he must pray the ships will not abandon the effort. *Sometimes we found 5 fathoms, and by and by 7, and within two casts with the lead 9, & then 8, next cast 5, & then 6, & then 4, & then 9 again, and deeper.* In the distance waves crest over the reef *out of the main sea into the inner waters.*

At last the *Hopewell* breaks free. August 15, *towards evening,* the long-anticipated moment arrives. Capstans moan as the anchors unwind and grind fast. They have reached Hatorask Island.[16] Ahead lies Port Ferdinando, a break in the barrier island chain. And through it, in the distance, White glimpses Roanoke.

Three long years have passed since White last stood here. Years of struggle, years of bitter disappointment. In his mind's eye, he relives that awful day, the air nauseatingly warm, an image of a vividly colored dress, the hem trailing across wet sand and foam, swaying to the motion of Eleanor's hand. White lingers on deck. His granddaughter, Virginia, will be three years old. Suddenly, he is jarred from his reverie. Heart pounding, he observes *a great smoke rise* on the island *near the place where I left our colony in the year 1587*. The *Hopewell* has been sighted! *Which smoke put us in good hope that some of the colony were there expecting my return out of England.* Three years too late.

Fires and False Hope

The next morning — one wonders if White has slept at all — the boats are readied and *we commanded* the master gunner to prepare artillery: two minions and a falcon, *and to shoot them off with reasonable space between every shot, to the end that their reports might be heard to the place where we hoped to find some of our people.*

Nerves jangling, White steps into a shore boat, the planking bowing under his feet. It all seems so unreal. Sailors crowd the deck above, blocking out the sun, shouting as the vessel is lowered into the sea. White steadying himself as the bottom smacks the water. In muted understatement, he says only that Captains Cocke and Spicer *& their company with me* pull away from the ships.

Shots rocket out from the *Hopewell,* cracking the air with their report, startling seabirds into flight. Before White is halfway to shore, *we saw another great smoke to the southwest of Kindrikers Mounts.* Was it a signal?[17] Discussion follows. Kenricks Mounts lay on the island of Hatorask, in the opposite direction from Roanoke.[18] Yet if someone has heard their report, if the shallops have truly been seen, then far better to go *to that second smoke first.* A detour. The boats are beached on the island and the men work their way south on foot through sand and scrub, the way proving *much farther than they think.* Hopelessly so. A wafting mirage tantalizingly out of reach. Each step an eternity, *so that we were very sore tired before* — at last — *we came to the smoke.* But when they came abreast of it, *that which grieved us more* was the utter disappointment of finding . . . absolutely nothing. Only a smoldering fire; *we found no man nor sign that any had been there lately.* And, worse still, *nor yet any fresh water in all this way to drink.*

In his haste, White has been understandably careless. In addition to carrying no water he has lost another valuable day. The men retrace their steps to the boats only to find the sailors lugging empty water casks ashore. The operation has just begun: the crew will not stop midway. Thus, *wearied,* the party has little choice but to head back to the *Hopewell,* and *so we deferred our going to Roanoke until the next morning.*

Unfortunate Accident

The following morning, already *being the 17 of August,* the company is *prepared again to go up to Roanoke.* But then another complication, another needless delay. Captain Spicer* has chosen this moment to send *his boat ashore for fresh water,* tying up both time and vessel, *by means whereof it was ten of the clock aforenoon before we put from our ships.* Stinging disappointment gives way to frustration. Half the morning spent and White still powerless; only this time, cruelly, within very sight of Roanoke. His anxiety is apparent after Spicer's return when, rather than wait any longer, he impatiently strikes out alone. His party *halfway toward the shore* before *Captain Spicer* put off from his ship.[19]

As they near Port Ferdinando, the breach is clearly visible. Water rushes over shoals, forming a churning, sand-choked course. Too much water. And now White sees that the morning's delay was costly, for the tide is high; the channel transformed into a tumbling cauldron. To make matters worse, a stiff wind blows from the northeast *direct into the harbour so great a gale,* that the *sea break extremely on the bar.* High seas crash one into another *and the tide went very forceably at the entrance.*

There is nothing to be done but brave it. White's boat surges headlong into the breach, *not without some danger of sinking.* A sea crests over it, which *filled us half full of water.* They frantically pull on the oars, the boat reeling, nearly capsizing. The captain wrenches the vessel around before the next wave. A wild ride; but they are spared, thank Heaven, *by the will of God* and the careful steering of Captain Cocke. The shallop grinds against the sand on Hatorask Island and is *hauled ashore,* safe; though clothing, food, and shot are *much wet and spoiled.* Another lengthy delay; *most of our things are taken out to dry.*

From the security of the shore, White's company watches as Captain Spicer's boat makes its approach into the breach. And then a mistake. They have entered it wrongly, leaving the *mast standing up.* Utter silence as the men watch tensely. The boat is still negotiating well. They are halfway across and have almost made it when suddenly, *by the rash and indiscreet*

*Edward Spicer was captain of the *Moonlight,* the *Hopewell*'s consort.

steerage of Ralph Skinner his master's mate, the boat warps broadside into a swell. Rocked off balance, *a very dangerous sea break into their boat and overset them quite.* A shocking accident; horrible to witness. Sailors cling to the boat, *some hanging on it,* but the next sea bludgeons it hard onto the bar, forcing them to release their hold. Some stagger to their feet, *hoping to wade ashore,* but the sea *beat them down, so that they could neither stand nor swim, and the boat twice or thrice was turned keel upward.* The hull arcs into the air, Captain Spicer and his mate Skinner dangling helplessly from it *until they sunk* and are *seen no more.* Like many sailors, they cannot swim.

Captain Cocke, as *soon as he saw their oversetting, stripped himself, and four others that could swim very well reached them, & saved four.* But no more. There is a somber accounting of the dead. Those swallowed by the breach *were 11 in all, & 7 of the chiefest were drowned, whose names were Edward Spicer, Ralph Skinner, Edward Kelley, Thomas Bevis, Hance the Surgeon, Edward Kelborne, Robert Coleman.*

The death of Robert Coleman must grieve White greatly. A hook thrust into the pit of his stomach. For Robert Coleman is a civilian passenger. Not a sailor. Like White, he has come because his family is here. A Thomas Colman and wife were among the colonists of 1587.[20] To find them, Robert Coleman put up a valiant fight.

The accident triggers an unforeseen reaction among the sailors. *This mischance,* the death of Spicer's crew, *did so much discomfort the sailors, that they were all of one mind not to go any farther to seek the planters.* Another blow to White. He desperately informs them that they must and will go. Roanoke, he points, is just over there. They gape at him, these rough and burly sailors, wild with fear, and then at the wind-chopped surface of the broad sound. Roanoke lies within view, White shouts. The breach has been crossed, they must and will go! In *the end* and after the loss of much precious time, *by the commandment and persuasion of me and Captain Cook* [Captain Abraham Cocke], *they prepared the boats.* But not without misgiving. Until, *seeing the Captain and me so resolute, they seemed much more willing.* There is no turning back.

Roanoke

The day is quickly fading. Spicer's boat is righted and, with *19 persons in both boats,* they push into the water as the sun begins its descent, coloring the trees a rich, golden hue. Progress is slow, the water confronting the bow like cement. An hour passes. And another. The sun dips lower.

Eventually the whisper of dusk calms the chop as the wind dies away. Imparting a tranquillity to the shore, a softening of edges. Seabirds alight on the glassy water and nestle in, sleepily regarding the boats as they pass. In all this way, the crew has seen no one.

At last, Roanoke looms ahead, dark and forbidding. Night grips the island in a smothering hold. Drawing the boats toward the northern shore along a rim of gloomy foliage, the men make another mistake; for it had grown *so exceeding dark, that we overshot the place a quarter of a mile.* They have gone too far.

Like thieves, they steal back along the shoreline. The night air breathing warm and damp. They have barely turned around when a light glimmers across the water in the direction they had just been, *toward the north end of the island.* Again they reverse course and immediately row toward it, perceiving it to be a *great fire through the woods.* Wafting the pungent aroma of loblolly pine. Adrift in the warm sound, the men stop and listen. And are met with profound silence. Droplets trickle from the oars, spreading quiet ripples across water ruddy from the glow. Receding into darkness. Rivulets pool into the boat down the length of the wood.

Noise. White springs into action. They need noise. Someone on shore must be made to hear them! *We sounded with a trumpet, a call.* He quickly commands them to sing, anything; sing anything! Sea chanties, folk songs, ballads. And they do, chortling *many familiar English tunes of songs.* There is only silence. White shouts into the night. The crew joins him, a chorus of voices, *and called to them friendly.* Darkness all around. Disappointment rings in White's voice: *we had no answer.* With sinking spirits, the men give up and hunker down in the boats for the night.

Message from the Colonists

August 18. A red sun emerges from the sound in a bleeding mist, piercing the treetops. In the shallops, White's company is already awake. Stumbling ashore, they press through the woods to a smoking clearing, the fire of the previous night now smothered except for patches of *grass and sundry rotten trees burning about the place.* But nothing else. No people. No encampment. Like Hatorask, no sign of life anywhere. Another illusion.

Reeling from this disappointment, White plunges back through the brush to the shore, advancing around the north end of the island, *until we came to the place where I left our colony.* Three years ago. The entire route *by the water side* littered with footprints *of 2 or 3 sorts, trodden that night.* Disconcerting proof that at least someone in the darkness — several people — had been watching. Who hadn't come forward in friendship. White pushes ahead, the sailors following. Out of their element.

Scrambling up a sandy bank, White cries out. He has found something, an astounding discovery. Cut into a tree, *in the very brow thereof, were curiously carved these fair Roman letters: CRO.*

None of the company knows what it means. Nor can anyone be sure when it was written. The inscription, says White, was *well considered.* To all appearances, CRO spells nothing. No decipherable word. No hidden meaning. The message, indeed, remains obscure; but curiously, amid the excitement, White alone shows no surprise. He alone knows why it is here. The colonists carved the mysterious message into the tree because he had instructed them to do so.

Fifty Miles into the Main

It is a startling revelation. To explain himself fully, White would have to recount what had happened on Roanoke in 1587. The unexpected death of George Howe. The danger in which he left the colonists. The crime that had been committed: the reason for his leaving. Instead, he reveals only that they had considered relocating. At the time of *my last departure from them,* he says, they were *prepared to remove from Roanoke 50 miles into the main.*

Seized with dread that he would be unable to find them when he returned, they devised a plan, *a secret token agreed upon between them & me.* A way of ensuring a reunion *which was, that in any ways they should not fail to write or carve on the trees or posts of the doors the name of the place where they should be seated.*

But there is more, in this age of cyphers and riddles: *I willed them, that if they should happen to be distressed in any of those places, that they should carve over the letters or name, a cross ✠ in this form.* So that he would be assured of their condition, with no doubt about their state. White runs an anxious hand over the bark, where were *carved these fair Roman letters: CRO.* But no cross — *we found no such sign of distress.*

A Settlement Vanished

They are wasting time. Hoping for a better clue, White races toward the settlement clearing, where the colonists dwelt three years ago *in sundry houses,* the men scrambling after him. But as they enter the compound, he stops short, stunned. For before him is . . . *nothing at all.* There are no carvings on the door posts, for there are no doors anywhere. No doors, no houses, no sheds, no buildings; not a lock, not a board, not a nail. A bare clearing, void of life. As though the colonists had never been.

A chill sweeps over White, constricting his heart. Everything gone . . . but one thing. In the center of the compound is a high wooden palisade, artificially constructed of trees *with curtains and flankers very fort-like.* The place where the houses stood is curiously surrounded by it, *strongly enclosed.* White has never seen it before. There is no explanation for it. Not a soul here.

CRO. White stands amazed. He had not expected this. Without a more complete message, there is no way to determine where the colonists are. A rising panic. CRO is meaningless! And then he sees it: on *one of the chief trees or posts at the right side of the entrance* to the palisade, where the bark is scraped away. There, five feet from the ground, *in fair capital letters was graven CROATOAN.* Bold, prominent characters etched deeply into the wood, and — incredibly, wonderfully! — *without any cross or sign of distress.*

At last, the tension of three years' struggle, of months risking life and limb at sea aboard the *Hopewell,* all the danger and uncertainty and upset, releases in a flood. *Croatoan. He knows where they are. CRO.* Perhaps the men allow White a respectful moment alone, or perhaps they crowd around him in open jubilation. He has come so very far to be here.

Clues

Inside the palisade the men locate a few remaining items. Bars of iron, lead casts, four iron fowlers, iron sacker shot *and such like heavy things* in disarray, *thrown here and there, almost overgrown with grass and weeds.* Clues. *Heavy things* not easily transported. *Heavy things* — weapons — and that is all.

Leaving the sailors to search the grounds, White and Captain Cocke inspect *the point of the creek to see if we could find any of their boats or pin-*

nace, but we could perceive no sign of them. Nor of their armaments — the falcons and small ordnance — *which were left with them.* The picture is far from clear.

Meanwhile, there has been a discovery. *Some of our sailors meeting us, told us that they had found where divers chests had been hidden, and long since* dug up. The chests themselves are *broken up, and much of their goods spoiled and scattered about, but nothing left, of such things as the savages knew any use of, undefaced.*

White is shown the place, *in the end of an old trench, made two years past by Captain Amadas.* Odd he should say two years past — he really means five. The trench was dug in 1585. Five years ago. In his recounting of events, is White harkening back to the summer of 1587, when he was last here with his family? As though time had stopped then? It must seem incredible, now, as he gazes around, at this place where his house once stood, where his daughter Eleanor gave birth to her child, and they baptized her Virginia Dare. Where the people of Dasamonquepeuc and Croatoan once came in friendship, and he painted their portraits and knew them by name. Back when the future held dreams. The sailors pick over grounds that to them present such novelty.

White can only go through the motions now, his memory cluttered with old familiar scenes. *We found five chests, that had been carefully hidden of the planters, and of the same chests three were my own, and about the place many of my things spoiled and broken. . . .* He stares at them burst open in the trench, the spilled watercolors streaked with rain. Remembering the time, three years ago, when he had worried about their safety. Standing before the colonists and knowing *they intended to remove 50 miles further up into the main,* he had expressed fear that *his stuff and goods might be both spoiled, and most of it pilfered away.* They had assured him that his effects would not be harmed.

They had tried their best, burying the chest in the trench. White sifts through his belongings, *spoiled and broken.* What pains him most are not the objects he once thought valuable, but the items he can never replace, *my books torn from the covers, the frames of some of my pictures and maps rotten and spoiled with rain, and my armour almost eaten through with rust.* But possessions no longer matter. For *although it much grieved me to see such spoil of my goods, yet on the other side I greatly joyed that I had safely found a certain token of their safe being at Croatoan, which is the place where Manteo was born,* the people *of the island our friends.*

The Storm

There is nothing more to be seen. An empty compound bearing the imprint of lives once lived; a palisade; a few pictures, spoiled by rain. The men turn away, reboarding the shallops. But the misfortune that has dogged the rescue thus far continues unabated. Clouds scud across the sun and a wind picks up, raising a chop on the sound. Rowing *with as much speed as we could,* they push toward the sea, brine spraying from the bows, perspiration clinging stubbornly in the clammy air, portending a storm. The atmosphere is drenched, alive with electricity; all indications are *very likely that a foul and stormy night would ensue.* At Port Ferdinando, the channel roils higher than before, the ocean heaving and alive. Devourer of eleven men, hungering for more.

It is not until evening, *and with much danger and labour, we got ourselves aboard the ships, by which time the wind and seas were greatly risen, that we doubted our cables and anchors would scarcely hold until morning.* The *Hopewell* breaks free, abandoning water casks on shore, impossible to retrieve *without danger of casting away both men and boats.* Night passes fitfully, the ships plunging in the mounting swells.

The next morning, despite the weather, Captain Cocke agrees to set a course for the island of Croatoan, *where our planters were,* since the wind at least *was good for that place.* The anchor draws in with a shriek, fighting the sea. A cable snaps. The anchor spins away, taking a second down with it. Untethered, the ship drives *fast into the shore.* Toward the shoals.

The Captain barks orders to release the third anchor, *which came so fast home that the ship was almost aground by Kenricks Mounts: so that we were forced to let slip the cable end for end.* By accident, sheer luck, they fall into a channel of deep water and avoid being dashed to pieces on the bar. Otherwise, *we could never have gone clear of the point that lies to the southwards of Kenricks Mounts.*

Safe for the moment, *but not without some loss.* Only one anchor remains of an original four, and *the weather grew to be fouler and fouler; our victuals scarce and our cask and fresh water lost.* The near miss works a sobering influence. Willing enough to court disaster privateering, the *Hopewell*'s crew does not dare risk Croatoan.[21]

Reckless Wager

Knowing the Spanish treasure fleet will sail for Europe in the spring, White salvages plans, desperately begging the captains to reconnoiter in the Caribbean *either at Hispaniola, Saint John, or Trinidad, that then we should continue in the Indies all the winter following, with hope to make two rich voyages of one.*[22] Counting on the *Hopewell*'s greed to supply the will. A reckless wager. If God would only protect White another six months before *our return to visit our countrymen at Virginia.* His personal feelings bitter. Not enough time had been allotted for the search. The crew *regarding very smally the good of their countrymen* — his family, his daughter! — *determined nothing* more than merely *to touch at those places* where he might have found them.

Having urged his proposal *with earnest petitions,* White agonizingly awaits the decision. Aware that this will be his last chance to see his family again. The minutes tick by. Certain considerations are weighed: additional time spent away from England and the cost of refitting the ships for the winter, against the possibility of capturing a Spanish ship off guard, the potential for *purchase and spoils.* The odds are too great for the *Moonlight.* Her men decline, claiming a *weak and leaky ship.* They head back for England. The strain taking its toll on White as the *Hopewell* considers her options. Finally, *the captain and the whole company of the* Hopewell, *(with my earnest petitions), thereunto agreed.* They will winter in the West Indies. A course is charted for Trinidad, in the face of a rising sea.

Hurricane

There are times when the ocean seems uncannily human. Ask any sailor, and he will recount for you its many changing moods. Coy, playful, slumbering. Fierce. But worse than these is a rising sea, neither one thing nor the other. Frightening in its indecision. The sailor shudders, for deep down, far beneath the grim surface, he can feel the forces gathering. The energy and fury of the universe flowing together, coiling up tightly, twisting into a pounding tension. Explosively released.

August 28 it happens. The wind shifts. John White should have sensed the sea was against him from the first. The storm blasts up off the Carolina coast from out of nowhere, ushered in by a relentless booming that sounds like cannon. A wild storm, full of malice and greed. Howling winds buffet the ship, coiling the sails around the masts. The thundering gusts swirl from southwest to west and northwest. Wrenching the *Hopewell* away from its destination. A hail of lightning spikes pounds the sea with the noise of war. Captain Cocke braces above deck, roaring commands at his men, battling the sea.

He loses. Routed by the wind, the *Hopewell* is forced east in a direct line with the Azores. Away from the eye of the storm. White fervently praying, willing the captains to reoutfit then depart anew for the Indies or Virginia. While there is still time.

White Is Finished

At Flores in the Azores the *Moonlight* is spotted riding with four English men-of-war. A surprise. The leaky hull only an excuse to rejoin the fray, dodging inactive duty at Roanoke. News is had, too, of the long-absent *Little John,* left behind in the Caribbean months before. Its Captain, Christopher Newport, sports a gaping hole where his arm had once been. The limb *striken off* in a skirmish.[23] The West Indies would have been no safe place for White to winter. And all the while, the enemy sea and her ally the wind continue to play havoc with his plans, preventing a landing for provisions at St. George in the Azores. The *Hopewell* finally surrenders and sets a course for England.

October. *Saturday the 24. We came in safety, God be thanked, to an anchor at Plymouth.* The voyage is over. White's last chance to contact the planters has come and gone.

> *Thus may you plainly perceive the success of my fifth and last voyage to Virginia, which was no less unfortunately ended than forwardly begun, and as luckless to many, as sinister to myself. But I would to God it had been as prosperous to all, as noisome to the planters; & as joyful to me, as discomfortable to them. Yet seeing it is not my first crossed voyage, I remain contented. And wanting my wishes, I leave off from prosecuting that whereunto I would to God my wealth were answerable to my will. Thus committing the relief of my discomfortable company the planters in Virginia, to the merciful help of the Almighty, whom I most humbly beseech to help and comfort them, according to his most Holy will and their good desire, I take my leave from my house at Newtowne in Kylmore the 4 of February, 1593.*
>
> *Your most well wishing friend,*
>
> *John White*

2 A CASE OF MISSING PERSONS

Historians will leave it recorded to succeeding Ages, that the bright sun-shining and glorious days of England under Queen Elizabeth ended in a foul, cloudy and dark evening, yea in an eternal night. (Posterity . . . will impute the mass and heap of future calamities not so much to the adversaries' malice, as to the gross carelessness of these times.)

Courtiers to Elizabeth I, 1587[1]

The Investigation Begins

What we have is a case of missing persons on such a scale that it confounds the senses. An entire *town* is missing! One hundred and fifteen people — gone — from the tiny coastal island of Roanoke.* Without a trace. Our task is to try to make sense of it. First: Why have they disappeared? Second: Where are they? And eventually, from the evidence, a third, and chilling, question: Why have they remained lost?

At this point, however, it is not clear that a crime has even been committed. Governor John White saw his colonists settled on Roanoke. When he returned three years later, they were gone. These facts are from his word alone. Upon this foundation we will build our investigation.

The First Suspect

White's own behavior is somewhat suspect. It is clear that something had gone very wrong on Roanoke in 1587. Something that left the colonists wholly unprepared. In fact, for reasons we do not yet understand, they were in trouble. And yet White's action in the face of this apparent danger was to abandon the colony. Why would the Governor, the person most directly responsible for the welfare of the group, be the first to leave? And why, if they were safe at Croatoan three years later, did no

*Throughout this book, 117 is the number of the original colonists; 116 indicates the missing colonists without John White, who returned to England; and 115 the colonists minus John White and George Howe, who died before White's departure.

one come forward to meet the rescue ships? Especially since there was ample time to do so? How likely is it that the *Hopewell* went undetected? After all, she was firing cannon. There may be more here than meets the eye. Is White, in fact, guilty of a crime?

Not according to his own testimony. He alleges that it was not his decision to leave, but that *the whole company, assistants and planters, came to* him and *with one voice requested him to return himself into England.* Anticipating recriminations back in London, he initially refused to go and steadfastly *alleged many sufficient causes why he would not.* Not least among his fears was the scandal of public opinion, realizing that *he could not so suddenly return back again, without his great discredit, leaving the action, and so many, whom he partly had procured through his persuasions, to leave their native country, and undertake that voyage.*[2]

Curiously, and most significantly, his concerns appear concrete. There would seem to be specific, unnamed individuals *enemies to him, and the action,* who wish to poison his name and *would not spare to slander falsely both him, and the action, by saying he went to Virginia but politicly, and to no other end but to lead so many into a country in which he never meant to stay himself, and there to leave them behind.*[3]

These arguments sound convincingly personal, though admittedly such sentiments were a reflection of the times. It was an age when *the reputation and honour of a man doth master every other affection,*[4] when credit and respect were of vital importance. *A spotless name is more to me,* declares Avisa in a poem of the same name written by one of Raleigh's coterie, *than wealth, than friends, than life can be.*[5]

Indeed, there is some indication that White's fears were not ill-founded, and that such a stigma may have been attached to his name after his return to England, as it certainly has been by later historians.[6] Posterity has deemed him weak and ineffective, unable to control company and crew; too unassertive to deflect the forces ranged against him. But we shall see that this is a serious misjudgment, for those forces, once set in motion, were very powerful — indeed, too powerful to resist.

Who, then, is John White? Why did he go to Roanoke, what is his background? These questions demand answers, yet if we hope to solve the mystery of the Lost Colony by questioning its Governor, we will be disappointed. For when we open our investigation, we discover . . . John White is gone.

3 JOHN WHITE: GOVERNOR

And such as marks this world, and notes the course of things,
The weak and tickle stay of states, and great affairs of Kings,
Desires to be abroad, for causes more than one,
Content to live as God appoints, and let the world alone.

Thomas Churchyard[1]

John White: The Enigma

The records are missing. Or incomplete. Or deliberately concealed. Thus very little is known of John White: not his place of birth; not his age; not his family connections. Nor how he came to be associated with Raleigh, nor why he was a member of the Roanoke expeditions . . . nor, indeed, why he appears to have vanished completely after the bombshell announcement of his colony's disappearance.

The mystery surrounding him only deepens when we search for the answers. There is no John White mentioned for the Roanoke voyage of 1584, though we know, by his own reckoning, he was there.[2] Nor is his name among the list of soldiers and specialists resident on the island the following year. Except for a single notice in an anonymous 1585 ship's log, we would have no record of his being on the expedition at all.[3] There is almost no trace of him in any document. In a wild flight of fancy, we might almost suspect the all too common name of John White to be a pseudonym. A disguise, like that of Edward Kelley (aka John Talbot), scryer to the famed mathematician, Dr. John Dee. Or the satirists John Penry and Job Throckmorton, who both went under the name of Martin Marprelate to keep themselves from being killed. Or Bernard Mawde (alias Montalto), an agent to Secretary of State Sir Francis Walsingham. Assumed names were not uncommon.

Explain the omission as one will, the fact remains that here is the record and there is very little of John White within it. Odd, at the very least. His intimate connection with Raleigh might have guaranteed him, as it did others of this circle, some degree of notoriety. Historical reference might have derived from his office as Governor; and of an ill-fated colony at that. One might reasonably expect him to have been mentioned by some biographer of the day. Yet all we have is his single farewell letter to Hakluyt; and that is all.

The Artist

What, then, is left? Pieces of a puzzle, a tantalizingly vague outline. We do know that John White was an artist — though even this occupation is revealed to us only imperfectly. Seventy-five paintings are attributed to him. How many more — if any — lie among the many anonymous works from the period is impossible to say.[4] There is a John White entered into the musty guild registry of the Painter-Stainer's Company in London in 1580.[5] Certainly a match. But that tells us very little. What type of artist was he? Under whom did he study? To what Renaissance school does he belong? Hints to be teased from history. The first evidence presented to us is a portrait White drew of Calichoughe in the year 1577. In Bristol.

Martin Frobisher had just returned to England from his second Arctic expedition.[6] A mining venture to exploit a black ore found the previous summer by his unlikely passenger, Dr. John Dee. Using, it might be added, the dubious technique of a divining rod.[7] Assayers in London, and Dee himself, thought they had struck the mother lode.

But the 1577 voyage spelled disaster. On Baffin Island there was a misunderstanding, Frobisher's error; resulting in the bloody massacre of an entire band of Nugumiut on a cliff overlooking the sea. Frobisher, his ship's hold crammed full of ore, seized three Nugumiut and returned to England: a woman and child — Egnock and Nutioc — and an unrelated man named Calichoughe, who was injured in the capture.[8]

On Bristol's wharves, Frobisher's men unload the ore. Two hundred tons of black rock. Sparking an immediate gold mania. Metallurgists and assayers rush to the coast to test its worth. Investors tumble over themselves, calculating their returns. In the riot of excitement a comet streaks across the night sky, showering fireworks over the celebration.

In the harbor, beneath the angular trading houses, Calichoughe quietly plies his kayak. White seabirds circle overhead; over this lonely Nugumiut man, bleeding from internal injuries unsuspected by the crowds gathered onshore to watch.[9] Calichoughe, paddling a kayak, creates a sensation. Celebrated Flemish artist Cornelis Ketel hastens to Bristol to paint all three Baffin Islanders. Two of the portraits are intended for Queen Elizabeth. To be displayed in her palace at Hampton

Court, where they will be much admired by visitors.[10] There are plans afoot to transport the Nugumiut to London for a royal audience.

But there is another painter here in Bristol. He, too, composes portraits of the Nugumiut. In watercolors. In a style reminiscent of Dürer or the Flemish artist Breughel, or Lucas de Heere who painted another Inuit taken by Frobisher the previous year.[11] John White captures them with his brush. Sealskin parkas trimmed with fur; Calichoughe holding a bow; the kayak paddle. Egnock, with her little girl, Nutioc, tucked inside her coat, peering out from the hood. There is a certain sensitivity and realism in these paintings not found in others' works.

And then it all goes wrong. The celebration smoke settles chokingly around Bristol as Calichoughe's pain echoes out over the tidal wash. Frobisher's expedition is crumbling. The biggest maritime fiasco to date. Yet even with everything unraveling — after the ore is determined fool's gold and its financier cast into debtor's prison; after Calichoughe dies within weeks from his injuries; after the attending Bristol physician, Dr. Edward Dodding, is *bitterly grieved,* not over his death, but over the Queen's lost chance to view him; after Egnock and Nutioc succumb to fever days later — after all this tragedy and disaster, John White's paintings alone come shining through.[12] With a profound sense of humanity and compassion. They are the only redeeming feature of this whole episode. Who is this man, to paint like this?

A London Career

Watercolor was his speciality. His talent in this field was considerable. His known works, now in the British Museum, provide the only tangible evidence of John White. Yet what was his career? To what bent were his talents turned? Perhaps as a limner: a painter of portraits and miniatures like the famous Nicholas Hilliard?[13] These gentlemen artists were in much demand, painting locket and token portraits of royalty and nobles. In an age before photography, princes and statesmen collect keepsake mementos of their foreign counterparts. To put a face to a name; to know their associates.

There are techniques in White's work that suggest this: delicate brush strokes; opaque washes like those used in medieval illuminated manuscripts; gold and silver highlights. Yet White is also an innovator, a freethinker, a nonconformist. Anticipating watercolor methods not thought to have been developed until the eighteenth century — the use of light, rather than bold, outlines in lead; unconstrained strokes that imbue the drawings with a vivid sense of life; an awareness of the underlying texture and color of his medium, applying clear washes directly to the paper.[14]

Alternatively, White may have been a specialist in murals and decorative art, like Lucas de Heere, skills increasingly in demand to beautify the homes of wealthy patrons with startling depictions of ancient mythology, kingdoms, and exotic, cosmopolitan places. Currently all the rage. At Theobalds, Lord Burghley's estate, the twelve signs of the zodiac march across the ceiling of the grand hall *so that at night you can see distinctly the stars proper to each; on the same stage the sun performs its course, which is without doubt contrived by some concealed ingenious mechanism.*[15] White's vivid portraits of travelers from Turkey, Uzbekistan, and Greece might imply familiarity with the merchants of Constantinople; or perhaps such colorful characters frequented the trading houses of London or Bristol. If, indeed, White drew them from life.[16]

But if one were to follow a hunch, one might suggest a different course, placing White squarely within a field then only in its infancy. That of scientific illustrator. England was just beginning to make forays into the distant world: to India, Asia, Africa, the Americas. Recent expeditions had resulted in myriad discoveries, having an impact on an exhaustive number of fields: astronomy, mathematics, navigation, geography, cartography, botany, zoology, entomology, ethnography, publishing, and engraving.

The rise of English naturalists and explorers prompted an explosive demand for scientific illustration. Books on foreign travel were popularized by their scenes of faraway lands. The new scientists, such as Dr. John Dee, Richard Hakluyt, and Thomas Hariot — all intimate acquaintances of Raleigh, the last, indeed, in his employ — were in the vanguard of these discoveries. For a young artist it was a thrilling, stimulating environment indeed. The question is, was White there?

Jacques LeMoyne

White's connection with the skilled French artist Jacques LeMoyne de Morgues might indicate he was. LeMoyne had been a member of René de Laudonnière's Huguenot colony, which had been established on the St. John's River in Florida in 1564. After its destruction by the Spaniards, LeMoyne fled home to France, only to discover the attitude toward Protestants rapidly deteriorating. In 1572 the tension exploded in a bloodbath in Paris streets on St. Bartholomew's Day. For three days and nights Protestant Huguenots were slaughtered. The killings raged across France. Thirty thousand dead. On the Rhône, corpses floated so thickly that they choked the water.[17] LeMoyne must have hidden to preserve his life, as did a twenty-year-old English volunteer, hot for action in support of the Huguenots, who abandoned an education at Oxford University for this. Young Walter Raleigh, from Devon in the West Country.

After the St. Bartholomew's Day Massacre, LeMoyne moved permanently to London, one of many refugees pouring into the city. Later, Raleigh hired him to paint a visual record of Florida. This he did, creating an astonishing vignette of Timucuan Indian life: villages, harvests, celebrations, processions, even family picnics *with divers other things . . . lively drawn in colours at your no small charges,* Raleigh is reminded by Hakluyt — himself busily translating Laudonnière's narrative — *by the skilfull painter James Morgues, yet living in the Black-friars in London.*[18]

White must have been there, by the older man's side. Somewhere. Two of White's watercolors are based on LeMoyne's drawings of Florida Timucua — a man and a woman. The woman in a blue sarong of Spanish moss, the man's body laden with copper. Overall, in all of White's paintings, there is a vague sense of LeMoyne. A similarity in background detail, in poses, in the angles of composition.[19] Both artists made studies of ancient Britons and may have worked on some of them together. An effort, on White's part, to show that the people of Roanoke were not so very different from his own ancestors.

Expedition Artist

It was at this juncture, thanks to Raleigh, that a remarkable opportunity opened up for John White . . . Roanoke Island. He joined the first Roanoke expedition in 1584 as commissioned artist. In 1585 he was again *sent thither specially and for the same purpose,* to draw.[20] To bring home remote, strange lands to those who would never go there. To be England's eyes in the new world: faithfully recording the plants, animals, faces, and village life of the people he sees. It will change White forever.

Hakluyt's cousin, a lawyer, urged that American voyages include a *skilful painter* similar to that *which the Spaniards used commonly in all their discoveries, to bring the descriptions of all beasts, birds, fishes, trees, towns, &c.*[21] And so John White was commanded to faraway Roanoke, a skillful painter, hauling paper and lead and pigments and brushes and grinding stones into an unknown world.

White's depictions of botanical and zoological specimens made on the voyage attest to experience with scientific illustration. The surviving examples are marked by a considerable attention to detail. They are fresh, vivid, carefully labeled: the spidery veins in a plantain; the fins of a flying fish, splayed like an accordion; spinelike hairs on the leg of a land crab; the creamy underbelly of a baby alligator: *This being but one month old was 3 foot 4 inches in length and live in water.*[22]

Dr. Thomas Penny's work on insects entitled *Insectorum . . . Theatrum* included four of White's illustrations: a butterfly, two fireflies, and a gadfly from Virginia. White also presented him with a Virginia cicada. He was, said Penny, a *painter not uncelebrated. A most skilful painter.* A diligent observer of natural life both in the Caribbean and on the North American mainland. A yellow swallowtail, its wing tips singed a sooty black, bears the inscription: *From Virginia, America, given me by White, the painter, 1587.*[23] A poignant gesture. The fragile gift of a butterfly thoughtfully offered by White to Penny at a time when his own family was in such danger. Or perhaps he gave it earlier, before the colony's departure from England.

Botanist John Gerard also utilized White's work. His famous *Herball,* published in 1597, included a woodcut of a milkweed based on one drawn by *Master White, an excellent painter.* Indeed, the two men held avid discussions about a plant from the American Southeast. The Spaniards positively raved about it. White contributed to Gerard's knowledge of the root — and possibly supplied samples — of this *salsa parilla,* mangled into English as sarsaparilla and, finally, "sasparilla."[24]

Thomas Hariot's book about Roanoke, the *Briefe and True Report of the New Founde Land of Virginia,* was published in 1590 by Theodore De Bry. An expert engraver, De Bry illustrated the volume by cutting copper plates from originals *diligently collected and drawn* by White.[25] Wildly popular, the work raced through seventeen editions between 1590 and 1620, published in Latin, French, German, and English. It would be fully three centuries before anyone created a visual record as spectacular as John White and LeMoyne did of the Americas.[26]

The Family Man

In 1587 White is prepared to take a much more decisive step with regard to America. One that will be irreversible. On January 7 he is appointed

Governor of the City of Raleigh in Virginia and agrees to lead a company of planters across the Atlantic to establish it. White will emigrate permanently to the New World. His family will go with him.

But who are they? In all this time, we have heard nothing of them. White had been married, though his wife's name is unknown. She was probably deceased, for she is not mentioned among the passengers. Together, she and White had at least one child: a daughter, Eleanor.

Eleanor was grown and married at the time of the expedition, though we do not know how old she was. When she left for Roanoke, she was more than five months pregnant.[27] The age of consent for marriage in England was twelve years for girls and fourteen for boys, although most unions were contracted much later: half of all marriages took place with both parties well into their twenties.[28] Adding their ages together, John White was perhaps in his early forties in 1587.

What other family did White have? Some may have been present on the expedition. A Cutbert White is listed among the Lost Colonists. A brother, perhaps? A grown son? It would be surprising if a number of the colonists were not bound by blood to John White, since many had agreed to go, as he said, *through his persuasions.* Implying a closeness. Thomas Butler, a Lost Colonist, may have been related, since White counted Butlers in his family tree. It is just possible that Henry Payne was also. An original collection of White's watercolors appeared, in 1788, in the hands of a London bookseller named Thomas Payne, with their provenance far from clear.[29]

Governor of a Colony

If we are uncertain of White's family connections, we are equally in the dark as to how he was selected to govern the City of Raleigh. Perhaps the projected colony was his idea. He was certainly instrumental in gathering the personnel and arranging the logistics of the voyage. Raleigh wholeheartedly approved of him, claiming that he himself had *nominated, elected, chosen, constituted, made & appointed John White of London, Gentleman, to be the chief Governor there.*[30]

Eleanor's husband, Ananias Dare, was a London tiler and bricklayer, an occupation which has led to the assumption that White's own status was not above that of a common laborer.[31] But other causes might have brought two young people together: a shared religious conviction perhaps. And then there is White's fine italic hand, which speaks of education and class; his skill as a limner; his known contacts with men of substance such as Raleigh, LeMoyne, and Hakluyt; the fact of his being made Governor at all; his title of address as *master* and *gentleman*.[32]

A Distorted Image

By July 1587 White's colony had reached Roanoke Island and begun to settle in. Yet despite its hopeful beginning, something had gone quite wrong. One colonist had been murdered, and the horror of death hung like a pall over the rest. Panicked, they forced White back to England for help. He sailed away . . . and never saw them again. The 1590 rescue expedition failed. The Roanoke dream was dead.

After this, we know nothing of White's whereabouts. The trail ends abruptly . . . until 1593. In England Richard Hakluyt receives a letter dated February 4 from Newtown in Kilmore, Ireland, signed by White. The contents detail the sad events of the 1590 voyage, penned in response to a request Hakluyt had made when they were last together in London. The wording of the letter bears the stamp of finality. In other hands, it might have made a convincing suicide note. What was happening here? Could White merely have been going away? Had he indeed resigned himself to the colony's fate, as implied? Perhaps he wished to end further discussion. Or is it possible he no longer felt safe? Did John White know too much? The answers, in time, will become clearer, though they will never be brought fully into focus. Strangely, after the farewell letter was delivered, White was never heard from again.

John White of London, gentleman. Celebrated artist. Governor of Roanoke. Missing person.

The Search Broadens

In the absence of concrete information about White, the investigation logically should turn to the colonists. It is they who are missing. We might expect them, in fact, to hold the key to the puzzle or, at the very least, to furnish a clue. Instead, what they furnish is another dead end. What do we know of them? Who were they? And why did they emigrate thousands of miles to an unknown land? Did they hold certain political or religious convictions that might have a bearing on this case? What of their internal organization? Or their relationship to Raleigh? The answers to these questions may only be inferred. Because, curiously, there is scarcely any information on these people. Like John White, much about them is veiled in mystery. Their story, from start to finish, is an enigma. It would seem that we have both a Governor and his colony who simply can't be found.

Yet what if we make a wider sweep? What can we learn about the colonists by looking at the world in which they lived? A world which they left behind and which may provide a motive for their departure. England. What is it like at this moment in history? For the Lost Colonists do not owe their genesis to Roanoke. Everything in London bears on their story.

4 OF LONDON

London is a large, excellent, and mighty city of business, and the most important in the whole kingdom; most of the inhabitants are employed in buying and selling merchandize, and trading in almost every corner of the world, since the river is most useful. . . .

Frederick, Duke of Wirtemberg[1]

A City of Water

London is a very old, walled city. So old, in fact, that in the sixteenth century Roman artifacts and ruins are frequently unearthed layers below the current street levels — much to everyone's amazement.[2] Mute testimony to the strata of human life long sustained here by the Thames. Along the southern edge of the city the river charts a smooth course, gliding past the Tower, the wharves, the ruins of Baynard's Castle, the ancient monastery of Blackfriars by the western wall. Sweeping everything in. A history steeped in water.

Various streams, or bourns, once trickled down through the walled city, winding under bridges and along lanes, performing daily ablutions. Most are now vaulted over with brick and paved level with the street. The population grows rapidly, houses crowding so thickly upon one another that much of the drinking water is ruined and must be piped into the city through conduits of lead. The effect this has on the mind can only be guessed. Many thrill to the changes around them; others are critical and dislike what they see. And there are not a few who believe that the world is coming to an end.

Close to the Madding Crowd

Only recently has London come to be regarded as England's true capital, thanks to Queen Elizabeth. Her reign rolls along on an overwhelming tide of popularity. On the anniversary of her ascension, bells peal from a forest of steeples above the old city walls. *They are vastly fond of great noises that fill the ear,* a foreign visitor notes, *such as the firing of cannon, drums, and the ringing of bells; so that in London it is common for a number of them, that have got a glass in their heads, to go into some belfry and ring the bells for hours together for the sake of exercise.*[3]

Of the fourteen royal residences, the twenty-four-acre palace of Whitehall in Westminster west of the London gate is by far the most spectacular, envied as the largest palace in Europe. An incredible 1,500 courtiers and retainers maintain a constant bustle about the Queen, keeping a well-ordered Whitehall humming with activity. The kitchen alone is cluttered with departments: for poultry, for dairy, for produce, for pastries and confections, for seasonings, for butter, for vinegar, for baking, each with its own separate staff. All this requires an enormous intake of supplies: spices; candles; linens and bedding; rushes and flowers; bottles and glass; cutlery; mountains of firewood; annually, 2,500 tons of ale and beer; 33,024 chickens; 13,260 lambs; 8,200 sheep; 1,240 head of beef; and 60,000 pounds of butter.[4] Enough to keep an army of Londoners employed. Little wonder that gentlemen and merchants desert the country en masse *and do fly to London.*[5] To earn a living.

As for retailers, therefore, and handycraftsmen, it is no marvel if they abandon country towns, and resort to London; for not only the court, which is now-a-days much greater and more gallant than in former times . . . is now for the most part either abiding at London, or else so near unto it, that the provision of things most fit for it may easily be fetched from thence.[6]

Inside the city walls, London pulsates with motion, with an incessant din of hammering and hawking, the clank and call of a multitude of craftsmen. Here are ranged the great trade guilds of the masons, the weavers, the coopers, and the like. Saddlers, glovers, tanners, perfumers, upholsterers, soapmakers, needlemakers, haberdashers. A welter of specialists, all with their own arms and ceremony. All with an eye on the Royal Exchange, a massive edifice of brick and stone accommodating hundreds of merchants who meet twice daily to transact business.[7]

From the Royal Exchange, past the Pissing Conduit and down into Eastcheap along the waterfront, the fishmarkets and butchers' shambles are strewn, where more meat is sold in a day than Portugal consumes in a whole year.[8] Where the stench is overwhelming, and the filth of offal is channeled down to waiting dung boats on the Thames.

There is an insatiable appetite for luxuries and fads in a city that boasts enough markets to supply anything under Christendom. Londoners delight in foreign goods. Novelties crowd shop windows. And for a lark *we oft exchange our finest cloth, corn, tin, and wools for halfpenny cockhorses for children, dogs of wax or of cheese, twopenny tabors, leaden swords, painted feathers, gewgaws for fools, dogtricks for dizzards, hawkshoods, and suchlike trumpery, whereby we reap just mockage and reproach in other countries.*[9]

A Tourist Industry

Foreign princes travel to London just to see the sights. A voracious appetite for tour books keeps presses churning at an impressive rate. *London is the capital of England and so superior to other English towns,* raves a visitor sparing of pronouns, *that London is not said to be in England, but rather England to be in London, for England's most resplendent objects may be seen in and around London; so that he who sightsees London and the royal courts in its immediate vicinity may assert without impertinence that he is properly acquainted with England.*[10]

London streets, relics of an earlier age, are narrow and twisted, overwhelmed by the recent congestion of carts and coaches, *for the world runs on wheels with many, whose parents were glad to go on foot.*[11] For economy's sake, it is easier on everyone to travel by way of the Thames. Wherries, London's water taxis with comfortably upholstered interiors, line up along the bank *in great crowds,* vying for fares since customers *are free to choose the ship they find the most attractive and pleasing, while every boatman has the privilege on arrival of placing his ship to best advantage for people to step into.* When Swiss traveler Thomas Platter embarks on such a ride to see the sights, he is most astounded, not by the historic buildings but by the continuous line of boats on the Thames, extending the entire length of the city.[12]

The ever-popular St. Paul's Cathedral is a famous tourist landmark, a must-see on any itinerary. A sea of booksellers' stalls and printers' shops, drenched by colorful signs, laps its base. And, skulking around, the usual assortment of knaves, pickpockets, and thieves. People-watching promises never a dull moment, for amid the *jostling* and *jeering* crowd *you shall see walking the knight, the gull, the gallant, the upstart, the gentleman . . . the scholar, the beggar, the doctor, the idiot, the ruffian, the cheater, the Puritan, the cutthroat.*[13]

After attending the service, a favorite pastime is to climb the three hundred stone steps to the cathedral roof, paved with lead. Couples stroll there along the promenade on Sunday afternoons, taking in sweeping views of the rushing crowds below, the writhing city of London with Westminster poised regally in the distance along the rolling Thames.

The roof has also become, sad to say, a popular haven for graffiti artists. By all means, mocks the satirist Thomas Dekker, visitors must not neglect to pay the admission fee to the roof in order to experience the pleasure of defacing it. Pay *tribute to the top of Paul's steeple with a single penny. . . . Before you come down again, I would desire you to draw your knife, and grave your name . . . in great characters upon the leads . . . and so you shall be sure to have your name lie in a coffin of lead, when yourself shall be wrapped in a winding-sheet. And indeed, the top of Paul's contains more names than Stowe's Chronicle.*[14]

Lead roofs appear to be irresistible for this kind of thing. In 1581, despite raging political turmoil, the ousted Portuguese king, Don Antonio, on official state business to Elizabeth, manages to find time to etch an inscription on the tower roof behind Windsor Palace: *When Antonius the eloquent was compelled by war to seek help of the Queen, this inscription was made.*[15] Apparently the Eloquent enjoyed himself so much, he updated his autograph four years later.

The artistic pride of the city and *a work very rare* is London Bridge, its twenty graceful arches spanning the Thames. It is a marvel by night, spraying soft lights upon the dark river, water gurgling under the vaults below. Towering over it are expensive shops and wealthy merchants' houses *so that it seemeth rather a continual street than a bridge.*[16] The secretary of Frederick, Duke of Wirtemberg, waxed utterly rhapsodic about these *splendid, handsome, and well-built houses* dwelt in by *merchants of consequence,* stuffed with costly wares from around the world.[17] Guarding one such house is a disagreeable, spitting, and very alive camel; an unexpected visitor bonus.

In Come the Urbanites

Yet a change is coming over the citizenry. Unpleasant urbanites are sprouting up like mushrooms, whining cityfolk inured to none of the hardships of the countryside. Much to the profound disgust of their fellow countrymen. *Londiners . . . are in reproach called Cockneys and,* worse yet, *eaters of buttered toast.*[18] Lest this seem an unfair castigation, let it be known that there is an overall disdain of those who shun the wholesome food of the countryside. They, with their nice, *tender stomachs,* which cannot handle such fare, would find it lying *stinking in their stomachs, as dirt in a filthy sink or privy.*[19]

Such fastidiousness is not confined to cuisine alone, but has extended to the whole atmosphere of dining. A veritable mantra of culinary ritual is developing. Not least in the curious affair of placement settings: Venetian glass, pewter dishes and silver spoons are a prerequisite. Wood will no longer do. Tapestries, silks, *fine napery,* and plate garnish the homes of even the *lowest sort* in London.[20]

Such are the *London Cockneys.* The term is new, begging definition. They are held to be embarrassingly gullible, half-baked dolts, *utterly ignorant of husbandry or housewifery, such as is practised in the country, so that they may be persuaded anything about rural commodities.* The ever-popular *tale of the citizen's son, who knew not the language of a cock, but called it neighing, is commonly known.* Cock-neigh.[21]

The name is generally fixed on such who are born within the sound of Bow-Bell Church, and are tender enough and sufficiently ignorant in country businesses. Weak, *delicate, and silly folk.*[22]

The cherished opinion of rural England places London at the farthest extreme of frivolity. Small lapdogs are all the rage, sought *far and near to satisfy the nice delicacy of dainty dames and wanton women's wills.*[23]

These sybaritical puppies, remarks an incredulous and alliterating Harrison, are *meet playfellows for mincing mistresses to bear in their bosoms, to keep company withal in their chambers, to succour with sleep in bed and nourish with meat at board, to lie in their laps and lick their lips as they lie (like young Dianas) in their wagons and coaches.*[24]

No surprise that a popular London saying is *Love me, love my dog.*[25] One of the cleaner adages. The streets are rife with all sorts of irreverent witticisms and sacrilegious jests. Alongside somber and eloquent eulogies to the dead, one is just as apt to stumble upon inscriptions like the boisterous verse engraved on a locksmith's tombstone:

A zealous lock-smith died of late,
And did arrive at heaven gate,
He stood without and would not knock,
Because he meant to pick the lock.[26]

Or the epitaph of the worldly Thomas Elderton:

Here is Elderton lying in dust,
Or lying Elderton; choose which you lust. . . .[27]

It's an unusual attitude. Yet, for all this jocularity, all that glitters is not gold. Or, to quote another London saying, it's *not all butter that the cow shits.*[28]

Self-Indulgence

There are too many people in this city, and its effects are becoming evident in irritability and self-centeredness. Older forms of hospitality crumble. In the countryside, manors welcome visitors with a generosity as great on the day of departure as on that of arrival. Not so in London, where *men oftentimes complain of little room; and in reward of a fat capon or plenty of beef and mutton largely bestowed upon them in the country, a cup of wine or beer, with a napkin to wipe their lips and a "You are heartily welcome," is thought to be great entertainment; and therefore the old country clerks have framed this saying . . . upon the entertainment of townsmen and Londoners, after the days of their abode in this manner: The first is pleasant, and the second tolerable, the third is empty, but the fourth day stinks.*[29]

If city people no longer lavish hospitality on visitors it is, in part, because guests increasingly demonstrate a marked lack of gratitude in return. *A great housekeeper,* it is said, *is sure of nothing for his good cheer save a great turd at his gate.*[30]

The rudeness is in keeping with an overall atmosphere of self-indulgence. A shirking of personal responsibility. The guiding words of the past *lie open to the censure of the youth of our time,* complains the historian Camden, *who, for the most part, are so over-gulled with self-liking, that they are more than giddy in admiring themselves, and carping at whatsoever hath been done or said heretofore.*[31]

There is an alarming lack of discipline and self-control. Anger is allowed free rein; street brawls are common. Couples easily separate when tired of marriage. Even in the innocuous realm of cuisine, the swelling army of *pursy and corpulent* citizens indicates an absence of self-denial. In the past one dish was felt sufficient, now tables groan under the weight and variety of courses. Not even the most devouring glutton or *the greediest cormorant that is, can scarce eat of every dish in every course. Oh what nicety is this? What vanity, excess, riot, and superfluity is here? Oh, farewell former world!*[32]

Aiding and abetting the decadence are the entertainments of the day. There are plenty who spend their Sundays, not at church in the quiet contemplation of God, but in *dancing, dicing, carding, bowling, tennis playing, hawking, hunting, and such like.*[33] Admittedly, something is amiss when the city's most impressive laborers are those souls of industry in the workshops of the Marshalsea Prison, diligently turning out false dice for gambling cheats.[34]

Dancing to express a joyous frame of mind is one thing, say the critics, but now it is done entirely *in praise of ourselves,* night and day without moderation, and in all manner of *smooching and slobbering one of another, what filthy groping and unclean handling is not practised everywhere in these dancings? Yea the very deed and action itself, which I will not name . . . shall be portrayed and showed forth in their bawdy gestures of one to another.*[35]

These criticisms are no mere complaints by a scandalized generation, but express very real concerns about a society which yields to every desire. No thought to consequences. There is a flourishing of sexual gratification without restraint, embarrassing in its irresponsibility. *Mutual coition between man and woman,* returns the flippant reply, *is not so offensive before God. For do not all creatures (say they) . . . engender together?* Therefore, *they conclude, that whoredom is a badge of love.*[36]

Bastard births, a soaring population, and pandemic venereal disease rank among the many products of this age. Seldom discussed. Still, the call for change is hardly helped by one reformer's exuberant list of alternatives: the delights that *cometh by meat and drink, and sometimes while those things be expulsed and voided, whereof is in the body over-great abundance. This pleasure is felt when we do our natural easement, or when we be doing the act of generation* (with legal spouses), *or when the itching of any part is eased with rubbing or scratching.*[37]

Drinking and drunkenness wash over England like a tide. Drowning souls. There was a time when public houses were few and far between. But now every town, village, and street corner overflows with an *abundance of alehouses, taverns and inns, which are so fraughted with malt-worms night and day, that you would wonder to see them.* Often they sit drinking and carousing a whole week together, as long as the money lasts. *A world it is to consider their gestures and demeanours, how they strut and stammer, stagger and reel to and fro, like madmen, some vomiting, spewing and disgorging their filthy stomachs, other some . . . pissing under the board as they sit, which is most horrible, some fall to swearing, cursing . . . interlacing their speeches with curious terms of blasphemy to the great dishonour of God and offence of the godly ears present.*[38]

A welter of graphic and irreverent nicknames attach themselves to *such heady ale and beer:* the *huffcap, the mad-dog, father-whoreson, angels' food, dragons' milk, go-by-the-wall, stride-wide, and lift-leg, etc. . . . It is incredible how our maltbugs lug at this liquor . . . with such eager and sharp devotion as our men hale at huffcap till they be red as cocks and little wiser than their combs.*[39]

Social Disintegration

A slow rot is seeping through the city; a disturbing underbelly of London's wealth and power. A wilderness of slums. At Smart's Quay, a thieves' school instructs streetwise boys in the delicate art of pickpocketing. A way of survival, of keeping clear of vile debtor's prisons. Pedestrians, passing these places of incarceration, are horrified by *the pitiful cries* of the inmates, *lying in filthy straw and loathsome dung, worse than any dogs.*[40] As though dogs should be treated this way.

Examples of degenerate society prompt public outcry — unheeded — against the concentration of wealth into too few hands. Condemning the rich who expend great sums to nourish their sporting dogs while the poor go hungry. Begging for bread. *Money is like muck, not good except it be spread.*[41]

By way of proof, the depraved district of Southwark oozes like scum along the southern edge of the Thames. The repository of London's human offal. Sights here include the infamous Clink, a clerical prison for the incarceration of Jesuits, thieves, and pirates; Paris Garden with its abhorrent bear-baiting arena; gambling dens; prostitution rings and a jumble of whorehouses, taverns, and playhouses. Not the least of which are the Globe Theater and the Hope. Places of ill repute. Filled to capacity even *when the church of God shall be bare and empty.*[42] Theatergoers *flock thither thick and threefold,* asserting that the messages delivered in the plays are as good as any sermon.[43]

Better, at least, than Paris Garden. Better than the bear-baitings that take place on Bankside in the shadow of Lambeth Palace across the marsh. A putrid, vicious sport. In the middle of a lonely arena, a bear crouches, tethered to a stake. No one to help it. Spectators clamber onto risers for a better view of what is to come, eagerly placing bets as snarling mastiffs are released one by one on the terrorized animal. Cries of delight escape from the crowd as the bear hopelessly tries to ward them off. The dogs are specially bred for the purpose, champion prize fighters housed in a tenement of foul-smelling kennels behind the stadium, 120 in number. Too valuable to risk injury, the odds are stacked: the bear cannot bite — its teeth are broken short.[44]

The most grotesque attraction at Paris Garden is an old, blind bear securely fastened, then struck with canes and sticks by young boys. Bewildered and upset, it can neither see its attackers nor escape; innocent of any crime, too old to be threatening. These children are the hope for London's future, this their education. The cruelty hits home once when the animal pathetically unfastens its rope and flees to the safety of its own cage. It is enough to bring tears to the eyes, but doesn't. Instead its antics are greeted by howls of laughter.

To see a strange out-landish fowl,
A quaint baboon, an ape, an owl,
A dancing bear, a giant's bone,
A foolish engine move alone,
A Morris dance, a puppet play,
Mad Tom to sing a roundelay,
A woman dancing on a rope,
Bull-baiting also at the Hope;
A rhymer's jests, a juggler's cheats,
A tumbler showing cunning feats,
Or players acting on the stage,
There goes the bounty of our Age;
But unto any pious motion,
There's little coin, and less devotion.[45]

A Religion Called Money

If religion were once the answer, it is no longer. Clergy complain of low church attendance and a *general contempt of the ministry.* Money has become the worshipped god. Everyone *from the highest to the lowest, from the priest to the popular sort* is caught up in money. *A covetous man may well be compared to Hell, which ever gapeth and yawneth for more.*[46]

Classes of *thriftless* men and women spring up everywhere, earning a living as beggars, of which there are reckoned to be no less than *10,000 persons* in the realm. Some few are legitimate. The rest run scams, communicating among themselves in a thieves' *canting* language, counterfeiting illness and disease by the application of *corrosives* and poisons to their own skins *thereby to raise pitiful and odious sores and move the hearts of the goers by* to *bestow large alms upon them.*[47] Quite a fortune can be made in this way.

Scams extend even to craftsmen who churn out delightful products *curious to the eye,* costly to the purse. Shoddy work is quickly shuffled off to the first buyer. Artisans toil in *haste and a barbarous or slavish desire to turn the penny and, by ridding their work* make a speedy profit. If they *bungle up and dispatch many things, they care not how, so they be out of their hands.*[48] Even the magnificent mansions cropping up throughout the city *are rather curious to the eye like paper work than substantial for continuance.*[49] And so yet another saying is born to cover the work of such swindlers: *Claw a churl by the arse, and he shiteth in thy hand.*[50]

Not surprisingly, lawyers proliferate like flies, their numbers increasing incrementally with lawsuits filed. The *lawyers, they go rustling in their silks, velvets and chains of gold, they build gorgeous houses, sumptuous edifices, and stately turrets.* At the expense of others. *As long as one grease them in the fist, then your suit shall want no furtherance until the money is gone. . . . In presence of their clients, they will be so earnest one with another . . . but immediately after their clients being gone, they laugh in their sleeves, to see how prettily they fetch in such sums of money, and under the pretence of equity and justice.*[51] Little wonder that bringing suit is often more headache than it's worth. *The more ye stir a turd, the worse it will stink.*[52]

Decency has been so far displaced, cry the worthy, that blasphemy has become daily sustenance. Just see the farmers of Walden the year saffron plummeted on the Exchange! Forced to sell fully half their produce as cut flowers, they suffer a grievous economic loss. Yet no one is dead, or injured; crops remain intact. Rather than accept the clergy's advice and give thanks for abundance, Walden prays instead for scarcity and reviles God. They *in most contemptuous manner murmured against Him, saying that He did shit saffron, therewith to choke the market.*[53]

It is the end of an era. There is widespread belief that the world has gone mad. That the disintegration of English society is at hand. There is a meanness to the times. A self-indulgence. And a corruption. Too much wrong.

This is the world the colonists left behind.

5 OF POPULATION

It is a very populous city, so that one can scarcely pass along the streets, on account of the throng.

Frederick, Duke of Wirtemberg[1]

Birth Without Control

Perhaps the colonists leave England for the simple reason that there is no longer any room for them at home. A demographic explosion in the 1570s has launched a full-scale assault on the realm, London's booming population swelling to four times its previous size.[2] In Cordwainer Street Ward, grocer and twice mayor Thomas Knowles and his wife Joan churn out nineteen children.[3] No great rarity. *Some also do grudge at the great increase of people in these days, thinking a necessary brood of cattle far better than a superfluous augmentation of mankind.*[4]

Young people, *by marrying too soon,* propagate far more offspring than if they had waited until riper years and *do nothing profit the country but fill it full of beggars. . . .*[5] No one considers the consequences of their actions, even an action as sacred as bearing children — who increase exponentially: ten producing a hundred producing a thousand. Even death from disease and war offers no check upon a population careering out of bounds.

Rural Beauty: Twice the Charm

London's walls bow and groan from the weight of its massive population until they burst, disgorging into the suburbs. The surrounding countryside is quickly distended. East of Aldgate, development presses on to the common field and ruins it. This *common field . . . being sometime the beauty of this city on that part, is so encroached upon by building of filthy cottages* that it is scarcely wide enough for carriages to pass. Much *less is there any fair, pleasant, or wholesome way for people to walk on foot; which is no small blemish to so famous a city.*[6] No quarter is left untouched.

In developers' plans, there is no room for beauty, antiquity, or history. Suffolk House, a sumptuous mansion in Bridge Ward, is sold to merchants who *pulled it down, sold the lead, stone, iron, etc; and in place thereof built many small cottages of great rents.*[7] Indeed, land is at such a premium that the poor, lodging in the Queen's almshouses in Bishopsgate, have no qualms about accepting their welfare pensions and moving to cheaper districts, illegally leasing their former quarters *for great rent* and pocketing that money too. Forcing the beleaguered parish priest to *challenge tithes of the poor.*[8]

You have such teeming cities, mused a Hungarian visitor, *that unless you build them upwards so that houses scrape the sky, your land, however broad, will not support your people.*[9] An incongruous and overwhelming thought. Tall buildings blot out the sky.

Rural areas suddenly find themselves the object of intense interest from land investors. Soon the squeeze is on, and farmlands are ploughed under for development. Without regret. Available lands tighten up, crushing rural people and driving them off their holdings. By *encroaching and joining of house to house,* the country people are reduced to beggary, *devoured and eaten up. . . . Howbeit, what care our great encroachers?*[10]

An expanding population confined to a finite land mass makes a volatile cocktail. The population explosion nears critical mass, rising faster than the market can keep pace. Heaping up woes, inflation runs rampant. In the midst of this crisis, 1586 emerges as a famine year. The wool industry takes a tumble and bottoms out, resulting in tremendous losses and an alarming increase of landless indigents — unfortunate, in an age in which vagrancy is condemned as a felony.[11]

Timber! And the Trees Come Crashing Down

England's growth rate impacts the countryside in other ways; it is wedded to an unprecedented need for wood. There must be houses aplenty to accommodate everyone. Their size swelling far beyond the functional.[12] Shipyards hum with activity; saws bite into timber for masts, decks, and forecastles. For merchantmen and men-of-war; galleons, pinnaces, shallops, and barges; boxes and crates; and cranes and carts and wagons and warehouses. And lumber and mills.

The result is wholesale demolition. Nowadays *a man shall oft ride ten or twenty miles* for wood . . . *and find very little or rather none at all.* It is now possible to speak of individual groves remaining, as in Chatley

Moor, in Shropshire, in Amounderness, *and a moss near Manchester, not far from Leicester's house, although in time past not only all Lancashire, but a great part of the coast between Chester and the Solve were well stored.*[13]

A man would think, laments William Harrison, *that our laws were able enough to make sufficient provision for the redress of this error. . . . But such is the nature of our countrymen that . . . they will rather seek some crooked construction of them to the increase of their private gain.*[14]

Nor is it only woodlands that suffer, but water too. No river in Europe exceeds the Thames in fish production, despite public protest over man's *insatiable avarice* and all for *commodity's sake.* There are those of all ages who lament for nature. *Oh, that this river might be spared but even one year from nets, & etc!* cries Harrison.[15]

But such is our nature and so blind are we in deed that we see no inconvenience before we feel it, and for a present gain we regard not what damage may ensue to our posterity.[16]

Ah, America!

Our image of London is becoming more dimensional. To many it is a city exciting in its rapid change and multinationalism. Marred only by crowding. The prospect of unlimited land resources in America therefore holds enormous appeal.

Just as many Londoners, on the other hand, are appalled by the changes raging around them. With disapproval and dismay, they stand by as time-tested values crumble before social ills run rampant. To them, America offers the quiet promise of a different sort of life.

Who were the colonists? On which side of the debate did they fall? To consider this, there is still another aspect of London to view. . . .

6 OF RELIGION

Surely common election of ministers, and this deciding of matters in controversy by a multitude, will breed greater strife and contention, than without danger will be appeased.

Bishop John Cooper[1]

A Cry for Reform

Religion, during the reign of Queen Elizabeth, is in large measure a political concern. A strong church means a unified country in an age when religious divisions are spewing deadly civil wars across Europe. To prevent this, Elizabeth severs ties with the Vatican and forms the Anglican Church.[2] It is a uniquely English endeavor. In the interest of national security, allegiance to the Church is synonymous with allegiance to the Crown.

Nevertheless, a Puritan movement catches fire. At the universities, young people rebel against the *fanatical Catholic gang* controlling the administration, accusing Anglican officials of being too Catholic. At Trinity College, Cambridge, student protesters hack the tail off a horse belonging to the College Master, shearing its forelock into a popish crown. There are window smashings and other demonstrations, and on October 12, 1565, the fellows of St. John's College collectively tear off their surplices, greatly alarming the Chancellor and Tudor government officials.[3]

Reverend Turner of Wells — *old Doctor Turner* — an avid reformer, seizes the day by teaching his dog to leap up and steal the corner caps off the heads of visiting bishops.[4] Yet such champions of reform rarely advocate the overthrow of the Church. Continuing to operate as part of the established system, their protest is merely for more sweeping changes within it.

Counterculture

Separatists and nonconformists are an entirely different matter. Flourishing in underground communities in London, their identities are kept hidden from the authorities. With good reason, for their claim to worship *not in bondage and subjection, but freely and purely,* to hold separate assemblies and ordain their own ministers, is treason.[5]

What would happen, exclaims the Church, if a subject were allowed to determine what is tyrannical? Neither monarch nor master would be safe! What *lord of the council,* cries Matthew "Nosey" Parker, Archbishop of Canterbury, *shall ride quietly minded in the streets among desperate beasts? What master shall be sure in his bedchamber?*[6] Suspicions flare that Separatism will translate into a wider attack on education, class, and property. Indeed, Richard Bancroft, a member of the Court of High Commission and the first to expose the secret activities of the Separatists, links it to an international conspiracy.[7]

Martin Marprelate

Although most Separatists regard themselves as loyal subjects, they are increasingly distrusted. Fears of a plot are confirmed by the outbreak of the Marprelate Controversy in 1588, a series of political satires attacking Anglican abuses, composed by an anonymous "Martin Marprelate." Bishop Cooper immediately condemns the *railing comedy* as a *wicked and malicious* libel.[8]

What sayest thou, man? cries Martin, naming the bishops individually, though sparing John of London *(. . . for it may be he is at bowls, and it is a pity to trouble my good brother, lest he should swear too bad).* These lord bishops, *with the rest of that swinish rabble,* are *proud, popish, presumptuous, profane, paltry, pestilent, and pernicious Prelates.*[9]

The Marprelate tracts, though immediately outlawed, are wildly popular — even at Court. This only encourages the libelers to further *desperate boldness, as if they thought there were neither Prince, nor Law, nor Magistrate, nor Ruler, that durst control them or seek to repress them.*[10]

Martin lashes out with invective, enraging the clergy. *As long as Bishop Overton, Bishop Bickley, Bishop Middleton, the Dean of Westminster, Doctor Cole, Doctor Bell, with many others are living,* he mocks, *I doubt me whether all the famous dunces be dead. And if you would have an ill-sample of an excellent pulpit man, indeed, go no farther than the Bishop of Gloucester.* This man, while preaching at Worcester, *came at the length unto the very pith of his whole sermon, contained in the distinction of the name of John; which he, then showing all his learning at once, full learnedly handled after this manner. "John, John; the grace of God, the grace of God, the grace of God. Gracious*

John; not graceless John, but gracious John. John, holy John, holy John; not John full of holes, but holy John." If he showed not himself learned in this sermon, then hath he been a dunce all his life.[11]

Whitgift's Reign of Terror

Suddenly Separatists find themselves under attack on all sides. Cooper labels them the *most dangerous* element in the commonwealth, worse even than Papists, who pose *great perils.*[12] The Puritan party condemns them as *ignorant, rash and heady,* reducing discipline to *bedlam* with their *new-found equality,* infuriated by their desire to separate from a Church that merely needs reform.[13] The issue boils down to a single question: How much of a person's life should the Crown control? It is unreasonable, cry the Separatists, *that there should be thrust upon me a governor of whom the everlasting salvation or damnation of my body and soul doth depend . . . unless those upon whom he were thrust were fools, or madmen, or children, without all discretion of ordering themselves.*[14]

Autumn 1583. The turning point comes when John Whitgift is consecrated the new Archbishop of Canterbury. His regime is denounced by a shower of Puritan publications churned out from secret presses. Cambridge University erupts in protest, assailing Whitgift with slander nailed to college doors. Separatists and radical Puritans call on their members to *fight a good fight,* calling Whitgift's authority *Antichristian, ergo not to be obeyed.*[15] Their outcry, in turn, prompts a royal proclamation banning seditious literature, equating attacks on the Church with attacks on the government.[16]

Whitgift swings into action, pursuing dissidents with such rigor that even Burghley, Lord Treasurer of the Queen's Privy Council, condemns the policy as entrapment and smacking of the Inquisition. By 1587 Puritans can complain of *tyranny* and *dangerous days. I see a miserable desolation,* writes Richard Parker, *like to come upon us.*[17]

He is right. The crackdown begins in earnest later that year. Leaders of the Separatist movement are thrown into prison. Minute books of their clandestine meetings are confiscated and culled for the names of conspirators. A nationwide manhunt for Martin Marprelate is launched and prosecuted with vigor. Arrests proceed madly, but the Marprelate tracts remain unsilenced. The bishops, *like furious and senseless brute beasts . . . spare none, but with tooth and nail cry out, "Down with that side that favoureth the Gospel so! Fetch them up with pursuivants; to the*

Gatehouse Prison, to the Fleet, to the Marshalsea, to the Clink, to Newgate, to the Counter with them."[18]

Brownists

1593. Amid the furor, a Brownist bill is brought before Parliament, directed against a Separatist sect led by John Browne. Those who refuse to attend Anglican services are to be banished from England, the death penalty invoked against any who return. Raleigh, a Member of Parliament, opposes the bill, claiming there are twenty thousand Brownists in England. Who, he asks significantly, will take care of their families? Who will incur both charge and responsibility? One of Raleigh's shipping captains is a Brownist.[19] Are there others connected to him? Could he be thinking of White's colonists? Had he given compensation to the families of the missing?

May 28, 1593. John Penry, one of the authors of the Marprelate tracts, is executed. To espouse the cause of Separatism in this highly charged atmosphere is to assume very *Dangerous Positions* indeed.[20]

Lost Colonists as Separatists

Let us now return to the Lost Colonists and reexamine their behavior in their final moments on Roanoke. Something had gone wrong. They were in trouble. In the midst of it, John White returned to England for help. The sequence of events seems straightforward enough. Or does it?

The question is: Why was *White* the person sent back? Was the choice logical? If the colonists' situation on Roanoke was so perilous that they considered it essential to dispatch someone to England, why was the Governor of the colony the necessary selection? There can be only one reason. The sole characteristic that set White apart from the others was the fact that he *was* Governor. He was the single most important person in authority. He held the power.

This is a clue. It is reasonable to conclude from this that the problems the colonists were experiencing were not confined entirely to Roanoke. Somehow, they involved England. Otherwise, why send back the Governor? If the colonists anticipated that they would not receive a proper audience due to the fame and, therefore, inaccessibility of their patron Raleigh, White had only to delegate his authority to an appointed officer and send him home with a letter. At first this was what he tried to do. But the colonists begged him with great persistence. They seemed frantic. Why? Could their fear have had something to do with the enemies White said they had? These very enemies were the reason White did not want to go back himself, afraid that his return as Governor would jeopardize their credibility.

Where does the political situation in England fit in? Was there something in the nature of the colonists themselves that not only prompted them to go to America in the first place, but also convinced them that their petition in England might go unheard? That also explained why their project had enemies? If they as a group were in a weak position, they might certainly expect no outside help short of sending home the Governor himself. As incredible as it sounds, were they, in fact, political or religious dissidents? Or was there something more going on behind the scenes? It is time to examine what we know of John White's colonists.

7 THE COLONISTS

Now have they taken leave of worldly pleasures all,
That young and lusty were to live; and now to toil they fall.
That finely were brought up; yea now they bid adieu,
The glittering Court, the gallant town, the gorgeous garments new;
The bravery of this world, the pride and pomp of earth,
And look not backward any way to riches, race, or birth;
To worthy wife or friend, to babes nor nearest kin;
But only to the Lord above, and journey they are in.

Thomas Churchyard, embarkation poem[1]

The City of Raleigh

It is difficult to place the colonists. The historical record is meager. The contract detailing their arrangement with Raleigh to settle in America is missing. All writing and correspondence between them, nonexistent. Or misplaced. What we do know is that the colony was organized as a corporation under the title of *The Governor and Assistants of the Cittie of Raleigh in Virginea.* Papers were drawn and signed on January 7, 1587. The designated Governor was John White. Twelve colonists were named as Assistants. Together, they make up *the first founders* of the *original and renowned* City of Raleigh.[2]

The corporation, as organized, was largely autonomous. Raleigh retained jurisdiction over his North American holdings under the terms of his original patent, subleasing a portion to the colony. His personal seal, dated early 1585, reads: Walter Raleigh, Knight, and Governor of Virginia. However, the seal is later amended, omitting all mention of administering Virginia. *Walteri Ralegh: Militis: Gardian: Stannar: Cornue: et: Devon + Capitan: Gard: Reg: et: Gubernator: Insulae: de: Jersey.*[3] Governor of Jersey, but not Virginia.

The City of Raleigh was designed as a joint-stock corporation, and the individual colonists were expected to invest their own money. In return, each was to receive a grant of at least *five hundred acres to a man,* even if the initial investment, for whatever reason, were waived. This implies that many of the colonists, perhaps the majority, were wealthy enough to finance their own voyage, with a lesser number — tradesmen or servants — volunteering only *the adventure of his person.*[4] Whoever the colonists were, they clearly were not the begging poor.

A Trail Obscure

Despite the little information we have, we must try to work up a profile. What could the colonists' motivation have been for emigrating from England? To try their fortune or increase their wealth? Escape corruption? Avoid persecution? Were they strangers, or a group who knew each other intimately and functioned as a body? Any selection we make must fit the known facts and also contribute to our understanding of circumstances that, so far, appear inexplicable.

For the sake of argument, let us suppose that White's colonists were a Separatist congregation. Corruption and persecution would be their chief concerns. If so, then their voluntary departure from England on the eve of Whitgift's crackdown in 1587 was an extremely smart move. A smart move, but a very dangerous one. Because Raleigh was their only lifeline. An interesting hypothesis, for, were it true, it would explain unequivocally why the colonists assumed they would receive no help in England short of sending home the Governor himself to set matters right.

So far, so good. We continue. Very few of the colonists have been identified with any certainty.[5] The surnames are common, records patchy or nonexistent. The difficulty is compounded by choice. For example, a Mark Bennett is listed in the Essex records of the 1580s as a farmer. Was this the same Mark Bennett who was a Lost Colonist in 1587? We assume so, but we cannot be sure.

Tentative identifications indicate that the colonists were relatively influential. There was a John Jones, physician; a William Browne, goldsmith; an Anthony Cage, sheriff; a Thomas Hewet, lawyer; Thomas Harris, faculty at Cambridge; Richard Wildye, graduate of Oxford. Others were listed as gentlemen, though admittedly two had criminal records, having been jailed for theft.

Why Leave a Homeland?

If the colonists were merely lesser gentry or aspiring members of society, hungry for position, we would understand their eagerness to embrace all that America offered. Oddly, few seem to have done so. There were few volunteers. We might expect the incentive of five hundred acres to spark a land rush, land in England being scarce. It did not. In fact, far from prompting a headlong dash, White tells us that many of the colonists came only as a result of his *persuasions.*[6] *Master White,* said John Gerard, was *an excellent painter who carried very many people into Virginia . . . there to inhabit.*[7] His urging, his responsibility. Since the colonists were expected to finance their own voyage, and since the names identified thus far were people of substance who required considerable persuading in order to go, what are we to think?

What would induce people with financial interests in England to leave everything they owned and all that was familiar to make a long and perilous journey into an unknown wilderness from which they could not readily return?[8] Raleigh had difficulty mustering people even willing to *invest* in Virginia, let alone go and live there!

Furthermore, the colonists left England at a time when relations with Spain were deteriorating rapidly. In fact, the Spanish Armada was preparing for attack; a terrible fact known and dreaded throughout England. This was a war year! The majority of adventurers left wives and children behind to be sent for at a later date. So why would anyone abandon business and family in the face of such political turmoil? Panic was sweeping England, predictions were rife that the country would fall. The colonists must have been aware that resupply would be difficult. Why not wait until the crisis blew over? Without doubt, White had to persuade them! Still, how did he do it? And how did he convince nine young couples with children, a nursing mother, and two pregnant women to go?[9]

Separatists Again

Impossible . . . unless, and herein lies support for the theory, they were already a coherent body — a congregation even — beginning to feel the heat. The pressure intensifying from Whitgift on the one hand. The specter of the Spanish Inquisition looming with the Armada on the other. A body who knew White and trusted him. Who had very strong motives for forming a community far away from London, war or no war.

If not this explanation, then why the inordinate concern expressed by the colonists that their resupply on Roanoke might not be undertaken? If their apprehension stemmed only from the war, of being lost in the shuffle, what did they imagine White could accomplish that one of the Assistants could not? Certainly people of some stature — the goldsmith, the lawyer, the physician — would be able to make their cause felt in London. White may have been Governor, but he was merely an artist, wasn't he? Not a wealthy or powerful businessman with connections and associates who could make things happen. Yet, for some reason, they needed White to go. This is evident from a petition signed, not only by *the Assistants, but diverse others, as well women, as men,* to ask White — no, they *most earnestly entreated and incessantly requested,* in effect, begged White — to return to England *for the better and more assured help.*[10]

Without concrete proof, we have nothing more than a theory that the Lost Colony was a congregation of Separatists. What is the evidence? And is there a connection between this and their mysterious disappearance?

Mottoes and Crosses

Pieces of information, insignificant in themselves, may supply an answer when taken together. The coat of arms for Raleigh City, for example: a white shield emblazoned with a simple red cross. A roebuck in the first quarter, *set on a hart of concord.* The motto, *Concordia: Parva Crescunt* — in unity, the weak become strong. *Small things increase.*[11] A powerful statement for a small settlement with a great future, or for a persecuted congregation given latitude to thrive and prosper.

Crosses figure prominently in the colony's brief history. Is there something to the symbolism? St. George's cross, red on a white field — symbol of England, the triumph of good over evil — has a similar look. Without a hart of concord in its quarterings. But there was another cross connected with the colony. We have seen it in White's plea to the colonists to carve it as a sign of distress. Not their own symbol, the plain, unembellished cross. But a cross formé: ✠. A cross used in heraldry. The kind sewn onto the gowns of Anglican archbishops. A Catholic Crusader's cross. From whom did the threat come?

Enemies

It may have come from Whitgift. It certainly came from Spain. Spain, which sent out missions to sweep the Atlantic coast, searching for them.

If discovered, White's colony would have been destroyed as swiftly as Laudonnière's Huguenot settlement in Florida. Catholic Spain. The Inquisition. These are the entities to fear. *I willed them, that if they should happen to be distressed in any of those places, that then they should carve over the letters or name, a cross* ✠ in this form.[12]

By the time the Brownist bill was introduced into Parliament in 1593, the idea of utilizing North America as a religious refuge was at least ten years old. In 1583 Raleigh's brother, Sir Humphrey Gilbert, had hoped to settle Catholic recusants in Newfoundland, with Dr. Dee compiling lists of Catholic adventurers, promoting it as part of England's overseas colonization effort.[13]

There was talk of banishing dissident Separatists throughout Elizabeth's reign: to Scotland, to Canada. The Queen stipulating that they should not return unless they conformed. *Our land . . . likes not you,* writes Joseph Hall, . . . *when it is weary of peace, it will recall you.*[14] Emigration of dissidents was a one-way ticket.

We see Richard Hakluyt comparing White's colony to Laudonnière's Huguenot settlement in Florida, commending Raleigh for those *which are to be employed in your own like enterprise.* Like enterprise? What does he mean — similar because the settlement is in North America? Or because, like the Huguenots, they happen to be a reformed body? Preparing to hold a portion of the Queen's territory against Spain. Dedicating his English translation of Laudonnière to Raleigh, Hakluyt conceded that *no history heretofore set forth had more affinity, resemblance or conformity with yours of Virginia, than this of Florida.*[15]

So they were Protestants at the very least. Raleigh's 1593 defense of the Brownists, his employment of at least one as a captain and charges of atheism later leveled against him, contribute a not unconvincing picture that Separatism was exactly what White's colonists were all about.[16]

Unusual Behavior

But the strongest evidence comes from the behavior of the colony itself. On Roanoke, White appeared to exert very little authority as Governor and ultimately was persuaded to leave the island, against his inclination, by a vote of the entire company. Separatists *entirely abhor all difference of rank among ecclesiastics.*[17] The same held true among the laity.

This would account for White's lack of assertiveness, which has drawn sharp criticism as a sign of defective leadership. The obvious course for

White to have followed, as we have said, would have been to appoint an Assistant to return for help. When White attempted to do this, the result was *some controversies* between them *about choosing two out of the twelve Assistants, which should go back as factors for the company into England: for every one of them refused.* Far from a commanding presence as Governor, White *by much persuading* at last induced Christopher Cooper to leave, only to have him change his mind the very next day *through the persuasion of divers of his familiar friends.*[18]

On August 22, *the whole company, both of the Assistants, and planters, came to the Governour, and with one voice requested him to return himself into England.* Women also joined the petition, being *all of one mind, and consent.*[19] What can we make of this? This is no Anglican way to settle an issue! In both monarchy and Church, government is strictly hierarchical. Yet here on Roanoke, the colonists sound remarkably democratic. Hardly the behavior we would expect toward an Elizabethan governor. Yet it *is* the way Separatists might make decisions.

White's attitude toward Indian people was also unusual. Hakluyt endorsed proselytizing, *the gaining of the souls of millions of those wretched people, the reducing of them from darkness to light, from falsehood to truth, from dumb idols to the living god, from the deep pit of hell to the highest heavens.*[20] White embraced an entirely opposite view. His was one of warm affection and admiration, exhibited not only in his paintings but in his vow at Croatoan *to renew the old love that was between us* and to live together *as brethren and friends.*[21] Acceptance. Ralph Lane, commander of the Roanoke fort in 1585–1586, was more typical when he observed their land to be fertile and *fit to be civilly, and Christianly inhabited,* though at present *inhabited only with savages.*[22]

Preparation for the Journey

We have made a case from the evidence available that the Lost Colonists were Separatists. The implications of this — of why, for example, rescue efforts to locate the missing colonists were never rigorous — have yet to be determined. Certainly it must have played a part, though time may yet prove us wrong. However, one thing is clear: whoever the colonists were, they were very much on their own on Roanoke and, indeed, had been since the start of their journey. It was they who assumed control of the colony's administration. It was they, as investors, who outfitted the expedition. And it was they who were projecting themselves into an unknown land.

The colonists were briefed in the weeks before they sailed. An experienced Portuguese navigator named Simon Fernandez, one of the Assistants, was taken on as pilot. Hakluyt was employed to render Laudonnière's book on Florida into English, an example of Raleigh's *singular and special care* to prepare the colonists so that, noted Hakluyt, *by the reading of this my translation,* they might be *forewarned and admonished as well to beware of the gross negligence, in providing [in]sufficiency of victuals, the security, disorders, and mutinies that fell out among the French . . . that by others' mishaps they might learn to prevent and avoid the like.*[23]

Hakluyt busily compiled accounts of other North American expeditions. His *Divers Voyages,* which took so long in coming to press that his friend Thomas Savile of Merton College joked that it must have been crushed to death, provided an excellent handbook on early American travels.[24]

And then there was the testimony of David "Davy" Ingram, who claimed to have walked the entire length of North America from Mexico to the west of Cape Breton in 1569. For two whole months in 1582, and after thirteen years of neglect, Ingram was interrogated about the country by a group of officials headed by Secretary of State Sir Francis Walsingham.[25] He had found a captive audience at last. Recounting more than they needed to know. Musical instruments: one kind formed from a hollow cane struck against the thigh while seated. A very pleasing sound. Another, a drum like a tabor, covered with hide. He acts out dances, hums a few bars. Overwhelming his listeners: *This examinate can very well describe their gestures, dancing and songs.* Ingram repeats the half dozen sentences he remembers from their language. Words for "greeting," for "king," for "bread," for "sun." And of course, warming to his subject, the word for *the privities. Carmugnar,* he grins.[26]

All this information and more is shared with the colonists. Hakluyt further recommends a list of *dead victual* to carry in the ships. Items other voyages have found useful. Among the deceased provisions: salted pork and beef, oatmeal, rice, butter and honey, cheese, currants, raisins, prunes, olives, beans, peas, salad oil and vinegar, turnip and parsnip seed, radishes, carrots, cucumbers, cabbage, lettuce and endive, onions and garlic, thyme, mustard, fennel and anise.[27]

The Colonists

One hundred and seventeen men, women, and children.[28] Nine married couples. Wives and babies remaining in England, preparing to rejoin husbands. Nine children. Two infants born in America. George Howe, murdered on Roanoke. This constitutes all we know of the Lost Colonists. And we know their names:

Men
Morris Allen
Arnold Archard
Richard Arthur
Roger Bailie
Mark Bennet
William Berde
Henry Berrye
Richard Berrye
Michael Bishop
John Borden
John Bridger
John Bright
John Brooke
Henry Browne
William Browne
John Burden
Thomas Butler
Anthony Cage
John Chapman
John Cheven
William Clement
Thomas Colman
Christopher Cooper
John Cotsmur
Ananias Dare
Richard Darige
Henry Dorrell
William Dutton
John Earnest
Thomas Ellis
Edmond English
John Farre
Charles Florrie
John Gibbes
Thomas Gramme
Thomas Harris*
Dyonis Harvie
John Hemmington
Thomas Hewet
George Howe
James Hynde
Henry Johnson
Nicholas Johnson
Griffin Jones
John Jones
Richard Kemme
James Lasie
Peter Little
Robert Little
William Lucas
George Martyn
Michael Myllet
Henry Mylton
Humfrey Newton
William Nicholes
Hugh Pattenson
Henry Payne
Thomas Phevens
Edward Powell
Roger Prat
Henry Rufoote
John Sampson
Thomas Scot
Richard Shaberdge
Thomas Smith
William Sole
John Spendlove
John Starte
Thomas Stevens
John Stilman
Martyn Sutton
Richard Taverner
Clement Tayler
Hugh Tayler
Richard Tomkins
Thomas Topan
John Tydway
Ambrose Viccars
Thomas Warner
William Waters
Cutbert White
Richard Wildye
Robert Wilkinson
William Willes
Lewis Wotton
John Wright
Brian Wyles
John Wyles

Women
Joyce Archard
Alis Chapman
[?] Colman
Elyoner Dare
Elizabeth Glane
Margery Harvie
Jane Jones
Margaret Lawrence
Jane Mannering
Emme Merrimoth
Rose Payne

*He is listed twice. Were there two men by the name of Thomas Harris or did John White include him twice by mistake? Could one have been a child?

Jane Pierce
Wenefrid Powell
Audry Tappan
Elizabeth Viccars
Joan Warren
Agnes Wood

Children
Thomas Archard
Virginia Dare
Robert Ellis
Harvye
George Howe Jr.
Tomas Humfrey
John Prat
John Sampson Jr.
Tomas Smart
Ambrose Viccars Jr.
William Wythers

8 IN CERTAIN DANGER

I have had good experience of this world; I have known what it is to be a subject, and I now know what it is to be a sovereign. Good neighbours I have had, and I have met with bad; and in trust I have found treason.

Elizabeth I[1]

A Plan Gone Awry

Where do we stand in this investigation? We have 115 people missing from Roanoke Island. They may have represented a dissident Separatist congregation. Although initially it appeared that White abandoned them, he did not. He returned to England for help at their insistence. He is, therefore, ruled out as a suspect. Neither he nor Raleigh can be blamed for neglect, for sober efforts were made prior to departure to prepare the colonists for what lay ahead.

White himself had been to Roanoke twice before. As a result, he clearly understood the requirements for survival there. Two other colonists, James Lasie and John Wright, were also veterans of the earlier expeditions.[2] Their expertise would guarantee the inclusion of items indispensable for the voyage. White's twelve Assistants were carefully briefed.

Yet all the planning came to naught. On Roanoke the colonists exhibited extreme distress. One man lay dead, and evidently they believed others would follow. Nearing panic, the colonists — with one voice — forced the governor home for their *better and more assured help.* Expressing great fear over *certain our known, and apparent, lacks and needs.*[3] Despite all preparation. Despite all precaution. The question is . . . *what went wrong?*

A Grisly Reception

August 1587. The colonists reach Roanoke after a dangerous sea voyage occupying nearly four months. Rowing ashore, a shocking discovery is made: strewn about a clearing are the bleaching bones of an Englishman:

one of the fifteen soldiers stationed on the island, with whom they were to reconnoiter. Appalled, White's company pushes through the woods to the fort, only to find it abandoned and partly razed. The remaining portion, along with *necessary and decent dwelling houses,* is overgrown with melon vines *and deer within them, feeding on those melons.*[4] Something is terribly wrong.

Unable to account for the missing soldiers, White takes control. He promptly issues orders *for the repairing of those houses, which we found standing, and also to make other new cottages, for such as should need.* A temporary measure while he considers what to do. In particular, he is anxious *to learn the disposition of the people of the country towards us.* As though he anticipates ill will. The answer is forthcoming: George Howe, out crabbing, is found slumped facedown in a marsh, his body pierced with Secotan arrows. Leaving a wife and young son desolate in a strange land. We wanted *only,* White said of the neighboring Secotan, *to renew the old love that was between us, and them, at the first, and to live with them as brethren and friends.*

Impossible. White knows this, as do Lasie and Wright. How much of the story have they told the others? The atmosphere on Roanoke crackles with tension. Day-to-day events streaming out of control amid an aura of numbing disbelief. For White never intended to be here. *In fact the colonists never meant to settle on Roanoke at all.*

Startling Revelation

The destination is not, nor ever has been, Roanoke Island! White is emphatic about this. From the beginning, from the very first, the colony was to be established farther north on the Chesapeake Bay. Never on this dark and forbidding shore. Condemned by the past. White's words ring out almost frantically: they were to call at Roanoke only briefly, to rendezvous with the soldiers and then leave for *the Bay of Chesepiok, where we intended to make our seat and fort, according to the charge given us among other directions in writing under the hand of Sir Walter Ralegh.*

And yet they remain on Roanoke. The victims of a deliberate deception. In fact, as we shall see, they have been betrayed. *This* is the information White must convey to Raleigh. This is why someone must go back. To report that their forsaken condition on Roanoke means only one thing . . . *sabotage.*

PART TWO

A CASE OF MURDER

9 SABOTAGE

To Kingdoms strange, to lands far off addressed;
Alone, forsaken, friendless on the shore,
With many wounds, with death's cold pangs embraced;
Writes in the dust as one that could no more,
Whom love, and time, and fortune had defaced.
Sir Walter Raleigh[1]

Lurking in the Shadows

White's colonists severed ties to family and business in England and purchased a voyage that was to lead to a new life on the Chesapeake Bay. At the time, they had no way of knowing that someone had a far different agenda for them and had expended considerable effort to achieve it. They could not know that, contrary to carefully laid plans, they would be taken to Roanoke Island instead. And left there. This circumstance was dire enough, but to this was added a crushing blow that made their landing catastrophic. Something had occurred in Roanoke's past that made any hope of survival there impossible.

We do not yet know what that was, but there were certainly those present who did. John White knew. So did someone else on the expedition. Someone — other than Lasie and Wright — who had been there before. Who knew the story. Who was aware of the events that had taken place during the fateful winter of 1585–1586.

The roster of the second Roanoke expedition of 1585 included the names of James Lasie and John Wright, but we cannot accuse either of wrongdoing. Too little is known; they appear nowhere else in any record. In fact, the only possible link is a John Wright who subscribed to the later Jamestown venture.[2] This man was listed as a merchant with the East India Company and admitted to the Mercer's Guild in 1604, which might imply that he was a young man. Could he have been the son of Lost Colonist John Wright, left behind in 1587 with his mother in England? If so, it might explain his interest in the later Virginia colony. At this moment, we simply don't know. Aside from this curiosity, nothing conspicuous about Lasie or Wright exists.

The Peculiar Case of Darby Glande

There was another individual who had been on both voyages. One who departed with John White's company in 1587—but never reached Roanoke. And although he was present on Grenville's 1585 expedition, he insisted that he had gone against his will. His name was Darby Glande. Years later, he would impart his own strange story to Spanish officials in St. Augustine.[3] He said he was an Irishman. A soldier and a sailor. And on a ship loaded with wine and merchandise out of Brittany, he was captured by Raleigh's cousin Sir Richard Grenville and impressed into service on the expedition to Roanoke. He was forced to spend the winter of 1585–1586 with the military command stationed there, despite his protests, because the English refused to give him passage home. He returned to London with the rest of the company in the spring of 1586.

Rare as this adventure was, Darby Glande made the improbable claim that it had happened to him again. Astonishingly, he maintained that he had never intended to accompany White's colony to Roanoke in 1587, but had been seized and taken by force. How could this be? Such a bizarre action would not likely come from the hands of the John White we know. The profile simply does not fit. Could there be more to this story?

Murder

Our simple case of missing persons has come to an end. The situation has become much more complex. Clearly something was going on behind the scenes which bears investigation. The picture that is emerging is incredible: there are men, women, children, and babies stranded on Roanoke Island, in certain danger, having been placed in harm's way without adequate provisions. They are aware that their supply ships, which will be sent to the Chesapeake Bay, will never find them. Whoever was responsible for placing them on Roanoke knew this too. This fact dramatically changes our focus. The crime is nothing less than attempted murder.

Thus we begin anew. Yet what a case this is! There are no bodies, no suspect, and no motive! Darby Glande has yet to be charged.

Ready the Sails

1587. Three ships line the wharf in Portsmouth harbor: the *Lion* and two consorts — a flyboat and a pinnace.[4] John White, Governor of the colony, sails as Captain. His pilot is Simon Fernandez, who is also one of the twelve Assistants. Edward Spicer commands the flyboat. Three years from now, in a breach off Hatorask, White will watch him die. The pinnace is captained by Edward Stafford. White is acquainted with him from the Roanoke expedition of 1585.

Supplies are loaded aboard the vessels. Barrels of food, water, wine. Furniture to last a lifetime. Articles comparable to those destined for Jamestown years later: clothing, linen, wooden dishes, cups and saucers, candlesticks, frying pans, beds and bedding, pillows, napkins, buttons and thread, glue, carpentry tools, paper, wax, ink and parchment.[5]

The colonists bustle up the gangway, loaded with packages, herding their children before them. Rich with parting gifts of marmalade and butter, they are leaving the known world behind.[6] With them is Manteo, native to Croatoan Island, who is returning home from his second visit to England.[7] He is the colonists' link to the future. It is April 26.

No Turning Back

May 5. At night the convoy pulls into Plymouth harbor. It is the final stop before the Atlantic crossing. The two days spent in town are poignant. The colonists are the "in between." Neither here nor there. No longer of England, not yet away from her.

Plymouth's streets twist down to the harbor, narrowed by stone shops savoring of fruit pastries, breads, and sausages. Merchants and sailors bustle along the wharf, oblivious to the Roanoke venture, loading and unloading cargo. A colorful commotion. Seagulls wheel above the steps leading to the water, searching for food. And beyond the snug harbor and creosote and brine, the cliffs of Devon and Cornwall reach slender fingers out into the English Channel. Dotted with vessels. This is the last of England the colonists will ever see. *The 8. we weighed anchor at Plymouth, and departed thence for Virginia.*

A Harrowing Voyage

May 16. Only eight days out there is a problem. It unfolds so strangely that at first it is difficult to know what has happened. In the dead of night, off the dangerous Portuguese coast, Captain Spicer's flyboat is left stranded. An accident — or deliberate? She carries colonists as well as supplies. The other ships do not help; instead, they abandon her. *Simon Ferdinando, Master of our Admiral, lewdly forsook our flyboat, leaving her distressed in the Bay of Portingall.* There is nothing White can do.

June 22. The *Lion* and pinnace reach the Caribbean and anchor off Santa Cruz in the Virgin Islands, *where all the planters were set on land.* They remain for three days. Was this the rendezvous agreed upon should the vessels become separated? The company still hoping that the flyboat will reappear.

Poisoned Fruit

The colonists settle in. Cabins are built along the beach under an awning of dense foliage. After a month at sea, the lush shore with its tropical breezes and exotic fruits must seem like paradise. It isn't: *some of our women and men, by eating a small fruit like green apples, were fearfully troubled with a sudden burning in their mouths, and swelling of their tongues so big, that some of them could not speak. Also a child by sucking one of those women's breasts, had at that instant his mouth set on such a burning, that it was strange to see how the infant was tormented for the time.* How on earth did this happen? More to the point, who allowed it to happen?

The pilot, Simon Fernandez, has had more experience in the Indies than almost anyone in England, having received his training there in the service of Spain. This is no small matter, for before they can sail Spanish navigators must pass a rigorous course in the renowned pilot training school in Seville.[8] After months of lectures, examinants are brought to the Contraction House before a panel of twenty-five certified pilots and tested on their knowledge of the Indies. *Then the Pilot Major commandeth the examinant to spread a sea-chart upon the table, and in the presence of the other pilots to depart or show the course, from the bar of Saint Lucar to the Canary Islands, and from thence to the Indies, till he come to that place whereof he is to be examined.*[9]

The test is designed to evaluate a pilot's knowledge and experience. He is quizzed about *the rules of the sun and of the north-star, and how he ought to use the declination of the sun at all times of the year . . . another asketh him of the signs and marks of those lands which lie in his way to that haven whereof he is examined. And then another demandeth, that if his masts should be broken by tempest, what remedy he would use? . . . Others ask him what remedy if his rudder should chance to fail? Others oppose him about the account of the moon and of the tides? Others ask him if a pirate should take him and leave him destitute of his chart, his astrolabe, and his other instruments serving to take the height of the sun and of the star, what course he would take in that extremity?*[10]

Only when he has passed all questions to the panel's satisfaction is the applicant granted a license. In short, the pilot is a professional, an expert; a seaman of the highest rank.

Fernandez is a pilot. He has successfully guided both the first and second Roanoke expeditions through the Indies. He has earned a reputation for navigating these waters well. He knows which islands to avoid and which are beneficial. He knows where to stop for water and the best ports of call for trade.

So why, on this island in the West Indies, does Fernandez not warn the colonists of potential danger? And why would they assume that a strange fruit, growing in an unfamiliar land, is fit to eat? In fact, we would expect them to err on the side of caution. We would expect them *not* to sample anything they did not immediately recognize as absolutely safe. We must therefore conclude that someone told them it was edible. That the fruit would bring relief to the monotonous diet of hard tack and salt beef. That it would be a healthful dietary supplement to prevent illness. Who told them this? For eat it they do: the colonists consume their fill. The result is devastating. It will be a full twenty-four hours before the effects wear away. Faces thick and swollen. The baby howling in pain. A day and night of terror, wondering if they will recover.

Water, Water, Everywhere, Nor Any Drop to Drink

But there is more. Other surprises are in store, for the drinking water on Santa Cruz is poisoned. The colonists find nothing *but a standing pond, the water whereof was so evil, that many of our company fell sick with drinking thereof.* Not a little sick, but life-threateningly so. And *as many as did but wash their faces with that water, in the morning before the sun had drawn away the corruption, their faces did so burn, and swell, that their eyes were shut up, and could not see in five or six days longer.*

June 23. Those with strength remaining search the island for fresh water. White and a company of six climb to the top of a hill for a better view. Fernandez had promised abundant food, yet they see neither sign of *beasts, nor any goodness.* Only a flock of parrots. And then a jarring discovery. Returning to camp, White *found, in the descent of a hill, certain potshards of savage making.* The place is inhabited, though Fernandez *had told us for certain, the contrary.* They have unwittingly invaded another people's land, and have taken no defensive precautions.

White's dream for the City of Raleigh is dying. The colony, rapidly deteriorating. An unknown number of planters have been lost with the flyboat. Many of those remaining are blind. Others suffer from the poison they have ingested. And hanging over everyone, a critical shortage of water. *The other company had found running out of a high rock, a very fair spring of water, whereof they brought three bottles to the company: for before that time, we drank the stinking water of the pond.*

As complaints mount, Stafford departs in the pinnace for Beak Island, *being so directed by Ferdinando, who assured him he should there find great plenty of sheep.* Food for the colony, and presumably water too. Yet nothing comes of the search. Stafford rejoins them off Puerto Rico. The next three days pass *unprofitably in taking in fresh water, spending in the mean time more beer, than the quantity of the water came unto.*

It is here that two of the company defect. And here that we again pick up the story of Darby Glande.

Defection

The incident occurs on July 1 at Mosquitoes Bay, Puerto Rico.[11] Glande and another Irishman, Denice Carrell, are left behind. Of Carrell we know nothing; neither who he was nor why he deserted. Nor do we hear of him again. In view of this, we have no choice but treat his story as a dead end.

All the more reason to take a closer look at Darby Glande. A man of shifting identity: he is Darby Glande in 1585. White lists him as Darbie Glaven. Later, in a sworn statement, he calls himself both David Glavin and David Glavid.[12] Is this significant? Still, orthography was uncertain; it was not uncommon to spell names in a variety of ways. Regardless of what name he went by, we are dealing with the same individual.

After abandoning the ships in Mosquitoes Bay, Glande's next move is unclear, but he eventually makes his way across the island to the headquarters of the Puerto Rican Governor, Diego Menendez de Valdés. The same official who, in 1590, will report John White's presence aboard the *Hopewell*, bound for America. Destination unknown.

Warning

Glande, taken into Spanish custody, tips off Valdés that the English are preparing to settle a colony in North America, at a location called *Jacan*.[13] This is highly significant. Glande is very specific about the destination; he is not talking about the Chesapeake Bay, but the place to which he was brought by Grenville in 1585. The place where Raleigh's man brought him in 1585 and where Drake later arrived and carried him away. *Jacan*, for Glande, is Roanoke Island. Yet the colonists aboard ship know nothing of this. They think they are headed for the Chesapeake. How could Glande know of plans afoot to maroon the colonists on Roanoke unless he had been informed of this before his escape? Had he been told what to say?

There is more. Other ships, Glande warns, will follow with many additional settlers. The news jolts Spain to the core. English intrusion into this tightly controlled region is tantamount to invasion. It is this information that will prompt Spanish authorities to dispatch Captain Vicente Gonzalez in 1588 to scour the coast for White's colony. On the Outer Banks he will find a slipway for vessels. Other searches will follow and reams of paper will be expended in the frantic effort to find them. All this commotion stems from Darby Glande.

But what was his motive? Certainly Glande cherished no love for the English — an Irishman, captured by them twice. Yet this could hardly have prompted him to deliver himself into Spanish hands, to throw his life away. For a reward, he was impressed as a galley slave and served a seven-year term before securing his release in Havana.[14] Later, in a sworn deposition made while a free man and in the service of Spain, we see clearly that Glande did not instigate his own defection. Having been seized in London and taken aboard the *Lion* as far as Puerto Rico, he says he *was told to make his escape.*[15] He did it; he was ordered to do so.

This is curious. Nowhere does the record indicate that Glande was restrained during the voyage or confined below deck. Therefore, had the opportunity to flee presented itself, he would not have required much direction. Had he wanted to escape, he need only have watched and waited. He would not have lingered until he was told to go.

If the individual who instructed Glande to escape had been his London kidnapper, Glande might have said so. To be seized and then released without ceremony on an island in the West Indies defies explanation, and we would expect him to have registered some surprise. It makes no sense that someone would go to all the trouble of forcing him aboard ship, only to urge him to break free when the voyage was no more than half over. Yet never at any point does he inform Valdés that it was his captor who agreed to release him, but simply that he was told to escape.

It is far more likely that Darby Glande was a dupe. That the person who told him to run was neither friend, nor captor, but a third party. And that the escape was orchestrated as part of a larger plan. So there were two conspirators. The man who forced Glande aboard ship, and another who released him. The Irishman was a pawn to destroy White's colonists. If true, his dismissal on Puerto Rico was no coincidence, but a strategic maneuver. They were counting on Glande to alert the Spanish authorities. He had been to Roanoke before.

Who Else Remains?

In any case, since Darby Glande never completed the trip, it is clear that he is not the saboteur. Somebody else must be involved in the colonists' betrayal. Someone who had been present on Roanoke during the winter of 1585 and was aware of the jeopardy in which he was placing them (with Glande's warning to Spain as additional insurance), who was capable of seeing that the colonists never left the island. He and Darby Glande had come face to face. The question is, who was he? And who was his accomplice? We have eliminated White, Lasie, and Wright. None of the other colonists has ever been to Roanoke.

Perhaps we have needlessly narrowed our search. It is true that no one on White's voyage had been present during that fateful winter on Roanoke. But then that wasn't necessary: not as long as they had ears with which to hear. In other words, someone had only to know about the circumstances. To know about them and use them to his advantage. We have been overlooking the obvious. Was there a colonist aware of what had happened on Roanoke Island who never intended to remain in the City of Raleigh? His identity now is clear. It should have been all along.

Identity Revealed

July 1. The evening of Glande's defection. The ships enter Puerto Rico's Rojo Bay. White was here before, in 1585, to load salt from deposits on shore. Fernandez has promised to stop here again, and so in preparation, the colonists have busied themselves making *as many sacks for that purpose, as we could.* White arms a defensive party for protection, lest Spaniards appear from the nearby garrison of San German.

But Fernandez, *perceiving them in a readiness* to disembark, sends for White and, *using great persuasions,* urges him not to land. Although he has guided previous expeditions ashore in this exact place, Fernandez now produces many excuses *not to take in salt there, saying that he knew not well whether the same were the place or not: also, that if the pinnace went into the Bay, she could not without great danger come back, till the next day at night, and that if in the meantime any storm should rise, the Admiral were in danger to be cast away.*

Whilst he was thus persuading, he caused the lead to be cast, and having craftily brought the ship in three fathom and a half water, he suddenly began to swear and tear God in pieces, dissembling great danger, crying to him at the helm, bear up hard, bear up hard: so we went off, and were disappointed of our salt, by this means. Without it, the colony will have difficulty surviving. It is their chief means of preserving food.

A definite and terrifying pattern is emerging. The flyboat abandoned off Portugal, the futile search for supplies on Santa Cruz, the ingestion of poisonous food and water, the denial of salt on Puerto Rico, unnecessary delays, deception. Is the saboteur White's Assistant, Simon Fernandez?

The next day, sailing along the west end of S. Johns, the Governour determined to go aland in S. German's Bay, to gather young plants of oranges, pineapples,[16] *mameas, and plaintains,*[17] *to set at Virginia, which we knew might easily be had, for that they grow near the shore, and the places where they grew, well known to the Governour, and some of the planters: but our Simon denied it.*[18]

The Case of Alanson

Rather than land on Puerto Rico, where White is familiar with the terrain, Fernandez instead makes for Hispaniola to visit his friend Alanson, a French trader, who will furnish them *both of cattle, and all such things as we would have taken in at S. Johns.* But Fernandez never intends to land, *as it plainly did appear to us afterwards.* July 3. The ships reach Hispaniola *and bare with the coast all that day,* with the expectation, as promised, that the pinnace will be sent ashore to *the place where Fernando his friend Alanson was: but that day passed, and we saw no preparation for landing in Hispaniola.*

The following day, nearing the town of Isabella, and *we having knowledge that we were past the place where Alanson dwelt* and *no preparation yet seen* for going ashore, White confronts Fernandez. Demanding *whether he meant to speak with Alanson, for the taking in of cattle, and other things, according to his promise, or not: but he answered, that he was now past the place.* And, furthermore — another shock — Alanson is not even there. He *thought him dead,* Fernandez flippantly remarks, for the French ambassador told Raleigh that Alanson had been arrested and taken to Spain. So that *it was to no purpose to touch there in any place, at this voyage. The next day, we left sight of Hispaniola, and haled off for Virginia, about 4. of the clock in the afternoon.*

Pitiful Situation

We can only imagine the condition of White's planters. They have been en route since April, with little fresh food and water, though within sight of islands that might easily have provided both.[19] Eleanor Dare and Margery Harvey are nearly to term in their pregnancies. Another woman is nursing a baby. All three have special dietary needs.

By now the living quarters are stinking and filthy from three months of accumulated waste. Human excrement dribbling from privies directly onto the ballast in the hold of the ship. Pooling with rotten garbage from the galley. Raleigh has a reputation for well-designed vessels. Yet even he admits that to embark upon an ocean voyage is to endure *a rolling ship, to change the diet of soft bread and fresh meat for hard biscuit and salt beef, to drink unsavoury water instead of wine and beer . . . besides a world of other harms and hazards.*[20]

Satirist Thomas Churchyard summed it up in a poem:

> *And all for country's cause, and to enrich the same,*
> *Now do they hazard all they have; and so for wealth and fame,*
> *They fare along the seas, they sail and tide it out;*

They hail and stretch the sheets aloft, they toil and dread no doubt.
They feed on biscuit hard, and drink but simple beer,
Salt beef, and stock-fish dry as keck, is now their greatest cheer.
And still a fulsome smell of pitch and tar they feel;
And when sea-sick (God wot) they are, about the ship they reel.
And stomach belcheth up a dish that haddocks seek,
A bitter mess of sundry meats, a syrup green as leek:
Then head and heart doth heave, and body waxeth cold:
Yet face will sweat, a heavy sight the same is to behold.
But they must needs abide a greater brunt than this,
And hope that after hellish pains there comes a time of bliss.[21]

For White's colonists there will be no time of bliss. Only prolonged agony. On July 6 they arrive at the Caicos, *wherein Fernando said were two salt ponds, assuring us if they were dry, we might find salt to shift with until the next supply, but it proved as true as the finding of sheep at Beak.* This was their last chance. Fernandez is stalling.

Too Late to Plant

At last, the summer far advanced, the ships reach the southern limit of the Carolina coast. It is mid-July. Fernandez anchors to reckon his bearings; they lie dead in the water several days. It is impossible not to suspect a delaying tactic. Fernandez has conducted expeditions here before, successfully and with confidence. Raleigh's captains named one of the three entries through the Outer Banks "Port Ferdinando" in honor of his discovery of it in 1585. Earlier, he sailed to America for Raleigh's brother Gilbert, completing the trip in record time. Before the voyage he had been schooled by Thomas Hariot in the use of the latest navigational technology, *not without almost incredible results.*[22] Yet days idle away before Fernandez finally realizes that he has mistaken an offshore island for Croatoan far to the north and, *finding himself deceived,* they move on. He need only have consulted Manteo, native to Croatoan, who was on board and who certainly could recognize his own homeland.

The colonists' prospects for survival are bleak. The season is now too late for planting. Supplies from the Caribbean, which might have tided them over — salt, vegetables, and livestock — were not obtained. They will have no choice but to consume their own seed stock, leaving nothing to plant the following year. Their only recourse is to await the arrival of supply ships and, in the meantime, trade for food with the Powhatan nations of the Chesapeake Bay using irreplaceable pots, tools, and clothing.

But Fernandez steadily subverts the mission. The ships head north along the dangerous edge of the Carolina coast, *where in the night, had not Captain Stafford been more careful in looking out than our Simon Fernando, we had been all cast away upon the breach, called the Cape of Fear, for we were come within two cables' length upon it: such was the carelessness, and ignorance of our Master.*

Mutiny

July 22. Despite a harrowing passage, the ships arrive safely at Hatorask.[23] John White boards the pinnace *with forty of his best men* to visit Roanoke according to Raleigh's instructions. He is to hold conference with the fifteen soldiers stationed at the fort since 1586, *concerning the state of the country* and the Secotan people within it. Manteo is to be invested with authority over Roanoke and the town of Dasamonquepeuc. After that, the company will continue north to the Chesapeake Bay.

And then it happens. The final act of sabotage. As the pinnace carrying White and his men moves away from the ship, the accomplice, a *Gentleman by the means of Fernando*[24] *who was appointed to return for England, called to the sailors in the pinnace, charging them not to bring any of the planters back again, but leave them in the island, except the Governour, and two or three such as he approved, saying that the summer was far spent, wherefore he would land all the planters in no other place.*

The announcement explodes like a bombshell. The planters, helpless in the tiny pinnace, are stunned. White, finding his voice, must have urged the sailors to disobey Fernandez and receive them back aboard the ship, to preserve their lives. A desperate appeal to all that is humane! His efforts are futile. It *booted not the Governour to contend with them,* for they were of one mind to follow Fernandez. *Unto this were all the sailors, both in the pinnace, and ship, persuaded by the Master.* There is nothing White can do. It is mutiny. He is lucky to have his life.

Overwhelmed, the men quietly depart for Roanoke. There is still hope to be had from the soldiers in the fort. At the very least, the colonists can expect temporary shelter. The soldiers will be furnished by Raleigh, even if the colony's supplies bypass them for the Chesapeake Bay. Although rations for fifteen men will hardly feed one hundred and seventeen.

It doesn't matter. On Roanoke, the men make the grisly discovery. The *same night, at sunset* they *went aland on the island, in the place where our fifteen men were left, but we found none of them, nor any sign that they had been there, saving only we found the bones of one of those fifteen,* bleaching in a clearing. There will be no help from the soldiers: one dead, the others missing. The nauseating realization must wash over them like a tide: they have reached the end. There will be no supply ships to save them. Fernandez will notify England that the soldiers are dead.

Later, they will find the fort dismantled. White will order repairs to the houses overgrown with weeds and melon vine. New cottages will be built of brick and tile. And shock will settle in. A certain numbness. For this is Roanoke. They cannot survive.

Reunion

On the 25th there is a brief respite from the upset, a momentary victory over Fernandez. Captain Edward Spicer in the long-absent flyboat arrives at Hatorask, miraculously having found his way, though he has never been here before. The missing planters are reunited *to the great joy and comfort of the whole company: but the Master of our Admiral, Fernando, grieved greatly at their safe coming: for he purposely left them in the Bay of Portingall, and stole away from them in the night, hoping that the Master thereof, whose name was Edward Spicer, for that he never had been in Virginia, would hardly find the place, or else being left in so dangerous a place as that was, by means of so many men of war as at that time were abroad, they should surely be taken, or slain: but God disappointed his wicked pretences.* They survived, only to be doomed.

A Death and a Birth

The festive mood is quickly shattered. It would have been better if Spicer had never found Roanoke and had instead returned to England. They have — all of them — survived months of torment, only to be marooned on Roanoke Island. In the midst of this crisis, George Howe is slain.

Aware of their dwindling food supply, the colonists had gone into the marshes to hunt crabs. Howe strayed off alone, not realizing that hunters from the town of Dasamonquepeuc were also there. After deer. Even if he had known, he would not have understood the significance. He had not been to Roanoke before. They, *being secretly hidden among high reeds, where oftentimes they find the deer asleep, and so kill them, espied our man wading in the water alone, almost naked, without any weapon, save only a small forked stick, catching crabs therewithal, and also being strayed two miles from his company, shot at him in the water.* Piercing him with sixteen arrows. With clubs, they *beat his head in pieces.* Through the woods, among the houses, his young son awaits him in vain. George Howe Jr., a mere boy.

It was inevitable. White knows they can hardly expect less, given the circumstances of 1585. The colonists are not responsible for what happened. They are innocent of England's past. Yet they will pay heavily for the crimes that others committed . . . and someone in England will let them. George Howe's death deals a crippling blow. An envoy is rushed to Croatoan with Manteo, hoping to smooth things over. Leaders from towns throughout the Secotan country are invited to Roanoke for peace talks. There is nothing more the colonists can do.

August 18. Another, fleeting, surge of hope. Eleanor, *daughter to the Governour, and wife to Ananias Dare, one of the Assistants, was delivered of a daughter in Roanoke, and the same was christened there the Sunday following, and because this child was the first Christian born in Virginia, she was named Virginia.* They stand together on a carpet of loblolly pine, in a clearing of houses pressed against the sound. Momentarily forgetting the horror, they celebrate this new life, and imagine what might have been. White's granddaughter. Virginia Dare.

Plenty of Time to Linger

All the while, Fernandez remains at Hatorask. His excuse that the summer is too far spent to carry the planters the remaining hundred miles north to the Chesapeake Bay proves to be a lie when he tarries another thirty-six days leisurely preparing his ships. The vessels are emptied and scoured, laden with *wood and fresh water,* the men ordered *to new calk and trim them for England.* Activities that could have been accomplished far more easily on the Chesapeake Bay than on this rugged coast.

Although Captain Spicer remains friendly to the company, he can neither transport the colonists home, nor north where they wish to be. To disobey Fernandez would jeopardize his own life, and so the planters hopelessly *prepared their letters and tokens to send back into England,* to family left behind. Counting on the flyboat to deliver them.

Someone Must Go Home

August 21. The ships prepare to depart. As the colonists watch in despair, a violent storm slams into the coast. It is hurricane season. The *Lion* cuts cables and is forced out to sea, stranding most of the sailors on shore. Days pass and still *such a tempest* rages that the ship is lost from view and *we feared he had been cast away.* Roanoke closes in. For the first time their desolation hits home.

Curiously, even as he was marooning the colony, Fernandez had stated that White or an Assistant could return to the ships. Why he did so is unclear. Perhaps for show. In England he will maintain that it was too late in the year to complete the journey to the Chesapeake Bay. It will be his word against White's. The fact that he offered to bring a representative back will prove his good intentions. He may also know that White, or his colony, has enemies at home — who will work in his favor. Fernandez must be very confident indeed that he will not be charged with mutiny.

Day one of the storm. The colonists decide to send someone for help, but disagree sharply over who this should be. As the rain beats down, *some controversies rose between the Governour and Assistants* about choosing who will return to England. Everyone *refused, save only one, which all the others thought not sufficient.* At last, *by much persuading of the Governour,* Christopher Cooper agrees, only to change his mind at the urging of his friends, *so that now the matter stood as at the first.*[25]

White's Decision

The next day, the 22. of August, the whole company, both of the Assistants, and planters, came to the Governour, and with one voice requested him to return himself into England, for the better and sooner obtaining of supplies. White refuses, *alleging many sufficient causes.* He stands to be ruined by certain unnamed *enemies to him, and the action,* who will not spare to *slander falsely* both of them.

Far more importantly, the colonists are leaving Roanoke. They *intended,* White says, *to remove 50 miles further up into the main.* An attempt to preserve their lives. Yet he and the colonists will become separated. He struggles against a rising panic. His goods will be lost, ruined, or pilfered in the transport. He will find himself *utterly unfurnished* upon his return. Desperate excuses. He has a daughter and baby grandchild he will not leave behind. He is the Governor! He, least of all, should go!

Worse yet, he has led his daughter to this fate. Plans made so long ago in England unraveling so disastrously.

The next day, not only the Assistants, but divers others, as well women, as men, began to renew their requests to the Governour again. They have placed their faith in him. They will meet his objections and promise the *safe preserving of all his goods.* If any should be spoiled or lost, *they would see it restored to him.* They are begging him to go. A bond is drawn, signed *under their hands and seals* and *delivered into his hands* testifying the same:

> *for the present and speedy supply of certain our known, and apparent lacks and needs . . . we all of one mind, and consent, have most earnestly entreated, and incessantly requested John White, Governour of the planters in Virginia, to pass into England, for the better and more assured help, and setting forward of the foresaid supplies: and knowing assuredly that he both can best, and will labour, and take pains in that behalf for us all, and he not once, but often refusing it, for our sakes, and for the honour and maintenance of the action, hath at last, though much against his will, through our importunancy, yielded to leave his government, and all his goods among us, and himself in all our behalfs to pass into England.*

Painful Departure

August 27. The storm passes. In the early morning, the *Lion* and flyboat reappear and the seamen who up until this moment thought that they, too, had been stranded on Roanoke, eagerly leave. The vessels make last-minute preparations. Orders are given to hoist the sails. The flyboat weighs anchor and moves outside the bar, and still White has not made up his mind. The colonists' appeals are frantic. He must go before it is too late! Before all is lost! At last, *through their extreme entreating,* White is *constrained to return into England, having then but half a day's respite to prepare himself for the same.*

In the final, anxious moments, White urges *a secret token agreed upon between them & me,* that when they vacate Roanoke, *they should not fail* to carve the name of their destination *on the trees or posts of the doors.* Promise! A distraught father, leaving his family behind. *I willed them, that if they should happen to be distressed in any of those places, that then they should carve over the letters or name, a cross* ✠ in this form. White is insistent, searching beloved faces for signs of assurance. He embraces Eleanor for the last time.

Numbly, White boards the boat that draws him away from shore. His eyes clinging to the figures receding in the distance. Eleanor waving farewell. The hem of her dress trailing in the surf. The hope that all will be well must be feeble indeed. The soonest White can return will be spring. A winter Atlantic crossing has never been attempted.

A Rough Voyage

White refuses any further contact with Fernandez. He boards Spicer's flyboat, which sets a course for England, *where we hoped, by the help of God, to arrive shortly.*

But during the voyage, the winds are variable and *sometimes scarce.* Rotten water casks spring leaks; by September the supply reaches critical level. On the twentieth day out, off the Azores, a nor'easter strikes hard *which for 6 days ceased not to blow so exceeding, that we were driven further in those 6 than we could recover in thirteen days.* To make matters worse, the sailors are ill. Two die and are cast overboard, their rigid bodies splashing into the churning sea. And *all the beverage we could make, with stinking water, dregs of beer, and lees of wine which remained, was but 3 gallons, and therefore now we expected nothing but by famine to perish at sea.*

October 16. Land is sighted, but what land it is remains unknown. A hulk from Dublin and an English pinnace are anchored in the harbor, but they may as well be leagues away, for Spicer left his shoreboat behind on Roanoke. They are incapacitated. They will die within reach of land. As dusk settles, the sailors, through bleary eyes, spot half a dozen men rowing toward them from the English vessel. They are saved! From them, at last, *we understood we were in Smerwick in the west parts of Ireland.*

White and Spicer are transported ashore. The town is too small to supply food and medicines and so, on horseback, they race for help across the peninsula to Dingle Bay. White's horse thundering across the moor, hooves pounding above the cliffs. Knowing his family depends on this. Aboard ship, the death toll mounts, striking the steward, boatswain, and his mate.[26] Leaving but eight men standing. The rescue soon arrives. The men are transported ashore and helping hands bring the matter under control. White's problem, less obvious, is ignored.

The Official Report

White is frantic. He must get to England. In mounting agitation he searches ports for a ship, with no luck. Finally, on November 1, he finds one—a slow vessel bound for Southampton—and takes it. White arrives in England seven days later, only to discover he is too late. Fernandez beat him home. For three weeks he has been in London, presenting his story. Stafford has been back even longer. Long enough for Hakluyt to publish a book in October, enthusiastically proclaiming the trip a success. Dedicated to Raleigh, it hails the triumphant *late return of Captain Stafford and good news which he brought you of the safe arrival of your last colony in their wished haven.*[27]

In their *wished haven*? What can this mean, except that Stafford was the gentleman accomplice?[28] Cold fear must seize John White. For more than a month, he has battled storms, famine, and contagion to report his colony's plight as they struggle for their lives on Roanoke Island . . . one man already dead. Yet England is rejoicing: Stafford has assured the world of their safety.

Little wonder White feared for his credibility. We know that he met with Raleigh. But how much did he tell? Did he name names? The strange "farewell" letter to Hakluyt never disclosed the identity of the "gentleman." Or if it did, it was neatly edited out. However, Simon Fernandez was not similarly protected. White very definitely fingered him as the main conspirator. Which sounds incredible! Fernandez, after all, was an Assistant. Why would he, of all people, sabotage the colony? He will attribute the series of mishaps on the voyage to accident, and excuse his inability to land the colonists at the correct location to the lateness of the year. It will be White's word against his.

The problem is, as the problem was, that Fernandez lacks motive. The facts indict him, but without logical rationale he can hardly be charged. Could White provide the answer? Could anyone? It now seems apparent that we have been operating in the dark long enough. If Fernandez's motive cannot be determined by examining his behavior on the 1587 voyage out, we must investigate his activities prior to this date.

It was Fernandez who piloted the expedition to Roanoke in 1585. It was a voyage fraught with conflict, and a military mission that ended in profound tragedy. The record will show that Fernandez was in the midst of it. Although he left before the real trouble began in the winter of

1585, one thing is certain: Fernandez was allied to the principal players. He knew what subsequently occurred.

The time has come. We must face the horror. We must place ourselves on that voyage and understand firsthand what went wrong on the Roanoke expedition of 1585–1586. The second Roanoke voyage: the military.

10 THE SECOND ROANOKE EXPEDITION: GRENVILLE AND THE SECOTAN (1585)

If you touch him in the Indies, you touch the apple of his eye, for take away his treasure which is nervus belli, and which he hath almost out of his west Indies, his old bands of soldiers will soon be dissolved, his purposes defeated, his power and strength diminished, his pride abated, and his tyranny utterly suppressed.

Richard Hakluyt to Elizabeth I[1]

War Is Brewing

Greenwich Palace on the Thames. The New Year's festivities burst forth in an explosive extravaganza of revelry and merrymaking. There are garish masquerades and balls; music and pageantry; costly gifts bestowed upon the Queen. As though war in Europe were not brewing.

The card playing and dicing and dancing plash across the holiday, raucous days and nights of frolic and frivolity. Manteo and Wanchese, strikingly attired in brown taffeta, are a constant diversion. They are Raleigh's Indian guests, brought home from the first Roanoke expedition of 1584.[2] The palace audience tumbles over in side-splitting laughter at the antics of Richard Tarleton, comedian in the Queen's theatrical troupe. He challenges Elizabeth's little dog, Perrico de Faldas, to a duel.[3]

Outside, beyond the palace lights and laughter, the streets are cold.

1585. London. The year begins darkly. From the monastic gloom of the Escorial, Philip II of Spain is gearing for war. In France, the House of Guise casts its lot with the Catholic powers and enters *into a dangerous confederacy,* prompting fears of a formidable Holy League alliance.[4] Spanish troops converge on the Netherlands, sending shockwaves of panic throughout England. If the Low Countries fall, attacks will be launched across the North Sea against her. *And if he settle there, then let the realm say adieu to her quiet state and safety.*[5]

Twelfth Night, January 6. At the end of the celebrations, Raleigh is knighted as a reward for annexing the land of Virginia for the Queen. As he kneels before her in Greenwich Palace, Elizabeth lays a sword upon his shoulders. Raleigh, it is said, is *a man of marvellous great worth and regard, for his many exceeding singular great virtues, right fortitude and great resoluteness in all matter of importance.*[6] It is Sunday.

The time bomb over Europe is ticking. As the Spanish buildup steadily increases, Raleigh moves forward with secret plans to arrest it. He will lead a military expedition to Roanoke. Erect a base on the island.[7] And aim his mark at Spain. For Raleigh is aware, as are the top English military advisers, that Philip cannot attempt an invasion of England without a steady stream of New World gold. While Spain plots England's demise, the bold Sir Walter lunges at the dragon's underbelly.

The Spaniards, Hakluyt assures the hesitant Queen, are a *men most odious, not only to the people of the West Indies, but also to all Christendom and all the world beside.* The Italians are oppressed by them. The French *hate them for the most part worse than scorpions.*[8] As do the Prince of Hesse and the Duke of Saxony.

Money welds the regime together. Disrupt its supply and the Spanish war machine will grind to a halt. The frightening armies, monstrous weaponry and matériel support will all come crashing down. Nations *kept by great tyranny* will realize hope; *people kept in subjection desire nothing more than freedom. And like as a little passage given to water it maketh his own way, so give but a small means to such kept in tyranny, they will make their own way to liberty.*[9]

To block Spain in the Indies is to block Spain permanently. A desperate wager for *gold, for praise, for glory,* Raleigh's aim is nothing less than to topple the mighty Spanish empire.[10] And *the Spanish king shall be left bare as Aesop's proud crow, the peacock, the parrot, the pie, and the popinjay, and every other bird,* cries Hakluyt, *having taken home from him his gorgeous feathers, he will in short space become a laughing stock for all the world.*[11]

Raleigh's Campaign

A squadron is readied for Roanoke, the site of the offensive. Alarmed, a Spanish agent reports thirteen ships preparing, destination unknown.[12] In the House of Commons, Thomas Cavendish commissions a military expert to draw up notes on defense and fortification. Three hundred soldiers are conscripted for the enterprise, many drawn from combat in war-torn Ireland.[13]

From her navy, Elizabeth assigns Raleigh the warship *Tiger.* Mounted with two tiers of guns. An additional 9,600 pounds of gunpowder is carted out in crates from the Tower armory to ships waiting on the Thames. Royal prerogative is granted to impress mariners, soldiers, and provisions.

February 8. As a final act, Elizabeth recalls Captain Ralph Lane from military service in Kerry to head Raleigh's land forces.[14] Fresh from the Irish wars, he will transfer the ferocity of that campaign to Roanoke. Unrecognized at the time, this will be a significant factor in the fate of the Lost Colony.

April 9. The fleet is assembled at Plymouth. Commanding general is Raleigh's cousin Richard Grenville. Forty-three years old, from a wealthy and respected West Country family, he is known to be *a gentleman of very good estimation both for his parentage and sundry good virtues.*[15] Although he has never led a squadron, Grenville is an excellent choice.

Second in command, as High Marshal, is Thomas Cavendish. Ralph Lane, third in rank, sails as Lieutenant. Vice-Admiral of the fleet is Captain Philip Amadas, a Plymouth man. He led the first expedition to Roanoke in 1584. Simon Fernandez, Pilot Major, is third officer on the maritime side. These men, together with the ships' captains and Assistants, form a council of war and constitute the administration of the fleet. Aboard, too, are the specialists: John White, artist; Thomas Hariot, scientist and Raleigh's tutor; Joachim Ganz, a mineral man from Prague with expertise in copper; apothecaries and merchants to determine the value of medicines and commodities yet to be discovered. Sailing with them are Manteo and Wanchese, returning to their homeland after spending the winter in England. The full complement is six hundred men, divided between seven ships.[16]

Pirates and Privateering

May 1585. Escalation begins. Spain declares an embargo on English shipping. Merchant vessels in Spanish ports are seized, their crews subjected to the Inquisition. The *Primrose* of London barely escapes with the news, returning to England to a hero's welcome.[17] Under the embargo the English economy quickly collapses. Small businesses are crushed, and, with the outlet for cloth sealed up, the trade spirals into a depression. It is said that the *whole country is without trade and knows not how to recover it; the shipping and commerce here having mainly depended upon the communication with Spain and Portugal.*[18]

July. Hundreds of English privateering vessels are issued letters of reprisal to recoup their losses, swarming out upon the high seas in undeclared war.[19] The difference between privateering and piracy no more than a slip of paper bearing the government's stamp of approval. The distinction is utterly lost on Spain. The English, they say, *are good sailors and better pirates — cunning, treacherous and thievish.*[20]

Piracy finances expeditions on a colossal scale, and at great profit. Powerful London syndicates clean up, raking in money hand over fist. Shipping, warehouses, transport, and marketing contracts are all under their control so that goods are easily unloaded. Wealthy magnates unleash navies of two-hundred-ton merchantmen, converted into powerful men-of-war by the addition of heavy armament. These pirate ships carry fierce names, a terror to Spain: *Seadragon, Black Dog, Tiger, Scorn, Disdain, Dreadnought, Defiance, Malice Scourge, Revenge, The Spy, Wildman's Club.*[21]

A dance is begun upon the high seas of pursuer and pursued. The home market is quickly flooded with Spanish exotics: oil, sweet wines, figs, currants and almonds, oranges, lemons, spices and dyes. Contraband sugar is confiscated from Brazilmen in such tremendous quantities that soon more of it is found in England than in all of Europe.[22] Giving a phenomenal boost to the national economy. The English ecstatically add sweeteners to almost everything. Confections and pastries are invented daily.

Some privateers are out to get rich, recklessly pursuing the Spanish fleets. Foolhardy risk-takers: *The Wheel of Fortune, Poor Man's Hope, Chance, Desire, Costly.* And *Why Not I? They that risk for small things are pirates,* declares Raleigh.[23] Those who seek large prey, the millions in Spanish ducats, are in a different class altogether.

But patriotism has its part to play. The great sea battles are strikes against the Spanish tyranny now gripping Europe. English combatants challenge the empire in ships bearing names full of scorn: *The Virgin God Save Her, The Black Bishop, Gift of God, John Evangelist, Holy Ghost, Pagan.* The political climate steadily heats up. In London, Raleigh anxiously awaits news of his squadron.

The Domino Effect

Puerto Rico. Ship's log: *The 12. day of May, we came to an anchor in the Bay of Mosquito, in the Island of S. John.* The *Tiger* is all alone. The fleet had been battered by a storm in the Bay of Portugal and separated. A bad beginning. Grenville orders the men ashore to erect a fort, and assesses the damage. A pinnace will be constructed to replace the one sunk, for the expedition cannot continue without it. It is vital because it must transport new supplies to make up for those lost aboard the six missing vessels; it alone can maneuver the shallow sounds to Roanoke. *General Sir Richard Greenville and the most part of our company landed, and began to fortify, very near to the sea side.*[24]

They are observed. Eight Spanish horsemen materialize out of the forest. Grenville immediately rallies his soldiers, forcing a retreat of these *Spaniards, who by all possible means did their best endeavour by proffering of sundry skirmishes* to drive Grenville's men back into the sea. *But he, nothing appalled with their brags, kept his ground.*[25]

Clearly, the loss of the pinnace has caused an unexpected chain of events. It has forced Grenville's company ashore and alerted the Spaniards that significant plans are afoot. Even the activities of John White will be duly noted and reported to authorities in Seville by Hernando de Altamirano.[26] White, transferring banana plants and pineapples with brush onto paper. Painting an indelible record: a hermit crab, a mammee fruit, a scorpion, an iguana. A watercolor sketch of the fort.

The new pinnace is finally launched on May 23. They have been joined by the long-missing *Elizabeth,* Thomas Cavendish's vessel. The two will strike out alone. Grenville orders the fort set on fire. As choking palls of black smoke stream out over the water, an inscription is carved on the bark of a tree for their other ships, should they straggle in. Vying, for sheer verbiage, with something on the order of a gazetteer: *On May 11th, we reached this place with the Tiger and on the 19th, the Elizabeth came up and we are about to leave on the 23rd in good health, glory be to God. 1585.*[27] One wonders how big this tree must have been.

Factions

As the ships work their way through the Caribbean, relations deteriorate between Grenville and his third in command, Ralph Lane. The rupture is significant, setting the stage for the crisis to follow. At Puerto Rico's Rojo Bay, Lane is ordered ashore to load salt as troops from the Spanish garrison of San German watch ominously from a hillside. The salt loaded, Lane beats a hasty retreat to the ship, bitterly condemning Grenville for hazarding his life. *My telling him of it,* Lane complained, *bred the great unkindness afterwards on his part towards me.*[28]

June 1. Friction between the two men intensifies when the *Tiger* anchors off Hispaniola after capturing two Spanish frigates. Their crews are ransomed. With the money received, Grenville opens shop. Incredibly, *sundry Spaniards* come to the ships to trade and are *well entertained aboard . . . by our General.*[29] Governor Rengifo de Angulo is urged to visit at the first opportunity. A shrewd move; Grenville now has supplies.

Sir Richard Greenefeelde General, Lane fumes, *hath demeaned himself, from the first day of his entry into government at Plymouth . . . far otherwise than my hope of him, though very agreeable to the expectations and predictions of sundry wise and godly persons of his own country, that knew him better than myself.*[30] A vile trick. A stratagem designed to weaken Grenville's integrity, to impugn his character. Lane strengthens his own position by slander.

The company unravels into factions. There is acrid disagreement over leadership. It is apparent that Lane and certain gentlemen serving on the council, in particular a disgruntled Atkinson and Russell, feel that their *complaints* and opinions, taken in concert, must outweigh Grenville's decisions.[31] This is his first expedition; they hardly expect him to assume control. Yet Grenville is no figurehead. He has been placed in this position of authority because of his talents and his ability to carry out Raleigh's designs. He sails to Roanoke as both Admiral and General; head of forces on land and sea. Those aboard the *Tiger* do not like it at all. If they had hoped to dominate the voyage once away from England, they are disappointed.

Shipwreck

June 23. The morning breaks warm and muggy. The ships drift quietly along the Carolina coast, frigate birds pitching crazily among the masts. The scent of pine wafts across the deck as the *Tiger*'s watch takes a turn in an uneventful shift.

Then, without warning, shallows jut from the water. The dangerous shoals of Cape Fear loom all around. Sailors scramble from the hold, springing at the rigging in a furious effort to draw the vessel back. Sails flap sharply. Rope whirls wildly across deck, stinging the boards as the ship lurches starboard. The *Tiger* is overwhelmed, afloat in a sea of sand. Feverish minutes pass as the hull slips through a maze of twisted reef.

At last the *Tiger* claws free and continues shakily up the coast. The next time, in the far more dangerous waters of the Outer Banks, they may not be so lucky. Grenville, Lane mutters, has nearly caused the expedition *several times* to have *taken a final overthrow.*[32] Lane, who left his military charge in Kerry for this promotion, finds his power far short of his expectations.

Tension mounts as the ships coast northward, the barrier islands now clearly visible. Grenville is duly cautious, determined to avoid mishap. For three days the ships ride off the island of Wococon while depth soundings are made and recorded. All entries into the interior *are so by nature fortified to the seaward, by reason of a shoal and most dangerous coast above 150 leagues lying all along this, her majesty's dominion.*[33]

At last it is determined to bring the vessels through the entry at Wococon. Fernandez takes the helm and, as he coaxes the ship forward, misjudges the shoals. The *Tiger* runs aground hard, shuddering from the jolt. Men tumble to the deck; crates and cargo spill across the hold — slamming into bellowing livestock.

A heavy sea washes over the ship, driving it onto the shoal like a battering ram. Without time to recover, it is pitched hard against the bar again. And again. And again. Eighty-nine strokes in all. The *Tiger* lies exposed and helpless, repeatedly beaten, bathed in salt tears. And in this moment, unknown to John White, the fate of the Lost Colony is sealed forever. From here on, all ensuing events evolve from this disaster. *All our fleet struck aground,* Lane wrote, *and the Tiger lying beating upon the shoal for the space of 2 hours by the dial, we were all in extreme hazard of being cast away.*[34]

In the end, the *Tiger* is rotated and run aground *hard to the shore.* The ship, though damaged, is still intact *with her back whole, which all the mariners aboard thought could not possibly but have been broken in sunder.* And, though at least we *saved ourselves,* murmured Lane, it is not without loss.[35] Grenville's *ship was so bruised,* journalist Abraham Fleming reported in England, and *the saltwater came so abundantly into her, that the most part of his corn, salt, meal, rice, biscuit, & other provisions that he should have left with them that remained behind him in the country was spoiled.*[36] The season is too far advanced for planting.

The disaster bitterly underscores the lateness of their arrival. And *that wholly through the default of him that intendeth to accuse others,* Lane acridly notes. The fault of Grenville, who blames Fernandez. *Your honour's servant Symon FerdyNando,* Lane hotly informs Secretary of State Walsingham, *truly hath carried himself both with great skill, and great government all this voyage, notwithstanding this great cross to us all; as the whole gang of masters and mariners will with one voice affirm.*[37]

Butler's Campaign

As the cleanup of the *Tiger* commences, Grenville dispatches Corporal Richard Butler north to Hatorask Island, near Roanoke, to search for any of the fleet's missing vessels that may have arrived.[38] Miraculously, both the *Roebuck* and the *Dorothy* are sighted and retrieved.

After this, Butler's activity is unclear. The account is garbled. There are indications that he may have gone ashore, headed inland some sixty miles, and engaged in a skirmish with an unnamed Indian nation, enemies to those at Hatorask. He kills twenty. Little can be made of the story as it stands; as it is, the account is barely more than a comment in passing. Yet, as we shall see, it may hold a clue to the fate of the Lost Colonists.

Wanchese must have accompanied Butler north to Roanoke. We *sent word,* states an anonymous entry in the *Tiger* journal, *of our arriving at Wococon, to Wingino at Roanoke.* Wingina, *the King.*[39] But what else did Wanchese tell his leader? For he does not share Manteo's enthusiasm for England.[40] The difference in their attitudes is striking, obvious to all. Sullen since his arrival, Wanchese will not return to the ships. Nor will he enter the English chronicle again in any other capacity than that of an enemy.

The Secotan Country

July 11. A tilt boat, fitted with an awning, is readied for Grenville and *divers other gentlemen,* including Hariot and John White, for a trip into the interior.[41] The party totals four vessels; fifty men at the very least. Manteo is sent ahead to prepare the way.

The boats glide in formation away from Wococon, skirting the low, sandy keys hugging the island. Their route lies northwest across Pamlico Sound, which stretches to the horizon like a broad inland sea. The hours crawl by, forcing the barrier islands into distant retreat. All the while, the sun beats down upon the water, searing English faces blood red. Grenville is lucky to have an awning.

They near the mainland as dusk settles. In the evening light the eerie swamp forest presents a dark and forbidding aspect. Somewhere deep inside the impenetrable gloom of this *vast and huge* expanse, a whippoorwill's call echoes off cypress, tupelo, gum, and tulip.[42] The men pass the night on the beach under full guard along the hem of trees. Or, perhaps more likely, they tough it out in the boats; a bed of rough planks gently lapped by water. Trusting what is familiar. Avoiding the thickening shadows; the forest drenched in night noises.

The following day, the boats pull near the town of Pomeioc and apprehension melts away. Crowds throng the shore in greeting, an impressive sight. *They are a people clothed with loose mantles made of deer skins,* says Hariot, *& aprons of the same round about their middles; of such a difference of statures only as we in England. . . . And to confess a truth, I cannot remember that ever I saw a better or quieter people.*[43]

The English are conducted down a sandy path snaking inland. Each step taken draws this remarkable world closer, shutting out England, forcing every man's thoughts into himself. The trees grow more dense the deeper they penetrate, pressing in on every side. Suffocating. Luxuriant. Spanish moss drips from the canopy overhead, blotting out the light. Underfoot, the pine-needle carpet is stained purple from muscadine grapes spilling onto the ground. We *have discovered the main to be the goodliest soil under the cope of Heaven, so abounding with sweet trees, that bring such sundry rich and most pleasant gums, grapes of such greatness, yet wild.*[44]

They travel blindly through a dense world of shifting hues. Curtains of cadmium, cinnabar, sienna. A cardamom forest of towering trees. The spires soar above and all around them, a silent cathedral of shifting mood and light. An artist's palette, a symphony of color. And then a shadowy palisade in a clearing. They have reached Pomeioc.

Pomeioc

The Englishmen wind through a turnstile of aromatic wood and pass into the town. John White snatches at sketch paper and charcoal. Capturing impressions and shapes. Later, he will fill in everything with vibrant watercolor. *The entrance is very narrow as may be seen by this picture,* observes Thomas Hariot, narrating, *which is made according to the form of the town of Pomeioc. There are but few houses therein, save those which belong to the king and his nobles.*[45]

Children peer hesitantly from doorways. On both sides, a momentary shyness. The English, at a loss what to do, spread out trade goods produced in noisy shops in faraway London. We *offered them of our wares, as glasses, knives, babies, and other trifles, which we thought they delighted in.*[46] To the great relief of the *multitude* of English indigents, the Indian trade will provide *ample vent of the labour of our poor people at home, by sale of hats, bonnets, knives, fish-hooks, copper kettles, beads, looking-glasses, bugles & a thousand kinds of other wrought wares.* Mr. Ashley, a maker of playing cards in Butulph Lane, hopes to tap into this market. His workshop is littered with beads and trifles. *Looking-glasses, bells, beads, bracelets, chains or collars of bugle, crystal, amber, jet, or glass.*[47]

White sketches a picture of the chief's daughter, *of the age of 8 or 10 years,* clutching an English baby doll. *They are greatly delighted with puppets, and babes which were brought out of England,* comments Hariot. A much-loved little girl. What, exactly, did her father trade in order to buy it for her? The people, *perceiving our good will and courtesy, came fawning upon us, and bade us welcome.*[48]

As the afternoon wears on, John White and Thomas Hariot survey the surrounding countryside. There is a place behind the town, they are told, a perfect sphere of water. An inland lake. A *great lake called . . . Paquype.* They follow a wooded trail, damp and spongy underfoot, around knotty cypress knees jutting out of stagnant water the color of weak tea, tainted by tannic acid. Scarlet-headed parakeets tumble wildly into the air, frightened at their approach.[49] The path skirts trees the girth of five men, primordial giants draped in skeins of green vine. Tendrils curl, cascading downward, twisting over the ground below. Then without warning, incongruous amid the tangle, a ring of blue water.

A mesmerizing sight. Paquype, a white sandy bed beneath bands of turquoise water as luminous as any West Indian sea. The lake is shallow, barely four feet deep. Hot to the touch. On the shore a blue heron takes flight, its wings silently beating, rising gracefully above the treeline. A shiver. There is something wonderfully wild and lonely about Paquype. And alive.

Hariot seems oddly at a loss for words: *near the lake of Paquippe, there is another town called Pomeiock hard by the sea. . . . The country about this place is so fruitful and good, that England is not to be compared to it.*[50] Never compared to it. Later, amid the rushing throngs of London, how will he describe this place? How will he make anyone understand?

Only reluctantly, as shadows spread across the lake, do the men step back into Pomeioc. Into a human world. Into a great commotion, a bustle of activity. People laughing. Women unrolling woven mats across the plaza. A mosaic of color and pattern; a carpet of black and red and tan and orange. Wooden platters are laid out, piled high with savory meats and breads; bowls brimming with soups and stews. The company gathers around; English visitors on one side, the Secotan on the other. A speech is made, startling the soldiers, for it is likely that here, as in the Powhatan country to the north, formal words are spoken *with such vehemency and so great passions, that they . . . are so out of breath they can scarce speak. So that a man would take them to be exceeding angry or stark mad.*[51]

Darkness settles heavily around Pomeioc. The night air enveloping, warm, heavy with the drone of locusts and frogs. The visit makes for a festive atmosphere. Much laughter and joking as the food platters are passed around. *They keep their feasts,* says Hariot, *and make good cheer together in the midst of the town.*[52] Somewhere far away within the swamp an alligator growls. Inside the protective palisade walls, a comforting security. A surrendering to the calmness of the night.

Aquascogoc

In the morning the boats head west, hugging the mainland. They are now deep within the Secotan country, two days away from the ships anchored off the coast. By late afternoon they invade the waterside town of Aquascogoc. With each town visited, a world is mapped out. Unknown people and places becoming familiar. Again a welcome; again a trade. The people, observes Lane, are *most courteous, & very desirous to have cloth.* By London standards, the trade advantage is one-sided. They *esteem our trifles,* Hariot remarks, *before things of greater value.* It is, of course, relative. Hariot readily concedes that they seem *very ingenious* and *show excellencie of wit.*[53]

The town of Aquascogoc lies enveloped in cornfields. As the traders pack away their wares, the last, weak rays of sunlight play across the maroon corn silk spilling out of cobs fat and ready for harvest. The kernels, a riot of pink and white and purple, will be pounded in mortars into lavender-tinted flour. Worked into moist bread called *ponap,* the "corn pone" of English settlers.[54]

Offshore, Indian dugouts ride a crimson tide as the sun tumbles into the sound. Shimmering fire across the water. Fishermen, in grand silhouette, lay their nets, rhythmically casting and hauling in. Butterflies unfolding glistening wings of nettle fiber. A graceful dance. Eventually the boats, lit up by torches, will twinkle toward land. Drawn by the fires of Aquascogoc.

The domed houses gleam with muted light, illuminating woven wall patterns like stained glass, spilling warm shapes across the tamped ground outside. Each design different. Stars and geometrics; kaleidoscopic forms; birds and fish. Hariot cautiously enters a house, touching the beams gingerly to examine its construction. *Their dwellings are builded with certain posts fastened together, and covered with mats which they turn up as high as they think good, and so receive in the light.*[55]

Such *excellencie of wit* encourages the belief that the Secotan might readily embrace the Anglican religion. The task falls to Hariot, fluent in their language from days spent with Manteo and Wanchese at Raleigh's house along the Thames. *Many times and in every town where I came, according as I was able, I made declaration of the contents of the Bible.* The accoutrements of faith are produced: a Bible, a cross, a silver communion chalice.[56] For Aquascogoc the destruction has begun. July 15: the morning dawns clear and bright. On the surface nothing seems amiss; nothing portends that Aquascogoc will not survive another day.

Secota

The English embark, heading west through Pamlico Sound, and disappear around a coast cluttered with sand islands. Brackish spray flies hot against the wooden bowsprit. It is afternoon before they reach Secota, Wingina's capital, entering by an inlet that fronts the town. Houses, temple, and statehouse are ranged unevenly along an avenue amid fields of corn and family garden plots. The plan is open, airy, and inviting, *fairer* than the walled villages already visited. No palisade surrounds this place. At Secota the English are *well entertained.*[57]

An avenue runs through the center of the community like a heart line, crowded with houses and cornfields cleared back to back and pressing against the forest. Each is differently sown, providing three harvests; a steady crop of food. *Their ripe corn. Their green corn. Corn newly sprung.*[58] The first field is flanked by a column of pumpkins, not yet ripe. Green globes cradled by soft ground.

The avenue continues along the edge of the fields to the river *from whence they fetch their water.*[59] Women crouch along the bank, dipping deep within the river, receiving the water into hollow gourds. A tinkling of chimes as the vessels clink together, caught up from a nest of wet sand. A constant coming and going of women.

Hariot pushes through a verdant forest of *six or seven foot* corn stalks, his arm a machete, forcing a path. Suddenly, piercing cries and an insistent striking of a stick against wood are answered by a wall of black crows lifting into the air, jolted skyward as if struck by lightning. Vehement shrieking; a thundering of black bodies. Hariot shields his face, warding them off. The commotion issues from a woven hut perched atop a scaffold, housing a youth bobbing around like a marionette, yelling and wildly waving his arms. *In their corn fields, they build as it were a scaffold whereon they set a cottage like to a round chair . . . wherein they place one to watch. For there are such number of fowls and beasts, that unless they keep the better watch, they would soon devour all their corn.*[60] Indeed, deer are seen feeding at the edge of the field.

Hariot scrutinizes the corn; unknown in England. He runs his palm against a blade, turning it over, examining it with unrecognizing eyes. And is suddenly aware of being watched. Muffled giggles. A group of Secotan women are observing him in obvious delight. A European scientist in a woman's field of corn. *The women of Secotam are of reasonable good proportion. In their going they carry their hands dangling down,* open, direct, unguarded. They are clothed in *deer skin very excellently well dressed, hanging down from their navel unto the midst of their thighs.*

He gazes in wonder at the thin blue lines of tattooing winding around their bodies in graceful tendrils, along *their foreheads, cheeks, chin, arms and legs. . . . About their necks they wear a chain, either pricked or painted. They have small eyes, plain and flat noses, narrow foreheads, and broad mouths. For the most part they hang at their ears chains of long pearls, and of some smooth bones.* Then a postscript, added a trifle ruefully. *They are also delighted with walking into the fields.*[61]

Hariot beats a retreat and wanders along the river, where men are catching fish. There he observes other women following the proceedings with interest. Hariot gazing at them, gazing at the fishermen. *Doubtless it is a pleasant sight to see the people, sometimes wading and going, sometimes sailing in those rivers, which are shallow and not deep.* Girls, too, crowd along the bank. *They delight also in seeing fish taken in the rivers.*[62]

Green Corn Feast

The English seem relaxed here, owing perhaps to the town's larger size and a bustling commotion occasioned by the visit coinciding with a Secotan holiday, *a great and solemn feast whereunto their neighbours of the towns adjoining repair.* Indeed, guests arrive hourly *from all parts, every man attired in the most strange fashion they can devise having certain marks on their backs to declare of what place they be.*[63]

White and Hariot make a record of the preparing feast, bobbing in and out of the cooking area. White sketches fish grilling atop a barbecue.

And when as the hurdle cannot hold all the fishes, they hang the rest by the fire on sticks set up in the ground against the fire, and then they finish the rest of their cookery. Deep smoky flavors; skewers of hickory and pecan. *They take good heed that they be not burnt. When the fish are broiled they lay others on, that were newly brought, continuing the dressing of their meat in this sort, until they think they have sufficient.*[64]

The odor of exotic and delicious dishes wafts across town. Smoke from the barbecue billows out, bathing the houses along the street in a milky haze, floating out across the fields. Children laughing, playing to while away the time; content to surrender the honor of getting underfoot to Hariot and White. Old people crouch in doorways, chatting with friends from neighboring villages. Venison and oysters and garlic and mint. Dogs pacing hungrily underfoot; a vicious tussle over scraps of fat tossed on the ground. White paints a clay pot propped upright in a pool of white-hot embers. A woman stirs in berries, walnuts, chunks of meat. Their *women fill the vessel with water, and then they put in fruit, flesh, and fish, and let all boil together like a stew.*[65]

The food is arranged *into dishes and set before the company.* Soft-shell crab. Sweet persimmon cakes, blackberries, corn bread and fritters, rose-tinted china-briar jelly, beans simmered in garlic and grease. Field apricots. And the most important dish of all on this holiday: grated green corn soup. After *they have ended their feast they make merry together.*[66]

There is an easy rhythm to life here. The people, *void of all covetousness, live cheerfully and at their heart's ease.* Perhaps Hariot feels envy. Yet something is wrong. When do the English first notice it? A silver cup is missing. It was last seen at Aquascogoc. Left there? Lost? They believe it stolen. Either way, Grenville's men might easily have written it off. They have been fed and entertained in this land for days. At Aquascogoc, as elsewhere, they have received more than compensation from a trade in which they paid out *trifles.*[67] All will be sacrificed for a silver cup. Amadas and ten soldiers will return to Aquascogoc.

The Burning of Aquascogoc

The songs fade away over Secota as the morning sun rises above the swamp forest, staining the eastern horizon. The canopy overhead is alive with birds welcoming the day. Below, the soldiers drag their boats into the water. Amadas and his men are the first to depart, returning by the same route they came, toward Aquascogoc. Who ordered them there,

Grenville or Lane? Amadas's official position in Lane's government is Admiral of the Country. *The Admiral,* it is said, was sent to Aquascogoc.[68] Oars dip into the sound, steady, purposeful.

At Aquascogoc, startled faces turn toward the shore. The English boat sprawls like a beached whale on the sand, cast off from the remainder of the fleet. Amadas strides forward and demands the silver cup. His question must cause no little dismay. Relations begun so cordially days before, no easy thing to reconcile with the Englishmen's change of manner. Who has the silver cup? Was it a trade? Was it ever even taken? No matter; they promise its return. What else can they do? Amadas waits.

The sun mellows into dusk, the hours ticking by. No one comes forward. The time of negotiation is past. The town, strangely quiet. And then a notation is entered in the *Tiger* journal, a single chilling blow: *The 16 we returned thence, and one of our boats with the Admiral was sent to Aquascococke to demand a silver cup which one of the savages had stolen from us, and not receiving it according to his promise, we burnt, and spoiled their corn, and Town, all the people being fled.*[69]

Flames spurt up from Aquascogoc. Black patterns on house shingles melt and bleed as fire consumes them. Lighting up the night. Cornfields wither under a shimmering orange heat. Maroon tassels dripping bloody threads. The cobs roast then turn to ash, the harvest ruined. Smoke from the town spills over the forest, visible for miles. Along the beach, Amadas's boat pushes into the black water, dwarfed by the fiery holocaust. The houses collapse, spewing molten cinder. The boat, swallowed by darkness.

A single picture of White's survives of this place: a girl with strands of pearls and copper beads around her neck, her hair clipped into neat bangs.[70] What became of her? For the theft of a single silver cup Aquascogoc is razed, the food supply destroyed, the people dispersed. Harsh retribution: to teach the Secotan a lesson. Undoubtedly it does.

News of the burning must travel quickly throughout the Secotan country. Meetings are convened to try to make sense of so bizarre an action. The English have begun to exhibit traits more of an enemy than a friend. Dark deeds once begun . . . *If there fall out any wars between us and them,* writes Hariot, *what their fight is likely to be, we having advantages against them so many manner of ways, as by our discipline, our strange weapons and devices else, especially ordinance great and small, it may easily be imagined; by the experience we have had in some places, the turning up of their heels against us in running away was their best defence.*[71]

No resistance was offered at Aquascogoc. *All the people being fled.*

From towns throughout the Secotan country, they will beg food and supplies necessary to survive the winter without starving. Their condition will burden others. Extra mouths to feed. These English, so exacting of generosity and harsh in judgment! If a silver cup wrongfully taken is punished so severely, one might consider how the Secotan will respond to precious food stores depleted by soldiers without compensation. Worth more than any cup.

Insubordination

Wococon, July 18. Grenville's company regroups under a relentless sun, the ships weltering in the haze. He must decide what course to take. There is talk of aborting the mission. Raleigh's instructions were for Grenville to *tarry himself, or to leave some gentlemen of good worth with a competent number of soldiers in the country of Virginia, to begin an English colony there.*[72] Specifically, he is to leave Lane. Yet the wreck of the *Tiger* with all provisions, particularly given the attack on Aquascogoc, has destroyed all hope of remaining. Grenville determines that their only option is to return to England and renew the offensive in the spring. With fresh supplies.

But now the bitter divisions that have plagued the expedition for weeks congeal. Strenuous objections are raised immediately. The participants in the attack against Grenville are possibly Atkinson and Russell, certainly Lane. He pens a *bold letter* to the Secretary of State, spewing tirades against Grenville, who *intendeth to accuse others.* A growing faction is determined to stay, standing *resolute rather to lose our lives than to defer a possession to her Majesty.*[73] Lane may well have demanded compliance with the original plan of placing him in command. If so, he stands in direct opposition to Grenville's authority. The General, *by indirect means, and most untrue surmises,* Lane cries, very likely suspects him of insubordination.[74] In fact, mutiny.

Court-martial meant execution. In a calculated exaggeration, Lane informs Walsingham of *how tyrannous an execution, without any occasion of my part offered, he not only purposed, but even propounded the same, to have brought me . . . to the question for my life.* Harassed *only for an advise, in a public consultation by me given.*[75] Grenville, the tyrant. Irrational and unwilling to entertain others' opinions. Lane, the innocent.

July 21. Grenville's hand is forced. The fleet weighs anchor and sails north out of Wococon. Lane will stay on Roanoke. One hundred and seven men — less than a third of the available military complement — will remain with him. Altogether, *a weak number.*[76] Construction of the fort is begun at once on the north end of Roanoke Island. An expert on defensive works, Lane himself oversees operations.

Although he has had his way, Lane now realizes that Grenville will return home to inform both Walsingham and Raleigh of *sundry complaints, against sundry gentlemen, of this service.* He therefore fires off a series of letters: four to Walsingham — *to advertise your honour and that most truly concerning them;* another to the Queen. To Raleigh he forwards an entire book, *an ample discourse of the whole voyage.* It documents Grenville's usual *manner of proceeding . . . and particularly towards myself.* A *true copy of the whole discourse* will also be delivered to Walsingham, including corroborating *testimonies and depositions.*[77]

The attack is vicious. Lane urges Walsingham and other investors to remove Grenville from office, citing his *intolerable pride and insatiable ambition.*[78] A sly move, suggesting that Grenville has jeopardized their money.

August 25. The *Tiger* weighs anchor and Grenville sails for England, little suspecting that both Atkinson and Russell carry secret letters addressed to Walsingham. Two weeks later, the last of Grenville's squadron sails away, leaving Lane in command of 107 men without supplies in a fort on a remote island beyond the boundaries of the known world. Had Lane been less bold, he might have felt trepidation at the prospect. Had he been less bold, he would have had no need to fear.

Lane's actions, more than any link in the chain of events forged thus far, will directly seal the fate of the Lost Colonists. His behavior, both brutal and despotic, may be dismissed by many as a product of his age. As nothing more than wartime tactics, used in both the Irish campaign and the treatment of the Welsh before them. But there are others who will view any who commit such atrocities as sadistic, regardless of the age in which they live. Indisputably, Lane's tenure on Roanoke was a downhill spiral ending in enormous tragedy. As we have said all along, something happened on Roanoke Island. We must now discover what that was. And, in so doing, enter the world of a madman.

11 THE SECOND ROANOKE EXPEDITION: LANE'S COMMAND (1585–1586)

It is a shameful and unblessed thing to take the scum of people and wicked condemned men to be the people with whom you plant; and not only so, but it spoileth the plantation; for they will ever live like rogues, and not fall to work; but be lazy, and do mischief, and spend victuals, and be quickly weary, and then certify over to their country to the discredit of the plantation.

Francis Bacon[1]

Lane's Fort

July 29, 1585. Lane should have known better. Granganimeo, *brother to King Wingino,* has been brought aboard the *Tiger* for negotiations. He has granted the English request to live on Roanoke, but not without conditions: they will receive no help from his people.[2] No corn. No cultigens. No meat. Raleigh's exploring party the previous year has depleted their stock. To feed 108 additional mouths is impossible. There is the matter of Aquascogoc to consider. The Secotan will trade only surplus, which this year is unlikely. There are no guarantees.

In the light of the situation on Roanoke, and confronted by his own food shortages, Lane's obsession with staying at his post is appalling.[3] After his bitter condemnation of Grenville for exposing them all to danger in Puerto Rico, Lane's willful decision to occupy Roanoke commits himself and everyone else to a vastly more certain danger. And, in so doing, he sets in motion a tidal wave of destruction.

August 17. Construction of the fort is completed. Lane assumes command of his new headquarters as both Governor and General. Philip Amadas, as Admiral of the Country, is second-in-command. Captains Edward Stafford and John Vaughan[4] command two companies; if there are other officers present, they have not been identified. Of the soldiers at Lane's disposal, at least one, Edward Nugent, served with him in Ireland. Others have been conscripted, including Darby Glande, brought here against his will. Hakluyt had proposed sending soldiers to America who had returned from the wars in Europe and Ireland, that those who *might be hurtful to this realm may be there unladen.*[5]

Such troops, not surprisingly, prove so undisciplined that Lane finds himself, *in the midst of infinite business, as having amongst savages, the charge of wild men of mine own nation, whose unruliness is such as not to give leisure to the Governor to be almost at any time from them.*[6]

Nevertheless, Lane fully appreciates the implications of his position. To command this post, to ensure the addition *of such a kingdom as this,* is to topple the *tyranny* of Spain *(being the sword of the Antichrist of Rome and his sect).* Though there be no food in the country for his troops, they will prevail! Lane is embarking on a holy war. *Not doubting,* he enthuses, that God *will command even the ravens to feed us, as he did by his servant the Prophet Habakkuk.*[7] This campaign is Lane's great glory.

Falcons, harquebuses, armor, and ammunition are transported from the ships and stored inside the fort. The troops and guns presenting a far different spectacle to the Secotan than that of the exploring expedition the year before. Even then, whenever *we discharged any piece,* Barlowe had said, *were it but a harquebus, they would tremble thereat for very fear.* Hariot reports that the people of Roanoke *were amazed at the first sight of us.*[8] Little wonder.

The Indian village of Roanoke, a palisaded town of nine cedar houses, lies near Lane's fort on the north end of Roanoke Island.[9] Granganimeo is a *weroance* here, a leader. Raleigh's men, in 1584, were struck by his appearance and the respect and deference his people accorded him. His wife also exerted a commanding presence, though their first impression of her was of a shy and aristocratic woman, *very well favoured, of mean stature, and very bashful.* She came to the ships in the presence of *forty or fifty women always.*[10]

Wingina, Granganimeo's brother, was understood to be *the King* of the entire Secotan country. With Lane's soldiers here, he will shift his residence to Roanoke.[11]

A Pleasant and Fruitful Country

Lane's first step as commander is to dispatch Philip Amadas to the mainland north of Roanoke Island. A country situated against the uppermost reach of the sound, *to Weapemeocke.*[12] What his mission is later becomes clear. The Weapemeoc confederacy, headed by a man named

Okisko, consists of four small nations: the Yeopim proper, the Perquiman, Pasquotank, and Poteskeet. Allied to the Secotan.

West of the Weapemeoc are the Chowanoc, also a member of the alliance. Each day, knowledge is gained, writes Lane, *of some fertile and pleasant provinces in the main,* populously inhabited. The towns are *situated upon most delicate plats of ground, distant the one from the other not above 3 English miles.* Amadas saw crowds gathered *so as upon one of their holy days there hath been of my company . . . that hath seen above 700 persons, young and old together, on a plain.*[13]

For the soldiers, an anticlimactic beginning. These matters are the business of Hariot the scientist, *specially employed* by Raleigh to deal *with the natural inhabitants,* not enlisted men.[14]

A World of Observation

Hariot vigorously compiles a journal, stuffing it full of notes on Secotan gardens. *Pagatowr,* corn, the staple crop. We *have found here a Guinea wheat,* writes Lane, struggling to maintain investor interest, *whose ear yieldeth corn for bread, 400 upon one ear, and the cane maketh very good and perfect sugar.* Children suck it as candy for the *sweet juice.*[15]

There are beans, Hariot observes, called *okindgier,* which are simmered in broths, or sometimes they *bruise or pound them in a mortar, & thereof make loaves or lumps of doughish bread.* There are melons, squash, and sunflowers — a plant only marginally familiar: *a great herb, in the form of a marigold, about six foot in height. . . . Some take it to be planta solis: of the seeds hereof they make both a kind of bread and broth.* The gardens are planted in an apparent jumble, corn and beans trailing together. *The ground they never fatten with muck or dung,* Hariot adds incredulously.[16]

The journal is assuming compendious proportions.

Drought

As a relentless sun beats down, Hariot traipses through Roanoke gardens with a curiosity that might have been humorous in any other circumstance. But a serious problem is developing throughout the Secotan country, which will have a profound impact on events unfolding. The English are unaware of what is happening. What do soldiers know (or care) of farming? What do London merchants know of the land?

The blistering sun scorches the earth. Strangely absent is the suffocating humidity of the coast. The soil dries to sand. *The climate,* observes Lane, is *somewhat tending to heat.*[17] No rain. No rain for weeks. It is at last obvious to everyone what is happening. Roanoke is in the midst of a drought. What is not obvious is its severity: it will be the worst drought to hit the coast in eight hundred years.[18] Plants, succulent and green only weeks before, droop, curl — then die. Fruits shrivel on the vine. A dark blight creeps along the edges of corn blades dry as parchment. Sheaths split from cobs, exposing gaping rows of intermittent kernels. The *corn began to wither by reason of a drought which happened extraordinarily.*[19]

Of all the crops, corn is the most critical. A low yield is disastrous. A nonexistent one thrusts the Secotan into very desperate straits indeed. Panic ensues. Many attribute the calamity to their refusal to feed Lane's troops. Dreading judgment, they rush to Hariot, to the soldiers, desiring them *to pray to our God of England, that he would preserve their corn, promising that when it was ripe we also should be partakers of the fruit.*[20]

We Will Make You Christian

Taking the cue, members of the company renew their efforts at proselytizing. *Some religion they have already, which although it be far from the truth, yet being as it is, there is hope it may be the easier and sooner reformed.* Many are persuaded, Hariot declares, *that if they knew not the truth of God and religion already, it was rather to be had from us, whom God so specially loved than from a people that were so simple, as they found themselves to be in comparison of us.*[21]

To underscore his point, Hariot demonstrates the use of scientific gadgets: *the virtue of the loadstone in drawing iron, a perspective glass whereby was showed many strange sights, burning glasses, wildfire works, guns, books, writing and reading, spring clocks that seem to go of themselves . . . Whereupon greater credit was given unto that we spake of concerning such matters.*[22]

It would be surprising if the Secotan were not upset by these efforts. To destroy their religion is to destroy their entire way of being. Confounded and shocked, the Secotan world is reeling. And still no rains come.

Everything Under Christendom

Toward the middle of September, though we do not know precisely when, a surveying expedition is sent into the interior. Hariot presumably leads it, mapping out the country with parchment and quills, compasses, a cross staff, and calculation tables. The team includes Joachim Ganz, the metallurgist, who will search for ore into the very *bowels of the earth.*[23]

Part of their task is to conduct an inventory of marketable commodities. There is *daily discovery,* Lane boasts, *of somewhat rare growing that Christendom wanteth.* Wood of every kind: oak, pine, hickory, beech. *Cedar, a very sweet wood & fine timber; whereof if nests of chests be there made, or timber thereof fitted for sweet & fine bedsteads, tables, desks, lutes, virginals, & many things else (of which there hath been proof made already), to make up freight . . . will yield profit.*[24]

There are many *strange trees.*[25] Even more striking is their size. They are colossal. Secotan forest management is vastly different from anything Lane's company has ever known. In England large trees are felled first, leaving hosts of spindly saplings. It is common to regard this as normal; easy to forget that trees ever grew bigger than two hands around. Children growing up have known nothing else.

The Secotan, on the other hand, weed out saplings, leaving mature trees intact.[26] The undergrowth cleared, luxuriant trunks have room to expand to tremendous size. Unlike their English counterparts, Secotan children hide and play among giants, under a vast, living canopy. It is the greatest architecture in the world.

Pestilence

The region's commodities are both rich and abundant. Indeed *these parts do abound with the growth of them all,* says Lane, *but being Savages that possess the land, they know no use of the same.*[27] Had he wished the Secotan gone, he could not have willed it faster. The first sign was in the sky. On or about September 27 the surveyors first notice it. Directly south over the sound, at nine o'clock at night, a comet blazes close to earth.[28] Its trail is clearly visible with the naked eye. Hariot records the spectacle in his journal. And then everything changes.

The Secotan begin to die. The effects are sudden and devastating. Town after town falls victim to English microbes — to which there is no immunity — startling the surveyors with such a *rare and strange accident.* Yet some of Lane's men were ill upon their arrival on Roanoke: *sundry that came sick, are recovered of long diseases, especially of rheums.*[29]

The surveyors push through the land, trailing virulent epidemic in their wake. Within *a few days after our departure from every such town,* wrote Hariot, *the people began to die very fast, and many in short space; in some towns about twenty, in some forty, in some sixty, & in one six score, which in truth was very many in respect of their numbers. . . . The disease was so strange, that they neither knew what it was, nor how to cure it; the like by report of the oldest men in the country never happened before, time out of mind.*[30]

The implications of the epidemic are profound, not only in the sheer number of lives lost, but for the holes rent in the fabric of this close-knit society. Now torn asunder. Old people succumb, taking with them lifetimes of knowledge. Priests die, forever silencing religious doctrine and ceremonies and rites. Orators and leaders are struck down. Mothers, friends. The best cooks, the best craftsmen, the best fishermen, the best fighters. People whose lives have barely begun; a nation orphaned by raging disease that casts down multitudes without discretion. People with knowledge are dying. A way of life crumbles into dust.

Bone-chilling cries float through the swamp forest and along damp trails, swallowed up in the dense canopy overhead. Fires blaze into the night as death blackens the land. Lingering over every town is the foul stench of disease and decay. Exploding the Secotan world into chaos. Wingina, who frequently accompanied the surveying party, is seized with chills. He collapses, filled with infection, *so grievously sick that he was like to die, and as he lay languishing . . . and thinking he was in such danger for offending us and thereby our God, sent for some of us to pray and be a means to our God that it would please him either that he might live, or after death dwell with Him in bliss.* Pathetic requests similarly flow in from all quarters, from *many others in the like case.*[31]

Corpses lie rotting, the living barely able to bury the dead. The English watch as the Secotan dig *graves about three foot deep.* How many priests are left to perform the proper rites? *They believe also the immortality of the soul, that after this life as soon as the soul is departed from the body, according to the works it hath done, it is either carried to heaven . . . there to enjoy perpetual bliss and happiness, or else to a great pit or hole.*[32]

Enemies Among Us

The Secotan, bleary with sickness, eye Lane's men warily and *impute to us the cause or means thereof.* Relations deteriorate. Some came *to prophesy that there were more of our generation yet to come, to kill theirs and take their places, as some thought the purpose was by that which was already done.* And that the English *did make the people to die in that sort as they did.* That the epidemic is a visitation by God working on behalf of the soldiers, says Hariot, *we ourselves have cause in some sort to think no less.*[33]

As the surveyors move from town to town, they are no longer welcomed. The English warn that the *subtle device[s]* now practiced against them will call forth divine retribution. *Insomuch that when some of the inhabitants which were our friends, & especially the Wiroans Wingina, had observed such effects in four or five towns to follow their wicked practices, they were persuaded that it was the work of our God through our means, and that we by Him might kill and slay whom we would without weapons, and not come near them.*[34] If the Secotan think this, then it is clear that their view of Lane's men has changed. The English are now regarded as both hostile and vindictive.

The days shorten. The breezes scudding off the water grow brisk. October passes into November and morning finds frost upon the ground. Overhead multitudes of geese darken the sky. They descend from the heavens by the thousands on snowy wings, blanketing the swamps and sounds in the purest white. The surveying party retreats to Roanoke, having reached at least as far west as the town of Secota, but *winter also being at hand . . . we thought good,* says Lane, *wholly to leave the discovery of those parts until our stronger supply.*[35]

Grenville Returns Home

In England there is great rejoicing. In the West Country, amid a throng of well-wishers, Grenville's expedition returns home. The first to reach London is John Arundell, who left the Outer Banks some weeks earlier than the others. He is immediately granted an audience with the Queen at Richmond Palace, where, to great fanfare on Thursday, October 14, he is knighted as the first member of the squadron back.[36]

Raleigh's position at Court has dramatically altered in the intervening months since the fleet's departure. In July, as his ships were arriving at

Wococon, he was elevated to the office of Lord Warden of the Stannaries — the tin mines of western England — with judicial power over their parliaments and authority to collect taxes. This was followed, in September, by his promotion to Lord-Lieutenant of Cornwall, a position traditionally held by nobility. In October, Raleigh is returned as a Member of Parliament for Devon. Before the year is out he will be favored yet again: granted the office of Vice-Admiral of both Devon and Cornwall. His brother, Sir John Gilbert, is his deputy. Together, these offices make Raleigh the most powerful military figure in the whole of the West Country.[37]

With Arundell back, Raleigh travels to Plymouth to await Grenville's arrival. October 18. To the rejoicing of *divers of his worshipful friends,* Grenville enters Plymouth harbor, *being by the hand of God delivered from the dangers of the seas.*[38] And of Lane. Grenville sails, not on the *Tiger,* already safely in port, but on the *Santa Maria de San Vicente,* a Spanish carrack captured off the coast of Bermuda; the flagship of the Santo Domingo treasure fleet.

The *Santa Maria* weighs in at three hundred tons, laden with sugar and ginger. Grenville declares the cargo's worth at 40,000–50,000 ducats. His enemies from the *Tiger,* however, inform Walsingham that the haul is vastly greater. A Portuguese merchant claims the manifest totals 120,000 ducats, including gold, silver, and pearls. In an anonymous account sent to the Queen, the profits are racked up to more than a million.[39] Who did this? Grenville shrugs off the discrepancy as a reporting error, yet it, too, will figure in the disappearance of White's colony.

Details of Raleigh's meeting with Grenville are not recorded. Neither Lane's behavior, nor his libel, appears to have been made public. We do know that Grenville detailed for his cousin the stringent hygiene policy implemented aboard the *Tiger.* Lane heard about it; seven years later, he was still accusing Grenville of taking credit for health and safety measures that, he claimed, were his.[40]

It is apparent that Raleigh did not credit Lane's slander. Indeed, all indications are that he was happy with his cousin Grenville's performance. Lane's request to have Grenville removed from office went unheeded, and Raleigh again selected him to command the returning squadron.

Grenville, for his part, pens a polite, professional letter to Walsingham, denying the charge of embezzlement. *I have, God be thanked, performed the action whereunto I was directed as fully as the time . . . and all possibilities would permit me. I have possessed and peopled the same to her Majesty's use, and planted it with such cattle & beasts as are fit and neces-*

sary. . . . The commodities that are found there, are such as my cousin Raleigh hath advertized you of.[41]

Results of the Voyage

Grenville is true to his word. The *Tiger*'s hold is stuffed with *a great amass of good things* — samples of American products to confirm his report — to *avoid all suspicion of fraud.*[42] The most exciting product is *oyssan,* which is *as common there as grass is here.* From it the Secotan spin cloth. It is thought to be silk. If true, the import of silks from Persia, Turkey, Spain, and Italy would end; the trade would transfer to England. In London, experiments are made. A woman is hired to spin a sample into thread which is, indeed, determined to be silk. A *piece of silk grosgrain* is woven from it and *found to be excellent good.*[43]

The discoveries create a sensation at Court. The articles are eagerly passed around, examined by scientists, and snatched up into the hands of curiosity collectors. Walter Cope's famous London home is crammed full of amazing treasures: an Egyptian mumified child; Chinese porcelain; a flying rhinoceros; bells from Henry VIII's fool; holy relics from a Spanish ship; a horn found growing out of an English woman's head; a Mexican Madonna made of feathers; and fireflies from Virginia (which, Cope explains, are used in lieu of lights since the country is in perpetual darkness for nearly a month). Suspended from the ceiling, the entire length of the room, is an Indian canoe with paddles.[44]

Lord Treasurer Burghley's celebrated garden in the Strand has also benefited. Something of a national arboretum, it includes many rare and exotic plants from the Americas. An instant craze for foreign herbals and apothecary drugs from Virginia, Arabia, and the Mediterranean seizes the country: *It is a world also to see how many strange herbs, plants and annual fruits are daily brought unto us from the Indies, Americas . . . and all parts of the world . . . for delectation sake unto the eye and their odoriferous savours unto the nose they are to be cherished and God to be glorified.*[45]

England's foreign expeditions are becoming world renowned. Tourists, who once flocked to the palace of Hampton Court to marvel at the Queen's royal throne studded with *very large diamonds, rubies, and sapphires,* now gaze upon Cornelius Ketel's portraits of the Nugumiut man, woman, and child. At Windsor Palace sightseers are enthralled by a unicorn horn — a narwhal tusk — irreverently referred to as *that horn of Windsor.*[46]

Ha, ha, ha, ha! This world doth pass
Most merrily I'll be sworn;
For many an honest Indian ass
Goes for a unicorn.[47]

Cold War

Hand in hand with the excitement of discovery goes the mounting political crisis with Spain. Drake is let loose in the West Indies with twenty-one battleships, and Raleigh makes immediate arrangements to reinforce Lane's troops. A promotional campaign is launched, the products brought home by Grenville used to pique investor interest. *Inducements* prepared by Hakluyt's cousin of the same name, the *elder* Richard Hakluyt — a lawyer — are likely used too, although his muddled argument can hardly have been effective:

The *ends of the voyage are these: 1. To plant Christian religion. 2. To traffic. 3. To conquer. Or, to do all three. To plant Christian religion without conquest, will be hard. Traffic easily followeth conquest: conquest is not easy. Traffic without conquest seemeth possible, and not uneasy. What is to be done, is the question.*

If the people be content to live naked . . . then traffic is not. So then in vain seemeth our voyage, unless this nature may be altered, as by conquest and other good means. . . . Admit that they have desire to your commodities, and as yet have neither gold, silver, copper, iron, nor sufficient quantity to maintain the yearly trade: What is then to be done?[48]

Not helpful. A moot question anyway. December 10, 1585. Walsingham receives intelligence of a massive naval buildup in Iberian ports.[49] The invincible Armada is preparing. The goal: to invade England. In a single stroke, Lane's outpost on Roanoke is rendered obsolete. This is Armageddon. No fort half a world away is going to make a difference.

Revitalization

On Roanoke Island it is winter. The days are short and the nights cold and cheerless. Inside the fort the soldiers are idle. Contact with the Secotan is minimal. Having sustained crippling drought and disease, the village of Roanoke almost certainly withdraws inside itself, preoccupied with survival. Silence reigns over the island. A lull after the previous tumultuous months.

And then a shred of hope. In a Secotan town sixty miles from Roanoke, Hariot is told, a young man died and was buried, but came back to life. For *although his body had lain dead in the grave, yet his soul was alive and had travelled far in a long broad way, on both sides whereof grew most delicate and pleasant trees, bearing more rare and excellent fruits, than ever he had seen before or was able to express.* The path to Heaven. Yet the route was long and hazardous, beset with trials determined by the conduct of his life. At last the man reached an indescribably beautiful town of *most brave and fair houses* peopled by family and friends, ancestors who had gone before.[50] A place of comfort. No sorrow, no pain, no hunger, no falling away from ancient teachings.

A great revival is gripping the Secotan country, caused by calamity. The message is clear and powerful, full of promise and excitement: the Secotan must live in goodness and wisdom and courage, adhering to time-honored customs. They must not falter as they follow the path of truth and tradition that will lead to happiness in the world to come. They must remain Secotan. The tide is turning. Conversions will not now be easy. Nor will relations with Lane's men be so open.

Unrest

For the Secotan, life has become a day-to-day existence. The severity of the drought is incalculable, their corn crop destroyed. The damaged yield accounts for Hariot's ability to note such variety of roots and nuts gathered by them in lieu of cornmeal. *Okeepenauk,* wild potatoes, consumed *for want of bread.* Greenbrier root is chopped, pounded, and strained: its juice *maketh bread.* As do arrow-arum and golden club, chestnuts, chinquapin, and acorns. Consumed also *for want of bread.*[51]

The soldiers, on the other hand, fail to sustain themselves. As salaried combatants, they expect a commissary as their due. When it is not forthcoming, they press the Secotan to sell stores in exchange for copper. Even this fare is highly distasteful, *nor of that choice as otherwise might have been to our better satisfaction and contentment.* Indeed, there are some in the company who, Hariot complains, *were of a nice bringing up, only in cities or towns, or such as never (as I may say) had seen the world before. Because there were not to be found any English cities, nor such fair houses, nor at their own wish any of their old accustomed dainty food, nor any soft beds of down or feathers, the country was to them miserable, & their reports thereof according.*[52]

With the exception of Hariot's surveying team, few of Lane's men stray away from the fort or are *out of the island where we were seated, or not far, or at the leastwise in few places else.* The men grow bored and restless. To ease their hunger, or for sport, they kill and eat the dogs that wander into the compound from the Roanoke village; seizing them *as they came to our hands.* Worsening relations. The men who came merely for the promise of riches are rapidly disillusioned that *gold and silver was not so soon found.*[53] The only products of worth discovered thus far are pitch, tar, rosin, and turpentine. Marketable commodities: all four essential ingredients for London undertakers. As embalming solution.[54]

Tension mounts. Thomas Harvey, the Cape Merchant, bitterly reviles Manteo and Wanchese for misrepresenting the trade potential, causing him to lose his fortune — most of his goods spent for food — leaving him with nothing but the pleasure of being in a foreign country in *very miserable case.* Supplies are wearing thin. *Some want also we had of clothes.*[55]

The soldiers begin to commit acts of *misdemeanour and ill dealing* and are *worthily punished.* One is hanged. What his crime was is unknown. The expedition's martial instructions outline ten infractions subject to punishment. Three invoke the death penalty: the violation of *any woman;* the drawing of a weapon upon an officer; abandoning a post or sleeping on duty.[56] The soldier hanged by Lane might have done any one of the three. If, however, he abused a woman, the woman he abused was Secotan.

Pearls, Copper . . . and Gold

As winter progresses, too much attention is directed at the people of the country. The women draped in jewelry, the *chief ladies* wrapped in pearls *5 or 6 fold about their necks, bearing one arm in the same,* as in a sling.[57] Amadas, Lane's second-in-command, learned during the previous year's exploring expedition of a pearl fishery located on a river somewhere to the northwest, *in which there is found great store.*[58] The description places this squarely at the upper end of the sound in Weapemeoc territory. *This* is why Amadas was sent there the moment Lane touched down upon Roanoke. For pearls. He never found them, *not having yet discovered those places.*[59]

Lane's appetite was whetted, but the Secotan possess something far more important: copper. Or could it be gold? Granganimeo *himself had upon his head,* wrote Barlowe, *a broad plate of gold, or copper, for being unpolished we knew not what metal it should be, neither would he by any means suffer us to take it off his head, but feeling it, it would bow very easily.*[60] In trade, *copper carrieth the price of all,* especially if it is red.[61]

The Secotan glitter with copper necklaces, pendants, bracelets, and rings. Copper sparkles in their hair. Granganimeo wears a radiant *plate of copper* suspended from a chain, a sign of high status. Young dandies — his children *and other noblemen* — loop copper bands through their ears. At Secota, girls *of good parentage* are resplendent in delicate necklaces of *little beads of copper,* while their mothers are adorned with ghost necklaces of bluish tattooing, the color of oxidized pennies. Copper chains are even draped around religious statuary inside temples, which metal *they esteem more than gold or silver.*[62]

The truth is, Lane and his troops are tolerated because they have copper. Yet they are blundering into a world they little understand. Nor have they any notion of the consequences that will result from their seeking this wealth, or that the delicate balance between trade and war in this region hinges on it. It would be better had they let it alone. The ferocity of their involvement will drag many others to their deaths. Ultimately, Lane's obsession with copper will destroy the Lost Colonists.

12 CHAUNIS TEMOATAN AND A MURDER (1586)

If you voyage well in this your journey,
They will be the King of Spain's atomy
To bring you to silver & Indian gold
which will keep you in age from hunger & cold.
Thomas Hariot[1]

To Win Renown

Certain factors are converging. It is winter and food is scarce on Roanoke Island. Lane is told that game is more plentiful on the mainland. The soldiers are bored and dissatisfied, and increasingly difficult to control. The pearl fishery has yet to be found. Somewhere in the interior copper deposits exist and, very likely, silver and gold. To this is added one further fact: Lane's command has produced no great distinguishing discoveries.

The stories from Spain are too familiar. Cortés marched into Mexico and discovered Tenochtítlan, a city of staggering wealth and magnificence. Gold, silver, and precious gems; plazas pulsating with life; broad avenues, universities, and gardens. Pizarro found an empire in Peru, while the gold mines Columbus claimed in the West Indies catapulted Spain, overnight, from a third-rate country into the most powerful nation in Europe. Their *terror* is *great amongst us in England,* remarked Lane, but their reputation *doth altogether grow from the mines of his treasure.*[2]

Amadas returned from the Weapemeoc country in September reporting *fertile and pleasant provinces in the main . . . specially towards the west.* In this vague direction both pearls and copper were said to abound. *I mean with the favour of the Almighty,* Lane announced, *to visit that province and some part of the winter to pass there, being 140 miles within the main.*[3] A party was dispatched, but where they went or who made up the group is unknown. Hariot, certainly, for he said of these travels that *in the time of winter, our lodging was in the open air upon the ground.*[4]

The Reconnaissance

Wherever it went, the winter expedition returned to Roanoke at the end of February, to find Lane chafing at the bit. Hariot reported the land *farther into the main* to be richer, higher ground than the sandy scrub of Roanoke Island. The soil appears *to be fatter; the trees greater and to grow thinner; the ground more firm and deeper mould . . . more plenty of their fruits; more abundance of beasts; the more inhabited with people, and of greater policy & larger dominions, with greater towns and houses.*[5]

All very encouraging, but what Lane wants to hear is far more specific. Hariot discloses it at last: *a hundred and fifty miles into the main, in two towns, we found with the inhabitants diverse small plates of copper that had been made, as we understood, by the inhabitants that dwell farther into the country, where as they say are mountains and rivers that yield also white grains of metal, which is to be deemed silver. . . . The aforesaid copper we also found by trial to hold silver.*[6] Joachim Ganz confirms it. It is of exceedingly high grade.

But who are these copper manufacturers who dwell farther into the country? White's map depicts a hilly land to the west, along the Roanoke River, identified by the name of *Mangoak*. Mangoak, Lane explains, *is another kind of savages dwelling more to the westward of the said river.* They are a people *whose name and multitude besides their valour is terrible to all the rest of the provinces.*[7] These Mandoag will be intimately associated with the Lost Colonists, and we will have every reason to wish to know more about them.

Friends No More

February's end, 1586. Roanoke Island resumes its prewinter configuration. Lane's soldiers are reunited at the fort. It would have been better had they stayed away. As dogwood petals shower down, whitening the edge of fields as yet unsown, a second — and far more deadly — epidemic sweeps the island. As though there has not been enough suffering. Both Wingina and Granganimeo are infected. Wingina recovers, but Granganimeo is not so lucky; by March he is dead. The impact upon Wingina is profound: *upon the death of his brother,* he discards his own name.[8] From this point forward, he will be known as Pemisapan.

The situation on Roanoke, dormant all winter, becomes critical. Relations are severed with the English and *consultations* held.[9] There were,

Lane claims, *all matters proposed against us, which both the king, and all the rest of them after Grangemoe's death were very willing to have preferred.* Only Ensinore, Pemisapan's father, *opposed himself,* counseling that the English were dangerous and not to be provoked.[10]

Meanwhile, Lane's rations run out, forcing a complete dependence on the sale of food by the alienated Secotan. A recipe for paranoia. Lane immediately suspects treachery, ranting about the likelihood of *poisonings and such like,* which would *have assuredly brought us to ruin in the month of March.* For it is in this month, he claims, that Pemisapan plans to abandon his town on Roanoke and move inland, *to have run away from us.* Without them, the fort will be destitute — Pemisapan intending *to have left his ground in the Island unsowed, which if he had done, there had been no possibility in common reason (but by the immediate hand of God), that we could have been preserved from starving out of hand. For at that time we had no wares for fish, neither could our men skill of the making of them, neither had we one grain of corn for seed to put into the ground.* What military commander would have allowed himself to reach this state?

For Gold

Supply ships from England are expected daily and still Lane has little to show for his command. Obsessed by the illusion of gold, he determines to lead a company *farther into the country.* Strangely, he demands guides from Pemisapan and is thereby compelled to divulge the purpose of the mission, against his inclination. *I having been enforced to make him privy to the same, to be served by him of a guide to the Mangoacks.*[11]

At this point the story radically diverges from the truth. Lane's official version of events is that he is a victim of Pemisapan, who deceived him by claiming that two neighboring nations, the Chowanoc and Mandoag, were plotting against the English. Therefore, Lane insists that he did not send his troops north to search for gold, but to attack these allegedly threatening nations. Pemisapan, he complains, *did never rest to solicit continually my going upon them.*

Lane's boats accordingly push northwest along the mainland, past the Weapemeoc villages, and enter the Chowan River. The water, lapping steel-gray against the distant, imposing line of timber. The men cross the border and are now within the territory *and jurisdiction* of the Chowanoc. A most powerful nation, Lane reports, led by Menatonon, *the greatest Province and seignorie lying upon that river, and the very town itself is able to put 700 fighting men into the field.*

Presently the men draw abreast of *a town which we called the blind town, but the savages called it Ohanoak.* It *hath a very goodly corn field* and *is subject to Choanoke.* After this the river diminishes, contracting sharply until it *groweth to be as narrow as the Thames between Westminster and Lambeth.* Trees loom large on either shore.

Rounding a bend, the soldiers arrive at the Chowanoc capital. What it looked like or where it was located is not divulged: it must have been substantial. The Chowanoc with their large, vigorous towns held their own along the Mandoag frontier. In a clearing, a meeting of Chowanoc and allied Weapemeoc is in progress as the soldiers step onto the wet sandy beach. The drone of the Chowanoc council masks their approach. These are not people on guard, preparing war. Lane's men take them completely by surprise.

The troops attack. The suddenness of which *did so dismay them, as it made us have the better hand at them.* The compound erupts into chaos. People screaming. People fleeing. *If there fall out any wars between us & them,* Hariot commented, *what their fight is likely to be . . . it may be easily imagined; by the experience we have had in some places.*

Menatonon, *a man impotent in his limbs, but otherwise for a savage, a very grave and wise man,* is seized and tightly bound. As darkness falls, a guard is posted around the town, and in the wavering firelight Lane interrogates his prisoner. In the harsh exchange that follows, *Menatonon confessed* that Pemisapan forewarned him of Lane's expedition. This *confederacy against us, of the Choanists and Mangoaks,* Lane relays in a rage, *was altogether and wholly procured by Pemisapan himself . . . who sent them continual word that our purpose was fully bent to destroy them: on the other side, he told me that they had the like meaning towards us.* The entire business, he says, was orchestrated by Pemisapan.

The Truth

Lane is lying, and it is here that it becomes apparent. If his argument with the Chowanoc were due solely to the machinations of Pemisapan, then reparations would be made immediately. We would expect profuse apologies to Menatonon and an urgent attempt to rectify the situation, if for no other reason than for the injured parties to join forces and defeat the Secotan. Simple and deft politics . . . it never happens. Instead, Menatonon remains captive for the two days that the soldiers occupy the town. Lane viciously states that *the Chaonists . . . durst not for the most part of them abide us, and that those that did abide us were killed.*

We know that Pemisapan was closely allied to both the Weapemeoc and Chowanoc. The English clearly understood this. Why, then, would Pemisapan have urged Lane's soldiers to attack? Did he? His only possible motive could be the hope that the English would be defeated. A risky move! Chowanoc were killed. Had Pemisapan plotted Lane's demise, all he needed to do was call in his Chowanoc and Weapemeoc allies for a surprise attack. It is far more credible, certain even, that the story is Lane's invention to justify action. And that after Lane demanded guides, *having been enforced to make him privy to the same,* Pemisapan sent a desperate warning to the Chowanoc to beware of his arrival.

Close quarters with soldiers have taken their toll. Pemisapan himself plans to relocate from Roanoke to the mainland town of Dasamonquepeuc. Angered at the loss of his food supply, Lane prepares to commandeer what he wants by force, outlining a series of defensive works in the interior: *I would have raised my said sconce upon some cornfield,* he declared, *that my company might have lived upon it.* Pemisapan warns the Chowanoc.

Chaunis Temoatan

In the flickering firelight, Menatonon is cross-examined about *his own country and the disposition of his own men, but also of his neighbours round about him as well far as near, and of the commodities that each country yieldeth.* Lane will know their strength and what their countries provide. The relentless questioning reveals something else. Lane discovers the source of copper.

The copper mines are located deep within the interior, where *not only Menatonon, but also the savages of Morotico themselves do report strange things.* Access is controlled by the Mandoag. It *is a thing most notorious to all the country, that there is a province to the which the said Mangoaks have recourse and traffic up that River of Moratico, which hath a marvellous and most strange mineral.*

Menatonon's information is consistent with Hariot's winter report. To reach the copper mines, Lane will have to pass up the Roanoke River, into hilly country guarded by the Mandoag. *This mine is so notorious amongst them, as not only to the savages dwelling up the said river, and also to the savages of Choanoke, and all them to the westward, but also to all them of the main: the country's name is of fame, and is called Chaunis Temoatan.*

Lane systematically probes *all the savages that dwelt towards those parts* about the mine, *and especially of Menatonon himself.* They are brought before him, one by one, Manteo interpreting. The surrounding woods a profuse blush of redbud, a raging fire. Color bursting with anger. *The mineral they say is wassador, which is copper,* Lane explains with fervor, *but they call by the name of wassador every metal whatsoever: they say it is the colour of our copper, but our copper is better than theirs: and the reason is for that it is redder and harder, whereas that of Chaunis Temoatan is very soft, and pale.* Like gold.

Menatonon *promised me guides of his own men who should pass over with me, even to the said country of Chaunis Temoatan (for overland from Choanok to the Mangoaks is but one day's journey from sun rising to sun setting . . .) These things, I say, made me very desirous by all means possible to recover the Mangoaks, to get some of their copper for an assay.*

For Praise

Menatonon has outlived his usefulness. The following morning, the troops depart abruptly. Menatonon, Lane says, presents him with a rope of pearl, though *they were black, and naught, yet many of them were very great.* Odd, to be this critical of a gift. Menatonon was a prisoner and Lane his captor; the pearls were, in fact, the price set on Menatonon's head. I *having dismissed Menatonon,* Lane declared, *upon a ransom agreed for.*

As Menatonon quickly hobbles past the line of soldiers, free of his fetters, Lane barks a command. In one rapid movement there is a startled cry, a struggle, and someone is hustled aboard the pinnace. He is a boy named Skiko. He is Chowanoc. And he is Menatonon's son. Anguished shouts explode from the shocked and horrified village. All resistance useless for, as Lane has said, all who did so *were killed.*

For Glory

Oars creak as the wherry boats navigate back down the Chowan. Lane's record of abuse is mounting. Like his father, Skiko is subjected to interrogation concerning the Mandoag and copper. *Of this metal the Mangoaks have so great store, by report of all the savages adjoining, that they beautify their houses with great plates of the same: and this to be true,* Lane affirms, *I received by report of all the country, and particularly by young Skiko, the King of Choanoke's son my prisoner, who also himself had been prisoner with the Mangoaks, and set down all the particularities to me before mentioned: but he had not been at Chaunis Temoatan himself.*

I took a resolution with myself, Lane boasts, to reach Chaunis Temoatan. The boats crawl into the sound and swing west into the mouth of the Roanoke River, a waterway *most notable . . . and in all those parts most famous.* Yet the route upriver is strangely quiet. Ominously so. As they pull near the town of Moratoc, Lane scans the shore for signs of life and finds none. The town, inexplicably empty. Houses gape open, desolate, ghostly. Every village will be the same: abandoned, the inhabitants fled.

The boats glide on and silently pass into the land of the Mandoag. Lane's need for guides to Chaunis Temoatan *made me most desirous to have some doings with the Mangoaks either in friendship, or otherwise to have had one or two of them prisoners.* How little he knows them.

No Turning Back

Lane's intended meeting *with more either of the Moratiks, or of the Mangoaks* never takes place. For Pemisapan *in like sort having sent word to the Mangoaks of mine intention to pass up into their river and to kill them (as he said), both they and the Moratiks . . . abandoned their towns along the river and retired themselves* with their families and food stores *within the main.*

The Roanoke River begins to constrict. The banks, close and confining. Wisps of Spanish moss cling to trees choking the water, dark and oppressive. For days, the boats pass slowly upriver, meeting no one. Food stores dwindle away. The soldiers cannot locate so much as *a grain of corn in any their towns.* They are now 150 miles into the interior.[12]

I *advertised the whole company of the case we stood in for victual,* Lane complained, *and of mine opinion that we were betrayed of our own savages, and of purpose drawn forth by them, upon vain hope to be in the end starved, seeing all the country fled before us.* But the men are unanimous. As long as there is *one half pint of corn for a man, we should not leave the search of that river, and that there were in the company two mastiffs, upon the pottage of which with sassafras leaves (if the worst fell out), the company would make shift to live two days.* Gold fever: the men would rather starve *than be drawn back a foot till they had seen the Mangoaks, either as friends or foes.*

The two days pass and *we could never see man, only fires we might perceive made alongst the shore.* The Mandoag are watching.

The Mandoag

Day six. The wherries ride alone in the river. The soldiers' rations are now utterly spent. As evening shadows stretch across the water, suddenly *we heard certain savages call, as we thought, Manteo.* And then a profound silence. Not a rustle along the bank. Not a stirring. At Lane's insistence Manteo shouts back, as a song eerily floats out of the forest. The men confidently conclude it was *in token of our welcome to them.*

Manteo knows otherwise. He swiftly seizes a gun, yelling that *they meant to fight with us: which word was not so soon spoken by him . . . but there lighted a volley of their arrows.* Lane, in blind fury, rams the boat into shore in order to mount the guns, although the banks are high and steep. Weapons tumble onto the ground and are hastily readied, but the Mandoag remain concealed. The soldiers scramble up the bank and rush through the woods, clawing through a forest of branches, and come up empty-handed. The enemy, unnervingly invisible. The men pass an unsettling night ashore under heavy guard.

The next morning, before dawn, the soldiers withdraw, *which at my first motion,* said Lane, *I found my whole company ready to assent unto.* They hungrily kill the dogs and eat them as porridge. *I could allege the difference in taste,* Hariot noted dryly, recalling the dogs taken and eaten from Pemisapan's village, *of those kinds from ours, which by some of our company have been experimented in both.*

Riding with the current, the men retreat, regaining the mouth of the river in half the time it took to ascend. In the Weapemeoc country along the northern edge of the sound, fish weirs are raided but afford meager relief. The inhabitants of these villages, too, *were fled.* Easter Sunday, April 2. The soldiers reach Roanoke Island, having *as narrowly to escape starving in that discovery before our return, as ever men did.*

Homecoming

The Secotan, Lane alleges, believed him dead. In his absence, *they had raised a bruit among themselves that I and my company were part slain, and part starved by the Chaonists and Mangoaks.* Ensinore thought differently, warning *that they amongst them that sought our destruction, should find their own.* As confirmation, while the soldiers were still a hundred miles away, were some *that by sickness had died among them: and many of them hold opinion, that we be dead men returned into the world again. . . .* This opinion is strengthened when Lane materializes out of the territory of the dreaded Mandoag, *whose very names were terrible unto them.*

Menatonon, meanwhile, sends pearls *for a present* — Lane claims, his thinking increasingly distorted — *or rather as Pemisapan told me, for the ransom of his son, and therefore I refused them.* Skiko is too important to release. In the summer, Lane will search for the pearl fishery *with the guides that Menatonon would have given me, which I would have been assured should have been of his best men, (for I had his best beloved son prisoner with me) who also should have kept me company in an handlock with the rest foot by foot all the voyage overland.*

Pemisapan's Conspiracy

Great politics are afoot. The Weapemeoc, allied and subordinate to the powerful Chowanoc, send twenty-four delegates to Pemisapan. All *his savages* met *in council then with him.* The subject of the meeting is unrecorded, but clearly Menatonon is struggling to save his son. Pemisapan agrees to help, ordering his men to build fish weirs for the fort and to sow enough corn to sustain the troops for a year.

April 20. Ensinore dies . . . and everything changes. He was *no sooner dead,* Lane charges, *but certain of our great enemies about Pemisapan, as Osacan, a weroance; Tanaquiny and Wanchese most principally, were in hand again to put their old practices in use against us.*

In the midst of this crisis, Skiko escapes. The young boy flees from the fort, scaling the earthen ramparts, and is spotted. An alarm sounds. There is yelling and running, and Skiko is dragged by rough hands back inside the jail. There he lies, huddled on the floor, his thin legs bound in heavy iron manacles. He is allowed movement by shackles that slide along an iron bar screwed into the floor boards. *Skyco, the king Menatonon his son my prisoner,* Lane cries, *who having once attempted to run away, I laid him in the bilboes, threatening to cut off his head.* Pemisapan furiously intervenes, *being persuaded that he was our enemy to the death.* He *did not only feed* Skiko himself, daily coming to the fort, *but also made him acquainted with all his practices.*

Pemisapan's conspiracy, wholly provoked by Lane's aggression, unfolds in earnest. Skiko will be freed; by force. Pemisapan, joined by Okisko of the Weapemeoc, musters eight hundred bowmen. With *great quantity of copper,* Lane reports, Pemisapan buys Mandoag mercenaries. The rescue is scheduled for June 10, 1586, during a ceremony to solemnize *any great person dead.* In this case, Ensinore. The Weapemeoc will attend. The Mandoag, *who were a great people,* will combine with the "Chesepians" to the number of seven hundred at the town of Dasamonquepeuc opposite Roanoke Island.[13] They will wait until darkness. The attack will begin when a signal fire is lit.

Strategy

Details of the plot are available from Lane only. The first stage of the plan, he claims, is put into effect. The Secotan *did immediately put it in practice that they should not, for any copper, sell us any victuals whatsoever.* Lane is forced *to disband my company into sundry places to live upon shellfish, for so the savages themselves do, going to Ottorasko [Hatorask], and other places fishing and hunting while their grounds be in sowing and their corn growing.*

Was there ever a conspiracy? Could Lane have been so delusional that he mistook the normal Secotan pattern of gathering as a sign of hostility? The villages had few, if any, resources upon which to draw — the drought had seen to that. Unlike the soldiers, the Secotan did what was necessary to survive.

Lane's men refuse to disperse. The *famine grew . . . extreme among us.* The Secotan, meanwhile, collect crabs and oysters, mussels, scallops, and lobster. The rivers yield sturgeon *most plentiful.* In desperation, Captain Stafford is dispatched with twenty men to Croatoan *to feed himself, and also to keep watch if any shipping came upon the coast.* They likely ate Croatoan food stores. This alone would account for restrictions imposed upon John White by a desperate Croatoan the following year.

Soldiers, in companies of twenty, are sent to Dasamonquepeuc *to live off* oysters and roots. Pemisapan, who relocated there specifically to avoid Lane, *to withdraw himself from my daily sending to him for supply of victual for my company,* is pursued. Lane's assessment of the situation is nothing short of fantastic: he *was afraid to deny me anything,* he raves, *neither durst he in my presence but by colour, and with excuses, which I was content to accept for the time, meaning in the end as I had reason, to give him the jump once for all: but in the meanwhiles, as I had ever done before, I and mine bare all wrongs, and accepted of all excuses.*

Lane is clearly operating under a gross distortion of reality, unable to make a connection between his aggression and his victims' actions. He has driven them to conflict, then reacts with paranoia at their response. This puts Lane's complaints against Grenville in better perspective. His madness is becoming increasingly evident. Menatonon, despairing over his son, *had given us many tokens of earnest desire . . . to join in perfect league with us, and therefore were greatly offended with Pemisapan and Weopomiok* for telling *such tales of us.*

June 10 is fast approaching. Lane knows of the rescue plan. His informant, he claims, is Skiko. Who has volunteered the information. The boy in leg irons. The boy whose head Lane threatened to cut off. Lane is lying! Skiko has not been brainwashed by his captors. It could not happen, for he is visited daily by Pemisapan, who continually encourages him with promise of deliverance. Skiko is aware of his father's capitulation and his nation's efforts to save him. He himself has bravely tried to escape.

In fact, Skiko was forced to talk. Isn't this the real reason Lane threatened him with torture? Pretending to cut off his head? To force him to betray Pemisapan? Lane's own explanation is bogus: *the young man finding himself as well used at my hand as I had means to show and that all my company made much of him* — the boy was held in leg irons in a jail! — *he flatly discovered all unto me.* Not credible. The same *was revealed unto me,* Lane continued, *by one of Pemisapan's own men the night before he was slain.*[14] Our disbelief needs no further confirmation.

Treachery

Events move rapidly. May 31. Lane notifies Pemisapan, *to put all suspicion out of his head,* that an English supply fleet is fast approaching *(though I in truth had neither heard nor hoped for so good adventure)* and that he wishes *to borrow of his men to fish for my company and to hunt for me at Croatoan.* That night, he said, *I meant by the way to give them in the island a canvisado* — an ambush — ordering his men to seize *all the canoes* to prevent news of the attack reaching Dasamonquepeuc.

The sun swings low and curls up into the sound, trailing a cloak of orange across the sky. Tethered dugouts rock together as the tide washes in, bringing an English boat ever closer. Soldiers leap from it into the cold brine and lash the canoes to the back of the vessel. A guard is posted on shore on the darkening sand: anyone leaving the island for Dasamonquepeuc is to be captured.

Two Secotan swiftly take to their boats, but the commanding officer *overthrew* them. He met with a canoe, Lane said, *and cut off 2 savage's heads: this was not done so secretly but he was discovered from the shore, whereupon the cry arose.* The soldiers pepper the beach with gunfire. Secotan rush for cover; *some three or four of them at the first were slain with our shot, the rest fled into the woods.* In the mêlée, one of Pemisapan's chief men, Osocon, smashes the manacles binding Skiko and rushes him away from the fort. They are caught. In the night, Lane reported, he was found *conveying away my prisoner, whom I had there present tied in a handlock.* The second attempt to rescue Skiko has failed.

Massacre

Lane's boats steal across the sound as dawn breaks. Beaching on the sand near Dasamonquepeuc, Lane *sent Pemisapan word* that he was come *to complain unto him of Osocon.* The inhabitants gather around Pemisapan, tense and wary: *the king did abide my coming to him, and finding myself amidst 7 or 8 of his principal weroances & followers (not regarding any of the common sort), I gave the watchword agreed upon.*

Lane raises his hand and emits a single bloodcurdling scream: *Christ our victory!* Shots explode. Weapons belch flame and smoke, spraying bullets. Shrieks of terror fill the air; women and children fleeing in all directions, overwhelmed. Bodies crumple into the dust *and immediately those of* Pemisapan's *chief men and himself, had by the mercy of God for our deliverance, that which they had purposed for us.*

The king is *shot through* with a pistol and left *lying on the ground for dead.* The soldiers, *busy that none of the rest should escape,* fail to notice that he is only wounded. Suddenly he leaps up and races through the carnage, bolting past Lane's men. An aide-de-camp jerks his gun around. As Pemisapan plunges into the trees, he is struck *thwart the buttocks by mine Irish boy with my petronel.* Edward Nugent, *an Irish man serving me,* and Lane's deputy provost take off after him. Moments later, Nugent emerges from the woods *with Pemisapan's head in his hand.*[15]

This fell out the first of June, 1586.

Drake's Arrival

June 8. Lane's headquarters. Notice arrives via Captain Stafford at Croatoan that a fleet of twenty-three sails is sighted. Drake's squadron. Three days later, a meeting between the commanders takes place. In answer to Drake's offer of assistance, Lane requests food and ammunition: *calievers, handweapons, match and lead,* clothing, boats and their crews. In return, he extends Drake *such thanks unto him and his captains for his care both of us and of our action,* though *not as the matter deserved.* Lane also asks to be relieved of *a number of weak and unfit men for my good action.*

June 13. The transfer of supplies and equipment is only half completed when suddenly *there arose such an unwanted storm and continued four days that had like to have driven all on shore.* Tremendous thunderclaps rock the coast and *hailstones as big as hen's eggs* lance into whirling sea spouts *as though heaven and* earth *should have met.*[16] Lane's men rush to the ships and *left things so confusedly,* Hakluyt reports, *as if they had been chased from thence by a mighty army and, no doubt, so they were, for the hand of God came upon them for the cruelty and outrages committed by some of them against the native inhabitants of the country.*[17] A vessel that Drake is preparing, having aboard two of Lane's officers and many of his men, is *carried away with the tempest and foul weather.* Significantly, they desert.[18] Clear of the storm, they set a course across the Atlantic, back to England.

The loss of the ship strikes a tremendous blow. Lane's desire to locate the Chesapeake Bay *to the northward, if any there be, which was mine intention to have spent this summer in the search of, and of the mine of Chawnis Temoatan,* is dashed.[19] Meeting with his officers, *their whole request was to me* to return home with Drake.

Roanoke is abandoned. The weather continued *so boisterous* that the boats foundered and *most of all we had,* including maps, *books and writings, were by the sailors cast overboard, the greater number of the fleet being much aggrieved with their long and dangerous abode in that miserable road.* Divine retribution does at last come into play. The string of Menatonon's pearls *I lost,* said Lane, *with other things of mine,* which were cast in the sea.

A World of Terror

June 19. The exodus is complete. The troops board Drake's fleet and sail away.

Lane has inflicted deep wounds on Roanoke that will never heal. During his brief tenure on the island, he has destroyed food stores and forced the Secotan, under starvation conditions, into maintaining troops who never should have been there. He has crippled them with debilitating epidemics; decimated populations; cut down their government and religion. He has savagely attacked towns without provocation; captured a king and held his son hostage. He has brutalized them with intimidation, threats, deceit, and murder. His obsession with the copper mines of Chaunis Temoatan will wreak untold misery and eventually topple the balance of power within the region. He has reduced their world to a shambles. He has beheaded Wingina.

Ten months after his arrival, Lane leaves this world behind.

PART THREE

A CASE OF CONSPIRACY

13 THE LOST COLONISTS (1587)

For among my people are found wicked men: they watch, as fowlers lie in wait; they set a trap, they catch men.

Jeremiah[1]

Resupply

With sickening clarity, we now see that White's colonists cannot hope to survive on Roanoke Island. Too much has happened; too much is lost.

After Lane's hurried departure, Raleigh's long-awaited supply ship put in to the Outer Banks *immediately after* the soldiers' removal *out of this paradise of the world.*[2] Finding no one, it returned with all provisions. Two weeks later further shipping arrived under Grenville's command. The complement included four hundred soldiers and sailors and a large store of supplies.[3] Unwilling to leave the fort unmanned, Grenville deposited fifteen soldiers on the island under the care, appropriately, of a Master Coffin and a certain Chapman. He, too, returned to England.[4]

John White and the Colonists

July 1587. The fifteen soldiers are gone. A bleaching skeleton, all that remains. John White understands that his colony is in danger; and all the while, anchored off Hatorask are the ships that could have taken them to the Chesapeake Bay and away from all this. Before Fernandez's sabotage. Before he delivered them to their deaths. For that is exactly the colonists' sentence.

White's first order of business, as we have seen, was to provide for the families' immediate comfort, ordering the houses to be repaired and others built. While this was progressing, George Howe was killed. Catching crabs, separated from the others.

It is now possible to understand White's account more fully. Circumstances that did not make sense before are clear. July 30. White does the only thing he can do. Twenty colonists are ferried to Croatoan by Captain Stafford, Lane's former officer, along *with Manteo, who had his mother and many of his kindred dwelling in that island.*[5] Croatoan, *the place where Manteo was born.* They come to ask the fate of the fifteen soldiers, but they have also come — bless John White! — *especially to learn the disposition of the people of the country towards us, and to renew our old friendship with them.*

The reunion does not begin smoothly. *At our first landing,* said White, *they seemed as though they would fight with us.* The envoys, startled, reach for their guns. Seeing this, the people *turned their backs, and fled.* Croatoan is John White's last hope. As they disappear from view, his spirit sinks in despair. It was not supposed to happen this way! On every side, misfortune. But wait! All is not lost: for Manteo *called to them in their own language.* Stopping, turning, the people of Croatoan stare in disbelief. These English clothes of his. And then recognition. All at once, they *threw away their bows and arrows, and some of them came unto us, embracing and entertaining us friendly.* The relief is overwhelming.

But scars are visible. Perhaps the presence of Stafford causes unease. Stafford, who led his men to Croatoan the previous year to plunder stores of food. Lane's orders. Despite the friendly embraces and signs of acceptance, the Croatoans desired *us not to gather or spill any of their corn, for that they had but little.*

We answered them, assures White, *that neither their corn, nor any other thing of theirs should be diminished by any of us.* Though the colonists' own supplies are not sufficient, *our coming was only to renew the old love that was between us, and them, at the first, and to live with them as brethren and friends.*

The First Roanoke Expedition

White had been there *at the first.* In 1584, a more innocent time. Captains Amadas and Barlowe had led the voyage of exploration onto this coast *which smelt so sweetly . . . as if we had been in the midst of some delicate garden, abounding with all kind of odoriferous flowers.* Ashore, the company had scrambled through woods of richly scented loblolly and live oak, where wild muscadine clung to the branches in such profusion, indeed *so full of grapes, as the very beating and surge of the sea overflowed them,* declared an amazed Barlowe . . . *as were incredible to be written.*[6]

Clambering to the top of a sand hill, the men whooped in exultation, firing off a volley of shot. *Under the bank or hill whereon we stood, we beheld the valleys replenished with goodly cedar trees, and having discharged our harquebushot, such a flock of cranes (the most part white) arose under us, with such a cry redoubled by many echoes, as if an army of men had shouted all together.*[7]

The Secotan came forward boldly, *never making any show of fear or doubt.* Granganimeo, arriving in grand state, was accompanied by *forty or fifty men, very handsome and goodly people, and in their behaviour as mannerly and civil as any of Europe.* As the Englishmen approached, *he never moved from his place . . . nor never mistrusted any harm to be offered from us but, sitting still, he beckoned us to come and sit by him, which we performed.*[8] Now he is dead.

How different it was then. A year after Lane's carnage, White humbles himself at the outskirts of Croatoan and earnestly pleads that he has come neither to fight nor seize their goods, but to live *as brethren and friends: which answer seemed to please them well,* and they *requested us to walk up to their town.*

Croatoan

White follows his hosts into Croatoan, guiding his small party into a world so familiar, so rich with memories. A world the colonists have seen only through his eyes and the vividness of his brush. The fact that they can be welcomed into this community, after all that has passed, is an astounding tribute to the generosity of Croatoan. They offered White friendship, *and there feasted us after their manner.*

For the colonists, the release of tension is profound. After weeks of uncertainty and betrayal, despair and abandonment, this friendship at last means they are not alone. Though the prospects are bleak, the future unaltered, contact with the people of Croatoan creates an illusion that all is not lost. For both sides, it is a much-needed respite from the turmoil, a friendship amid the pain. The way life might have been.

Nevertheless, the past intrudes: the Croatoans *desired us earnestly that there might be some token or badge given them of us, whereby we might know them to be our friends when we met them anywhere out of the town or island. They told us further, that for want of some such badge, divers of them were hurt the year before, being found out of the island by* Lane's soldiers.

To illustrate their point, White's company is led inside a house. Across the dimly lit room they discern one of Lane's casualties. The victim reclines on a pallet, who *at that very instant lay lame, and had lain of that hurt ever since: but they said, they knew our men mistook them, and hurt them* by mistake. They quietly murmured, says White, that *they held us excused.* There will be no more talking this day.

August 1. A conference is held. The first concern is the disposition of the Secotan towns that have been injured by Lane, specifically *the people of Secota, Aquascogoc, & Pomiock.* White begs his hosts to mediate in order to restore peace; *willing them of Croatoan, to certify the people of those towns, that if they would accept our friendship, we would willingly receive them again, and that all unfriendly dealings past on both parts should be utterly forgiven and forgotten. To this the chief men of Croatoan answered that they would gladly do the best they could.*

Peace talks are scheduled to take place within seven days, to which the leaders of the towns are to send answer that the friendship has been accepted. Meanwhile, *we also understood of the men of Croatoan that our man, Master Howe, was slain by the remnant of Wingina's men, dwelling then at Dasamongueponke.* A remnant, all that is left. Wanchese, White is informed, is still alive among them. News is had, also, of the fifteen soldiers *left at Roanoak the year before* by Grenville, who were *suddenly set upon by 30 of the men of Secota, Aquascogoc, and Dasamonqueponke.* Two soldiers were killed. The others escaped by boat, and were last reported departing from an island near Hatorask. Never seen again. The colonists conclude their business, and *the same day we departed friendly.*

That the people of Croatoan can do nothing to help White is likely. Wingina is dead. A chasm of bitterness exists that cannot now be bridged. No *people in the world carry more respect to their King, nobility, and governours,* Barlowe had noted, *than these do.* Wingina *is greatly obeyed, and his brothers and children reverenced.* And the English killed him. Nothing can be done now for John White. The people of Croatoan know that the colonists are already dead.

The Love That Was Between Us

August 8, 1587. The date for reestablishing peace with the Secotan has come and gone. White, *having long expected the coming of the Wiroances of Pomeiok, Aquascoquos, Secota, and Dasamonguepeuke,* is disappointed, *seeing that the seven days were past . . . and no tidings of them heard.*

What follows is one of the most horrible and inexplicable occurrences in the sequence of events thus far. Just before dawn someone orders an attack on Dasamonquepeuc in revenge for the slaying of George Howe. Captain Stafford, White, and twenty-four colonists carry it out. The action stands in sharp contrast to White's expressed sentiments — his desire to renew *the old love that was between us* and to live together *as brethren and friends.*

August 9. In the morning, *so early that it was yet dark,* the men land near Dasamonquepeuc and fan out through the woods. In the center of the town a campfire is burning with *some sitting about it,* and *we presently set on them.* The *miserable souls,* White laments, *herewith amazed, fled to a place of thick reeds . . . where our men perceiving them, shot one of them through the body with a bullet.* Hotly pursuing them, the Englishmen abruptly stop. For *we were deceived.* These are not the residents of Dasamonquepeuc, but *our friends, and were come from Croatoan.* The colonists have done exactly what Manteo's town most feared. Having failed to recognize their identifying badge, they shot them.

How did this happen? The attack flies in the face of the vastly different peace policy White had just initiated. Surely he knew the past could not be so easily forgotten, or corrected in a day! And that Howe's death, though tragic, was a direct result of Lane's sweeping reign of terror. Peace can hardly be accomplished by massacring a village. Nor is it likely that White, as Governor of a vulnerable and defenseless colony, would commit them and the Secotan to a never-ending spiral of murder and revenge. Even if he hoped to eliminate the remnant of Wingina's men at Dasamonquepeuc, White had to have known that the towns of Pomeioc, Aquascogoc, and Secota would avenge them. An attack was suicide.[9]

It is evident that there is more to the story. Fernandez maroons the colonists, but Stafford continues to ferry them to Croatoan and Dasamonquepeuc though not, significantly, to the Chesapeake Bay. It is Stafford who returns to England proclaiming *the good news* that they had arrived safely *in their wished haven.*[10] We already suspect his involvement.

Perhaps the sequence of events was different: George Howe is killed. Stafford, Lane's former officer, argues for an attack as a continuance of last year's policy.[11] White, not wishing for an escalation of hostility and instead desiring peace, buys time to try his way first. Accordingly, Stafford conveys White's delegation to Croatoan — and is present at the discussion about identifying badges.

Nothing comes of White's Croatoan conference. A week passes and nothing is heard from the Secotan towns. Under the circumstances, and owing to expected delays, White might reasonably have waited longer. After all, the leaders may not have come forward, but neither were there renewed hostilities. In time, White's peaceful overtures might have smoothed things over.

Instead, someone decides that the season of diplomacy is over. The time *to defer the revenge* having run out, a move is made against the *remnant* of Wingina's men *which were left alive.* To finish the job. If Stafford were responsible, the act represents a final insurance against the colonists' survival, negating White's unanticipated peace efforts at Croatoan. How else could it have happened that the single fear the people of Croatoan had — to be fired on by mistake — was the very thing that occurred? That the one action calculated to alienate the colonists' only friends at Croatoan was accomplished? We have no other explanation for so atrocious a crime. The colonists are stranded. The Spanish on Puerto Rico are notified of their presence. The Secotan are attacked. The colonists will not survive.

No Turning Back

There was no real hope for the colonists anyway. Fernandez prevented White from obtaining supplies in the Caribbean. They will get none from the Secotan. Ships scheduled for their resupply will bypass Roanoke and search for the colony along the Chesapeake Bay.[12] Not finding it, they will give up. Nearing panic — we clearly see why — White is sent back to England *for the better and sooner obtaining of supplies, and other necessaries.* And to notify Raleigh of Fernandez's betrayal. In the meantime, the colonists have no choice but to leave. They *are prepared to remove from Roanoak 50 miles into the main.* They are trying to survive.

Our simple case of missing persons is far behind us, though where the colonists are must still be determined. We have established that a crime was committed: the expedition was sabotaged by someone who knew what had happened on Roanoke under Lane's command. By someone who notified Spain via Darby Glande and ordered an attack on Dasamonquepeuc. What is now chillingly obvious is that the intended fate of the colonists was death. What we are investigating is a case of mass murder.

Fernandez is clearly a suspect. However, in spite of the evidence stacked against him, we are left with a nagging problem: motive. Why would Fernandez deliberately sabotage a venture in which he had a part? Which would mean his death if he were convicted? And which implies a personal grudge against 117 people? There is no answer.

What if, in fact, Fernandez had no motive? At one time, he had been a pirate and, by all accounts, one most notorious.[13] Now he legally privateers. Men like Fernandez live by their wits, not by principles. Money is a strong incentive. If he actually had no vendetta against the colonists, and there is nothing to suggest that he did, we must entertain another possibility. Was he merely a hired gun? Fernandez may not be our killer after all.

Who, then, is behind him? And protecting him? Who in England would gain from the colonists' destruction and would like to see them stopped? Perhaps someone working for Spain. But, then, would Fernandez be involved? He began his career in Spanish service, but that was before Spain invaded Portugal and forcibly annexed the Azores, his homeland. Fernandez is Protestant, has become an English citizen, and will soon take an English wife. He is reviled by the Spaniards as a traitor and heretic. He will join the English ranks to fight against the Armada. It is not likely that he is working for someone with Spanish sympathies, or for Spain itself.

Moreover, it is curious that Spain never found the location of the colony.[14] Although tipped off by Darby Glande, it is obvious that he was unable to steer them to it, to pinpoint its location along the miles and miles of unbroken coastline. Glande was not a navigator and did not have a pilot's map to chart his course. For his pains, he was condemned to seven years as a galley slave. Perhaps the Spaniards thought he had deceived them. Evidently whoever kidnapped Darby Glande and released him on Puerto Rico intended the action as an insurance policy, a bait. Spain grabbed it, expending great effort to discover Roanoke. Yet they are ancillaries in this picture, not principal players. Spain is not the answer.

Perhaps the colonists' enemy was someone with a hatred of Separatists. If our theory regarding White's colonists were correct, someone may have thought he would do a service to the Crown by eliminating them. Yet their removal from the realm effectively put an end to any political threat they posed. So why risk a criminal prosecution by killing them?

The colony does not appear to have been much of a threat to anybody. What was once a grave concern to Spain must now be largely academic, with the invincible Armada in the offing and England expected to fall. If Separatists, the colonists are now quietly tucked away. No need to elevate them into martyrs. There appears no plausible motive for wanting them dead. And perhaps that is precisely right. . . . There *is* no motive. By focusing on White's colony, we may have been looking in the wrong place entirely.

What if the killer *were not after the colonists at all?* What if they were only incidental victims and the real quarry was the person who would be most hurt by their failure? The person who benefited from their settling America and confirming his patent? *What if the target were Sir Walter Raleigh?* We must be careful what we say! For were this true — if we so much as entertain this as a possibility — then we are stumbling into something far greater than we ever imagined, and we must be bold enough to see it through.

14 RALEIGH'S RISE TO POWER

But envious brains do nought (or light) esteem,
Such stately steps as they cannot attain.
For whoso reaps renown above the rest,
With heaps of hate shall surely be oppressed.
Walter Raleigh[1]

Bold as a Lion

Raleigh was born in 1552 at Hayes Barton, in Devon, the youngest of five sons.[2] His father provided a comfortable country living, though the family name had once been greater. Raleigh attended Oxford and the Inns of Court. He was bright, ambitious, energetic, possessed of a sense of destiny and a heroic notion of valor. With his friends, he was boisterous, often in trouble for brawling and for playing practical jokes. He was a freethinker, inquisitive, with a wide range of interests and talents. He grew to be the quintessential Renaissance man.

June 11, 1578. Fortunes change. Raleigh's brother, Sir Humphrey Gilbert, is granted a patent by the Queen to discover and occupy North American lands not inhabited by Spain.[3] Twenty-six-year-old Raleigh and his brother Carew captain a reconnaissance mission. Raleigh's pilot is a Portuguese pirate, *a thorough-paced scoundrel,* named Simon Fernandez.

Thomas Churchyard, a friend from the West Country, learns of the venture in his usual way, by sending his son into the vendors' stalls of St. Paul's churchyard to overhear the gossip. As the expedition sets sail, his poem championing the exploits of Gilbert and his reckless brothers is read before Elizabeth at an entertainment:

This strange adieu of yours doth argue noble hearts;
And in your breasts are noble gifts, and many noble parts . . .
You might have walked the streets, as other gallants do,
Yea kept the court and country both, in Paul's have jetted too,
If mind had not been drawn to things of greater weight,
And had not hearts held up your heads another kind of height.
Perhaps in idle days, you would set men awork,

And call them to account in haste, that close in corners lurk:
And ask in open place, how they would spend their time,
And if they say they have no mind the lofty clouds to climb,
Yet would you wish they should see what on earth is found,
And search the proof, and sail by art, about the world so round.
At home to tarry still, but breeds gross blood and wit;
Then better with the falcon fly, than here on dunghill sit.[4]

Despite such promising beginnings, the accolades and frivolity, the brothers, with their boundless energy and intellect, will learn something on this expedition about jealousy. *Some people happy think a greedy hope of gain, And heaps of gold you hope you find, doth make you take this pain,* chortles Churchyard. *Let the world now speak the worst, and babble what they please.*[5] Their detractors are cheered when news that a leaking ship, storms, and desertions have plagued the expedition. It ends in failure and Gilbert's fortune is lost.

Life at Court

1580. Rebellion breaks out in Ireland against England's rule. Raleigh, now twenty-eight, tries his hand as a soldier of fortune, captaining troops at the front. Autumn 1581. Raleigh, highly critical of the handling of Irish affairs by Deputy Lord Grey of Wilton, boldly counsels a different approach. It is rumored that the Queen summons them both to Court to air their differences on Irish policy. Raleigh *had much the better in the manner of telling his tale, insomuch that the Queen and the Lords took no slight mark of the man and his parts, for from thence he came to be known and to have access to the Lords and then we are not to doubt how such a man could comply to progression.*[6] Raleigh quits his post in Ireland and remains at Court.

After the rigors of the Irish campaign, the leisurely pace of Whitehall must be overwhelming. Inside, the hallways and bedchambers are luxurious, strewn with sweet herbs and nosegays of perfumed flowers whose smell, visitor Levinus Lemnius remarked of English homes in general, *cheered me up and entirely delighted all my senses.*[7] Outside, the grounds boast a magnificent flower garden, full of walks, and an orchard for more solitary retreats. *From the palace is a very stately passage to the Thames where the Royal barge* is moored, manned by a staff of forty-two, in which Elizabeth can *pass at her pleasure the pleasant stream.*[8]

Pleasant indeed. The Thames is *very clear* and teeming with *an infinite plenty of excellent, sweet, and pleasant fish* sporting near the riverbank. And if the Queen or her legion of courtiers grow weary of this sight, they may retire to *the tennis courts, the bowling allies, cockpits, and other places of exercise* on the palace grounds. Or play a card game of primo. Summer entertainments include fireworks and water pageants featuring nymphs and mechanical dolphins.[9]

Old Nobility and the Nouveau Riche

If Raleigh's arrival in royal society were sudden and unexpected, his subsequent rise was meteoric. He quickly adapts to this world, and cuts a dashing figure. He is *a tall, handsome and bold man* (six feet tall, a good nine inches above average), with *a most remarkable aspect.* Black hair, exquisitely trimmed. *His beard,* noted Aubrey, *turned up naturally.*[10] Queen Elizabeth is clearly taken with this fascinating newcomer from the West Country. *And truth it is that she took him for a kind of oracle, which nettled them all.*[11]

To understand the fear Raleigh generates, one must understand the times. In Tudor England, merchants and lesser gentry are on the rise, becoming rich and powerful while older landed families find their influence eroding. A revolution is occurring.[12] Peers no longer fill the highest levels of government, while income from service at Court fails to rise with an inflated economy. Meanwhile, London and an urban merchant class balloons. *Certainly the making of new gentlemen bred great strife sometimes amongst the Romans, I mean when those which were "novi homines" were more allowed of for their virtues newly seen and showed than the old smell of ancient race.*[13]

Their exalted position threatened, the nobility bitterly close ranks. Gentlemen, once defined solely by wealth, are now judged according to how their money is made. Merchants, who work in worldly trades, are hardly of the same cut. The *opinion of nobility rejoice much in their own conceit, because it was their fortune to come of such ancestors whose stock of long time hath been counted rich. . . . And though their ancestors left them not one foot of land, or else they themselves have pissed it against the walls, yet they think themselves not the less noble therefore of one hair.*[14]

Yet the aristocracy cannot fail to notice the large numbers of new men rising rapidly to the top. The old moneyed families respond by abruptly shifting focus. Near-fanatical emphasis is now placed on education and appropriate behavior as indications of status. *Honours should change manners*, or so they say.[15] Nobility is a way of living, a sharing of tastes, a mastering of social graces. *For new nobility is but the act of power, but ancient nobility is the act of time.*[16]

Status

A clamor is raised, demanding the enforcement of laws that legally define the clothing styles allowed each class. Though merchants wear *fine and costly* garments, their wives are prone to outlandish display *both in attire and costly housekeeping*, and *cannot tell when and how to make an end. . . . I might here name a sort of hues devised . . . to please fantastical heads, as gooseturd green, pease-porridge tawny, popinjay blue, lusty gallant, the devil-in-the-head (I should say "the hedge"), and suchlike.*[17]

Diet is another status symbol. The number of dishes served by the nobility *(whose cooks are for the most part musical-headed Frenchmen and strangers)* is staggering. Each day *they have not only beef, mutton, veal, lamb, kid, pork, cony, capon, pig . . . but also some portion of the red or fallow deer, beside great variety of fish and wildfowl . . . so that for a man to dine with one of them . . . is rather to yield unto a conspiracy with a great deal of meat.*[18]

Gentlemen and merchants battle it out at the table, their banquets *often comparable herein to the nobility of the land.* Although, admittedly, spiced with a fondness for the ridiculous: jellies *of all colours* molded into *flowers, trees, animals and fruits;* marzipan *wrought with no small curiosity, tarts of diverse hues . . . sugarbread, gingerbread, florentines, and sundry outlandish confections, altogether seasoned with sugar.*[19]

Pedigree

As the lesser gentry begin to rival the aristocracy in extravagance, pedigree is seized upon as the ultimate determinant. Old blood outranks new. Genealogists map out impressive family trees — fabricated or otherwise. Suddenly everyone must *boast and vaunt themselves of their ancestors . . . saying, and crying with open mouth: I am a gentleman, I am worshipful, I am honourable, I am noble, and I cannot tell what: my father was this, my father was that: I come from this house, and I am come of that.*[20]

The College of Heralds is deluged with thousands of petitions for coats of arms, despite uproar over suspected bribery, forgery, and the granting of fake heraldry. True is the saying that *every Cock is proud on his own dunghill.*[21]

The Centrifugal Tudor Force

Such rivalry, on a national level, centers around the Crown. The most influential in the land are no longer the most wealthy, but those with the closest ties to Elizabeth. *A friend in Court is worth a penny in purse.*[22] Younger nobility resort to the city to curry favor, hoping to make their mark.

It is an expensive gamble, requiring a massive outlay of funds to create a competitive image amid a Court obsessed with physical appearance, novelty, and foreign tastes. Little wonder that the young hopefuls who *fly to London* find money flowing through their hands like water.[23] There are few openings at Court, the odds far greater for failure than success. With such lofty stakes, *he that is afraid of every grass,* quips Camden, *must not piss in a meadow.* Excellent advice. Many lose their fortunes. With interest rates soaring at 10 percent and above, others are forced to sell off manor lands to pay London debts, thereby accelerating their downfall.[24]

Maintaining a Competitive Edge

Into this elite world Raleigh steps with apparent ease. With no connections, without years of struggle, he enters the Court and at the very top. He is soon in Elizabeth's most intimate circle: *true it is,* says Naunton, *he had gotten the Queen's ear in a trice and she began to be taken with his elocution and loved to hear his reasons to her demands.*[25]

Yet Raleigh's position is exceedingly precarious. His staying power has yet to be determined, and there is no one to protect him but the Queen. Should he lose his footing, there will be no one to protect him at all. It is said that on the windowpane of Greenwich Palace, Raleigh etches the lines: *Fain would I climb, yet I fear to fall.* And the Queen's coy answer: *If thy heart fail thee, climb not at all.*[26]

Raleigh will climb. After all, *faint heart never won fair lady.*[27] Yet what kind of stout heart is necessary to win a Queen? And, once there, to keep her? For those fortunate enough to be admitted into Elizabeth's circle, the worries are far from over. There is continual pressure among the courtiers to maintain position, to distinguish themselves in order to keep from being supplanted. *The rising unto place is laborious, and by pains men come to greater pains. . . . The standing is slippery, and the regress is either a downfall, or at least an eclipse, which is a melancholy thing.*[28]

Fashion is public statement, and courtiers engage in a fierce competition of outlandish display. A gentleman, Harrison remarks, once trying to describe English attire at last gave up *and only drew the picture of a naked man, unto whom he gave a pair of shears in the one hand and a piece of cloth in the other, to the end he should shape his apparel after such fashion as himself liked, since he could find no kind of garment that could please him any while together; and this he called an Englishman.*[29]

Starched cambric, holland, and lawn are mounted layer upon layer into ponderous ruffles, segregating shoulders from head, *whereof some be a quarter of a yard deep, yea some more.* Should a gust of wind or storm *chance to hit upon them,* reports an incredulous Philip Stubbes, *then they go flip flap in the wind, like rags flying abroad, and lie upon their shoulders like the dishcloth of a flute.* Their origin is equally baffling, though perhaps *the Devil, in the fullness of his malice,* he proposes, *first invented these great great ruffs.*[30]

Farthingale dresses, popular at Court in the 1580s, are hooped with whalebone and exploded out by twenty yards of expensive cloth, making it difficult to sit down. Elizabeth's gowns, as one might expect, are spectacular, generously dusted with pearls and precious gems. One royal dress glitters with 365 diamonds, one for each day of the year. *Such is our mutability that today there is none to the Spanish guise, tomorrow French toys are most fine and delectable . . . and by and by the Turkish manner is generally best liked.*[31]

So too with men's attire: *the short French breeches make such a comely vesture that, except it were a dog in a doublet, you shall not see any so disguised as are my countrymen of England,* notes Harrison dryly. Indeed, adds an overwhelmed Stubbes, the doublets are *no less monstrous than the rest. For now the fashion is to have them hang down to the midst of their thighs, or at least to their privie members, being so hard-quilted, and stuffed, bombasted and sewed, as they can very hardly either stoop down, or decline themselves. . . . Now what handsomeness can be in these doublets which stand on their bellies . . . (so as their bellies are thicker than all their bodies beside) let wise men judge.*[32]

Courtiers frantically compete for the Queen's affection in dancing, poetry, and other accomplishments. *Truly it is a rare thing with us now to hear of a courtier which hath but his own language. And to say how many gentlewomen and ladies there are that, beside sound knowledge of the Greek and Latin tongues, are thereto no less skilful in the Spanish, Italian, and French, or in some one of them, it resteth not in me. . . .* Though the cynic might detect a certain superficiality to it all. *Would to God the rest of their lives and conversations were correspondent to these gifts!* cries Harrison. *For as our common courtiers (for the most part) are the best learned and endued with excellent gifts, so are many of them the worst men when they come abroad that any man shall either hear or read of.*[33]

The Queen's Favorite

Raleigh is different. Along with a handsome physique and splendid appearance, none can deny that he is also blessed with a brilliant intellect. He is the *wonder of the world for wit.* A keen observer, he soaks up everything. *He was no slug; without doubt he had a wonderful waking spirit, and a great judgment to guide it.*[34] An original thinker, *he could make everything he read or heard his own, and his own he could easily improve to the greatest advantage. He seemed to be born to that only which he went about, so dexterous was he in all his undertakings, in Court, camp, by sea, by land, with sword, with pen.*[35]

To vie with the nobility, and indeed to ridicule them, Raleigh cuts a figure to rival a prince. He dresses magnificently (some say flamboyantly) amid a resplendent court, his clothes glittering with rubies, diamonds, and pearls. His palace footwear is so bespattered with jewels, exclaims Drexelius, a visiting Flemish priest, that they are *computed to be worth more than six thousand, six hundred gold pieces.* Raleigh is, Drexelius adds, *the darling of the English Cleopatra.*[36] He plays the perfect courtier, mocking the role, doing all by extremes. And is hated because of it. He was, said Aubrey, *damnable proud.*[37]

The Queen, in high good humor, flirtatiously nicknames him *Water:* pun on the Devon pronunciation of his own name. He is her Water, her *Shepherd of the Ocean.* And she is Cynthia, goddess of the ocean's fate.[38] *Master Water Rawley is in very high favour with the Queen's Majesty; neither my Lord of Leicester nor master Vice-Chamberlain in so short time ever was in the like. . . . I have heard it credibly reported,* said Maurice Browne, *that Master Rawley hath spent within this half year above 3000 pounds. He is very sumptuous in his apparel, and I take it he hath his diet out of the privy kitchen, but all the vessels with which he is served at his table, is silver with his own arms on the same. He hath attending on him at least thirty men. . . . The whole Court doth follow him.*[39]

Raleigh's rooms within the palace are luxurious. His bed, it is avidly reported, is draped with a green velvet spread bordered with silver lace, and the four posts are garnished with white feather plumes. He is provided with all worldly pleasures yet, it is said, conducts himself well toward everyone. *He was such a person (every way) that . . . a Prince would rather be afraid of than ashamed of. He had that awfulness and ascendency in his aspect over other mortals.*[40]

The Queen grants Raleigh further favors, subsidizing his Roanoke ventures indirectly through privileges and estates. 1587: Raleigh receives his greatest honor, the coveted Captain of the Queen's Guard.[41] The head of Elizabeth's private bodyguard, he will defend her in these turbulent times from countless assassination attempts, standing watch at her chamber door and accompanying her on walks about the grounds. On summer progresses and journeys, he will ride at the front of the corps in shining silver armor, spangles of jewels sewn on shoes, sleeves, and cap. He will be closest to her always.

Deadfalls and Traps

Life at Court promises glamor, stimulation, and social accomplishment. But all the skills in the world cannot hide a certain ugliness permeating the palace halls. A desperation is visible in the courtiers swarming over Whitehall, scrambling for office. Too few positions to fill. Sir Philip Sidney, having received a military appointment in the Low Countries, is stung by evil words spoken at Court behind his back. *I understand I am called very ambitious and proud at home,* he writes from the field, *but certainly if they know my heart they would not altogether so judge me.*[42] His uncle, the illustrious Earl of Leicester, as reward for being the Queen's longtime favorite, finds himself the object of a scurrilous volume entitled *Leycesters Common-Wealth:*[43] a libel accusing him of plots, poisonings, sexual perversion, and political intrigue.

Raleigh's own rise has been too rapid. Too dramatic. He is denounced as a manipulator, a fraud, a deceiver. The palace walls swell with cutting jibes about his low birth. Once, when the Queen was playing a song on the virginals, the Earl of Oxford, eyeing the vertical movement of the hammer mechanism, loudly remarked within her hearing that *when Jacks went up, heads went down* — when knaves such as Raleigh are elevated to favor, the old aristocracy is thrust down, out of the way. The joke circulates around Court. Raleigh, the *Jack of an upstart.*[44]

Jealousies develop into cliques, nowhere more evident than in the Queen's own Privy Council. Lord Burghley versus Sir Francis Walsingham and the Earl of Leicester; the Earls of Sussex and Arundel versus Leicester, Leicester versus Burghley; Sir Nicholas Throckmorton versus Burghley; Sir Nicholas Throckmorton versus Leicester, then Walsingham. *The principal note of her reign,* says Naunton, *will be that she ruled much by faction and parties, which she herself both made, upheld, and weakened as her own great judgement advised.*[45]

Both Hatton and Leicester are accused of doing away with their opponents. Leicester, in particular, maintains two physicians on his payroll — the Italian Julio Borgarucci and the Portuguese Roderigo Lopez, both expert in poisons.[46] Sir Nicholas Throckmorton died at Leicester's house after eating a salad; Margaret Tudor, the Queen's relative, succumbed to poison after his visit. Walter Devereux, the Earl of Essex, passed away believing Leicester poisoned him. Amy Robsart, Leicester's first wife, died from a fall down the stairs. Rumor had it that his assassins first broke her neck and poisoned her. His second wife, Lady Douglas Sheffield, whose husband he poisoned, accused him of poisoning her too — her hair and nails falling out as evidence.[47]

When a royal marriage between Queen Elizabeth and the French Duke of Alençon appeared imminent, sniper shots were fired at his representative. A deviation from form, still all indications point to Leicester.[48] Yet reckless as he is, the Court harbors far deadlier foes. Were one to have an enemy, one could only hope it were not Burghley or Walsingham. Steady, quiet, and lethal. It is they who wield the greatest power.

To Win Enemies

For Raleigh, a crisis is imminent. One he cannot avoid. It springs from contempt and jealousy, from a dangerous structural problem inherent within the Court. It is created by Elizabeth's need to balance incredibly powerful and volatile factions in this rapidly changing society. To prevent England from exploding into civil war like those raging across the rest of Europe, Elizabeth deliberately produces a power vacuum in which no one party achieves absolute authority. In essence, a brokered anarchy. She *ruled much by faction,* keeping everyone off balance.

Individuals are supported, then undermined as soon as they become too powerful. An illusion is created that anyone can gain control. As a consequence, those without stature are led to believe that they can make it to the top, if only those in favor are removed. To do this, they employ slander, outrageous libel, forgery, and preposterous fabrications — often encouraged by the more powerful, who use them as pawns in a larger and deadlier game. The Court is full of *men seeking to please and win favour by slander . . . such as make up their own buildings with other men's ruins, and delight to say anything that may entrap the guiltless.*[49] One is lucky if it ends at this: false imprisonment and murder are all too common.

A molten viciousness lies beneath the polished floors of Whitehall, ready to erupt. Traps are set, poison laid. Men of wit and vigor proceed boldly, unaware that conspirators are plotting their undoing. The attack will catch them off guard. Lies and false accusations spew forth, dragging them down with a meanness out of all proportion to circumstances. Those oppressed are not always the guilty. *I fear the malice of some discontented persons,* said Burghley, *wherewith the Court is overmuch sprinkled.*[50]

Little wonder that Raleigh, who bursts onto the scene from the remote West Country to achieve unrivaled influence, is easily the *best-hated man in the world.*[51] Yet everyone close to the Queen suffers envy and slander. The question is, who among Raleigh's enemies was powerful enough to bring him down? And escape blame? And why? Why would someone so seek his ruin that they would destroy Roanoke and 116 innocent people to see that it happened?

15 POLITICAL TURMOIL

And in very deed it is most apparent that riches are the fittest instruments of conquest. . . .

Richard Hakluyt[1]

Forbidden Territory

January 1569. A stinking, broken-down ship named the *Minion* limps into a Cornwall harbor. Along the quay, onlookers gasp at the sight of the grisly crew. Pale, skeletal faces; bony hands clawing at proffered food. Here they are: fifteen men, all that remain of John Hawkins's squadron, which left Plymouth harbor in six ships little more than a year before.[2] More shocking still, the *Minion* belongs to the Queen.

Hawkins had gambled. He ventured trading ships into the Spanish West Indies, violating international law. The English were not supposed to be there. On May 4, 1493, from a room in the Vatican, Pope Alexander VI — a Spaniard — decreed this, touching pen to paper and neatly dividing the world between Portugal and Spain. All other nations excluded.

In the Mexican harbor of San Juan de Ulloa, Hawkins's ships were attacked by a fleet under the command of the Spanish Viceroy. Most of his crew was slaughtered. Survivors were subjected to the Inquisition: burned at the stake or made galley slaves for life. *If all the miseries and troublesome affairs of this sorrowful voyage,* Hawkins lamented, *should be perfectly and thoroughly written, there should need a painful man with his pen.*[3] From this point forward, the *military and sea-faring men all over England . . . desired war.*[4]

Holocaust

The basis of it all is power. Spain's conquest of the Indies has generated the wealth necessary to fuel that power. When Philip II ascended the throne in 1556, Spain controlled fully one half of Europe.[5] *The effect of these treasures* was rightly foretold by Peter Martyr of Anghierra, cried

Hakluyt, *whereby all the world shall be under your obeisance.*[6] Spain is mustering the most powerful army and navy money can buy.

One by one, the countries in Europe fall. King Philip's military regime is gathering nations and power and wealth and momentum. The *proud, hateful Spaniards* are destroying world peace through *servitude, tyranny,* and oppression.[7] Creating chaos, inciting insurrection. Spain's armies are unleashed upon the land. The upheavals cause waves of terror in England. *Hath not he these many years given large pensions to numbers of English unnatural rebels? . . . Hath not he divers times sent foreign forces into Ireland furnished with money, armour, munition, and victuals? Hath not he sent round sums of money into Scotland? . . .* The havoc wreaked in the Holy Roman Empire and the Low Countries *is like to work in other places unless speedy order be taken to hinder it.*[8]

Spain's powerful ally is the Vatican; the Iberian army operating as the *sword of the AntiChrist of Rome.*[9] A counterreformation is launched, a holy war bent on unseating Protestant leaders from power. Spanish-funded seminaries in Rome and Rheims churn out priests to foster sedition. Catholic recusants in England champion the claim of Mary Queen of Scots to the English throne; the Pope calls for Elizabeth's deposition.

Catalysts of War

1568. The year Hawkins is attacked by Spain. In the Low Countries shocking events are unfolding. Seven states within the Netherlands have declared themselves free. They are the United Provinces, their champion the Protestant William the Silent, Prince of Orange and Governor of Holland, Zealand, Utrecht, and West Friesland. There have been riots. In Antwerp, a mob descended upon the Cathedral of the Virgin and desecrated more than seventy altars: smashing the organ with axes, trampling holy wafers underfoot, toppling a giant crucifix by pulling it down with ropes and chopping it into bits.[10] The Spanish responded by dispatching troops to quell the rebellion, *to lay the yoke upon a most free nation.* And *(as if their freedom were now quite lost),* Spain's top military commander, the Duke of Alva, is sent in to restore control.[11]

In Brussels, martial law is declared.[12] Fear clings palpably to the city. The inhabitants hide in their houses, gripped by a terrible dread, speaking to no one, going out only when necessary, conscious of the watchful eyes of the soldiers. Businesses are shut down and trade grinds to a halt, leaving the streets deathly quiet. Ports and exits from the country are sealed and the Inquisition swings into action. February 16, 1568. The entire population of the Netherlands is condemned to death. Catholics as well as Protestants are marked for extermination; the latter for the crime of heresy, which is treason; the former for having allowed it to happen.[13]

Incapable of carrying out the full sentence, Alva creates a Council for Disturbances to determine who shall die. Twelve criminal judges constitute the tribunal. In the Netherlands, they are referred to as the Council of Blood.[14] The nation is gripped by *a constant fear of death.*[15] Friends and neighbors turn informant in a frantic effort to preserve their own lives. Arrests proceed without warning, as many as fifty people at a time tried and condemned. In Valenciennes, fifty-five citizens are beheaded at once.[16] New prisons are built, unable to keep pace with the arrests. Wealthy merchants are exterminated, their estates seized to fuel the Spanish treasury.

A Year to Remember

In England, the holocaust in the Netherlands takes its toll. Elizabeth is amazed that *she is changed so much and become so thin.*[17] Cries go up from neighboring Denmark, fearful that Spain will invade them next and that *the Enemy of Mankind* shall continue to *water the seed of war, which he had sown in the Netherlands, with the blood of men.*[18]

December 1568. To suppress the Dutch rebellion, Spain borrows tremendous sums of money from Genoa. As the vessels carrying it enter the Channel, French Huguenots give chase, forcing them to seek refuge in English ports. But by this time, news of Spain's massacre of Hawkins's crew is trickling into London. The Genoese loan, amounting to £400,000, is confiscated by Elizabeth and deposited in the mint at the Tower of London.[19]

Spanish reaction is immediate. *Upon which very day, to wit, the 29th of December, the Duke of Alva being in a furious rage seized upon the Englishmens' goods everywhere in the Netherlands and kept the Englishmen prisoners . . . the Duke of Alva intended this against the English for a terrour.*[20] How gravely he underestimates the Queen! Elizabeth, *nothing terrified,* responds in kind, impounding Spanish ships which were, indeed, a greater number.[21] Spain then imposes an embargo on England, forbidding *oil, alum, sugar, spices or other such like commodities* to enter the country, arresting English merchants and delivering them to the Inquisition.

Hostilities escalate and the *wound* is made *to fester, which in the beginning might easily have been healed.*[22]

Ireland, 1568.[23] England's exposed western flank. Ireland is a nation divided between traditional Celtic chiefdoms and powerful Anglo-Irish feudal lords who have controlled vast tracts of territory since the time of the Norman invasion. Neither is loyal to the English Queen. Spaniards have begun trading here, supplying both parties with arms and ammunition — and propaganda. They are promised aid to restore their former power and liberty, though neither the Celts nor the lords would welcome the control of the other. Bitter fighting breaks out in Munster between factions supported by the Queen and those backed by Spain and the Vatican. The movement is crushed by Raleigh's brother Humphrey Gilbert, sent to Ireland as Munster's new command.

Scotland, 1568.[24] The year of momentous events continues. Mary Queen of Scots, imprisoned the year before by her own lords while her infant son, James VI, is crowned king, escapes and flees across the border into England. Yet Mary has repeatedly claimed the English throne as her own. She is rigorously backed by her Catholic relations, the French House of Guise. And by Spain. And by the Vatican. Whitehall is greatly alarmed, with good reason, that English Catholics will rally to her cause. Mary is taken into custody and confined.

The Northern Rebellion

1569. Elizabeth's worst nightmare is realized. Revolution erupts in fury across the north of England.[25] The Northern Rebellion is led by the Catholic lords of Northumberland and Westmorland. Supported by Spain. It is triggered by the arrest of the Earl of Norfolk following his engagement to the imprisoned Scottish Queen, a thrust for power that would have placed him on both the Scottish and English thrones. Elizabeth is tipped off to the plot by the mysterious Dr. Dee, acquaintance of Raleigh and perhaps also spy, who warns the Queen to beware of Norfolk, that he has surrounded himself with a network of agents.[26]

The rebellion, once begun, is waged as a religious war. The northern force, between five and ten thousand strong, sweeps from town to town under Catholic banners and Crusaders' crosses, trampling Bibles and tearing Anglican prayerbooks. The Earl of Norfolk, they cry, will be freed in the name of Catholicism, and Mary Queen of Scots placed on England's throne.

In reality, it is a power play. The feudal nobility resents the privileges lost at Elizabeth's hands. They take up arms to defend the old order, *lest the ancient nobility of England should be trodden under foot by new upstarts, and their country delivered for a prey to strangers.*[27] The Queen, outraged, raises a massive army against them. The rebellion dissolves in the face of overwhelming odds.

The Pope's Bull

From the Vatican, Pope Pius V issues a bull of excommunication. A declaration of war against Elizabeth, it frees her subjects from their oath of allegiance and calls for her overthrow. The bull is found nailed to the Bishop of London's door in St. Paul's on a May morning in 1570. *The alarm publicly expressed by the people here, and their fears of being ruined,* writes Spanish agent Antonio de Guaras from London, *are perfectly incredible, and the whole talk at Court consists of discussions as to how they will defend themselves or how they will perish.*[28]

Yet the bull has an unexpected effect. A groundswell of patriotic fervor, scarcely seen before, emerges as a direct result of the threat to the Queen. Intense sentiments of nationalism and loyalty find expression in impassioned vows to defend Elizabeth from harm. The Pope's condemnation is referred to derisively as *the great Bull and certain calves* received, *specially the Monster Bull that roared at my Lord Bishop's gate.*[29]

The Ridolfi Plot

1571. The Vatican steps up its campaign. A list of Catholic sympathizers within Elizabeth's own Court is drawn up by an Italian agent named Roberto Ridolfi. A new plot is hatched.[30] Elizabeth will be assassinated.

In Dover, a spy named Charles Bailly is seized carrying a packet of coded letters from Ridolfi to Mary Queen of Scots. He is apprehended by Lord Cobham. A search reveals a cypher key sewn into the lining of his coat. The letters disclose Ridolfi's list of Catholic sympathizers. Cobham never turns it over to the authorities, for his own name is on the list. He forwards the packet to Mary's agent, who, aided by the Spanish ambassador, replaces the letters with innocuous forgeries. The fakes are then passed on to Lord Burghley.

Charles Bailly is thrown into the Marshalsea Prison. As luck would have it, William Herllie occupies the adjoining cell. All of London knows Herllie, a tormented Catholic prisoner. He is visible from the street through the iron grates, a feeble skeleton bound in leg irons, fed only bread and water. Bailly, affected by his condition and by way of encouragement, confesses the Ridolfi plot. What he does not know, until far too late, is that Herllie is a spy on Burghley's payroll.[31]

Burghley now knows of the plot, but cannot act without hard evidence. He can only watch and wait. Proof comes at last in the form of incriminating letters sent to Bailly. But they are in code and, without a cypher key, cannot be read. Reeling from his recent betrayal, Bailly refuses to talk, even when transferred to the Tower and racked. Until one dark night, when a man enters Bailly's cell and identifies himself as Dr. John Story, celebrated Catholic prisoner and sufferer for the faith. He convinces Bailly to provide the cypher in order to ingratiate himself with Burghley as a double-agent. Incredibly, even after the previous Herllie-Burghley affair, Bailly complies. In the morning he delivers the key to his interrogators, only to discover that the real Dr. Story is incarcerated elsewhere and that his nocturnal visitor was an impostor.

Arrests for the Ridolfi plot begin. In the twelve years of Elizabeth's reign, no peer has been executed. Ridolfi changes everything. The Duke of Norfolk is the first to be beheaded, following the conviction for high treason of forty-eight others. Cobham is arrested. Both the Scottish agent and the Spanish ambassador are expelled from the country.[32]

There is an immediate crackdown on Catholics. They, in turn, point the finger at Burghley. *He is a great heretic,* the ousted Spanish ambassador indignantly informs Philip, *and such a clownish Englishman as to believe that all the Christian princes joined together are not able to injure the sovereign of this country, and therefore treats their ministers with great arrogance. This man manages the bulk of the business, and by means of his vigilance and craftiness . . . thinks to outwit the ministers of other princes. . . . This to a certain extent he has succeeded in doing.*[33]

Peace or War?

In April 1572 Dutch Protestants step up their revolt against Spain by seizing the city of Brill. Gilbert joins the fray, commanding a volunteer squadron to Zealand with Elizabeth's approval. Raleigh has quit Oxford and is fighting in France, itself racked by civil war as Huguenots under

Admiral Gaspard de Coligny battle with royalist troops. He marches with his cousin Henry Champernowne under the black standard of Count Montgomery: *Let valour end my life.*[34]

Unfortunately, the royalists only scoff at the English volunteers and their inability to employ longbows. Archery in England is now largely a pastime. It is reported in London that the French, *deriding our new archery never hesitate in open skirmish, if any leisure serve, to turn up their tails and cry, "Shoot, English!" and all because our strong shooting is decayed and laid in bed. But if some of our Englishmen now lived that served King Edward the Third in his wars with France, the breech of such a varlet should have been nailed to his bum.*[35]

August 22, 1572. St. Bartholomew's Day. French royalist troops open fire on unarmed Huguenot civilians. Paris streets are awash with blood. By order of Catherine de Medici, Coligny is assassinated. Thirty thousand Huguenots are slaughtered; all who aid them are marked for death.[36] Raleigh is lucky; he survives. So does another Englishman in Paris — Francis Walsingham, then Elizabeth's ambassador. There are those who claim that his role in the Huguenot uprising is not insignificant, and that his intriguing extends to the Low Countries as well.[37]

Officially England is neutral. Elizabeth's ministers, chiefly Burghley, caution diplomacy. And yet her swashbuckling Devon volunteers prosecute an undeclared war, now spilling over into the Caribbean. In the summer of 1573, Francis Drake — *Drago* to the Spaniards — targets Spain's silver depot at Nombre de Dios in the Isthmus of Darien, Panama. With the assistance of a local people known as the Cimarrones, the "wild ones," mostly slaves escaped from Spanish mines, Drake attacks. Victory is complete; the loot incredible. The ships, groaning with treasure, can carry home only a small portion. In desperation, the men discard the silver, cramming the vessels only with gold.[38]

Sunday, August 9. Drake arrives in Plymouth harbor while church service is in progress. News of the plunder roars through the streets like wildfire. The church doors burst open and people spill out in a mad rush to the wharf, leaving the preacher without a congregation.[39] But beyond Plymouth, Drake receives no accolades, for England and Spain are on the verge of a détente. For the moment, diplomacy has won.

London, the night of October 14. Sir John Hawkins is riding along the Embankment past the Middle Temple with a friend. Suddenly a figure lunges out of the darkness. Hawkins is stabbed and falls to the ground. His assailant is a law student named Peter Burchet, returning from a Puritan rally at Whittington College. He has mistaken Hawkins for Sir Christopher Hatton, rumored leader of the Privy Council's Catholic faction.[40] Although Hawkins recovers, panic over a Puritan conspiracy flares.

Sir Humphrey Gilbert and the Forward-Thinking Men

By the winter of 1575 Raleigh's brother Gilbert is back home in London. George Gascoigne, a poet and fellow soldier, springs up his friend's stairs at his residence in Limehouse *and being very bold to demand of him how he spent his time in this loitering vacation from martial stratagems,* is immediately led into the study. Gilbert flourishes a discourse penned to his elder brother John, proving that his ideas about a voyage to Cathay via North America are neither rash nor irresponsible. John had been appalled by a plan that *then seemed strange* and, indeed, *impossible.*[41] But Gilbert is made of sterner stuff. With his motto *Quid non?* ("Why not?") he cries passionately that he *is not worthy to live at all, that for fear, or danger of death, shunneth his country service, and his own honour, seeing death is inevitable, and the fame of virtue immortal.*[42]

Gilbert's study is filled with scribblings, figures, files on exploration, navigation, sea charts, and even his own invention: a nautical instrument with a variable compass. Gascoigne, overwhelmed and excited because his own kinsman, Martin Frobisher, is ready to embark on a similar voyage of discovery, borrows Gilbert's manuscript.[43] That evening, amazed, he hauls out cosmographical maps and charts, testing Gilbert's figures against the tables of Dutch mapmaker Abraham Ortelius. They prove to be accurate.

Gascoigne, at *mine own greater presumption,* rushes his friend's letter to a printer. It goes to press on April 12, 1576, as *A Discourse of a discovery for a new passage to Cataia* by Humphrey Gilbert. His motto "Why not?" on the front cover. Gascoigne urges the Queen to reward Gilbert with as much enthusiasm as she punishes offenders. Having thus discharged his duty to both friend and country, Gascoigne bows out, signing his letter *from my lodging where I march amongst the muses for lack of exercise in martial exploits, this 12 of April, 1576.*[44]

Gilbert, the idealist, the soldier, the impatient man of action, now finds himself in the midst of a circle of London intellectuals. These are men who have more in common with Raleigh than himself. Richard Hakluyt the elder, a lawyer. His younger cousin of the same name, a geographer, cosmographer, and publisher. Both are vitally concerned with overseas colonization. They spend their time collecting data from sailors and merchants returning from exotic ports. William Camden, an historian. Thomas Hariot, Raleigh's young protégé, a graduate of Oxford and mathematical genius with an interest in navigation and inventions.[45] Antwerp merchant Emanuel van Meteren, whose cousin Abraham Ortelius is a celebrated geographer and cartographer. His maps are indispensable on English ships. And, of course, Dr. John Dee, who earns his keep as royal astrologer, drawing horoscopes for the Queen and her Court. In his own day he is likened to Merlin the magician, whose figure is portrayed as Dee with his long white beard and flowing artist's gown.

Dee is also the foremost mathematician and scientific authority of the Elizabethan Age.[46] He and his brilliant pupil Thomas Digges are famous for mapping out a spectacular supernova that appeared for seventeen months in the constellation of Cassiopeia in 1572. Elizabeth often visits his home and laboratory at Mortlake, entranced by his recent inventions: a ten-foot cross staff named a "radius astronomicus," mounted in a frame that swings up to observe the night sky; specialized compasses; prisms, optics, and refractions. Once, in a field outside his house, he showed Elizabeth, Leicester, and her entire entourage a distorting mirror that twisted their images out of proportion, to their great delight. Elizabeth startling him by laughing out loud.[47]

These are exciting, forward-thinking days. There are lively discussions on the northeast and northwest passages, cosmography, and navigation. Dee's range of interests is phenomenal: mathematics, geography, cartography, ancient Greek and Arabic astronomy, the zodiac, meteorology, alchemy, and even telepathy. He conducts experiments on the time-space continuum and the fourth dimension. Mechanical devices intrigue him.[48] He invents a lifelike raven and a jay, complete with feathers, a mechanical caw, and flashing eyes. This, in imitation of a fascinating experiment he observed in Nuremberg with a mechanical fly, which was released at a dinner table, buzzed around the heads of the invited guests, and softly landed in its inventor's palm.

Dee's private collection of four thousand volumes and seven hundred manuscripts is the greatest scientific holding in the country, a forerunner of the national library. Many are important works dating from the Middle Ages, salvaged from spoil and rot in decaying monasteries, *gotten as in a manner out of a dunghill.* Dee refers to it as *our museum,* and his home is virtually *haunted* with multitudes who consult his library and pose to him all manner of philosophical, geographical, and mathematical questions.[49]

Members of this scientific circle immediately latch on to Gilbert's plan, supporting the northwest passage in writing, proving that it can be done. Hakluyt accumulates accounts of Spanish expeditions, hoping to spark excitement. *For he who proclaims the praises of foreigners, rouses his own countrymen, if they be not dolts.*[50] Colonization and a passage to China would thwart Spain's trade monopoly.

North American Base

There is, however, talk of more direct action: Spain's homebound treasure fleet.[51] Ships from Cartagena and the Isthmus rendezvous in Havana with the Mexican and West Indian fleet. Between March and June they convoy home under hundreds of sail. Guarded by men-of-war. Leaving the protected Florida Strait, they randomly alter course across the Atlantic, making interception difficult. Gilbert proposes a Bermudan base from which to attack the fixed portion of the route, with English ships sent there *as secretly as they may.*[52] Yet Bermuda is too visible — how is secrecy possible? The idea of a hidden base on the North American coast congeals.

November 6, 1577. After meeting with Dee, Gilbert submits *A Discourse How Her Majesty May Meet with and Annoy the King of Spain,* cautioning the Queen to beware of their pretended friendship since *their fair words ought to be held but as mermaids' songs, sweet poisons.* Spain's sea forces must be weakened, either through direct attack or under the pretense of letters patent to North American lands. Under *colour of discovery.* Without the Indies assailed, *it were but labour lost.*[53]

Gilbert's Patent

1578. As spring approaches, a wax image of the Queen is found lying in Lincoln's Inn Fields, its heart pierced with a metal pin.[54] Dee is urgently sent for and declares it nothing more than a malicious prank, intended to scare Elizabeth. It does, and rumors that the Queen is dead send panic through the streets, with people rushing to the palace gates to ascertain the truth of the report. Within months, Gilbert's patent is granted.[55] Though, to his disappointment, he is instructed not to attack Spain.

Nevertheless, an alarmed Bernardino de Mendoza, Spanish ambassador to England, reports meetings held in the Earl of Leicester's own room, the Queen present, in which it is argued that robbing the treasure fleet is their only protection, *unless they could establish a footing on the coast, for thus they would prevent so much money coming to your Majesty.*[56]

The elder Hakluyt, with a lawyer's *burning zeal,* ceasing neither *day nor night*, draws up plans on North American colonization for Gilbert, urging settlement in a temperate zone that might grow olives, figs, or grapes.[57] Yet the 1578 expedition, as we have seen, failed.

Invasion and Assassination

Before Gilbert's plans have time to recover, a staggering report arrives in the autumn of 1579 that papal troops are landing in Ireland, electrifying all of England with fears that the *fire was like to spread into every corner of the realm.*[58] Bitter fighting breaks out anew.

February 1580. Spain invades *the rich kingdom of Portugal.* The move is triggered by the death of King Henry and the people's election of his nephew, Don Antonio, as successor. Ignoring this, Philip sends in troops under the Duke of Alva, and *in 70 days subdued all Portugal.*[59] Don Antonio flees and receives immediate support in England, despite residual anger over Portugal's participation in the papal demarcation of the world. For *God that sitteth in heaven laugheth them and their partitions to scorn.* It is said that as Portuguese officials passed near Quidiana on their way to sign the Pope's partition, they were accosted by a Portuguese child guarding his mother's laundry. The boy asked if they were the ones *come to divide the world with the Emperor? And as they answered yea, he took up his shirt behind and showed them his buttocks, saying unto them, "Draw your line through the midst of this place."*[60] The joke eases tension in London.

Later in the year, with England in turmoil, Drake returns to cheering crowds from a voyage around the world. The incredible navigational feat has been performed only once before—by Magellan. Drake's homecoming is spectacular: the hold of the *Golden Hind* overflowing with gold, silver, jewels, and silks. Even the ballast is replaced with silver! The Queen's investment nets her nearly 4,700 percent return.[61] To a tremendous fanfare and with throngs crowding the wharf, the Queen boards the *Golden Hind* and knights the triumphant Drake.

In London, Mendoza furiously orders that the plunder be restored. The Privy Council deliberates on the matter while the entire kingdom anxiously awaits the Queen's decision. Her pronouncement rings out like thunder: the plunder will not be returned. England will not acknowledge the 1493 papal demarcation. Under the law of nations, the sea is declared free and unrestricted. England will plant colonies in the Americas on lands not already inhabited by any Christian prince.[62]

March 18, 1581. The Dutch cartographer Mercator reports shocking news from Antwerp.[63] On Sunday, a young Spaniard hoping to collect the 25,000 gold pieces Philip II had put on the head of the Prince of Orange entered the palace unseen and shot directly into the Prince's face. The bullet entered above the right jawbone and exited from the left side of his head. Leaving him choking on his own blood, the young man fled but was overtaken on the way out. Drawing his sword, he fended off his attackers until they hacked him down. Later, emptying his pockets, they found them full of little metal crosses, a prayer scribbled on a scrap of paper, and the stub of a green wax candle. In Antwerp, the Duke of Anjou — brother to the King of France — received the news at a birthday party. It was said that he beat his head against the wall three times, then cried out loud. The Prince still lives, though the country is greatly shaken.

Tension permeates England. In June Londoners are shocked to discover the cross in West Cheap vandalized.[64] The kneeling Virgin Mary is defaced, baby Jesus stolen from her broken arms. The image is found encircled with ropes, tilted and likely to fall, as though the vandals were frightened away in the act. Bleak days. England finds itself increasingly isolated. Elizabeth is reduced to a single ambassador — in Paris — and only the French and Spaniards maintain embassies in London, more for espionage than peace.

Gilbert's Last Voyage

As the Spanish threat edges closer, Gilbert struggles to get another North American expedition off the ground. His patent, granted in 1578, expires in six years if a colony is not established. Staggering under the charges of outfitting such a venture, he is bailed out by Raleigh. He is Gilbert's truest and most steady supporter, attests Walsingham's agent Maurice Browne, giving him anything he requires. Including £2,000 in the form of a ship, the *Bark Raleigh*.[65]

From Richmond Palace, Raleigh pens a hurried letter to Gilbert, signing it *Your true brother* and enclosing a golden *token from her Majesty, an anchor guided by a lady, as you see.* It is inset with twenty-nine diamonds.

At each point on the anchor, and near the lady's hand, are attached great pearls. A ruby sparkles from her crown.[66] Yet, sadly, the talisman will fail to protect Gilbert. Raleigh will never again see his brother alive.

June 11, 1583. Gilbert's fleet sets sail. The voyage is plagued with trouble from the start. They are besieged by chronically bad weather. Sickness and arguments break out among an increasingly disillusioned crew. Heading south after revictualing in Newfoundland, one of the ships runs aground, drowning a hundred men. Gilbert is blamed for the accident. Terminating the voyage, he sails home in a small, grossly overladen frigate rather than share the comfort of his larger flagship, forced to *be so over hard* on himself because of slanders that he was *afraid of the sea.*[67]

In the midst of the Atlantic, the vessels are beset by *very foul weather.* By evening, raging winds drive such towering waves that the sailors, *which all their lifetime had occupied the sea, never saw* anything *more outrageous.* In the darkness, St. Elmo's fire crackles along the mainyard, *an evil sign of more tempest* ahead. At midnight on September 9, the lights on the little frigate are suddenly snuffed out. Hayes, captain of the flagship, reacts in horror. *For in that moment, the frigate was devoured and swallowed up of the sea.*[68] Arriving home at Dartmouth, Hayes rows ashore through a thick mist to report Gilbert's death to his brother John. Perhaps Gilbert's greatest epitaph was that written by the young poet Stephen Parmenius in the months before they embarked: *I was able to recognize that you are a man of such stature and spirit as deserves to be remembered forever by posterity . . . God speed!*[69]

A World Gone Mad

The fate of England lies in the balance. Assassination attempts against Elizabeth mount into the hundreds, all linked to efforts to liberate Mary Queen of Scots. 1584. One Francis Throckmorton, hauled to the Tower by Walsingham and racked, confesses to having encouraged the French Duke of Guise, Mary's relative and Spain's ally, to invade England with an army. The Pope calls on English nobles to stand ready when the troops land.

Dee, overseas in Prague, uncovers evidence that Mendoza is linked to the invasion plot.[70] In January the ambassador is charged with conspiracy and expelled from the country to his *great rage and fury.* He departs threatening war, accusing *the Queen and council by way of recrimination with detaining the Genoese's money, with assisting the Estates of the*

Low-Countries, the Duke of Anjou, and Don Antonio, and with the depredations of Drake.[71] And Raleigh: his mind now bent to the problem of saving the kingdom. The energetic young upstart at Court will soon be considered Spain's most formidable enemy.

Raleigh: A Hero's Rescue

We finally see Raleigh and Roanoke in perspective. March 25, 1584. Raleigh is issued Gilbert's letters patent to North American lands.[72] Impatient of diplomacy, he will confront the Spanish threat as Gilbert intended. By creating a North American naval base for privateers. A staging area for a direct attack on Spain. Hidden along an inaccessible coast, Roanoke Island will act as a refueling and supply station for swarms of pirate ships riding the swells, awaiting the returning treasure fleets. The Spaniards fear this greatly — as does one of Raleigh's countrymen.

July 4, 1584. Raleigh swings into action with the first Roanoke voyage. Captains Amadas and Barlowe, the pilot Fernandez, John White, *well furnished with men and victuals,* sail into the Outer Banks and establish peace with the Secotan. Roanoke Island is selected as a site for the base. In Europe the Netherlands falls. Antwerp, the last holdout, surrenders to Spain while Raleigh's men reconnoiter.[73]

Six days later, July 10, 1584. Throckmorton is executed. In Holland William the Silent is assassinated on the very same day, *being treacherously shot with three bullets out of a gun by Balthazar, a Burgundian.*[74]

October. The Roanoke expedition returns. Hakluyt presents the Privy Council with a *Discourse on Western Planting,* intended to convince the Queen to undertake Raleigh's venture as a state project. There is great urgency. If she and her Council delay, he warns, *let them assure themselves that they will come too late and a day after the fair.*[75]

October. At Walsingham's urging, Leicester forms a Bond of Association for the mutual protection of the Queen. It is composed of men from all across England, of all *degrees and conditions.* Thousands attach their names to a document as a pledge of allegiance, swearing to defend Elizabeth's life with their own and to impose the death sentence on any who threaten it. Rumors pour in *from all parts that great dangers were at hand.*[76] From Prague, Dee forwards a cryptic message: the *creatures of the Scorpion* plan a strategic attack upon the Forest of Dean.[77] Philip's agents will set fire to the timber necessary to enlarge the English navy.

Characteristically, Leicester proposes that Mary Queen of Scots be poisoned.[78] Walsingham objects, demanding a formal judicial inquiry. He has other plans. Panic grips the country that the *utter desolation* of England is imminent. Terrorized that they, too, will *fall into such miserable servitude and bondage as all those countries are oppressed withal, that in times past have been famous kingdoms and other flourishing estates, and are now languishing and spoiled provinces, subdued to the thraldom of the Spaniards.*[79]

Amid the tumult, fears of black magic spread like mania. Dee is accused of casting spells, a crime punishable by death. Someone, it would seem, would like to eliminate him as a spy. Reports run rampant of citizens prone to fits, with slurred speech and ashen color who waste away and die. With lead conduits for drinking water, witchcraft is a less likely culprit than lead poisoning.[80]

War at Our Door

London's streets are swollen by European refugees, crowding an already overcrowded city. They relay horror stories of Spanish atrocities, reviling Spain as *the foam of the sea, others gave them names of the beasts which are most cruel and living of prey which they have in their country. There were some likewise that called them Tuira, as one would say, the Devil's good grace.* Philip is *insatiable.* He will stop at nothing short of becoming Lord *of all the earth.*[81]

War is inevitable, yet the English treasury, bankrupt from the previous reign, does not have the money to prosecute it. The people are exhorted to bear the burden of defense since *the whole world . . . even the kingdoms and countries round about us (to us a world), stand at this day garboiled and oppressed with troubles and stirs; we, even we alone, here in this our England . . . sit us still every man in his own home, having freedom at the full to praise God in his sanctuary, and safety at the full to follow our affairs in the commonwealth.* And therefore, *for the procuring of peace, war must be undertaken.* For their own safety, *large provisions of money* must be amassed.[82]

Spring 1585. Grenville commands the second Roanoke voyage, the military. It is partly subsidized by the Queen through Raleigh's privileges and the right to impress men and provisions. Six hundred soldiers are transported to Roanoke Island, their departure almost coinciding with Philip's seizure of English shipping. They are a step closer to open war.

While Ralph Lane's soldiers are constructing the fort on Roanoke Island, Raleigh sends a squadron to knock out Spanish fishing fleets in Newfoundland, and Drake is dispatched to raid the West Indies. Spanish reports fling back the news in horror. Drake has sacked Santo Domingo. Cartagena is demolished. His men have sunk or taken all the warships in the Caribbean. All artillery and weapons. In Newfoundland, Raleigh's squadron attacks and captures seventeen vessels.[83] December 1585. Rumors of a planned Spanish invasion of England filter into London. The Armada is preparing.[84]

At Richmond Palace, Elizabeth's Court erupts in wild rejoicing at Drake's return and his bringing Lane's troops safely home. He is, Elizabeth says, *her pirate.* He regales them with stories of the fall of Santo Domingo, a city far larger than London. In half a year, he boasts, he has destroyed what Philip cannot rebuild in twenty, even with all his millions in gold.[85]

Lane, incredibly, also puffs himself up as the returning hero, notwithstanding the devastation and misery he has wrought on Roanoke. Grenville is slandered and Raleigh defends him, creating drama within the drama. Lane busily composes letters to friends, confirming the presence of precious metals in Virginia and expressing his intention to return again as soon as possible.[86] To Raleigh's credit, he never does.

Mobilization

1586. The country is preparing. English militia musters have been raised and warning beacons installed along the coast. Towns are fortifying, amassing supplies. The vulnerable counties of Devon and Cornwall are considered the most likely to face invasion. Their defense falls upon Raleigh's shoulders as Vice-Admiral of the West Country. A jingle forms on frightened lips: *When hemp is spun, England's done.* A dire prophecy, explains Bacon, *whereby it was generally conceived that after the Princes had reigned which had the principal letters of that word hempe (which were Henry, Edward, Mary, Philip, and Elizabeth), England should come to utter confusion.*[87]

These are intense times, with intense pressures. The imminent threat of Spanish invasion exacerbates the many personal and political conflicts already existing within the Court. Given Raleigh's high favor with the Queen, his unprecedented rise to power, and the numerous coveted privileges heaped upon him, we might assume envy to be the primary motive. Perhaps it was. But was Raleigh merely a victim of Court jealousy? Or was he a threat to a more serious political agenda? Raleigh and Roanoke were loose cannon. Unrestrained by Parliament or Privy Council, his actions received approbation directly from the Queen. War was brewing. In whose way had he stepped?

We must now discover who among Raleigh's enemies intended to destroy him. Any one of the key players in Elizabeth's Court might have had the power. Leicester: a Privy Councillor, long the Queen's favorite, might have felt displaced by Raleigh. Hatton: also a Privy Councillor, was rumored to harbor Catholic sympathies. Also a favorite, now in Raleigh's shadow. Burghley and Walsingham: Elizabeth's most powerful ministers. Both easily wield enough authority to ruin him, though neither possesses clear motive. The petulant Earl of Essex: Raleigh's sworn rival, introduced to Court in 1587. Too late to destroy the Lost Colony, but perhaps not completely innocent of the crime. These are our chief suspects. They alone have the power to bring Raleigh down.

16 THE PLAYERS

For such is the malice of wicked men, the Devil's instruments in this our age, that they cannot suffer anything (or at least few) to proceed and prosper. . . .

Sir Anthony Parkhurst[1]

The Earl of Leicester

It could have been any of them. Leicester, Hatton, Burghley, Walsingham. If we assume that one of these four — possibly aided by the Earl of Essex — is guilty, we must learn enough about each of them to eliminate suspects. The question is, who stood to gain the most from Raleigh's removal? Or, conversely, who among them suffered the most by Raleigh's presence?

The handsome and gracious Robert Dudley, Earl of Leicester, of noble birth, has been Elizabeth's longtime favorite.[2] A Privy Councillor within the Queen's innermost policy-making circle, his power is so great that he is referred to by his detractors as *the Prince*, and England as *Leicester's Commonwealth.*[3] Driven by ambition, he is a *respecter of his own advantages.* A man, said Camden, who *preferred power and greatness . . . before solid virtue.*[4] Unprincipled and unscrupulous. He is the *heart* and *head* of the realm, and it is said that the Queen, in her youth, was very much in love with him.[5] But Leicester is aging. He can no longer compare with the dashing figure of Raleigh, who has risen so quickly to favor.

Is the enemy Leicester? He certainly had the means, by virtue of his power, to subvert Roanoke and, indeed, has stood accused of far worse crimes. However, Leicester infuriated his enemies precisely because of his boldness. The acts of murder, bribery, and coercion with which they credit him are reckless, with little attempt at secrecy, relying for protection on his position at Court. To destroy Raleigh by subtly doing away with White's colony hardly sounds like his style. It was a crime requiring a meticulous calculation of cause and effect, patience to design and execute, and a long wait for uncertain results. Whoever secured Fernandez's betrayal had to be sure that someone else might not call at Roanoke and effect a rescue. Leicester could not guarantee this. There would need to be a contingency plan to ensure that Raleigh's colony would be unsuccessful. Leicester's method is direct.[6] If his detractors are believed, had he wished to eliminate Raleigh, Leicester would simply have poisoned him.

Nor does there seem to be any real animosity in Leicester's rivalry with Raleigh. After all, good looks are hardly a motive for murder. 1582: Raleigh accompanied Leicester on a diplomatic mission to Antwerp as part of his suite. 1583: they were so far from being enemies that Maurice Browne informed his friend John Thynne that Leicester alone could influence Raleigh and that they supported one another.[7]

The truth is Leicester may have been wearying of the courtier game. By 1587 he has been playing for twenty-eight years. His staying power is time-tested. He endured Hatton's rise to favor and found his own position unmarred. Nor was it affected by Raleigh. Indeed, it has been suggested that Raleigh was introduced to Court by Leicester as his protégé, a handsome replacement with assured loyalty.[8] In 1578, at the age of forty-six and having relinquished the idea of becoming King consort, Leicester married Lettice Knollys and incurred the Queen's wrath. Yet even this storm blew over. Very little can shake his influence with Elizabeth. In fact, Leicester has climbed as high at Court as one can go. And knows it.

Leicester's later life has been devoted to the steady accumulation of honors and preferments. Leicester has money. It is rumored that he is the richest man in the country and that the Queen herself would have money enough if Leicester would only share his bank account. The Earl's own friends admit that he has *the whole realm . . . at his own disposition.*[9] Lands, possessions, seignories, lucrative office. Raleigh has nothing over Leicester.

In 1585, when Leicester allowed the Netherlands to dub him Governor and Captain-General of Holland, Zealand, and the United and Confederate Provinces, without the Queen's knowledge, conferring upon him absolute authority, she was furious. Rumors flew that her anger was fueled by Raleigh. Elizabeth immediately denied this, ordering Walsingham to assure Leicester of Raleigh's continued benevolence and loyalty. Walsingham obeyed, carefully noting that this *I write by Her Majesty's command.*[10] Not his own. In the end, it was Raleigh who smoothed things over, disclaiming the *pestilent* reports that accused him of being *rather a drawer back, than a fartherer of the action where you govern.*[11]

1585: they are conciliatory. 1586: Leicester receives repeated confirmation of Raleigh's good will. At Leicester's request, Raleigh convinces the Queen to send English personnel to work the mines in the Low Countries. At his request, Raleigh puts in a good word for one Jukes for the office of the backhouse, with favorable results.[12] Clearly, by the time of John White's departure, Raleigh's usefulness to Leicester has not run dry.

There is no motive. Raleigh's rise to fame has never hurt Leicester. Leicester is an aristocrat; Raleigh is not. Leicester has wealth, preferments, and power; Raleigh has less, and none have diminished Leicester. Leicester is the Queen's "Sweet Robin"; Raleigh has not displaced these affections. As we have seen, Leicester is able to use Raleigh to advantage. For what it is worth, they share a common political position toward Spain. Curiously, Leicester is a sworn enemy of Ralph Lane and was charged, in 1584, with reducing him to disgrace and financial ruin.[13] Little wonder Lane grabbed at Roanoke. If Raleigh's opinion of him plummeted after the 1586 Roanoke fiasco, then Raleigh and Leicester share this sentiment as well. There is evidence that the two are, in fact, on very good terms. We will eliminate Leicester.

Sir Christopher Hatton

Hatton, like Raleigh, is not of noble birth.[14] He caught the Queen's eye as a result of his good looks and dancing ability as a theater performer while a student at the Middle Temple in 1564. He was admitted to Court, touted as the royal favorite, appointed Captain of the Queen's Guard and later Lord Chancellor. His preferments are many; he is wealthy, holding the highest salaried royal office. By his contemporaries, Hatton is described as an honest man of mild disposition. Reserved, discreet, and even wary.[15] Fair in his conduct of office. Rich in friends, a generous patron.

Hatton's passionate devotion to Elizabeth is legendary. If he has a fault, it is this. Fiercely loyal to his mistress, he never marries. His friend Edward Dyer cautions him to be a trifle less ardent.[16] Lovesick and unwise, Hatton is not above pouring forth petulant invective whenever he feels neglected. Such a man might well regard Raleigh with mortal aversion, for Raleigh can outdance Hatton, just as his handsome looks outshine him. Indeed, his introduction to Court was so alarming that Hatton sent the Queen a miniature gold bucket as a symbol of his fear of being displaced by "Water." The Queen returned an olive branch and a dove, assurance that he would not be destroyed by the flood. Still deeply depressed two months later, Hatton presented Elizabeth with a jewel cut like a fish prison, the Queen replying that he pleased her more *than any waterish creatures.*[17]

Yet Hatton's star had already begun to set. Edward de Vere, the Earl of Oxford, enjoyed great popularity at Court, briefly eclipsing Hatton's fame, even on the dance floor. Rumors swirled that Hatton secretly harbored Catholic sympathies and that he was not averse to eliminating a political rival. Raleigh, and indeed most of England, believed that he had done away with the Earl of Northumberland, found shot to death in his cell in the Tower in 1585. The incident was ruled a suicide, although a national inquest had to be conducted to clear the name of one Thomas Bailiff, Hatton's servant, to *satisfy the multitude.*[18] If Hatton is guilty, his technique is as direct as Leicester's, hardly in keeping with the subtlety required for Roanoke.

Hatton possessed opportunity and means, but the method was certainly not his. What about motive? Though initially jealous of Raleigh, did Hatton have continued reason to resent him? The answer is no. When Raleigh was admitted to Court, Hatton's promotions did not end. As one rose, so did the other. Raleigh was not usurping Hatton, but following his trajectory.

In 1587, moreover, Hatton was not strong enough to scuttle Raleigh's mission. While someone was busily planning the Roanoke sabotage, Hatton had his hands full maintaining his own footing — not at Elizabeth's Court — but at the bar. His appointment as Lord Chancellor in April upset the great London lawyers, who organized a boycott of him.[19] Their animosity stemmed from the fact that the office was traditionally filled by churchmen and nobility, not common courtiers. *Hatton,* said Camden, *was advanced to it by the cunning Court-arts of some, that by his absence from Court, and the troublesome discharge of so great a place, which they thought him not to be able to undergo, his favour with the Queen might slag and grow less.*[20]

Neither means, motive, method, nor opportunity fit Hatton to the Roanoke crime. Nor is his character or temperament up to the task. Mild when challenged, his responses — to Raleigh's entry at Court and his reception at the bar — are those of a depressive. He performs his official functions well and has come to share the highest affairs of state with Burghley, Walsingham, and Leicester. Even so, he does not wield much personal power, nor is his political following strong. In fact, Hatton is more a follower than a leader. *He was a gentleman,* confessed Sir Robert Naunton, . . . *that could soon learn the discipline and garb both of the times and court. The truth is, he had a large proportion of gifts and endowments, but too much of the season of envy, and he was a mere vegetable of the court, that sprung up at night, and sunk again at his noon.*[21] Hatton is the least likely of the four to be able to pull Raleigh down.

Lord Burghley

Our suspects are reduced to two. Burghley, born William Cecil, elevated to the peerage and created Baron Burghley of Stamford Burghley in 1571.[22] Trained in law, a Knight of the Garter, he became Elizabeth's first appointment upon ascending the throne. 1572: relinquished his position as Principal Secretary to Walsingham to become Elizabeth's Lord Treasurer. Sober, formidable, and immensely talented, he serves as her chief and lifelong adviser. *Of all men of genius,* said Camden, *he was the most a drudge; of all men of business, the most a genius.*[23]

Burghley's management of the state is single-minded and relentless. His goals well-defined: to strengthen the Queen's power, to rejuvenate the economy, to promote the Reformation. Meticulous in his conduct, Spanish ambassadors denounce him for directing the country with an iron fist, so much so that agent de Guaras referred to him as the King of England.[24] In the 1569 Northern Rebellion, nobles lashed out in open revolt — supported by Leicester — to remove the Queen from his influence. It failed, and Cecil — now Lord Burghley — enjoys the Queen's confidence more than ever.

Burghley favors diplomacy, not war. Ever cautious, he decries its expense as disastrous to England's economy. In the Privy Council he presides over a faction adamantly opposed to the war party offensive of Leicester and Walsingham. National defense is Burghley's consuming interest. Along the exposed West Country coast, in particular, he relies heavily on Raleigh and his cousin Sir Richard Grenville for reinforcement. To protect the realm, Burghley operates a defensive spy network, laboring tirelessly to ferret out plots against the Queen. As a young man, Walsingham first entered government service under him; through Burghley he learned the intelligence trade.

Considered one of the two most powerful men in government, Burghley, by virtue of his position and elaborate surveillance network, has both means and opportunity to destroy Roanoke. But did he? His career has been noteworthy for his reputation as a faithful and incorruptible minister.[25] Elizabeth openly admires him for these traits and for his sound judgment.

Burghley is a professional; he operates by the rules. Although he is known to entrap spies and force confessions under threat of the rack, none of this is illegal in the Elizabethan age. When an aristocrat named Anthony Babington was condemned to death for conspiracy and the Queen called for torture beyond the prescribed sentence, it was Burghley who convinced her to respect the law. In 1585, having refused a bribe, Burghley could *marvel* that anyone could think him capable of abusing his office. *Let them make* use, he countered, *of any one proof wherewith to prove me guilty of falsehood, injustice, bribery; of dissimulation, of double dealing in advice, in council either with her Majesty or with the Councillors.*[26]

Though contemptuous of enemies, Burghley is not always willing to press his advantage. Once when Elizabeth was upset with Leicester, Burghley vowed not to inflame the Queen's anger against him further.[27] In fact, probably the worst act he ever committed against Leicester was in 1585 — after more than twenty-five years of enmity between them — when Burghley confiscated copies of the scandalous book *Leycesters Common-Wealth* under direct order of the Queen — only to redistribute them to his friends at Court, including Elizabeth herself![28] The taciturn minister was not entirely humorless.

Although Burghley possessed the means and opportunity to sabotage White's colony, his method was inappropriately direct. Nor is there obvious motive. Clearly, it was not financial: Burghley is wealthy. His salary as Lord Treasurer is the highest-paid royal office next to that of Lord Chancellor.[29] This is augmented by a substantial income from revenues and perquisites.

In addition to a mansion in Covent Garden, Burghley maintains two palatial estates: Stamford Baron in Northamptonshire and the famous Theobalds, north of London, with its elaborate murals, art galleries, Italianate courtyards, and gardens. Considered one of the most exquisite homes in England, Theobalds is a retreat for foreign dignitaries and princes and a favorite of Elizabeth herself.[30] It is said that *no king need be ashamed to dwell there.* The *garden is close adjoining and of immense extent,* raved the Duke of Wirtemberg's secretary, *and as the palace is really most magnificent, so likewise . . . is no expense spared on the garden.*[31] Spanning two full miles, it is a magnificent riot of flowering roses, lilacs, cherry and plum, columbine and gillyflower, tended by John White's friend, botanist John Gerard.[32]

Burghley's motive was not financial — nor was it personal. His position at Court was influential and secure. Burghley was an indispensable elder statesman, not a courtier vying for rank. His relationship to Raleigh was cordial, respectful . . . perhaps even friendly.[33] At the time of the Roanoke crime, in 1587, Burghley's interests lay in paving the way at Court for his son, Robert Cecil, who was to be appointed to the Privy Council in 1591. For the duration of his father's lifetime, Robert Cecil counted Raleigh as a close friend.[34]

Burghley's only possible motive, therefore, would have to be professional: Did Roanoke threaten English security? Would unprovoked attacks against Spanish shipping result in war for England? Would the venture drain the treasury? Opposed to piracy in principle, Burghley could hardly be expected to approve of a military base on Roanoke that encouraged assaults on Spanish vessels.[35] But White's colony wasn't military. Burghley himself considered North America fair game.

There is something in Burghley's character, too, that would make his sabotage of the Roanoke venture unlikely. Burghley is a survivor. He has weathered the storms of rapidly changing politics many times before: serving first the Protestant Edward VI; then the Catholic "Bloody" Mary, who condemned hundreds of Protestants to death; and now the Anglican Elizabeth.[36] Burghley is a statesman capable of accommodation. Aware that the position of favorites is short-lived, he is more likely to use Raleigh to advantage rather than exert the effort to oust him. And so he does. Unless further evidence presents itself, we will eliminate Burghley.

Sir Francis Walsingham

We are running short of suspects. The investigation is taking an ominous turn, one we would rather avoid. We are entering very dangerous waters indeed and, alarmingly, find ourselves swept toward one inescapable conclusion. There is only one individual who could have commanded Fernandez to sabotage the Roanoke voyage. Only one individual who could have ordered him to maroon 117 innocent people on a remote island halfway around the world, far from home and without help. Only one individual who had the right combination of power, method, means, motive, and opportunity: it was Walsingham. And he got away with murder.

Surely this cannot be! Walsingham is Elizabeth's most powerful official. Principal Secretary. Secretary of State. He and Burghley control the top echelon of government. Before he is through, his political career will span seventeen years. The tentacles of his power are so far-reaching that he is undeniably the most influential figure in Elizabethan England. If we are to accuse him, we had better be able to produce hard evidence.

When we open Walsingham's file and read its contents, we find that he was born about the year 1532.[37] He graduated from Cambridge and studied law at the Inns of Court. A solid beginning. During Queen Mary's reign, he went to Italy. To Venice. Studied Roman civil law at Padua University. Padua! We may have something here. Red flag! Venice was a hotbed for the new Machiavellian statecraft, and the university its training ground. Students from across Europe flocked there to study its practices. Very interesting, for if Walsingham were a Machiavellian, his methods would be well defined. Political power is everything. The end justifies the means. However unscrupulous, attain the upper hand even if that means deception, treachery, and lies.

For the true Machiavellian, every action relates to this goal: all associations, all conversations, all friendships and activities are devoted to accomplishing this end. The old notions of chivalry and trust are dead. Enemies are defeated not by force but by a thorough understanding of their weaknesses. It is a world of betrayal. Of catching an opponent off guard, of false promises and adroit dealing. The key to the system is information. Through spy networks and espionage, it is obtained at all costs and by any method. As Walsingham once said, *intelligence is never too dear.*[38]

Lacking the normal avenues to power — nobility of birth, wealth and connection — Walsingham might very well have sought to achieve it through Machiavellian means. For achieve it he did, and rapidly. 1568: enters government service as an aide to Burghley in the collection of foreign intelligence. 1570: Ambassador to France. 1573: assumes Burghley's position as Principal Secretary, the equivalent of Secretary of State. Five short years: he has reached the top.

Walsingham shapes the office to his own ends. His government policy will mold England into a world power, provided Elizabeth acts as a forceful leader of Protestantism. It is a course that will set her at direct odds with Philip of Spain. To a cunning political analyst like Walsingham, the trend is clear. Protestantism is a rising ideological force; the old Catholic order is crumbling.[39] To oppose Spain is merely to abandon a leaking ship.

Leicester, taking his cue, supports Walsingham. Mendoza decries them both as *extremely self-seeking,* conducting state business *under cloak of preserving their religion.* As James VI observed of Walsingham's Protestant fervor, *notwithstanding that outward profession, he is a very Machiavelli, and he counselled* James *to use religion for his people's obedience.*[40]

Secret Service

To serve his needs, Walsingham constructs the most elaborate spy system in the world. Far greater, even, than Burghley's. *They note him,* says Naunton, *to have had certain curiosities and secret ways of intelligence above the rest.*[41] His intricate network of surveillance is a veritable underworld; mysterious circles of intrigue and espionage, secrecy and conspiracy. *Dextrous was he in finding a secret,* noted William Winstanley, *close in keeping it.*[42] Rumor has it that he maintains hundreds of spies on his payroll; in 1582 they number at least five hundred.[43]

He was, remarked Camden, *a diligent searcher out of hidden secrets, and one who knew exactly well how to win men's affections to him and to make use of them for his own purposes, insomuch as in sagacity and officious services he surpassed the Queen's expectation, and the Papists found fault with him as cunning and subtle in close carrying on his designs and enticing and decoying men into dangers.*[44]

No one knows who is a spy. Agents within Walsingham's network are unaware of each other's identity. On occasion, multiple and redundant espionage systems are used as additional security, spies spying on spies.[45] On Leicester, on Burghley. And, most certainly, on Sir Walter Raleigh. Walsingham employs master code-breakers and encoders, such as the experts John Somers and Thomas Phelippes, along with handwriting specialists and forgers, like Arthur Gregory. Spies are planted in people's homes, along the roads, in the workplace. In prisons. Quiet observers in Walsingham's pay. Family members betray each other; servants spy upon their masters.

Sensitive material passes back and forth across the country from clusters of agents, penned in invisible ink concocted of milk and lemon juice, disguised in cipher and crypt. Messages are intercepted. Smuggled documents are ripped out of the lining of clothing, the pages of books, the false bottoms of trunks, the soles of shoes. Walsingham posts searchers at every English port and along mail routes. Agents report to him from Rome, Venice, Milan, and Florence. The Vatican and the Spanish Court. The Low Countries, France, and Germany. Constantinople, Algiers, and Tripoli.

In Walsingham's Debt

Many of Walsingham's spies are in debt to him for their lives. It is his policy of conscripting such people that finds Egremont Radcliffe, in the Tower for conspiracy, released to become an assassin and a spy. That makes agents of priests and seminary students branded as traitors, like Gilbert Gifford. That creates confidants of men like Bernard Mawde, in prison for extortion. That rescues pirates about to be hanged . . . such as Simon Fernandez.[46]

Fernandez first came to Walsingham's attention at the height of his career as a pirate, operating out of south Wales in association with the notorious John Challice.[47] The Secretary of State quietly observed the Azorean's activities but did nothing, despite the vehement protest of the Portuguese ambassador, Francisco Giraldi, who accused Fernandez of murdering seven Portuguese sailors. 1577: following an incident involving Challice, the thirty-nine-year-old Fernandez is arrested in Cardiff and hauled to London on charges of piracy. A furious Giraldi promising evidence *enough to hang him.*[48]

After an inquest, Fernandez is mysteriously released. So is Challice. Giraldi excoriates Walsingham, demanding justice. Yet, in light of Spain's secrecy, Fernandez is valuable. Maps of American waters are restricted, Iberian pilots strictly licensed, and foreigners banned from Spanish vessels, even as passengers. Fernandez once worked for them; he knows their routes well. Piracy is a capital offense. But instead of greeting the hangman's noose, both Fernandez and Challice are found a year later piloting Gilbert's 1578 expedition to America. What sort of deal was worked out? Fernandez is identified as *Walsingham's man.*[49]

Manipulation

As relations with Spain deteriorate, Walsingham entrenches himself in a cold-war policy sharply at odds with the peace efforts of Burghley and the Queen. Alarmed at his army of spies and political maneuvering, both distrust him. Spain declares Walsingham to be the archenemy. *This Walsingham,* exclaims an impassioned de Guaras, *is of all heretics the worst.* He is *the right hand of [the Prince of] Orange* and, he warns, *any evil may be expected from him.*[50]

Walsingham is engrossed in a great game of chess. The board pieces are Elizabeth, Burghley, Leicester, Mary Queen of Scots. *He served himself of factions as his mistress did.* Philip II, the French House of Guise, Catherine de Medici, the Pope. *This Spanish proverb was familiar with him: Tell a lie, and find a Truth.* William of Orange. Don Antonio, the Portuguese pretender. *And this, speak no more than you may safely retreat from without danger.*[51] Walsingham's strategy is nothing less than to checkmate the Catholic League.

Walsingham's dexterity in employing and instructing his spies goes far toward promoting England's interests, which he certainly has at heart.[52] The diligence and care that both he and Burghley take in exposing the *daily attempts and conspiracies* against Elizabeth have saved her life on more than one occasion.[53]

Yet Walsingham is a dangerous man. He is known to pursue his own policy independent of the Queen's. This is treason. Any lesser person would have been hanged. 1576: he goes too close to the edge. While Elizabeth is pursuing détente with Spain, Walsingham promotes rebellion in the Low Countries. The Spanish Governor of Antwerp warns the Queen that aid to the rebels will be regarded as an act of war. She, in turn, calls on the Prince of Orange to submit. Despite this, and while peace negotiations continue, Walsingham, Leicester, and their supporters in the Privy Council conduct clandestine meetings with Dutch rebels. Indeed, Walsingham continues to support Protestant insurgents throughout Europe, advising the Prince of Orange to make overtures to France in order to goad Elizabeth into action.[54]

For the love of God, madam, Walsingham once exploded at the Queen, *let not the cure of your diseased state hang any longer on deliberation. Diseased states are no more cured by consultation, when nothing resolved on is put into execution, than unsound and diseased bodies by only conference with physicians, without receiving the remedies by them prescribed.*[55] Burghley and the Queen negotiate, Walsingham acts.

Walsingham also laid the foundation of the civil wars in France and the Low Countries. . . . Upon which occasion he told the Queen at his return from his embassy to France, "That she had no reason to fear the Spaniard; for though he had a strong appetite and a good digestion, he had given him such a bone to pick as would take him up twenty years at least, and break his teeth at last: so Her Majesty had no more to do but to throw into the fire he had kindled some English fuel from time to time to keep it burning."[56]

Sir Walter Raleigh

Whitehall stairs, with detail of Durham House, from Visscher's view of London

Elizabeth I, Armada Portrait

Woman and child of Pomeioc, by John White

Indians fishing, by John White

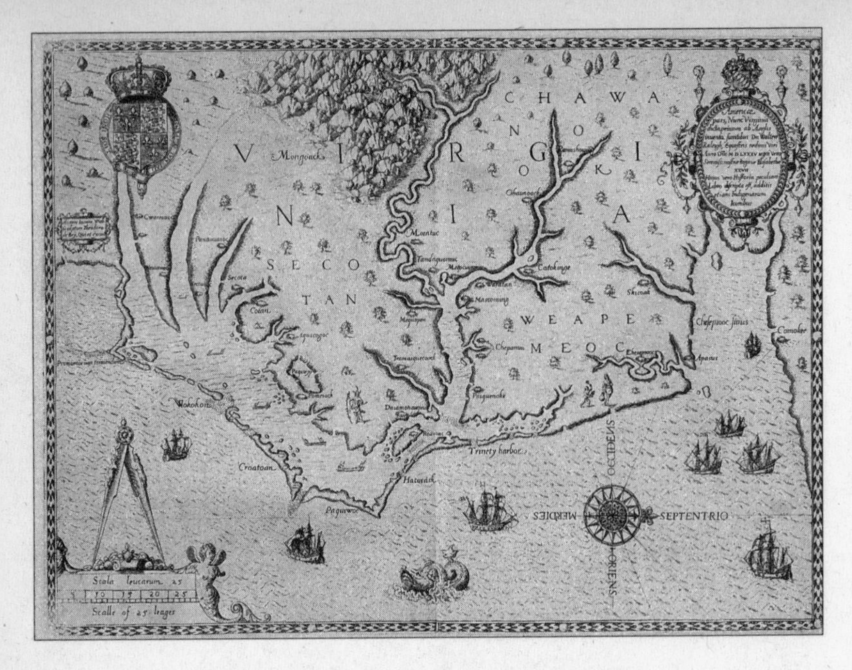

John White's map of eastern North Carolina

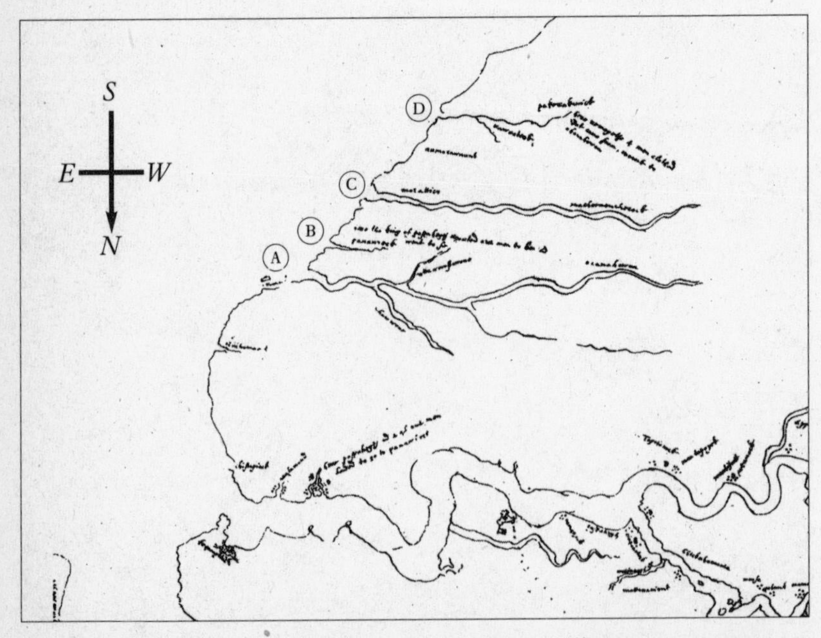

Detail from the Zúñiga map, depicting the James River (at bottom) and four waterways south: A) Chowan River; B) Cashie Creek; C) Roanoke River; and D) Tar River

Sir Francis Walsingham

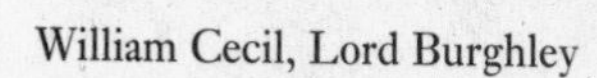
William Cecil, Lord Burghley

Lord Robert Dudley,
Earl of Leicester

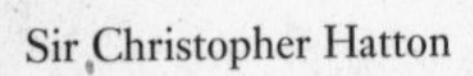

Sir Christopher Hatton

A Master of Deception

While Elizabeth prevaricates on important issues, assassination attempts against her multiply at a furious rate. Occurring too often to be coincidental. Some, incredibly, are staged by Walsingham himself—as a means of forcing her hand.[57] The Jesuit instigator Robert Parsons charges the Secretary with selectively reporting to the Queen, fabricating news, and fomenting wars and unrest in neighboring nations.[58]

Everywhere, it seems, Walsingham is mistrusted. The followers of the Prince of Orange express such deep suspicion about his character that the Secretary of State is forced to confront the Prince.[59] March 1575: after English merchant vessels are seized by Orange as part of a blockade of Spanish-held Antwerp, Elizabeth flies at Walsingham, accusing him of inciting the incident.[60]

A Free Agent

1578. The case against Walsingham mounts. At a time when the Queen is promoting peace in the Low Countries, Egremont Radcliffe claims under torture that he was hired by Walsingham to assassinate the Governor of the Netherlands.[61] Walsingham calls it slander. *He was ranked among the Togati,* William Winstanley reports, *chief of those that laid the foundation of the Dutch and French wars, which was another piece of his fineness, and of the times.*[62] Walsingham *might have been compared to the fiend in the Gospel that followed his tares in the night; so did* he his *seeds of division in the dark.*[63]

The same year, Walsingham infuriates Elizabeth by advancing the Dutch a loan £5,000 thick, with the expectation that the royal treasury will make it up. It does not, and the Queen's rage at Walsingham is as at *some notorious offender.* He, in turn, cautions her to beware, for *it standeth not with her Majesty's safety to deal so unkindly with those that serve her faithfully.*[64]

1581 finds Walsingham privy to a plot with Henry of Navarre, future king of France, to attack Spain directly. Henry would regain the occupied territory of Navarre, overrun by Spain. What concessions Walsingham would receive from France are unknown. Nothing comes of the negotiation, and it is unlikely that the Queen ever heard of it.[65] This in itself is revealing. It should come as no surprise, then, that Walsingham instructed Sir Edward Stafford, ambassador to France, to send the Queen information containing only the bare essentials. But *let me,* he added, *know all.*[66]

That same year, aboard ship, pilot Simon Fernandez shocks the fleet's chaplain, Richard Madox of Oxford, by declaring *I am at war with the King of Spain.* When the astonished priest asks how this could be, since he is now an English subject and Spain and England are at peace, Fernandez coolly responds that he has *a free pardon from five Privy Councillors for carrying on war with Spain.*[67]

Cunning as a Fox

Walsingham is indeed a master of Machiavellian politics. His vision for England is such that he is willing to pursue it at all costs, even when in direct opposition to merchant interests, the old Catholic nobility, Burghley, and the Queen herself. He has been accused, rightly or wrongly, of manipulating even the heads of European states to his ends. What would happen, then, if someone were to get in his way?

1578. The Duke of Alençon, son of Catherine de Medici and heir to the French throne, is in the way. To cement an alliance with France, a match is proposed between Elizabeth and the Duke, whom the Queen affectionately terms *her Frog.*[68] Outcry from the London populace is immediate. A flurry of pamphlets denouncing the match suddenly appears, inflaming talk of revolution should the marriage proceed, creating such a furor that it is called off. In Paris, the authorities angrily identify Walsingham as the agent behind the agitation.[69]

1585. Burghley is in the way, opposed to sending the military into the Netherlands. More significantly, a suit put forward by Walsingham for income from farming of the customs is strenuously opposed by Burghley — *a matter I found did greatly touch me in credit,* Walsingham informs him, *having waded so far therein as I had done. . . . And thereupon I did plainly resolve with myself that it was a more safe course for me to hold you as an enemy than as a friend.*[70]

To counter Burghley's influence over the Queen, slanders are spread that he is the enemy of the Huguenots and the Dutch, that he lives too luxuriously, and that he controls the Queen. It is said that he keeps the country in a stranglehold. Walsingham is responsible for the smear campaign, although he adroitly allows Burghley to suspect Leicester.[71] Both men know the Lord Treasurer's sensitivity to slander: in 1572 the *Trea-*

tise of Treasons was published in Antwerp, a stinging attack against Burghley which upset him tremendously. It is no coincidence that these libels are now dredged up and reused. *I confess,* Walsingham later admitted to Burghley, *I sought up such information as heretofore (unsought for) have been given unto me, that might any way touch your L.*[72]

Burghley asked him to name his informants and Walsingham declined. *If I might do it with the credit of an honest man, I would not fail to satisfy your Lordship therein. Besides it might reach to such persons as are not to be called in question.* Privileged, powerful sources. Walsingham denied Burghley's charge that he had directed one of his agents to an exchequer to *search of some matter that might touch you.* In the end, Walsingham shifted to outright entrapment, employing no less a person than Herllie, Burghley's own spy, to try to bribe him into aiding the Dutch![73]

The Greatest Intrigue of All

But of all the individuals in Walsingham's way, none was more so than Mary Queen of Scots. Her case is very instructive. Ultimately it will involve the Lost Colonists themselves, however indirectly. 1586: Walsingham uncovers Babington's Conspiracy, a plot to assassinate Elizabeth, and Mary Stuart's hand plays out. Her complicity will lead to her execution.[74]

The plot takes shape at the instigation of one Anthony Babington, *a young gentleman of good birth, rich, ripe-witted, and learned above most of his years.*[75] Gilbert Gifford, a recusant, joins them, along with another man — Robert Poley. If caught, neither will be convicted: both are Walsingham's agents. And although Babington thinks that *the very sun was a stranger* to their plans, the Secretary of State is following their every move.[76]

The Setup

The conspirators meet in St. Giles' Fields and in crowded places, at St. Paul's and the Three Tuns Tavern. A method of communication is devised with the imprisoned Scottish Queen whereby a local brewer smuggles notes to her in an ale cask. Babington immediately sends her a letter, revealing their plans with the assurance that the Pope, Spain, the Duke of Guise, and the Prince of Parma are all poised for invasion. Mary responds enthusiastically.

Walsingham easily intercepts the correspondence: the brewer is his agent. Mary's letters are delivered to her guard, Sir Amyas Paulet, another Walsingham man, who passes them to code-breaker Thomas Phelippes. They are then sent back to Paulet, who hands them to the brewer, who turns them over to an unnamed agent, who hands them back to Paulet, who forwards them to their destination. It is all a matter of security: neither the brewer nor the anonymous agent is aware that the other is a spy.[77]

With Mary Stuart's incriminating letter to Babington in hand, Walsingham has enough evidence for a conviction. *Thus far,* said Camden, *had Walsingham spun this thread alone, without acquainting the rest of the Queen's Council.*[78] Ballard, one of the plotters, is arrested in August for being a priest. *I knew full well what a master in the art of deception was this Walsingham,* lamented Father Weston, Babington's clergyman, *and how powerful in accomplishing whatever his mind was set upon.*[79]

Panicked, Babington flees for asylum to the home of a government official who offers help: none other than Sir Francis Walsingham! Realizing — too late — the trap laid for him, Babington escapes. Racing through the dark streets to Westminster, he changes clothing with fellow conspirator Robert Gage, who in turn trades garments with another named John Charnock. Then *immediately they withdrew themselves into Saint John's Wood near the city, whither also Barnwell and Dunn made their retreat. In the meantime, they were publicly proclaimed traitors all over England. They . . . cut off Babington's hair, disguised and sullied the natural beauty of his face with the rind of green walnuts and, being hardly put to it by hunger, they went to a house of the Bellamies near Harrow on the Hill. . . . There were they hid in barns.*[80]

August 14, ten days later. The conspirators are caught and hauled into London, to everyone's indescribable relief. The *city testifying their public joy by ringing of bells, making of bon-fires, and singing of psalms.* The peals of Lambeth Palace are answered across the Thames in the belfry of St. Margaret's in Westminster *for joy of the taking of the traitors.*[81]

The conspirators, examined for days, *cut one anothers' throats by their confessions.*[82] In September all of them — with the notable exception of Poley and Gifford — are hanged on a scaffold in St. Giles' Fields. Elizabeth orders Burghley to shield Mary, recoiling from the thought of prosecuting a kinswoman and anointed Queen. But the Bond of Association that Walsingham shrewdly created in 1584 binds her under parliamentary law to appoint a tribunal to try the Scottish Queen. Over Elizabeth's objections, Mary is tried at Fotheringhay Castle in October before a commission of forty-six.

The Trial

No witnesses are summoned for the trial, despite a government statute dictating that no prisoner can be condemned without the testimony of two witnesses present. Evidence against Mary stems solely from the statements of her secretaries, Claude Nau and Gilbert Curle, *who notwithstanding were absent from the trial.*[83] Both men are threatened, both offered pardon if they condemn the Queen. For his part, Nau maintains that he did *stoutly oppose* the accusation against his mistress, which *appeareth not by the records.* Twenty years later, he was still proclaiming her innocence.[84]

Conviction hinges on Mary's damning letter to Babington, in which the plot against Elizabeth *was commended and approved.*[85] The correspondence is missing. The commissioners are furnished with only Walsingham's copy of the original, prepared by the master forger Thomas Phelippes, himself absent from the trial. Mary, fighting tears, swears she neither wrote it nor approved of the assassination, and that *Babington might confess what he list, but it was a flat lie.* Her enemies, she cried, *might easily get the ciphers* she used, *and with the same write many things forgedly and falsely.*[86] Indeed, Babington recalled a postscript on Mary's letter, requesting the names of the conspirators. It was Phelippes's handiwork *cunningly added,* says Camden, *in the same characters.*[87]

On the stand Mary hotly accuses Walsingham of entrapment; that the forgery had been committed *to bring her to her end.* The scathing accusation brings Walsingham to his feet. The courtroom falls silent. *I call God (said he) to witness that as a private person, I have done nothing unbeseeming an honest man, neither in my public condition and quality have I done anything unworthy of my place. I confess that, out of my great care for the safety of the Queen and realm, I have curiously endeavoured to search and sift out all plots and designs against the same.* Then, alluding to Ballard, but strangely ignoring Babington, he remarked: *If I have tampered anything with him, why did he not discover it, to save his life?* Even more incredible is what happens next. Mary — an anointed queen — immediately apologizes to Walsingham, begging him *not to be angry* and praying that he give as little credence to those who slandered her *than she did to such as accused him.*[88]

The Verdict

October 25. The Commission finds Mary Stuart guilty. The sentence is death. Ugly murmurings are heard across England, charging that the Bond of Association was designed to entrap her.[89] The trial is condemned as a farce, allegations made *that spies and emissaries were employed by crafty dissimulation, counterfeit letters, and other cunning devices to circumvent her.* Indeed, Mary's own secretaries *seemed to be bribed and corrupted with money.*[90]

Elizabeth wavers. Pronouncement of the verdict is delayed five weeks while she weighs the appeals of both Scottish and French embassies. Meanwhile, in a now familiar pattern, someone spreads *false rumours and terrifying reports* in order *to strike the greater terrour into the Queen,* to scare her into signing the death warrant. *That the Spanish fleet was already arrived at Milford Haven; that the Scots were broken into England; that the Duke of Guise was landed in Sussex with a strong army; that the Queen of Scots was escaped out of Prison and had raised an army; that the northern parts were up in rebellion; that there was a new conspiracy on foot to kill the Queen, and set the City of London on Fire; yea, that the Queen was dead.*[91] Walsingham's technique is disturbingly effective.

Execution

With the Queen irresolute, the Stafford Conspiracy unfolds. Its author is Walsingham.[92] William Stafford, the brother of Elizabeth's ambassador in Paris, owes Walsingham a favor. Following orders, he visits Chateauneuf, the French ambassador in London, and broaches the idea of assassinating Elizabeth by laying gunpowder under her bed. The man he suggests for the job (a Walsingham spy) is lodged in Newgate prison. It is a setup. Walsingham immediately informs Elizabeth of the plot. Chateauneuf's secretary is apprehended at the jail and Chateauneuf is placed under house arrest. The results are threefold: the French cannot intervene for Mary's life with their ambassador restrained; Elizabeth, terrified, signs the death warrant; Walsingham gains favor by exposing the plot.

Elizabeth commands William Davison, *Walsingham's creature,* to swear out a warrant for Mary's execution.[93] Davison immediately does so; he shows the warrant to Walsingham and then, contrary to the Queen's instructions, delivers it to the Privy Council. The following day Elizabeth orders it stayed, but the Council rushes it to Fotheringhay Castle and sends for an executioner. Incredibly, Thomas Harrison, Walsingham's secretary, will later admit to forging Elizabeth's signature on the death warrant itself.[94] He also claims to have aided Phelippes in fabricating all of Mary's correspondence which implicated her at the trial. On the morning of February 8, 1587, Mary Queen of Scots is beheaded.

This is how to eliminate a queen. Walsingham orchestrated it from start to finish. We can never know how many in his pay contributed to her downfall, but the same Machiavellian technique could easily have eliminated 116 men, women, and children on Roanoke Island and, in so doing, destroyed Raleigh's power.

But did Walsingham do it? He had opportunity: as a Privy Councillor within the Queen's Court, he occupied the highest level of government and had a thorough understanding of Raleigh's plans. He also had means: a vast spy network with loyal personnel who could execute the assignment — secretly, swiftly, effectively. More than anyone else, Walsingham had the ability to sabotage Raleigh's Roanoke venture. The subtlety and minute reckoning of cause and effect required of such an operation is consistent with his method. He would work out every detail of Roanoke and factor in contingency plans. Walsingham called in favors: Fernandez was indebted to him for his life. We have seen the elimination of opponents who stood in his way. Rivals much stronger than Raleigh — an anointed queen! — have been brought down.

Walsingham once observed that *violent diseases must have violent remedies.*[95] If so, what disease did Raleigh represent? If we can answer that, we have motive. And then Walsingham alone will possess all four criteria for murder.

17 THE MOTIVE

The Times were partial and malignant, and Malice blind, which forgeth Crimes against the Innocent; but Justice clear-sighted, which being the venger of wicked facts, is to be expected from God.

Elizabeth I[1]

A Master Plan

Walsingham is the Queen's Principal Secretary. Secretary of State. Master politician. Machiavellian. He has spent his career painstakingly advancing certain political ends. He has balanced parties against one another on a razor's edge, accurately judged the repercussions of each minute maneuver, negotiated deals, and manipulated the most powerful heads of state with such finesse that they never suspected his subtle engineering behind their own responses.

Walsingham's politics are vastly larger than the picayune jealousies of Hatton or the self-aggrandizement of Leicester. His adversary is king of the most powerful empire in the known world. Walsingham operates according to a master plan, his methods worked out well in advance. Whatever his personal motivation may be, this is certain: Walsingham is a strategist. His purpose is single-minded, his challenge to remain one step ahead of the game, meticulously calculating move and countermove. Exploiting the psychology of his opponent.

Loose Cannon

Despite his careful work, Walsingham has never been a favorite with the Queen. *Walsingham had been employed in several embassies and other matters of state for many years before she could be prevailed with to make him a knight, notwithstanding it appears that he frequently asked it.*[2] Perhaps she is afraid of his power. Walsingham's greatest obstacle is not statecraft, but Elizabeth. His difficulty is convincing her to adopt his policies and not do everything by halves. It is a virulent source of frustration to him to be *so greatly crossed.*[3] In politics timing is everything. Walsingham succeeds partly by playing on the Queen's fear, partly by utilizing factions within the Privy Council to his advantage.

Enter Raleigh: brilliant, energetic, full of ideas, Elizabeth's darling. Were he merely a courtier, all might have been well. Were he content to play the part of the Queen's lover, amass honors, and leave politics alone, there would have been no trouble. But Raleigh is a far different personality. He is a thinker, a problem-solver, a driving force with a hero's frame of mind. He will go after Spain and he will do so boldly. As did his brother Gilbert.

Raleigh's actions are directly in the way. Little does he realize that his brash thrust at the West Indian caravels stands to undo years of Walsingham's careful maneuvering.[4] That his patriotic strike at the enemy is thwarting a meticulously designed program of cause and effect, of diplomacy and dealing. The Queen, ignorant of her Secretary's design, grants Raleigh warships and ammunition, the right to impress soldiers, and a vast territory in America in which to create a base. Raleigh is a loose cannon. Walsingham must restrain him.

To Bid Everything

If Raleigh's cross-purposes were Walsingham's only motive for murder, we might be hard-pressed to prosecute our case. It is difficult to prove after the fact, and much of Walsingham's activity was, by its very nature, conducted in the dark. Fortunately, there is another motive, much more concrete and far more personal.

The elimination of Mary Queen of Scots was Walsingham's crowning achievement. His removal of Elizabeth's greatest rival was the culmination of eighteen years of unceasing effort.[5] It has cost him untold resources, both human and financial. Many agents were involved, some over a period of years, working their way into trusted positions. As reward, Walsingham hopes to receive a portion of the conspirator Babington's estate, confiscated by the Crown. Yet in the weeks and months that follow the exposure of the plot, he sinks to the lowest point in his career. Why?

There is more than honor and reputation at stake. We sense a desperation, and when we look more closely at Walsingham's file we find something alarming. Walsingham did not merely want Babington's estate, he *had* to have it. He required it. *In fact, Walsingham needed the money.*

Finances . . . and Debt

Walsingham's spy structure is too costly. Largely his own creation, it is conducted with only partial government subsidy — most of the expenses are out of pocket.[6] Walsingham's agents are notoriously well paid. It is said that he doles out *large sums.*[7] Figures are unavailable for the substantial amount he spends on diplomatic entertainment and overseas operations. The only certain thing that can be said is that Walsingham's campaign against Philip, the wealthiest monarch in the modern world, comes at tremendous cost.

1578. Walsingham advances £5,000 to the Dutch rebels in the expectation that Elizabeth's loan will follow.[8] It does not; the money is lost. 1581. Walsingham, heavily in debt to the Crown, requests Hatton to persuade Elizabeth to relieve him of its pressure.[9] 1584–1585. The cost of the secret service soars to £10,030. 1586. It reaches an all-time high of £13,260. How much of this does Walsingham pay? His annual salary as Principal Secretary is only £100.[10]

In addition are the demands of life at Court. The cost of a London residence with its inflated rates is compounded by compulsory gifts to the Queen, which entail huge expenditure. New Year's Day, 1576: Walsingham presents Elizabeth with a glittering *collar of gold,* ornamented with a pair of opal serpents and *a pyramid of sparks and diamonds, in the top thereof a strawberry with a rock ruby.*[11] Walsingham is living beyond his means.

Sir Philip Sidney

A financial crisis is looming. Yet neither Walsingham's spy network, nor loans to Dutch rebels, nor expensive London living, nor diplomatic entertainments precipitate it. It occurs on October 17, 1586: the day Sir Philip Sidney died.[12]

Sidney is the Earl of Leicester's nephew. He is handsome, chivalrous, and highly popular at Court. He is also overwhelmed with debt. 1581. He begs the Queen for a grant, apologizing that *need obeys no law and forgets blushing.*[13] 1583. At the age of twenty-nine, the likeable Sidney marries Walsingham's daughter, Frances. If the Secretary of State hoped for the match to be lucrative, he is wrong.

In 1585 Sidney escapes his domestic woes and goes to war in the Netherlands. Commanding a detachment outside Zutphen, he is surprised by an enemy convoy. Shot in the thigh, he dies of gangrene. All of

London mourns the loss. Sidney's body is transported back to England in state, the ship decked out under black sail. In a private chamber Walsingham holds a legal will in clenched fist. Incredibly, it stipulates that he shall inherit his son-in-law's staggering debts along with those of his parents. The sale of Sidney's estate does not equal a third of the amount.[14]

Walsingham has only himself to blame. When Sidney left for the Low Countries, he conveyed a letter of attorney to Walsingham, authorizing the sale of lands to appease his creditors. Preoccupied with Babington's conspiracy, Walsingham failed to act. Sidney's death nullifies the conveyance; the lands cannot be sold. And *as I did hear,* Burghley comments, *you had good authority to have sold lands for discharge of the debts both of the father, the mother, and the son. But if your authority shall die with him for lack of foresight in making the conveyance . . . that you have, as the lawyers' term is, assumed upon yourself, you are in very hard case.*[15]

In fact Walsingham is in dire straits. Overwhelmed with the enormity of his obligation, he informs Leicester that the funeral must be discreet. Ignoring him, Leicester mounts a spectacular affair. Three hundred paid mourners outfitted in black — at Walsingham's expense — accompany a parade of nobles and officials to a splendid military funeral at St. Paul's Cathedral.[16] *Sir Philip Sidney, dying indebted to the Flushingers seventeen thousand pounds for which Walsingham was bound, Leicester refuseth to make payment of one penny out of his land.*[17]

In desperation, Walsingham petitions the Queen for the vacant Chancellorship of the Duchy of Lancaster for the income it provides. Leicester opposes the appointment, preferring his own candidate. Elizabeth turns Walsingham down.[18] Stung by disbelief and rage, Walsingham quits the Court in December, only days after Mary Stuart's proclamation of death is read. *I would not spend so long a time as I have done in that place,* Walsingham flung at Burghley, *subject to so infinite toil and discomfort, not to be made Duke of Lancaster.*[19]

Babington's Estate

The Queen is rich as a result of Anthony Babington's execution. The considerable fortune from his estate is forfeit to the Crown. Elizabeth immediately orders its assessment: rental income from the magnificent Babington Hall; three manors in Lincolnshire: Winterton, Houghton-on-Ham, and Houghton-Bickering; Lee Manor in Derbyshire along with six parcels of land and tenements; tenements at Kingston and Thrumpton in Nottinghamshire, at Bredon, West Terrington, and Harrick.[20]

March 17. Babington's estate is granted in its entirety as a reward to a faithful servant. He is also to receive *all goods, personals, and moveables* of Babington's possession, the Queen reserving for herself only an unusual clock.[21] By now Walsingham has returned to Court, the rupture with Elizabeth mended, though his finances are as precarious as ever. What better way to alleviate his need than with Babington's own money? There is only one problem. The recipient is not Walsingham at all . . . but *Sir Walter Raleigh!* The gift bears the royal stamp of the Great Seal, conveyed without fee.[22] It is an enormous blow to Walsingham.

Motive

Without realizing it, Raleigh has become Walsingham's worst enemy. His military activity is unpredictable and unrestrained. He wields far too much power and has foiled Walsingham's bid for Babington's estate. If Roanoke succeeds, Raleigh stands to be the wealthiest and most powerful man in the realm.[23] The easiest way to destroy Raleigh is to deprive him of this. But there is more to it than that: Walsingham wants the Virginia patent . . . and has had an eye on it since the days of Raleigh's brother Gilbert.

18 THE GAME

And as we see in experience, that dogs do always bark at those they know not . . . so it is with the inconsiderate multitude. Who, wanting that virtue which we call honesty in all men, and that special gift of God which we call charity in Christian men; condemn, without hearing; and wound, without offence given: led there by uncertain report only. . . .

Sir Walter Raleigh[1]

Rastell's Conspiracy

A similar crime had been committed before. Fernandez's stalling; his betrayal of John White; his claim that the summer was too far spent; his mutiny: very neatly done, but hardly original. Surely Walsingham, as Secretary of State, had access to the records and knew it had happened before. It was an easy matter to replicate John Rastell's voyage of 1517.

Rastell had been the first to propose colonizing Newfoundland.[2] An expedition was mounted, endorsed by Henry VIII, and partly funded by the Earl of Surrey, then Lord Admiral.[3] The Earl offered the services of his man, John Ravyn, as purser. And then he sabotaged the voyage.

Before the fleet left England, Ravyn stalled every step of the way. At Dartmouth, at Plymouth, at Falmouth, he delayed the expedition with flimsy excuses, promising supplies that should have been provided before they set sail. Days wore away. The time available to establish the colony diminished rapidly. In Plymouth, Ravyn drove the ship aground, causing a leak and further loss of time. Finally, having run out of excuses, Ravyn turned Rastell and his company out of the ship and abandoned them on the coast of Ireland, claiming that the summer was too far spent to try for Newfoundland. Did Walsingham coach Fernandez in the exact lines to say? The sailors, under Ravyn's sway, did as told and sailed away.

When the case came to court, Ravyn was not indicted. The Earl of Surrey protected him.[4] Rastell was condemned by posterity — as was John White — for ineffective leadership on a ruined voyage. But we must take careful note of how easily an alibi is established. Surrey was the guilty party. In fact, unlike Walsingham, he openly admitted to having instructed Ravyn to take *the ship into his own hand.*[5] Yet Surrey was a major shareholder in the enterprise! No one could quite believe that he would sabotage his own investment.

It is next to impossible to subvert a mission from the outside. Surrey's pose as an investor enabled him to position Ravyn on the expedition with enough authority to destroy it. Fernandez — Walsingham's man — was both an Assistant and Master of John White's ship. Yet no one at the time, and few since, dared accuse him of any crime more sinister than neglect. His financial investment as an Assistant guaranteed that few questioned his innocence. *If a man would cross a business,* observed Bacon, . . . *let him pretend to wish it well, and move it himself in such sort as may foil it.*[6]

Carleill's Bid

In terms of North America, Walsingham does "pretend to wish it well." 1574. Sir Richard Grenville — his ships in readiness — finds his license to explore the Pacific coast abruptly revoked. At Walsingham's urging, Drake revives the plan, receives permission to go, and sails around the world, robbing Grenville of a hero's accolade.[7] Walsingham repeatedly promotes his men to garner lucrative expeditions, most of which were first proposed by Raleigh's forward-thinking family.

1577. Gilbert submits his *Discourse How Her Majesty May Meet with and Annoy the King of Spain.* It argues cogently for a base from which to launch a two-pronged attack against Spain's West Indian fleet and her Newfoundland fishery. 1578. He is given patent to discover and occupy North American lands.[8] The monopoly expires in six years if permanent settlement is not established. The first expedition fails.

1581 finds Walsingham backing a curiously similar project with Drake: to occupy Brazil and create a base in the Azores to waylay the Spanish treasure fleet. If successful, what would this have done to Gilbert's plans? The expedition never gets off the ground.[9]

1582. Gilbert makes a final desperate attempt on North America before his patent lapses. To raise the necessary capital, he subgrants land to Catholic investors. They petition Walsingham for permission to settle a colony.[10] Two circumstances follow which subsequently appear highly suspicious: first, Walsingham, his stepson Christopher Carleill, and Catholic investor Sir George Peckham interrogate David Ingram about the Chesapeake Bay and his travels by foot to Cape Breton. Second, the Spanish ambassador — tipped off by someone — threatens the Catholic investors with death if they persist in their settlement plan. The effect is immediate. Money is not forthcoming and Gerard and his investors drop out entirely. A year later Gilbert drowns at sea and either Peckham or his son — curiously unafraid of the Pope's threats — publishes a discourse dedicated to Walsingham to attract investors in a new North American voyage.[11]

November 1582. Hakluyt is in Bristol, drumming up merchant support for Gilbert's voyage. A last-ditch effort at fund-raising. Mayor Thomas Aldworth pens an eager letter to Walsingham offering Gilbert a ship, all expenses paid. Very generous — but it does not appear that Walsingham ever informs Gilbert.[12]

February 1583. Gilbert is in despair. Capital is not forthcoming and it is strongly suggested that he relinquish his patent and let someone else try. Gilbert urgently writes to Walsingham, like the fly pleading with the spider, answering objections the government has raised about his competence. He begs permission to leave the country, *especially seeing I have her Majesty's grant and licence under the Great Seal of England for my departure.*[13] In a frantic effort to finance his trip, Gilbert sells his own estate.

March 11, 1583. Walsingham responds to the long-neglected offer from the Mayor of Bristol. His delay, he says, was due to *certain causes.* Aldworth is informed that Gilbert's ships will depart within ten days and their vessel may accompany him. Preposterously short notice! Walsingham suggests that it follow, then, as *soon after as you may.*[14]

That very same day, Walsingham asks Hakluyt to deliver a letter to Aldworth. The Mayor thanks Walsingham for the *letters* — implying more than one — concerning a voyage to America *lying to the Southwest of Cape Breton.* So *this* is the outcome of the David Ingram interview with Peckham and Carleill, but whose voyage is it? The Mayor thanks Walsingham for his disposition for the benefit of Bristol — suggesting favors received — and at a gathering of merchants, *caused your letters being directed unto me privately, to be read in public, and after some good light given by M. Hakluyt unto them,* every man present unanimously pledged *the sum of 1000 marks and upward* and offered a ship and a bark *to be left in the country under the direction and government of your son-in-law Master Carleil, of whom we have heard much good.*[15] Carleill, not Gilbert?

April 1583. Carleill publishes a discourse on his intended voyage in the hope of attracting investors from the Muscovy Company, who claim prior monopoly over the same lands covered by Gilbert's patent. They agree to back Carleill provided he secure their privileges.[16] The plan falls through. May 1583. With the expedition faltering, Walsingham's friend, the Earl of Shrewsbury, subscribes to Carleill's voyage *rather than it should fail, for his friend's sake.*[17] Yet only Gilbert's ships depart.

September 1583. Hakluyt, also something of a loose cannon, is sent to Paris by Walsingham as chaplain and secretary to Sir Edward Stafford. He remains there until 1588. Dr. Dee is also hustled out of the way. Before he goes, he reports peculiar nightmares: I had a *dream of being naked and my skin all over wrought with work like some kind of tuft mockado, with crosses blue and red.* That same night, he dreams of Walsingham.[18]

Dee may have been a spy.[19] In 1583 he and Duke Albert Laski, Prince of Poland, held divination sessions with a crystal ball rigged with optics to create illusions, including that of a lithe spirit named Madimi. She warned Dee about Walsingham. He and Burghley, she said, *are joined together and they hate thee. I heard them when they both said, thou wouldst go mad shortly. Whatever they can do against thee, assure thyself of. They will shortly lay a bait for thee, but eschew them. They have determined to search thy house, but they stay until the Duke be gone.* Dee was cautioned to trust neither; he was surrounded by spies. *See them, and be not seen of them; dost thou understand it?*[20]

Raleigh's Patent

June 11, 1583. Gilbert's fleet departs. In September he is reported dead. Hakluyt and Dee are hurried out of the country. And Walsingham, in the interests of his stepson Carleill, makes a bid for Gilbert's patent. By November it is considered a done deal. Carleill's friends — Sir John Hawkins and Sir Francis Drake — compose poetry in honor of the proposed venture.[21] January 1584. A certain M. Steventon is sent around the country gathering subscriptions to finance the expedition.

March 1584. Surprise. Sir Walter Raleigh, the one variable outside Walsingham's control, receives Gilbert's coveted patent from the Queen, eclipsing Carleill's efforts. Despite profound shock over your brother's death, John Hooker praises Raleigh, you have *levelled your line for the good of your country* and *did not give over.*[22] Carleill can do little more than accompany the first Roanoke expedition.

1585. The story is not yet over. Walsingham submits a curious plagiarism to the Queen under the familiar title of *A Plot for the Annoying of the King of Spain.*[23] It poses Gilbert's argument for an attack against the Spanish fishing fleet in Newfoundland. Raleigh's supply ships, intended for Lane's fort and which might have saved it from evacuation, are diverted for the job.[24] Drake's ships, sent to the Caribbean and the Outer Banks where Raleigh's should have been, bring Ralph Lane home. Meanwhile, Lane's defamatory libel against Grenville reaches Walsingham's hands. As we have seen, Grenville captures a Spanish carrack, the *Santa Maria,* and reports its value at forty thousand ducats. An anonymous letter to the Queen assesses its worth at more than a million, charging Grenville with embezzlement. The lines are clearly drawn. The English, it is said, *will stomach a matter vehemently, and a long time lodge an inward grudge in their hearts.* Walsingham, in particular, will *cherish a plot for some years together . . . his spies waited on some men every hour for three years.*[25]

1586. A costly secret service, Babington's Conspiracy, and Sidney's debts cast Walsingham into financial ruin.[26] December 1586. He is turned down for the Duchy of Lancaster. He leaves the Court in anger and stays away until February — ample time to work out the details of the Roanoke sabotage.

March 1587. The final straw. Walsingham, returned to Court, urges Drake to invade Portugal on behalf of Don Antonio to ignite a rebellion against Spain. It has taken three months to obtain the Privy Council's permission. Drake is ready to sail when his entire crew deserts. Scared away, Spanish ambassador Mendoza claimed, by Raleigh. He *is very cold about these naval preparations, and is secretly trying to dissuade the Queen from them.*[27] Drake finally sails in April as White's colonists depart. Raleigh will never again step in Walsingham's way.

Raleigh and Leicester

1587. The political configuration is changing. The long-standing Leicester-Walsingham alliance dissolves and Walsingham moves closer to Burghley.[28] Within the year, his daughter rallies from Sidney's death to marry Robert Devereux, Earl of Essex.[29] Twenty years old, of aristocratic birth, Essex was educated at Trinity College, Cambridge, under the tutelage of John Whitgift, the future archbishop. He is intrepid, he is spoiled . . . and he is Leicester's stepson. Leicester may have suspected Walsingham of arranging the marriage as a means of siphoning off his money to repay Sidney's debts. He may have been right. In any case, Leicester cannot have been happy. His relationship with Essex is notoriously poor.

Walsingham is fitting pieces into place. During the summer, while the Roanoke sabotage is in progress, he is busy at home setting Raleigh up for a fall. Essex is now at court, and Walsingham slyly informs his agent that Raleigh is opposed to Leicester on account of *the mislike of E. brought in, as he supposeth, by L.*[30]

July 26, 1587. Leicester is commanding the Queen's forces in the Netherlands. The city of Sluys falls to Spanish troops, and Walsingham attributes this to Leicester's arrogance. His agent suggests that Leicester should be removed from duty. Walsingham immediately notifies Leicester that the Queen is angry, the result of enemy slander. *I find there is some dealing underhand against your L., which proceedeth from the younger sort of our courtiers that take upon them to censure the greatest causes and persons that are treated in council or serve her Majesty.* Raleigh is a younger sort of courtier.[31] He has a history of criticizing his superiors. William Herllie informs Leicester that the ringleader is Raleigh, acting *either of his ill-nature* or out of jealousy.[32]

November. Leicester returns to England just as Raleigh is called away to attend to his Vice-Admiral's duties in the West Country. *In men's absence from Court,* Walsingham cautions, *envy oftentimes doth work most malicious effects.*[33] Who made it necessary for Raleigh to leave? Leicester is back, and *even Sir Walter Raleigh,* it is reported, *did not escape suspicion of ill done to the Earl, from which cause grew his sudden departure to the west country the day before the Earl came to court.*[34]

Smear Campaign

With a wedge driven between Raleigh and Leicester, a smear campaign is launched. The first target is Roanoke. When Lane arrived home in the autumn of 1586, he did so singing the praises of Virginia and its rich mines. Yet strangely, despite such testimony, a new sort of rumor emerges. Roanoke is barren, it says, not worthy of investor interest. It promises only misery.[35] *Do not let the envenomed shafts of your enemies and rivals trouble you. . . ,* Hakluyt consoles Raleigh. *Go on, I say, follow the path on which you have already set foot, seize Fortune's lucky jowl, spurn not the immortal fame which is here offered you.*[36] The damage done by false report is only the beginning.

The next to come under attack is Raleigh himself. Walsingham, assisted by Essex, projects Raleigh as an upstart with far too much power.[37] They say he has an ill nature, that he secretly plots Leicester's ruin. He disrupts the tranquillity of the Court. He is without family name. The Queen is too easily swayed by him. During an entertainment, her comedian Richard Tarleton revels in the gossip, loudly proclaiming: *the knave commands the Queen!*[38] Suddenly Raleigh, whom *the whole court doth follow* in 1583, is now the *best-hated man of the world, in Court, city, and country.*[39]

Walsingham has done a thorough job. *He could,* it is claimed, *overthrow any matter by undertaking it, and move it so as it must fall.*[40] He has cast suspicion upon Grenville and played upon the aristocrats' envy of Raleigh. The mighty Leicester, who might have defended him, now doubts his loyalty. The Queen herself is criticized for entertaining such a low-born courtier. Essex gathers his friends into a faction, gaining strength for a final overthrow. White's colonists are marooned on Roanoke; Raleigh's North American plans will fail.

Yet if Walsingham ordered the sabotage of John White's colonists, he would have had to ensure two things. First, that they would never be rescued. Second, that the Queen would not take Raleigh's side. In both cases, Walsingham succeeded.

19 THE FALL

For what we sometimes were, we are no more;
Fortune hath changed our shape, and destiny
Defaced the very form we had before.
Sir Walter Raleigh[1]

John White's Return

It was hopeless. White's colonists — who had enemies, who may have been Separatists — left England in 1587 to very little fanfare to settle along the Chesapeake Bay. Raleigh prepared them well before they departed. Fernandez, an expert pilot, offered himself as one of the Assistants. The colonists were safely loaded aboard ships with children, belongings, and supplies, and sailed away from Plymouth to a new world.

Imagine Raleigh's surprise, then, when John White reappears in England in November. On the twentieth, they meet in London. White discloses the awful news that the colony is marooned on Roanoke and delivers *letters and other advertisements* concerning the *state of the planters.* Raleigh's reaction is immediate: *whereupon he forthwith appointed a pinnace* to be sent to Roanoke with supplies. With the invincible Armada mobilizing, Raleigh's duties in the West Country as Vice-Admiral are pressing. Nevertheless, putting all other matters aside, he *also wrote his letters unto them,* says White, *wherein among other matters he comforted them with promise, that with all convenient speed he would prepare a good supply of shipping and men with sufficiency of all things needful which he intended, God willing, should be with them the summer following.*[2]

There is no record that the pinnace bearing Raleigh's letters and emergency provisions ever went to Roanoke. Perhaps it did get away after all, though there had been an order for a general stay of shipping since October 9. The official reason for this was the Armada, though England had known of Spain's preparations for more than a year and a half.[3] In fact, that spring Drake had sailed into Cadiz harbor and crippled the assembling fleet, wrecking Spain's invasion plans for 1587.[4] In October, then, the threat was far less than it had been for months. So why the order?

October 18. Fernandez was in England, having beaten White back by three weeks. Stafford was in London even earlier. Both men knew that White would arrive shortly. Both men, and their employer, knew what he would tell Raleigh. A rescue team sent to Roanoke was easily anticipated. Who controlled the special Council of Shipping and Mariners that ordered the stay? Was their October resolution to detain all vessels merely a coincidence?

Grenville's Rescue Attempt

If we give Walsingham and the Privy Council the benefit of the doubt regarding shipping in October, we cannot easily dismiss what happened next. As promised, Raleigh prepared a fleet, scheduled to reach Roanoke the following summer. Grenville was charged with outfitting it from his home in Bideford.[5] All that White's colonists had to do was survive a single year.

By winter it is obvious that the October moratorium on shipping is not being heeded. Raleigh informs his brother John that *there is little regard taken of the general restraint made . . . but that every man provideth to go for Newfoundland and other places at their pleasures.* As Lord Lieutenant of Cornwall and Devon, it is — ironically — Raleigh's job to detain all vessels. He makes an exception. John, his deputy lieutenant, is told to let Grenville *steal away.*[6]

Grenville readies *seven or eight ships and pinnaces* for his fleet, a great number — as large a complement as his 1585 military expedition. Such arrangements can hardly remain secret for long. Curiously, word leaks out that he is bound for the West Indies. Raleigh must deem this a much wiser move than admitting they are headed for Roanoke.[7]

March 1588. Grenville is ready, *only staying but for a fair wind to put to sea.*[8] White anxiously scans the harbor, waiting for a break in the weather. All is excitement. And then something terrible. A rumor: *at the same time, there was spread throughout all England such report of the wonderful preparation and invincible fleets made by the king of Spain joined with the power of the Pope for invading of England.* The Armada is rebuilding. *Ancient prophecies* spread like wildfire, portending *strange and wonderful events for the year.* The fall of kingdoms. The end of the world. A lunar eclipse occurs in Elizabeth's zodiac sign of Virgo, a bad omen. At the ruins of Glastonbury Abbey an earthquake reveals a marble tablet, purported to contain Merlin's prophecy of doom and ruin. The Privy Council hurries a book into print refuting such grim prognostications.[9]

We have seen Walsingham's technique before: he spreads panic to achieve his desired ends. Is that what is happening here? Grenville immediately receives a letter from the Privy Council confining his ships to their berths on account of the Queen's *daily advertisement* of Spain's preparations.[10] Whose job is it to give the Queen daily briefings but Walsingham?

Yet ships did leave. Sir George Carey — Leicester's friend and the Queen's relative — got vessels out. So did John Watts. The Spaniards themselves sighted four English ships in the West Indies in early July, which must have left England in the spring.[11] Specifically, the ships that are not allowed to sail are Raleigh's.

Grenville is *straightly charged and commanded in her Majesty's name* to have his ships *prepared to be in a readiness to join with her Majesty's navy as he shall be directed.* Grenville has no choice but to notify the Privy Council that he awaits their instructions. April 9. The Council issues an oddly worded statement, as though Grenville had volunteered his fleet on impulse, rather than in obedience to their orders. Because he informed them, it says, of his willingness to serve, *their Lordships could not but allow his purpose therein.*[12] Raleigh's ships are to be delivered to Drake. To Drake! Walsingham's hand is written all over this.

The letter goes on to say that Grenville may *employ in his intended voyage* any ships too small for Drake's service. This does not mean, however, that Grenville will be permitted to go. He will not. Considering the danger *of this present time and his knowledge and experience in martial affairs . . . he himself should remain in those parts where he now was, to give his assistance and advice to the Lieutenants of Cornwall and Devon.*[13] His orders are, incredibly, to assist Raleigh.

And so *Sir Richard Grenville,* White bitterly writes, *was personally commanded not to depart out of Cornwall. The voyage for Virginia by these means for this year* was *thus disappointed.*[14]

Thwarted

This has to have been deliberate. Although the Privy Council alerted Drake to the delivery of Grenville's ships, other ships detained in port for his use were never mentioned.[15]

Not one of Grenville's vessels was ever employed against the Armada. Drake already had enough shipping for his needs. He returned Raleigh's fleet at the end of August, after all opportunity for sailing to Roanoke was lost. Although it is true that the ships were kept until after the Armada was defeated, Drake must have known much earlier that he did not need them. The Lord Admiral, Lord Howard of Effingham, thought so too. On Grenville's behalf, he sued for compensation, charging that Drake needlessly took the ships *over and above his warrant, yet by order from the Council, as Sir Richard Grenville and he hath to show.*[16]

John White and the Brave

Despite this blow, White is not idle. In panic — his daughter in grave danger, family and friends in distress — and *notwithstanding* the Privy Council's order, he *laboured for the relief of the planters so earnestly* that two cramped boats are finally returned for his use: Grenville's thirty-ton *Brave* and the twenty-five-ton *Roe,* both far too small to sail across the ocean unescorted.[17] White is desperate.

The boats are fitted out anew. White can do little more than pace along Bideford harbor, exactly as he did a month before, gazing at the proceedings from the stone bridge spanning the River Torridge. Biscuit, meal, and vegetables are loaded into holds far too small to carry much. The relief White had hoped for will be negligible.

April 22, 1588. The boats leave the Devon coast. White rides in the *Brave,* captained by Arthur Facy. Fifteen colonists sail with him, family members, perhaps. Those who had been left behind. If the weather is favorable, White can expect a two-month crossing, placing them on Roanoke at the end of June.

May 6. One hundred fifty miles off the island of Madeira, plans change. A French pirate ship from La Rochelle, twice their size, attacks. The *Brave,* pressed for its life, has no choice but to *fight to help ourselves.* Lighting a cannon, they blast the enemy master gunner, striking off his shoulder. Their own gunner takes a bullet in the head. The exchange is sharp and quick. Pirates swarm aboard the *Brave,* grappling hand-to-hand *without ceasing one hour and a half.* A pike hurls through the air and catches Captain Facy in the face. It plunges through his head.

Other Frenchmen, grubby from the fight, wrench open White's supplies; *they robbed us of all our victuals, powder, weapons and provision saving a small quantity of biscuit to serve us scarce for England.* White must have lunged to save them, determined to preserve his family. As reward, a sword glints through the air and strikes his head hard, followed by a whirring pike, which sinks into flesh. *I myself,* White said, *was wounded twice in the head, once with a sword, and another time with a pike, and hurt also in the side of the buttock with a shot.* Three of the male colonists are injured, *whereof one had 10 or 12 wounds.*

The *Brave* surrenders. The Frenchmen unload the cargo, stealing all, and *left us not at their departing anything worth the carrying away.* The *Brave*'s survivors feebly repair the rigging and mend the torn sails. *By this occasion,* White charges, *God justly punishing our former thievery of our evil-disposed mariners, we were of force constrained to break off our voyage intended for the relief of our colony left the year before in Virginia, and the same night to set our course for England,* leaving the colonists *not a little distressed.* The rescue has failed.

The Invincible Armada

Spring 1588. Spain gears up for its naval attack on England. For *a terrour,* they publish the extent of their preparations, *which verily was so vast throughout all Spain, Italy and Sicily, that the Spaniards themselves were amazed at it, and named it the Invincible Armada.* Pope Sixtus Quintus blesses the venture, cramming 290 Mendicant monks and priests aboard vessels named for saints to prosecute the Inquisition.[18]

In England the Queen assembles a volatile Council of War: Raleigh, Grenville, Lane, Lord Grey. The kingdom's troops are far too few; therefore Raleigh urges a radical plan of attack: hit the Spaniards by sea before they can land. The English navy is redesigned, the ships lowered to gain nimbleness and speed. Lord Admiral Howard takes Raleigh's prototype, the *Ark Raleigh,* as his own. One of England's greatest vessels, it will head the Royal Navy for a decade. Swiss tourist Thomas Platter, visiting London in 1599, buys a souvenir miniature of Raleigh's ship to take home to Basle.[19]

There is no time now to think of any Roanoke rescue. Of John White, we have no word; possibly he is still recovering from wounds. Were he near Plymouth, he would have seen the English fleet bristling with cannon, flags, and pennants flapping, *bearing the royal arms of England and other emblems in bright colours.* The hulls, splashed with reds and blues and other *diverse colours,* carved with figureheads of tigers, dragons, and lions.[20] At Mortlake, Dr. Dee is busy forecasting the weather, predicting severe gales in the North Atlantic and receiving nightmarish visions of ships' forecastles rising up from the sea.[21] Everybody waits.

July 19, 1588. The Armada edges into the English Channel in an immense arc. The terrifying fleet rears up *with lofty turrets like castles, in front like a half-moon, the wings thereof spreading out about the length of seven miles, sailing very slowly, though with full sails, the winds being as it were tired with carrying them, and the ocean groaning under the weight.*[22]

The said Spanish fleet, being the best furnished with men, munition, and all manner of provision, of any that ever the ocean saw, and called by the arrogant name of Invincible, consisted of 130 ships: in which were 19,290 soldiers; 8,350 mariners; 2,080 galley-slaves; 2,630 great ordinance.[23] An English victory seems inconceivable.

But it comes. Raleigh's flagship, commanded by Howard, *thundered thick and furiously.* The English vessels sallied forth and *charged the enemy with wonderful agility and nimbleness.*[24] Raleigh was right. It was a total rout. Severe gales arose to finish the job. Of the Spanish ships, *there returned home 53 only. . . . Of the 91 great galleons and hulks there were missing 58, and 33 returned. . . . Of 30,000 persons which went in this expedition, there perished . . . the greater and better part.*[25]

England erupts in wild rejoicing, parades, and celebrations the likes of which were never seen before. A commemorative coin is struck in Zealand depicting the Armada *flying with full sails, and this inscription, Venit, vidit, fugit, that is: It came, it saw, it fled.*[26] Discovered among the wrecked Spanish vessels are appalling torture devices intended for the Inquisition: iron boots with wedges, manacles, thumbscrews, and *strange and most cruel whips.*[27] The grisly trophies are deposited in the Tower of London.

Thus the magnificent, huge, and mighty fleet of the Spaniards (which themselves termed in all places Invincible) such as sailed not upon the ocean sea many hundredth years before, in the year 1588 vanished into smoke.[28]

Complaints to the Queen

By all rights, Raleigh should be the hero of the day. Yet, oddly, as the festivities proceed, he and Grenville are sent away to clear the Irish coast of Spanish wrecks. For the first time in a long while, Walsingham is in the Queen's favor. At Burghley's urging he finally receives the coveted Duchy of Lancaster.[29] His protégé Essex is making rapid headway in Elizabeth's regard. The tables have turned, but why?

Let us assume, for the moment, that something was said. White returned from Roanoke in the autumn to face his enemies, claiming an outrageous story of mutiny and betrayal by one of his own Assistants. This would have thrust Raleigh into the unenviable position of accusing Walsingham of sabotage. To have made such a slanderous claim at that juncture to a Queen besieged by *malignant rumours,* while Walsingham's spy network was providing daily and accurate information about the impending Armada, might understandably raise Elizabeth's ire.[30] The timing was bad: with attack imminent, the country had far greater concerns. Under the circumstances, no one was likely to believe Raleigh. Or care. Many more lives than White's colonists' were at stake.

After the Armada the situation would be little better. With the victory celebration booming, Raleigh's complaints could only come as an unwelcome distraction — ungrateful at best — amid the patriotic fervor. John White's enemies will roundly condemn him as a liar. The whelp Essex and his faction are ever ready to denounce Raleigh for his recriminations, calling him an acerbic troublemaker whose combative nature disrupts the peace of the Court. He takes too much credit for the defeat of the Armada. He is too independent. With Burghley safely in Walsingham's camp, Raleigh's single defender is Leicester. Yet soon after the Armada's defeat, Leicester is dead from a fever, which many suspect was caused by poison.[31]

Whatever the source of Raleigh's trouble, there is no denying that he passed into a period of disfavor that has no other ready explanation. He speaks of *errors* made and, later and much more sarcastically, of *great treasons,* for which he is punished.[32] Was accusing Walsingham his error?

Exile to Ireland

As a final insult, Essex challenges Raleigh to a duel. He refuses and is laid open to mockery. *So that finding his favour declining,* says Naunton, Raleigh decided *to leave that terra infirma of the Court for that of the waves and by declining himself and by absence to expel his and the passion of his enemies, which in Court was a strange device of recovery. But that he then knew there was some ill-office done him, yet he durst not attempt to mend it otherwise than by going aside, thereby to teach envy a new way of forgetfulness and not so much as think of him. Howsoever, he had it always in mind never to forget himself.*[33]

Raleigh leaves the Court for Ireland, followed by an increasing round of slander, *for public envy is as an ostracism,* declares Francis Bacon, *that eclipseth men when they grow too great.*[34]

My Lord of Essex, a gleeful Sir Francis Allen informs a friend, *hath chased Mr. Ralegh from the Court, and hath confined him into Ireland.*[35] "Mister," not "Sir." Raleigh's actions are declared deceitful, *a fraud bought at the price of many woes.* Valued people, condemned by association, are likewise *forgot* and *doth strange and wild appear.*[36] John White, perhaps, with his bizarre tale of betrayal and deception, his incessant demands for a rescue ship. Once celebrated painter, now strange and wild, an object of scorn.

Clues in Rhyme

In Ireland, riding out the storm, Raleigh befriends the poet Edmund Spenser. Because of him, *The Faerie Queene* will be completed and published and Spenser's reputation will be secured for posterity.[37] Deeply depressed, Raleigh composes his own verses. Those dating from this period bear examination, for they may well furnish us with clues. They tell the story of blinding pain, of a man beset with *contention,* a victim of betrayal: Raleigh has lost the Queen's love.[38]

> *Yet more than this, a hope still found in vain,*
> *A vile despair, that speaks but of distress;*
> *A forc'd content, to suffer deadly pain,*
> *A pain so great, as cannot get redress;*
> *Will all affirm, my sum of sorrow such,*
> *As never man, that ever knew so much.*[39]

Beneath Raleigh's theme of love's betrayal, is there a hint of another betrayal? We must understand that Elizabethan writing characteristically employs double entendre. Concealed within verse are allegories and allusions to real persons and events. *The Faerie Queene* is packed with *certain signs,* Spenser confides, *here set in sundry places,* that *he may it find.*[40] Shakespeare counted on his audience to understand and decipher the many veiled references and jokes embedded within his plays. Clues to be teased out. In 1594 the hugely popular *Willobie His Avisa* surged through six editions before exhausting itself: all because the poetry contained clues to a contemporary sex scandal. The anonymous Willobie admitted that *though the matter be handled poetically, yet there is something under these feigned names and shows that hath been done truly.*[41]

Nothing is as it pretends to be. So what does Raleigh write? He composes "As You Came from the Holy Land of Walsingham" and, as if that were not enough, sets it to a traditional ballad called "Walsingham." He could hardly be more direct! Poignant and desperate, the poem speaks of a man afraid of abandonment, of being left *all alone, all alone as unknown.*[42] Themes of a fall from grace, broken promises, pain, and betrayal are all here.

There is no redress, Raleigh says. *Complaints cure not.* He has lodged them and they have angered the Queen. *A secret murder hath been done of late.* To acquit herself *this answer did she make: mistrust (quoth she) hath brought him to his end, which makes the man so much himself mistake, to lay the guilt unto his guiltless friend.* Raleigh accused Walsingham — or initially Leicester? It backfired and only harmed White, for *if I complain,* he says, *my witness is suspect.*[43]

Raleigh admitted that he wrote something to Elizabeth, composed in *furious madness,* alternating from *woe to wrath.*[44] To no effect. Betrayed by his enemies, his ability to save John White's family is impaired.

As in a country strange without companion,
I only wail the wrong of death's delays;
Whose sweet spring spent whose summer well nie done,
Of all which past, the sorrow only stays.

Whom care forewarns, ere age and winter cold,
To haste me hence, to find my fortune's fold.[45]

No one who reads Raleigh's lines ascribes them to mere literary convention.[46] The politics surrounding the failed Roanoke ventures lend a poignancy to his images of being lost and alone in an unfamiliar land.

The Merchant Agreement

March 7, 1589. Raleigh is back at Court, and so is his old fighting spirit: *I am in place to be believed not inferior to any man,* he heatedly writes to his cousin, Sir George Carew, *to pleasure or displeasure the greatest; and my opinion is so received and believed as I can anger the best of them.*[47]

In a damp London room, nineteen merchants attach their names to a paper, agreeing to venture *money, merchandise,* and *shipping* for Virginia. William Sanderson, a wealthy London businessman married to Raleigh's niece, must have put the tripartite deal together.[48] Raleigh, White, and the merchants will mount another Roanoke expedition.

Raleigh has already spent a staggering £40,000 on the Roanoke ventures: his purse drained by the purchase of ships, equipment, soldiers' pay, and supplies. The annual cost of the Queen's administration is less than £30,000 per year. *I have consumed the best part of my fortune,* he informed Leicester in 1586, *hating* Spain.[49]

Raleigh needs these merchants. The slanders raised against Roanoke after the return of Lane's expedition have deterred other investors. Hakluyt called it treachery. *There have been,* Hariot affirms, *diverse and variable reports, with some slanderous and shameful speeches bruited abroad by many that returned from thence. . . . Which reports have not done a little wrong to many that otherwise would have also favoured and adventured in the action.*[50] Raleigh is right when he says that *it is not Truth, but Opinion, that can travel the world without a passport.*[51]

Yet no ships are sent to Roanoke in 1589. It is not until May 1590, a month after Walsingham's death, that John White is able to return at last.[52]

John Watts

February 1, 1590. Activity on the Thames grinds to a halt. There has been another Spanish scare; outbound shipping is again confined to port. *There were at the time,* said White, *three ships absolutely determined to go for the West Indies.*[53] The *Hopewell,* the *John Evangelist,* and the *Little John.* Their owner is John Watts, head of the great London syndicates, successful privateer, high-wheeling capitalist. Spain calls him England's greatest pirate. Watts is a self-made man, decked out in jewels and chains of gold; immensely wealthy, propertied. His associates are his ships' captains. Privateering experts, every one, with a style all their own. In 1591 they were reported off Havana, provoking a fight, sending an enraged Spanish governor a steady stream of love messages and tokens.[54]

At the time the stay was ordered, White was in London searching for a way back to Roanoke.[55] Ignoring the stay, Watts's ships head for Plymouth. Swiftly packing and gathering provisions, White entreats Raleigh to *procure licence for those three ships to proceed on with their determined voyage.* If a deal can be struck to force Watts to carry supplies, *the people in Virginia (if it were God's pleasure) might speedily be comforted and relieved without further charges unto him.*

Raleigh is quick to act. While White rushes to Plymouth, he obtains license from the Queen, informing Watts that his ships may leave the country provided he transport John White to Roanoke. Order is taken that Watts *should be bound unto Sir Walter Ralegh* for the hefty sum of *three thousand pounds* — Raleigh's man of business remembers it to be five — *that those three ships, in consideration of their releasement, should take in and transport a convenient number of passengers, with their furnitures and necessaries, to be landed in Virginia.*[56]

February's end. Plans are laid amid a stir of commotion. The colonists are readied, White's heart bursting at the anticipated reunion. And then it happens again. Despite the Queen's license, *the order set down by* Raleigh is ignored and Watts's bond never taken. *But rather in contempt of the aforesaid order, I was by the owner and commanders of the ships denied to have any passengers or anything else transported in any of the said ships.* Familiar faces, vessels, the harbor docks stream out of focus. Becoming grotesque. *I made great suit and earnest entreaty,* cries White, *as well to the chief commanders as to the owner of the said ships.* But they stand resolute, allowing only White aboard with a single chest, *no, not so much as a boy to attend upon me.*

White casts about in panic, receiving from his *daily and continual petitions* only *cross and unkind dealing.* Raleigh is far away in London, unaware of what is happening, for *the scarcity of time was such that I could have no opportunity to go unto Sir Walter Ralegh with complaint.*

What good is a single chest to anyone? White the painter, pathetic, bravely fighting, eyes brimming with tears. He must not now even recognize himself. What an incredible choice! White must know that if he leaves England without supplies, his arrival on Roanoke will be as good as nothing. Three years wasted; he will return in exactly the same condition as when he left. For this, he has spent agonizing years braving famine and storms, ridicule and pirate attack. He has been shot and wounded. If White boards Watts's ship now without supplies, he will only share the colonists' fate.

March 20, 1590. The *Hopewell, John Evangelist,* and *Little John* put to sea from Plymouth harbor. Defying the Queen's order, they sail without colonists or supplies. Was Walsingham behind it? The decision might well have been made before his death. Essex? Burghley's son Robert Cecil, perhaps? Then edging into their camp. Or was White himself so condemned that he could expect no more than *cross and unkind dealing*? If the colonists were Separatists, were they held in such contempt that no one cared?[57] March 20, 1590. The *Hopewell, John Evangelist,* and *Little John* put to sea from Plymouth harbor. John White is on board.

Raleigh Condemned

We already know the story. White reaches Roanoke to find the settlement abandoned and the houses gone. The colonists, he learns, are safe at Croatoan, though a storm prevents his finding out for sure. He is forced back to England. We will not hear of John White again for three whole years.

Meanwhile, the slander so well sown against Raleigh in 1589 continues to sprout and flourish even after Walsingham's death. February 1592: Jesuit Robert Parsons charges Raleigh, enemy of Spain, with atheism. The gossip-mongers have a field day. *'Twas basely said of Sir W.R.,* mused Aubrey, *to talk of the anagram of Dog.*[58]

A rash of publications follows, decrying the *True Causes of the Great Troubles* besetting England.[59] Raleigh, significantly, is accused of the loss of life of voyagers and mariners, and of damaging England while enriching himself through militarism and ambition. What would happen, Parsons demands, if Raleigh were made a member of the Privy Council? He would persecute those opposed to his libertine views![60] An epicurean. A freethinker. Separatist sympathizer. A loose cannon.

Following on the heels of this scandal is a rumor that Raleigh is betrothed to Elizabeth Throckmorton, one of the Queen's maids of honor. Others say they are already married.[61] Idle tongues pounce on the gossip. *Nay sweet Sir Walter!* his sweetheart exclaimed. *Sweet Sir Walter! Sir Walter! At last, as the danger and the pleasure at the same time grew higher, she cried in the ecstasy, Swisser Swatter, Swisser Swatter! She proved with child, and I doubt not but this Hero took care of them both, as also that the Product was more than an ordinary mortal.*[62]

July 1592. Queen Elizabeth, in a rage, hurls the lovers in the Tower. Raleigh's *disgraces* leave him fair game for his enemies, *like a fish cast on dry land, gasping for breath.*[63] In prison, he writes "The Lie."

Go soul the body's guest
upon a thankless errand,
Fear not to touch the best
the truth shall be thy warrant:

Go since I needs must die,
and give the world the lie.

Say to the Court it glows,
and shines like rotten wood,
Say to the Church it shows
what's good, and doth no good.
If Church and Court reply,
then give them both the lie.

. . . Tell men of high condition,
that manage the estate
Their purpose is ambition,
their practice only hate:
And if they once reply,
then give them all the lie.

. . . Tell fortune of her blindness,
tell nature of decay,
Tell friendship of unkindness,
Tell justice of delay.
And if they will reply,
then give them all the lie.[64]

October. Raleigh is released from the Tower but banned from Court. Four months later, a strange letter is sent to Richard Hakluyt postmarked Ireland. Signed by John White, it details the sad events of his failed 1590 voyage to Roanoke Island, and commits his colonists to *the merciful help of the Almighty.*[65] The tone is resigned. The wording bears an odd stamp of finality. And then John White is gone.

White was never heard from again. No paintings made after his voyage to Roanoke are known to survive. There may not have been any. No other letters have ever been found. Perhaps his sorrow was too profound — *light griefs find utterance, deep griefs are dumb.*[66] Perhaps his accusations against Simon Fernandez were extended to Walsingham, the most powerful man in Elizabeth's government. Perhaps he paid for that. There is always the chance, of course, that White found a way back to Roanoke, though we have no proof of this. In any case, White is gone.

Spring 1594. Attorneys liquidate the estate of Ananias Dare.[67] Absent from England seven years, he is presumed dead.

PART FOUR

WHO ARE THE MANDOAG?

20 RALEIGH'S SEARCH

It is true that I never travailed after men's opinions. . . .

Sir Walter Raleigh[1]

Mace and Gilbert

The Queen's anger could not last forever. In May 1597, after five years of banishment, Raleigh leaves the countryside for London and resumes office at Court. Once there, he renews his efforts to retrieve White's colony.

We know very little about these rescue attempts. There are no surviving records of any of the expeditions. In 1599 Florida Governor Gonçalo Mendez de Canço dredged up an unlikely hero in the form of our old friend Darby Glande, now a soldier in the St. Augustine garrison, who said that White's colony was still alive; that two relief boats went to Roanoke with planters, clothing, supplies, and tools in 1594.[2] He had got the story from Richard Hawkins's men, captive in Havana.[3] True or not, we have no way of telling.

What we do know is that by 1602 there had been five rescue attempts — and all five had failed. Raleigh *hath sent* relief expeditions, John Brereton declared, *five several times at his own charges. The parties by him set forth performed nothing; some of them following their own profit elsewhere; others returning with frivolous allegations.*[4] It was a Herculean effort to send them out anyway, in days when an expedition to North America was tantamout to a voyage to the moon, with a price tag to match.

March 1602. Raleigh outfits yet another expedition to *find those people which were left there in the year 1587.* This one will be different. *At this last time,* says Brereton, *to avoid all excuse, he bought a bark, and hired all the company for wages by the month.*[5] To entirely eliminate privateering. Samuel Mace of Weymouth will head the expedition. Hariot briefs him, preparing a Secotan vocabulary and a list of copper items recommended as trade for sassafras. Sale of the aromatic wood in Europe is expected to offset the exorbitant cost of the voyage. *Kecow hit tamen?*[6] Hariot remembers. *What is this?* A useful phrase.

Nothing comes of all the planning. Who was Mace's pilot? Perhaps he had never been to the Outer Banks, for he missed the mark entirely. The ship reached the coast a full 120 miles southwest of Hatorask. Mace spent a month encamped in the sand, lading sassafras and sarsaparilla, spicebush, and a bark that tasted like cinnamon. By July it was reported that the inevitable summer storms were upon them, so that *when they came along the coast to seek the people, both in the islands and upon the main, in diverse appointed places, they did it not, pretending that the extremity of weather, and loss of some principal ground-tackle, forced and feared them from searching the Port of Hatarask, to which they were sent.*[7]

May 1603. Raleigh sends out two more vessels.[8] The first, under Bartholomew Gilbert, departs for the Chesapeake Bay. Gilbert is killed on shore; the expedition finds nothing. The second bark is captained by Mace. He, too, is unsuccessful. Not finding the missing colonists, he returns to an England in which everything had changed.

Long Live the King!

March 24, 1603. Richmond Palace shrouds itself in the blackest mourning. For the first time in forty-five years no joyful bells peal; no bonfires light up London's streets. Anguish is written on every face. Queen Elizabeth is dead at seventy. It is the end of an era.

The Queen was brought by water to White-hall,
At every stroke the oars did tears let fall . . .
I think the barge-men might with easier thighs,
Have rowed her thither in her people's eyes.
For howso'ere, thus much my thoughts have scanned,
She'd come by water, had she come by land.[9]

May 7. King James arrives in London to a muted fanfare. The Queen can no longer protect her beloved Raleigh. Enemies — now including Burghley's son, the politically ambitious Robert Cecil — warn James to beware of his power.[10] At a palace party for Elizabeth the previous December, a friend had spoofed Raleigh's name. *Raw Ly,* he quipped, *the foe to the stomach, and the word of disgrace, shows the gentleman's name with the bold face.*[11] Now, as King James turns a jaundiced eye toward Raleigh, the first words from his lips are *I have heard Raw-ly of thee.*[12]

Go echo of the mind,
A careless truth protest;
Make answer that rude Rawly
No stomach can digest.[13]

Arrested for What Thou Art

July 1603. While Gilbert fatally steps ashore on North American soil, equally fatal steps are being taken against Raleigh in England. It falls out suddenly. On the trumped-up charges of high treason, James orders Raleigh arrested and thrown in the Tower. His many offices and privileges are revoked . . . including rights to Roanoke Island. No evidence is produced against him until months later; all is withdrawn before the trial.[14]

In Spain, Philip II is dead. His successor, Philip III, offers reconciliation to King James provided Raleigh is eliminated. His list of offenses is long: he opposed Spain in Ireland, France, and the Netherlands.[15] He was a key player in the defeat of the Armada. His spectacular 1596 raid on Cadiz wiped out fifty-seven men-of-war in their own harbor and was regarded as the most humiliating defeat at the hands of the English. More so than the Armada. A year later Raleigh successfully attacked the Azores. He opposed Spain in Parliament and in counsel to the Queen. He invaded the Americas with intent to kill. Roanoke was more than a dire threat: it was a direct challenge to the empire and kept Spanish patrols frantic for years. Raleigh is a war criminal. An Elizabethan, from a bygone era. Grenville, Drake, Hawkins, Frobisher, the old sea dogs are dead. It is another England altogether.

I know that I lost the love of many, for my fidelity towards Her, Raleigh said of Elizabeth, *whom I must still honour in the dust; though further than the defence of Her excellent person, I never persecuted any man.*[16]

Tried Out of His Life

Thursday, November 17, 1603. Without evidence or witnesses, denied legal counsel, Raleigh is tried by the King's Attorney-General, Sir Edward Coke. His enemies sit as jurors to convict him — Robert Cecil among them. It is judicial murder.[17]

Thou art a monster! Coke rasps. A *viper!* The most *vile and execrable traitor that ever lived!* After he condemns Raleigh as a *Spider of Hell,* even the court intervenes, ordering Coke to restrain himself.

I want words sufficient, blasts Coke, *to express thy viperous treasons.*

I think you want words indeed, Raleigh calmly replies, *for you have spoken one thing half a dozen times.*

Thou art an odious fellow, Coke breathes, *thy name is hateful to all the realm of England for thy pride!*

It will go near, Raleigh rejoins, *to prove a measuring cast between you and me, Mr. Attorney.*[18]

At the end of the day the verdict comes in: Raleigh will die. This would never have happened, Lord Chief Justice Sir John Popham thundered at him, *if you had . . . not suffered your own wit to have entrapped yourself. . . . It is best for man not to seek to climb too high lest he fall. . . . You have been taxed by the world with the defence of the most heathenish, blasphemous, atheistical, and profane opinions,* a too *eager ambition* and a *corrupt covetousness.*[19]

The courtroom is stunned. The brutality of Coke's conduct has alienated even his staunchest supporters. Raleigh *behaved himself so worthily, so wisely, so temperately,* said an eyewitness, *that in half a day the mind of all the company was changed from the extremest hate to the extremest pity.*[20] Lord Hay had the audacity to inform the King that whereas he would have walked a hundred miles to see Raleigh hanged, he would now walk a thousand to save his life.[21] Were it not for an *ill-name, half-hanged in the opinion of all men,* admitted Sir Dudley Carleton, *he had been acquitted.*[22] Later, one of Raleigh's judges, Sir Francis Gawdy, swore upon his deathbed that the *justice of England was never so depraved and injured as in the condemnation of Sir Walter Raleigh.*[23] King James, in fact, does not dare execute Raleigh, but condemns him to the Tower for life, banished — like the Lost Colonists — from the world.

Nothing but a Joke

With Raleigh out of the way, interest in Virginia soars, even as White's Lost Colonists become the stuff of comedy. The 1605 play *Eastward Hoe* by George Chapman, Ben Jonson, and John Marston features an ostentatious Sir Petronel Flash in need of money for a voyage with Captain Seagull and comrades — the fool and his friends.

Quicksilver: Well, dad, let him have money; all he could anyway get is bestowed on a ship, now bound for Virginia. . . .
Security: Now, a frank gale of wind go with him, Master Frank! We have too few such knight adventures. Who would not sell away competent certainties to purchase (with any danger) excellent uncertainties? Your true knight venturer ever does it. . . .
Seagull: Come, boys, Virginia longs till we share the rest of her maidenhead.
Spendall: Why, is she inhabited already with any English?
Seagull: A whole country of English is there, man, bred of those that were left there in '87; they have married with the Indians, and make 'hem bring forth as beautiful faces as any we have in England.[24]

John White is absent from this picture. He and his tragedy belong to the past.

21 JAMESTOWN

For what we sometimes were, we are no more;
Fortune hath changed our shape, and Destiny
Defaced the very form we had before.
Sir Walter Raleigh[1]

A Sighting!

Raleigh's Virginia title is up for grabs. Chief Justice Popham — the very man who condemned Raleigh to death — forms a company of gentlemen and merchants to exploit his claim. Supporting him is Raleigh's old friend turned enemy, Sir Robert Cecil, and Attorney-General Sir Edward Coke.[2] January 1606. The London Company charter is granted.

Curiously, among the King's petitioners are *divers of his Majesty's loving subjects* who, during Elizabeth's reign and *at their own great charge and expense,* planted and inhabited Virginia.[3] Who are they? Investors, or relatives of Lost Colonists? None is mentioned by name.

April 1607. Captain Christopher Newport, Bartholomew Gosnold, and 105 colonists sail into the Chesapeake Bay. A reconnaissance locates the southernmost tributary, renamed the King's River. Forty miles from its mouth, in the country of the Paspahegh, a nation of the Powhatan Empire, the English construct a settlement dubbed "Jacobopolis." Colonist George Percy writes home calling the place James-Fort, a name more akin to the English town of *Chelms-ford.* A vast improvement. Easier on the tongue. It is also known as James Town, remarks Dudley Carleton, *but the town me thinks hath no graceful name.* The Paspahegh, Percy added, *murmured at our planting* there.[4]

While the fort is being built, Newport commands a boat farther inland, crossing into the territory of the Arrohattoc, another Powhatan member nation. At a bend in the river called Poor Cottage, they stop short, wholly startled, for *we saw a savage boy, about the age of ten years,* reports an incredulous George Percy, *which had a head of hair of a perfect yellow and a reasonable white skin, which is a miracle amongst all the savages.*[5] A miracle? Or a Lost Colonist? The English stand amazed. Yet why were no questions asked? The event was astonishing enough to be recorded — surely they must have found out more! Five miles away, Newport's men are entertained at the Arrohattoc capital, presented with mulberries and cakes and guides for their journey. They converse; the King is generous and friendly. There is every opportunity to question the boy. Instead, they let him slip away.

Far away in London, in his cell within the Tower, Raleigh keeps abreast of the discoveries. The sighting is chilling news. Hope of renewed contact with the Lost Colonists may have prompted him to urge more aggressive action. Someone certainly did. Newport, who had returned to England, is again dispatched to Virginia — with specific instructions to search for White's company.

Hard Times

Newport reaches Jamestown on January 2, 1608. But as his supply ships edge into their moorings, the fort is alarmingly quiet. The stench of rotting corpses permeates the air.

The sight that greets Newport is appalling. Of an original 105 colonists deposited at Jamestown just eight months before, only thirty-eight are alive. They had, the planters cried, grown *very bare and scanty of victuals.* Unwilling to hunt or fish even to support themselves, they starved to death. Compounding the problem, illness seeped through the settlement, explained Percy, caused by drinking river water that at low tide was *full of slime and filth.* The result was the *bloody flux* — diarrhea so violent that stools were laced with blood. The colonists' *pitiful murmurings and outcries* were chilling, some howling, some screaming long into the night. Some died *three or four in a night; in the morning, their bodies trailed out of their cabins like dogs to be buried.*[6] In addition to this were mutinies, bitter factioning, and relations with the nearby Paspahegh that ran from bad to worse.

The Search

The search for the Lost Colonists would have ended before it ever began had not fate intervened. Coincidentally, on the very morning of Newport's arrival in Virginia, Captain John Smith returned to Jamestown after a month spent in the interior — with information about White's colony. The story is nothing if not exciting. Seized by hunters while traveling upriver, Smith was brought before Opechancanough, King of the Pamunkey and brother of Wahunsonacock, ruler of the thirty-nation Powhatan Empire. He claimed they got along well, Opechancanough taking *great delight* in learning about English ships and tales of the sea. In return, *what he knew of the dominions he spared not to acquaint me with, as of certain men clothed at a place called Ocanahonan, clothed like me.*[7]

The news electrifies Jamestown. John White's colonists are still alive! Twenty-three years after the English last saw them. Days later, Smith met the *Emperor* Wahunsonacock at his capital of Werowocomoco. *The people at Ocamahowan he also confirmed, and the southerly countries also, as the rest . . . he described a country called Anone, where they have abundance of brass and houses walled as ours.*[8]

Inquiries are swiftly made. The Paspahegh king, Wowinchopunk, adds yet another dimension to Jamestown's mounting arsenal of information. The Lost Colonists are well known. The King agreed *to conduct two of our men to a place called Panawicke, beyond Roonoke, where he reported many men to be apparelled.* Did he really volunteer to guide them? For when a pinnace carries the party downriver to Warraskoyack, the point of departure, Wowinchopunk refuses to enter the interior. What can the English know of the Mandoag? Instead, *playing the villain and deluding us for rewards,* he *returned within three or four days after, without going further.*[9] The English attribute it to malice. Yet over the course of the next several months, the Powhatan show a uniform reluctance to enter the interior. Could it be that Wowinchopunk was afraid?

Spain. September 10, 1608. Philip III receives intelligence from London spy Pedro de Zúñiga. Contained in the packet is a folded piece of paper, the tracing of a map sent home by John Smith.[10] It was obtained, Zúñiga reported, from an Englishman — probably Captain Francis Nelson — lately returned from Jamestown. The map indicates known English settlements in North America: the one at Jamestown; and two farther south, occupied by White's colony.

One More Try

September's end, 1608. Months pass. Newport returns to Virginia with a second supply, including additional colonists, food, weapons . . . and firmer instructions. *How, or why,* Smith complains, *Captain Newport obtained such a private commission as not to return without a lump of gold, a certainty of the south sea, or one of the lost company of Sir Walter Rawley, I know not.*[11] But such the commission is.

Snatching up a pen, Smith promptly fires off a letter, scratching away in his own defense. To the Treasurer and Council of Virginia, Sirs: *I received your letter, wherein you write that our minds are so set upon faction . . . that we feed you but with ifs and ands and hopes, and some few proofs; as if we would keep the mystery of the business to ourselves. . . .*[12] Jamestown, it is feared, is deliberately concealing information.

Not surprisingly, Newport pursues the mines first. They are located west of the Powhatan, in high country above the cataracts that bridle all the rivers draining into the coast, among an enemy nation known as the Monocan; or perhaps south, in the territory of the Mandoag. A five-piece barge intended for the discovery is vastly unsuitable: *to be born by the soldiers over the falls,* Smith complains, *Newport had 120 of the best men he could choose. If he had burnt her to ashes, one might have carried her in a bag; but as she is, five hundred cannot, to a navigable place above the falls. And for him at that time to find in the South Sea, a mine of gold; or any of them sent by Sir Walter Raleigh: at our consultation I told them was as likely as the rest.*[13]

Newport returns empty-handed and sails for England, leaving Smith to carry out the search. *But during this great discovery of thirty miles,* Smith grumbles, *(which might as well have been done by one man, and much more, for the value of a pound of copper at a seasonable time), they had the pinnace and all the boats with them, but one that remained with me to serve the fort.*[14]

Company officials' *strange conceits* of finding wealth or colonists are enjoined to a threat: *they kindly writ to me,* charges Smith, *if we failed the next return, they would leave us there as banished men. . . . Had my designs been to have persuaded men to a mine of gold . . . or some new invention to pass to the South Sea, or some strange plot to invade some strange Monastery . . . what multitudes of both people and money would contend to be first employed?*[15] Monastery? A seclusion of religious people, he means. An odd statement, surely. Is Smith calling John White's colony Separatists?

Smith knew plenty of *them called Brownists,* later complaining that many went to Virginia, *pretending only Religion their governour,* when in fact it was *their pride and singularity and contempt of authority; because they could not be equals, they would have no superiors: in this fool's Paradise . . . they have paid soundly in trying their own follies, who undertaking in small handfuls to make many plantations, and to be several Lords and Kings of themselves, most vanished to nothing.*[16]

December 29, 1608. Smith and thirty-eight men set out from Jamestown for Powhatan's capital of Werowocomoco. That night, they bivouac in the territory of the Werraskoyack. As frost stiffens the grass in a sheath of white, Smith meets with Werraskoyack leader Tackonekintaco.[17] To test their friendship, he requests guides for a probe south into the Chowanoc country. Ice snaps from cold logs laid on the fire, spewing cinders into the trees. The answer comes back hollowly: Smith will have his way. Michael Sicklemore, *a very honest, valiant, and painful soldier,* is provided with two Werraskoyack men and *directions how to search for the lost company of Sir Walter Rawley, and silk grass.*[18]

Sicklemore is gone for three months. We know nothing of his journey other than that he carried presents to the Chowanoc leader. Not a shred of evidence beyond this has surfaced thus far. Not a single accounting of the Chowanoc, their current condition, towns visited, or discussions made. The reason is simple: the information was suppressed. The London Company was protecting its investment. Expedition members were legally bound to conceal all discoveries, and they did. Smith, as acting President, swore an oath of office to *keep secret all matter committed and revealed unto me* . . . until such time that *publication shall be made.* Nothing was printed without consent of the King's Council.[19] As we shall see, it was never in their interests to disclose the whereabouts of White's colony. The meager information we have is deliberately vague.

All Dead

March 1609. A single notice appears in John Smith's memoirs. *Master Sicklemore well returned from Chawonock, but found little hope and less certainty of them were left by Sir Walter Rawley. The river he saw was not great, the people few, the country most overgrown with pines. . . . But by the river the ground was good, and exceeding fertile.*[20] It reads like an epitaph. Indeed, further interest in the region was stilled for many years to come. But what did Sicklemore really discover? There is every indication that the news gleaned from the Chowanoc was not encouraging. This does not mean, however, that Michael Sicklemore found nothing.

With the Chowanoc reconnaissance ended, Smith had only to investigate the Mandoag. Another Powhatan nation was called upon to prove its fidelity—and bravery: the Quiyoughquohanock. *So that Nathaniell Powell and Anas Todkill were also, by the Quiyoughquohanocks, conducted to the Mangoages to search them there.*[21]

Southward they went, says Smith, *to some parts of Chawonock and the Mangoags to search them left by Sir Walter Raleigh; for those parts to the Town of Chisapeack hath formerly been discovered by Master Heriots and Sir Raph Layne.*[22]

It is spring. Redbud blossoms bleed ruddy into dogwood bursting forth in such fury that the woods appear cloaked in snow. Dogwood winter. As the petals sift on to the forest floor, Smith breathes the cold official pronouncement. Sicklemore, Todkill, and Powell searched for the Lost Colonists. *But nothing could we learn but they were all dead.*[23]

22 WAR ON THE POWHATAN

It is the sinfullest thing in the world to forsake or destitute a plantation once in forwardness; for, besides the dishonor, it is the guiltiness of blood of many commiserable persons.

Sir Francis Bacon[1]

The Great Deception

It was a lie, pure and simple. White's colonists were not dead. Smith knew it. The London Company knew it. Raleigh knew it. So did the Virginia Council at Jamestown. Yet the legal fiction was created — and would stick for nearly four hundred years.

Were such a thing true, Jamestown officials would need to explain why an inordinate amount of time was spent with the London Company in an effort to locate the dead. Were it true, the May 23, 1609, summons of Thomas Hariot to quiz him about the experiences of Raleigh's personnel in Virginia hardly seems necessary. In response to their questions, Hariot submitted *an alphabet that he had contrived for the American language, like Devil's* writing — to be used by Jamestown investigators probing south toward Roanoke.[2]

Instructions were immediately issued to Jamestown's new interim Governor, Sir Thomas Gates, to search for the Lost Colonists *in the part of the land inclined to the south . . . and if you find them not, yet search into this country; it is more probable than towards the north.*[3]

July 1609. From London, Zúñiga informs Philip III that Raleigh, *whom they consider here a very great personage,* conveyed certain information to the Council. *I have a paper which Walter Raleigh wrote,* Zúñiga says, *who is a prisoner in the Tower . . . it ought to be translated because it is the original which he had and when it is finished we shall compare it with the chart which they have caused to be made, and by it, the way which they will take will be understood.*[4] To which map will Zúñiga compare it? To the one he already has indicating survivors of White's colony?

There is much to this story that we do not know, but what we can be sure of is this: the Virginia Council in London was notified by Smith that the Lost Colonists were alive. Their instructions to Gates prove this. The Powhatan supplied specific information regarding the colony's whereabouts. Unfortunately, Smith's searches were only halfhearted and made against his will, though understandably so in light of Jamestown's condition. No proof that the colonists were dead was ever obtained. In fact, investigations into the Mandoag country, as we shall see, definitely indicated they were not. Despite the gag order concealing reports, we have glimpsed behind closed doors enough to warrant a closer inspection.

Yet something was looming on the horizon. An undercurrent of unrest, thrusting attention away from White's colony. That something was war.

The Starving Time

Jamestown has no food. Supply ships come, but they also bring more colonists. Too many planters are unwilling to fend for themselves, despite their own looming mortality. They reach crisis level, then sink even lower. The winter of 1609 is Jamestown's starving time. *The allowance,* remembers Robert Johnson, . . . *was only eight ounces of meal and half a pint of peas for a day . . . mouldy, rotten, full of cobwebs and maggots . . . which forced many to flee for relief to the savage enemy.* Savage enemy, he calls them. Yet the Powhatan, who never asked for such a visitation, are the colony's only source of food. Unless what they ate most *unnaturally* be counted: *the flesh and excrements of man,* the corpse of *an Indian, digged by some out of his grave* three days after burial. They *wholly devoured him.*[5]

Jamestown sinks into an appalling morass; were it not for their human form, England would never recognize these sons who *looked like anatomies crying out, We are starved! We are starved!* Two years later, nothing is changed: *so lamentable was our scarcity that we were constrained to eat dogs, cats, rats, snakes, toadstools, horse hides and what not, one man out of the misery that he endured, killing his wife powdered her up to eat her, for which he was burned.*[6] Robert Johnson speaks glibly of savages; what presents a more savage picture than Jamestown?

War on the Powhatan

May 23, 1609. Sir Thomas Gates is dispatched to Jamestown with authority to impose martial law, if need be, to reestablish order. His instructions make it clear that relations with the Powhatan are deteriorating. For Wahunsonacock *and his Weroances, it is clear even to reason beside our experience,* Gates is informed, *that he loved not our neighbourhood and therefore you may no way trust him, but if you find it not best to make him your prisoner, yet you must make him your tributary.*[7] Loved not our neighborhood? Since when? In 1607 Gabriel Archer had declared that *our best entertainment was friendly welcome.*[8] What changed were Jamestown's demands.

They *will never feed you,* Gates is told, *but for fear.* You are to *seize into your custody half their corn and harvest and their weroances and all other their known successors at once.* Their children are to be taken and reeducated so that *their people will easily obey you.* Priests are to be imprisoned so that they no longer *poison and infect them their minds* with religion, and *we pronounce it not cruelty nor breach of charity to deal more sharply with them and to proceed even to death with these murderers of souls.*[9] The Virginia Council are adept manipulators. Brainwash the children, remove the religious leaders. Control a people.

1609. Zúñiga writes to King Philip about Wahunsonacock. *I understand that as soon as they are well fortified,* he said, *they will kill that King and the savages, so as to obtain possession of everything.* 1610. War is declared.[10]

The Peace Movement

News of atrocities against the Powhatan filters home. The Paspahegh were attacked. Jamestown soldiers prodded Wowinchopunk's children into boats, rowed them into the bay, and disposed of them by *throwing them overboard and shooting out their brains in the water.* Governor De la Warr had their mother arrested as a prisoner of war, then ordered her stabbed. Reports multiply. A Nansemond village was incinerated, temples looted, the royal corpses dragged out onto the sand and robbed of their pearl and copper adornments.[11] This is more than war; it is barbarity.

England erupts in massive protest. Critics condemn the theft of Powhatan land, charging that Jamestown is no better than Spain, glossing robbery under *cunning and coloured falsehoods.* Promoters cry this isn't true: Spain urged Catholicism whereas *our invasion, much more current, and so far different,* is not intended to bring the Powhatan *out of the frying pan into the fire, but to make their condition truly more happy.*[12] All outgoing mail from Jamestown is censored. *You must take especial care,* Jamestown is warned, *what relations come into England, and what letters are written.*[13]

There will be no war, Johnson croons in the midst of the fighting, because Wahunsonacock will be won over *by fair and loving means, suiting to our English natures, like that soft and gentle voice, wherein the Lord appeared to Elias: How honourable will this be, in the sight of men and of ages to come?*[14]

Protesters react in anger. *Many good religious devout men,* declares a shocked Smith, *have made it a great question, as a matter in conscience, by what warrant they might go to possess those countries which are none of theirs, but the poor savages.* The Virginia Company bewails the *vulgar opinion* and *clamorous and tragical narrations* thus spread by *foul mouths* that *have divided the universal spirits of our land.*[15]

As propaganda, the Company dredges up the Lost Colonists. The English right to settle Virginia, Robert Johnson lashes back, stems from John White. It was *long since discovered, peopled, and possessed by many English, both men, women, and children, the natural subjects of our late Queen Elizabeth, of famous memory, conducted and left there at sundry times. And that the same footing and possession is there kept and possessed by the same English, or by their seed and off-spring, without any interruption or invasion, either of the savages (the natives of the country) or of any other Prince or people (for ought we hear or know) to this day.*[16]

But Robert Johnson, while vindicating Jamestown, makes a terrible mistake. He says the Lost Colonists are alive! Yet this simple truth will soon become clear: the Virginia Company cannot prosecute an unpopular war without White's colonists dead.

A World Oppressed with People

The crisis in Virginia is complicated by the fact that England suffers from massive overpopulation. It must be remedied: either the birth rate must be reduced, the people must emigrate, or both. Those who favor emigration point out that North America is not yet deforested; its land is *as good, or rather better than any we possess. . . . If this be not a reason sufficient to such tender consciences; for a copper kettle and a few toys as beads and hatchets,* the Powhatan *will sell you a whole country.*[17]

But if the Powhatan will really sell their whole country for baubles, why is a war necessary? Protesters, not fooled, decry the seizure of

Powhatan territory despite Jamestown's claim that it is *not unlawful that we possess part of their land.*[18]

It is clear that the only way to get the country behind the war is to turn the Powhatan into villains. Enter William Strachey.

William Strachey was born in Saffron Walden, the town that had once had such a problem with God and cut flowers.[19] A gentleman, he hob-nobbed in London with Ben Jonson, John Donne, and denizens of the Mermaid Club in Bread Street. People who know Raleigh. June 1610. William Strachey arrives in Jamestown as the new secretary of the colony. 1611. He composes a manuscript entitled the *Historie of Travaile into Virginia Britannia.* It circulates widely; a copy is sent to Raleigh's friend, the Earl of Northumberland, imprisoned in the Tower. Raleigh must have read it.

At the height of the protest against the war, something new had been needed to turn public opinion. Strachey provided it and, indeed, may have believed it. Wahunsonacock, he said, *murdered White's colony.*

23 REQUIEM

Wahunsonacock doth often send unto us to temporize with us, awaiting perhaps but a fit opportunity (inflamed by his bloody and furious priests) to offer us a taste of the same cup which he made our poor countrymen drink of at Roanoak.

William Strachey[1]

A Power Play

The news explodes across London; bursting into parlors, intruding on every conversation. White's colonists are dead. The Powhatan massacred innocent Englishmen! The rumor is repeated on trembling lips — though it is not true. There is no proof that the Powhatan did anything of the kind.

So who, or what, in Jamestown was responsible for the Powhatan murder story? Did Strachey invent it? Was it propaganda to create an enemy? To seize Powhatan lands? Or did Wahunsonacock himself concoct the tale to intimidate Jamestown?

Whatever its source, Jamestown seized upon it. King James *hath been acquainted,* Strachey reports, *that the men, women, and children of the first plantation at Roanoak were by practice and commandment of Powhatan (he himself persuaded thereunto by his priests) miserably slaughtered without any offence given him either by the first planted (who twenty and odd years had peaceably lived intermixed with those savages, and were out of his territory) or by those who now are come to inhabit.* A clever ploy, associating the murder of White's colony with the current events at Jamestown. King James *has given order,* Strachey adds, that the Powhatan *shall be spared, and revenge taken* only upon the priests. Hereafter, Powhatan subjects *must depend on his Majesty* for guidance, *acknowledging him for their superior Lord.*[2] The thirty nations will pay James tribute. It is all about money.

The Versatile Smith Reader

It is odd, to say the least, that Smith never mentioned a massacre in his conversations about the Lost Colonists with Wahunsonacock or the kings of Pamunkey, Werraskoyack, Paspahegh, or Quiyoughquohanock. In fact, each provided information that the colonists were still alive. Was the massacre edited out of Smith's writing? Perhaps. But how, then, do we explain the fact that he sent search parties to the locations the Powhatan specified? If the colonists really had been exterminated, then Newport's instructions to look for them, which Smith found so odious, would not have to be carried out.

The truth is that Smith *never* said that Wahunsonacock murdered the colonists. Samuel Purchas did. *Powhatan confessed that he had been at the murder of that colony,* Purchas wrote, *and showed to Captain Smith a musket barrel and a brass mortar and certain pieces of iron which had been theirs.*[3] Hardly proof — the items could have come in trade from anywhere. Stranger still, Smith's *General History,* written between 1623 and 1624, and a reworking of his earlier *Proceedings,* no longer mentions Lost Colony survivors. That information was removed and replaced by an entirely new episode. Smith, who had claimed he was extremely well treated during his captivity, now says he was dragged to an altar and that Powhatan's men gathered with clubs *to beat out his brains.*[4] He was saved from death, he said, by Pocahontas. One of the versions is false.

Search No More

The explanation that the Powhatan murdered the Lost Colonists is too neat and tidy. Were it believed, then Jamestown could justify wiping out the Powhatan. The implications are profound: from the moment war is declared, no further searches are made. Strachey's story and thirty years of ensuing hostility destroy any information we might have recovered.

Jamestown *laws divine, moral and martial,* article 38: *No soldier may speak or have any private conference with any of the savages without leave of his captain, nor his captain without leave of his chief officer, upon pain of death.*[5] In England, even Smith complains that *although I have tired myself in seeking and discoursing with those returned thence* from Virginia, *few can tell me anything but of that place or places they have inhabited, and he is a great traveller that hath gone up and down the river of James Town, been at Pamaunke, Smith's Iles, or Accomack.*[6] No more than fifty miles. No one can verify or gainsay the Lost Colony murder story. And thus, for four hundred years, it has stood.

Execution

The principal players are fast disappearing. Raleigh, by order of King James on the former charge of high treason, is condemned to death, having been released long enough to make a voyage to Guiana. Rumor had it, recalling John White's misfortune, that Raleigh had intended to abandon his men there. *Another slander was raised,* he said, *that I would have gone away from them and left them.*[7] Queen Anne and her father, the King of Denmark, *begged his life;* others pleaded on behalf of Queen Elizabeth, who *so dearly respected* him.[8] James remained unmoved. You have *been as a star at which the world has gazed,* said the King's Attorney-General to Raleigh, *but stars may fall, nay they must fall when they trouble the sphere wherein they abide.*[9]

October 29, 1618, 9 A.M. Amid immense throngs of supporters, Raleigh is executed. *Thus died that Knight,* says John Shirley, *who was Spain's scourge and terror . . . whom the whole nation pitied, and several Princes interceded for; Queen Elizabeth's favourite, and her successor's sacrifice.*[10]

James is sharply condemned for his action, even within his own Court. The commotion continues for weeks without end. The Spanish ambassador anxiously reports that the outpouring of grief shows no signs of abating.[11] A Ned Wymark is hauled before the Privy Council to explain his comment that Raleigh's head *would do very well on the shoulders of* the Secretary of State. Wymark mumbles that what he meant was that *two heads are better than one.* Wymark — a relation of John White? He counted Wymarks among his kin.[12]

Wahunsonacock also dies this year — of a broken heart, they say.[13]

The Curious Travels of John Pory

It is not quite true that after Strachey's statement was released to the public no further searches were made for the Lost Colonists. There was one. One person in Jamestown did indeed believe the colonists were still alive. His name was John Pory.[14] A graduate of Gonville and Caius College, Cambridge, he entered the university a year after John White's colony sailed for Roanoke. He counted Raleigh as a friend. 1619. Pory is sent to Jamestown as the newly appointed Secretary of Virginia.

April 18, 1622. At Bow Church in London the Reverend Patrick Copland preaches a sermon, startling the congregation with news that hints of the Lost Colonists. *Master Pory* is to be encouraged, he says, *for his painful discoveries to the southward as far as the Choanoack.*[15]

Could it be? Was Pory renewing the search at last? Virginia Dare would be thirty-five years old. Pory was the first to make contact with the Chowanoc since Michael Sicklemore's failed expedition thirteen years before.

In February last, announced the Virginia Company, Pory discovered a country *(the great King giving him friendly entertainment, and desirous to make a league with us). . . . The Indians have made relation of a copper mine that is not far from thence, how they gather it, and the strange making of it.*[16]

The *King there told him,* a 1649 report confirmed, *that within ten days' journey westward towards the sun setting, there were a people that did gather out of a river sand, the which they washed in seives, and had a thing out of it, that they then put into the fire, which melted & became like to our copper, and offered to send some of his people to guide him to that place. But master Pory being not provided with men as he would have had of English,* returned to Jamestown.[17] He had been very close to finding the Lost Colonists. Closer, perhaps, than he ever knew.

March 1622. Before John Pory can return to the Chowanoc with better supplies, bitter fighting erupts again between the English and the Powhatan. An attack on Jamestown leaves 350 dead. Among them, Nathaniel Powell.[18] The English launch horrendous reprisals. It is bedlam. Pory quickly ships for England, lucky to get out alive. His sorrow may only be guessed for, surprisingly, his stake in the matter was personal. Pory's sister Anne married Robert Ellis.[19] A Thomas Ellis and son Robert were Lost Colonists. *And thus we left seeking our colony, that was never any of them found, nor seen to this day, 1622.*[20]

24 DEEP IN THE INTERIOR

In few words, mysteries are due to secrecy.
Sir Francis Bacon[1]

Where Are the Lost Colonists?

Our murder investigation is drawing to a close. John White's colonists were deliberately sabotaged and left for dead on Roanoke Island. Were it prosecuted, we would have a good case against Walsingham as perpetrator, with Raleigh as his intended victim. Essex we suspect of collusion: he was a useful tool. Slandering Raleigh, he effectively covered the crime and prevented a rescue. Contrary to received wisdom, the Spanish Armada had little to do with it. Other ships made it to the Indies despite the war. Raleigh's did not; someone made sure of it, and, in that sense, the Armada provided a convenient excuse. The awful truth of the Lost Colony is that it was never lost at all. Instead, it was deliberately concealed, prevented from contacting the outside world. John White, reduced to misery.

This is a murder case, not a case of missing persons. Still, the fact remains, 115 people have gone from Roanoke Island, and we must find them. The only hard evidence we have comes from their own hands: they said they were going to Croatoan. This barrier island was *where Manteo was born* and the people *our friends.*[2] So how, then, twenty years later, did Jamestown pick up reports that White's colonists were living in scattered villages deep within the interior? What are the pieces to this puzzle? If Virginia Company officials had only investigated more thoroughly, we would not now be asking questions.

The Colony Divides

We have several facts at our disposal. To begin with, the colonists were not killed on Roanoke Island. All the evidence indicates that the evacuation was orderly and complete. The site was dismantled and everything methodically removed except the heaviest items — weapons — which were left behind. Despite Stafford's violent attack on Dasamonquepeuc, Wingina's men took no reprisals. They stayed away. It is a phenomenal tribute to the Secotan and, perhaps, to the nature of White's colonists themselves, that there was no cross or sign of distress.

Nevertheless, the company clearly could not stay on Roanoke Island. Lane, as well as Stafford, had seen to that. Betrayed, left to die, and entirely alone, the colonists prepared to leave the island until such time as John White could effect their rescue — if indeed he could convince anyone in England of their plight. Before he left, it was discussed: *they intended,* White said, *to remove 50 miles further up into the main presently,* where they *mean to seat themselves.*[3]

The question is, did they? What about Croatoan? Someone went there, at any rate. They said so. Yet Croatoan was on the coast, not fifty miles inland. Moreover, its people were both unwilling and unable to feed 115 additional mouths, as they had made abundantly clear. They told us, White said, *not to gather or spill any of their corn, for that they had but little. We answered them that neither their corn, nor any other thing of theirs should be diminished by any of us . . . which answer seemed to please them well.*[4]

It is not unreasonable, then, to propose a separation.[5] The colony divided; what else could they do? The majority moved inland fifty miles, where food was abundant and the Chowanoc friends. A smaller number of White's colonists — Eleanor Dare and Margery Harvie, who had recently given birth; the woman with a nursing baby; a handful of men, perhaps, to keep them company — went to Croatoan to wait for White. This is conjecture, but certainly Eleanor Dare might logically have refused to leave the coast without her father. Residence at Croatoan made perfect sense. It was close to the sea; White was familiar with the place. Far easier to guarantee a successful reunion there than to leave detailed directions (on a tree!) to an uncertain destination in the interior. Those who remained behind would lead White to the main body of colonists.

Fifty Miles into the Main

It was decided; they were going. But why fifty miles into the main? The distance is specific and therefore must be of some significance. It could be that fifty miles was the limit of the Roanoke military base. When

Jamestown was first settled, the planters were advised that all the land, woods, and marshes within a fifty-mile radius of their seat was theirs to exploit.[6] Since White's instructions were merely to call at the fort before heading north, perhaps his beleaguered company wanted to make absolutely certain that they were clear of the Roanoke fort's claims. An interesting idea, because if White's colonists felt that they had no rights within that fifty-mile zone, then very likely they did *not* order the 1587 attack on Dasamonquepeuc led by Stafford. What we may be witnessing is a division between civilian and military.

On the other hand, fifty miles into the main would bring the colonists into the borderland between the Weapemeoc and Chowanoc countries. This was an ideal region southwest of the Dismal Swamp along the Chowan River. Amazingly rich, well wooded, plentiful. *Into the main and country, we found the soil to be fatter,* said Hariot, *the trees greater and to grow thinner, the ground more firm and deeper mould, more and larger champions, finer grass and as good as ever we saw any in England . . . more plenty of their fruits, more abundance of beasts, the more inhabited with people.* Even deer, because of *better feed,* were fatter.[7] Survival was the issue. Relocation to the Chowan River, therefore, was the best decision that could have been made.

So why have so many past investigations focused on the Chesapeake Bay? Much had changed since the City of Raleigh was first conceived of in England. There is no reason to believe, once the sabotage had occurred, that the colonists would stick to their original plan. Indeed, the greatest hope for their survival lay in intercepting White upon his return. White himself was very clear on this subject. If the colonists proposed removing fifty miles and no farther, then the Chesapeake Bay was no longer their intended destination. At least not until White returned. Perhaps not ever.

We must therefore direct our inquiry into the region in which White himself told us to look. The place to start is fifty miles into the main.

A Country Laid Desolate

It will be remembered that when John Smith questioned the Powhatan about the Lost Colonists, their advice was to search among the Chowanoc. Indeed, they seemed so certain that this was where White's company would be found that Michael Sicklemore was dispatched there first. From the accounts of Lane, Hariot, and Barlowe, what Smith expected him to find — along with the colonists — was a land *populously* inhabited, where villages lay *distant the one from the other not above 3 English miles,* and social gatherings brought *above 700 persons, young and old together, on a plain.*[8] Michael Sicklemore found nothing.

Instead, the picture the country presented was one of massive depopulation. The land was fertile, yet *the people few, the country most overgrown with pines.*[9] Villages were gone, old fields reverted to stands of pine, one of the first trees to reestablish. Since Sicklemore reported that the river was narrow, he could not have penetrated farther south than the town of Choanoke, where the channel widened considerably. Yet even here, *the very town itself,* Lane said, *is able to put 700 fighting men into the field, beside the forces of the Province itself.*[10]

How could two accounts be so different? The answer lies in Hariot's own journal. The *people began to die very fast,* he wrote of the Secotan, *and many in short space; in some towns about twenty, in some forty, in some sixty, and in one six score, which in truth was very many in respect of their numbers.*[11] Disease. Contagion occurred everywhere in the Americas that Europeans made contact. In New England attrition rates soared to a horrendous 90 percent among the Wampanoag and their neighbors. In the south, Spanish soldiers in Luna's expedition could not even recognize the ravaged terrain before their eyes as the same rich, thriving land they had encountered twenty years earlier with de Soto. They thought they had been bewitched. It *pleased Almighty God,* South Carolina's John Archdale croaked, *to send unusual sicknesses among them, as the smallpox, etc. to lessen their numbers.*[12]

Disease struck the Powhatan. *I have seen the death of all my people thrice,* Wahunsonacock lamented to Smith at the founding of Jamestown, *and not any one living of those three generations but myself.*[13] A Virginia colonist noted Powhatan faces riddled with pock marks, *full fraught with nodes botches and pulpable appearances in their foreheads.*[14] The illness may well have spread north from the Chowanoc country. Menatonon traded with the Powhatan.

Suppose the explanation was as follows: the main body of White's colonists separated and moved inland to the Chowan River. The Powhatan confirmed this, claiming that they had settled at Ohanoac — slightly farther than fifty miles from Roanoke — but well within Chowanoc territory.[15] And there it must have happened. A sudden and precipitous population decline would account very well for the situation Michael Sicklemore encountered. Few people, few villages, old fields *overgrown with pines.*

Political Upheaval

But where were the Lost Colonists? Given this situation, we might expect Sicklemore to have found them quite easily. After all, they would have been immune to many of the European diseases that were crippling Indian populations. If an epidemic struck the Chowanoc, it might well have left White's people unscathed. Yet Smith reported that Sicklemore found *little hope and less certainty* of finding them alive. Could this mean they were not immune? Or had something else happened?

Very likely. To understand what it might have been, we must look again at the early accounts. At the friendships and animosities. The layout of the land. And when we do, we discover that Raleigh's men, in their haste to settle the country, completely ignored warning signs that should have been evident to all. The King, Barlowe had said, *is called Wingina* and his capital Secota.[16] During Lane's tenure he shifted residence first to Roanoke Island, then to Dasamonquepeuc on the mainland. John White's map refers to the whole region — including Aquascogoc and Pomeioc — as the Secotan country. The Weapemeoc and Chowanoc to the north, along the upper edge of the sound, were Wingina's allies. Enemies completely surrounded them.

Granganimeo *had a great liking of our armour,* recalled Barlowe, *a sword and diverse other things which we had: and offered to lay a great box of pearl in gage for them.* Their wars, he reported, *are very cruel and bloody, by reason whereof, and of their civil dissensions, which have happened of late years amongst them, the people are marvellously wasted, and, in some places, the country left desolate.*[17]

Why didn't the English pay attention to this? Raleigh's men were blundering into an area racked by internal strife! No one thought it important enough to matter. And perhaps it wasn't, then. The Secotan-Chowanoc-Weapemeoc alliance was formidable. Strong enough to survive enemy attack and keep trade relations on an even keel. But what would happen if the demographics changed?

Catastrophic population loss seriously disrupts the balance of power. In New England, when disease crippled the Wampanoag, it left the neighboring and enemy Narragansett unscathed.[18] Under pressure, the Wampanoag welcomed a Pilgrim alliance to guarantee their own survival. In the short term, they were saving their lives. Likewise, the Westo and Savannah of South Carolina *broke out into an unusual civil war and thereby reduced themselves to a small number.* In North Carolina, *I was told . . . of a great mortality that fell upon the Pamlico Indians,* reported

John Archdale, *as also, that a nation of Indians called the Coranine, a bloody and barbarous people, were most of them cut off by a neighbouring nation: upon which I said, that it seemed to me as if God had an intention speedily to plant an English settlement thereabouts. . . . It is a pity they should be further thinned with civil quarrels . . . and indeed I myself, their late Governour, prevented the ruin and destruction of two small nations.*[19] The great chiefdoms of the Deep South, following epidemics spread by de Soto's men, fell to civil strife.[20]

Chaos and political upheaval marched hand in hand with pandemic disease. It could hardly be otherwise. If we are right in assuming Chowanoc numbers drastically diminished, then the political ramifications would be grim. The Secotan were already weakened. Wingina's men reduced to *a remnant.*[21] By now the political situation would be getting shaky. The region had been a war zone from the very beginning.

Enemy Nations

We know that the Secotan were defensively allied with the Chowanoc and Weapemeoc. But why? Who were the enemy nations they guarded against? Barlowe identified two who lived to the south and west: the Pamlico and Neusiok. Both small, they were in league with *the next king adjoining towards the setting of the sun.* At least three nations lived in that direction. Which one was it? Tuscarora? Woccon? Coree, whose land may have extended west of the Neusiok? Whoever they were, the Secotan evidently held their own against them, though they engaged in *mortal war.*[22] There was, however, another region whose terrors were far greater.

Beyond the dark and gloomy swamp forests looming behind the Carolina Outer Banks, the land rises steadily into drier ground. A country of hills and dense hardwoods, a different world altogether. It will be the mid-eighteenth century before Europeans penetrate this vast wilderness, whose forested trails were dappled by only the scantiest light. In Lane's day, it was a country few cared to enter, for in it lurked a powerful people, *whose very names were terrible unto them.* So terrible, that no one dared to guide Lane there. He had to haul a young boy in a handlock to show him the way. Their name was Mandoag.[23]

Slightly to the north, Jamestown learned of another nation called Monocan, who inspired a similar dread among the Powhatan. They and the Mandoag may have been allied. *They have many enemies,* Smith noted of the Powhatan, *namely all their westerly countries.*[24] Here, too, guides steadfastly refused to conduct Smith's men into the interior beyond the fall line. When Newport's party neared the western outskirts of Powhatan territory on the James River, their Arrohattoc guide suddenly began spending the night aboard their boat. A request for conduct over the cataracts to the Monocan towns visibly upset the *weroance* Parahunt, who *sought by all means to dissuade our Captain from going any further,* said Archer, *also he told us that the Monanacah was his enemy and that he came down at the fall of the leaf and invaded his country.* Each autumn the Monocan descended the rapids to raid the Powhatan towns. Newport, *out of his discretion,* wisely *returned to his boat.*[25] The Monocan and their friends, agreed Thomas Jefferson years later, *waged joint and perpetual war against the Powhatans.*[26]

These nations of the Piedmont are not to be taken lightly. We now remember what Richard Butler said — or tried to say — in 1585.[27] Sent to Hatorask by Grenville, he landed and journeyed inland some sixty miles into enemy terrain. A skirmish followed; Butler says he fought on behalf of the people of Hatorask. The account is confused; it is difficult to make out what region he was in. What Butler tells us, however, is that the Secotan had near neighbors with whom they were in a state of war. These were very likely the Mandoag.

When we turn again to the Roanoke journals, we find ominous news. The disease that ripped apart the Secotan country never touched their neighbors. Whenever *any of their enemies had abused us in our journeys,* Hariot reported of the Secotan, *hearing that we had wrought no revenge with our weapons,* and fearful that that was how *the matter should so rest,* they begged that those who *had dealt ill with us might in like sort die.*[28] Their fear was very real. To tip the balance meant death.

Strachey Revisited

If we are right in assuming that sometime during 1587 the Secotan-Chowanoc-Weapemeoc alliance was disabled, what was the consequence? The balance of power certainly shifted; therefore the question we must ask is this: Did the Chowanoc, the nation closest to the Mandoag frontier, come under attack?

Strachey may have had the answer all along, although it is very likely that he misunderstood what he heard. Gates was instructed to find surviving Lost Colonists who *escaped from the slaughter of Powhaton of Roanocke.*[29] But what does that mean? "Powhatan" was a title the English applied to Wahunsonacock and his empire. In reality, however, it was the name of a town. Barbour derives its meaning from two words: *otani,* or "town," and *pauwau,* a "wise speaker."[30] The *Powhaton of Roanoke,* then, might refer to a main village on Roanoke Island. By extension, perhaps, its leader. Whoever he was, he was not Wahunsonacock.

Strachey's interpretation of what was a garbled story at best was that the Powhatan — that is, Wahunsonacock — murdered John White's men shortly before the arrival of the Jamestown colony, and after they had lived peacefully with the Powhatan for *twenty and odd years.*[31] But what if Strachey got it wrong? It certainly wouldn't be the first time various English expeditions were muddled together as one and the same. For it was true: immediately before *White's* colony arrived — *twenty and odd years* before Jamestown — there was indeed an attack on Roanoke. Grenville's fifteen soldiers were set upon by Wingina's men. Someone with an imperfect understanding of the language might well confuse this story and its reference to a *Powhaton of Roanoke* for Wahunsonacock, Powhatan of Virginia.

But there is yet another possibility to consider, a different interpretation entirely, which bears directly on the Mandoag question — which is that Strachey unwittingly merged two stories: (1) White's colonists *were* attacked; (2) but not by the *Powhatan of Roanoke* Island, or by the Powhatan at all, but by someone else. Wahunsonacock's officials were right when they insisted that the Lost Colonists were with the Chowanoc, even though search parties found no one there. Reduced by disease, the Chowanoc had been attacked on the frontier. By a lifelong enemy. By the Mandoag. If this indeed happened, the Chowanoc would have lost. White's colonists would have suffered the same fate.

If this is not the explanation, then we must somehow account for a riddle posed by Smith's investigators: *Why were there English prisoners among the Mandoag?*

Captives in War

Before we consider this startling development, let us examine how this would have occurred. If the Chowanoc were attacked by the Mandoag, what specifically would have happened to the Lost Colonists? How were wars conducted? Who lived and who died? Barlowe tells a story that he heard from Manteo or Wanchese while in England. The Secotan, he said, once revenged themselves upon the Pamlico by inviting thirty of their women and *divers men* to Secota for a feast, *and when they were altogether merry,* the Secotan *came suddenly upon them, and slew them every one, reserving the women and children.*[32] That was how wars were conducted: women and children survived.

Smith was fortunate enough to witness a mock battle staged by the Powhatan, with half of Wahunsonacock's subjects posing as Monocan. Only men were "slain." It was *contrary to the law of nations,* Opechancanough explained, to kill women during war.[33] Male captives, unless adopted to make up for prior loss or, less frequently, enslaved, were rarely spared. *They seldom make war for lands or goods,* Smith testified, *but for women and children. . . . Yet the Weroances, women and children they put not to death, but keep them captives.*[34] Strachey recorded that Wahunsonacock attacked the Piankatank in 1608, killing twenty-four men but taking home the women, children, and their king.[35]

Males who surrendered to their enemies were also spared. The Powhatan and Monocan issued conditions, reported Smith, that *whosoever were vanquished, such as escape, upon their submission, should live, but their wives and children should be prize for the conquerors.*[36]

Michael Sicklemore found no trace of an English presence along the Chowan River — no houses, implements, fence posts or rails. If White's colony had stayed there for any duration — the *twenty odd years* Strachey suggested — then we would expect to find something. Instead everything points to long decay. Events therefore must have moved rapidly after the colonists' relocation, after the sudden shift in the balance of power.

John White's original company included seventeen women and eleven children. At the very least, three adult women and their babies must have remained behind at Croatoan. Provided that those who moved inland to the Chowan River survived the first winter without succumbing to disease, starvation, or accident, and no additional children were born, then we might expect a maximum of twenty-two female and child captives to have been taken by the Mandoag.

Of the original eighty-seven males, we do not know how many stayed at Croatoan, or what the attrition rate was before the attack on the Chowan. Neither are we supplied with details of the encounter, nor figures for how many died in their own defense. Male prisoners were customarily put to death, though even this was not necessarily the case. A number may have surrendered, been adopted, spared because (as Assistants) they were leaders, or preserved for the value of their labor.

Perhaps two dozen survived; the figure is pure guesswork.[37] In any case, we might suppose that a rather large number of English men, women, and children were whisked away into the interior, possibly around thirty-five, though it easily could have been more, and certainly less.

It is important to remember that the Chowanoc interrogated by Michael Sicklemore did not tell him that the Lost Colonists were dead. Their answer was deliberately vague, for they truly did not know what had become of the captives. They were absolutely correct when they said that there was *little hope and less certainty* of their fate. The English were, after all, prisoners of the Mandoag. We recall that this was precisely the place that the Powhatan indicated Smith should look if he failed to discover the Lost Colonists in any of the Chowanoc towns. Accordingly, Nathaniel Powell and Anas Todkill were dispatched to the Mandoag. *But nothing could we learn,* Smith had said, but the colonists *were all dead.* This statement is absolutely false. It is time to come at the truth of Smith's report.

Powell and Todkill

It was never the case that Jamestown investigators failed to find evidence of the Lost Colonists. They simply did not disclose their discoveries to the public. What their probe actually uncovered is revealed in confidential instructions issued to Sir Thomas Gates in May 1609. The directive reads like a treasure map: *Four days' journey from your fort southwards is a town called Ohonahorn seated where the River of Choanocki divideth itself into three branches and falleth into the sea of Rawnocke in thirty-five degrees.* Here, *two of the best rivers will supply you, besides you are near to the rich copper mines of Ritanoc and may pass them by one branch of this river, and by another Peccarecamicke, where you shall find four of the English alive, left by Sir Walter Rawely which escaped from the slaughter.* They *live under the protection of a wiroane called Gepanocon, enemy to Powhaton, by whose consent you shall never recover them, one of these were worth much labour.*[38]

This is the information that Powell and Todkill returned in their report to John Smith! It is this chilling fact — that Lost Colonists were held by the Mandoag as slaves — that must have panicked company officials to the core and that they didn't want the English public to hear. Instead of publishing the report, therefore, both they and Smith covered it up and declared the colonists dead. The truth is that Jamestown was simply unable to repatriate White's planters; disastrous publicity for a struggling colony to bear. Circulating the story that the Lost Colonists were dead took the pressure off officials to mount an expedition — doomed to fail — to retrieve them, and lent an unexpected boost to the propaganda campaign against the Powhatan.

Yet we know that, in addition to the four colonists held by Gepanocon, others were confined elsewhere in the interior. The Smith/Zúñiga map, as we shall see, pinpoints their locations. Reports were duly forwarded to London. And then the Virginia Company entered something horrible in the Stationers' Register, December 14, 1609: *Intelligence of some of our nation planted by Sir Walter Raleigh, (yet alive), within fifty miles of our fort . . . as is testified by two of our colony sent out to seek them, who, (though denied by the savages speech with them) found crosses & letters, the characters and assured testimonies of Christians newly cut in the barks of trees.*[39]

So Powell and Todkill had indeed tried to speak with them! Without success. White's company, too, had struggled desperately to make contact. Held out of sight, they nevertheless communicated. The Virginia Company found *for certain,* reported an incredulous Emanuel van Meteren, *that some English are still alive there . . . they have had word and have found crosses carved on trees.*[40]

But Jamestown did not understand the message. Neither Powell nor Todkill, in the dark recesses of the forest, were sure of what they had seen. A doorway was opened on the Lost Colonists for the briefest of moments. A glimpse. And then White's survivors were hustled back behind an impenetrable wall of silence. Cut off forever, they had signaled their last SOS. A forest of trees etched with crosses.

The Mandoag Are Gone

It seems a simple thing, now, to find the Mandoag. To enter their world and reclaim White's people. But when almost within our grasp, the Lost Colonists again disappear. War is declared on the Powhatan, who are accused of their murder. Jamestown stops searching. A neat cover-up. It holds for four centuries.

1650. A merchant named Edward Bland makes a startling discovery. Acting on a rumor that Englishmen are alive to the south, deep within the interior, he hires an Appomattoc guide and descends into the forest. His journal details the whole of the journey into this haunting world, yet when he reaches the spot where the Mandoag should have been, Bland discovers . . . *There are no such people.*

25 WHO ARE THE MANDOAG?

The Mangoaks (whose name, and multitude besides their valour is terrible to all the rest of the provinces), durst not for the most part of them abide us. . . .

Ralph Lane[1]

Edward Bland's Strange Journey

August 27, 1650. The path over which the eight travelers ride is slick and choked with rain, the packhorses frothy from ploughing weary miles through clinging mud. Darkness descended hours ago, the thick forest blotting out even the meager light of the stars, so that the blackness is suffocatingly complete. Well into the night, long past the hour when he would have favored sleep, Edward Bland and his companions, led by an Appomattoc guide named Pyancha, struggle across Nottoway Creek and into *a Nottoway Town,* startling the inhabitants. It was *Sir Walter Rawleigh's observation,* Bland murmurs, that *Paradise was created a part of this earth.*[2] In 35 degrees north latitude.

This night is the first in an odyssey that will carry Bland into the depths of an uncharted wilderness, both geographical and human, and it is natural that his thoughts should turn to Raleigh, for his mission clearly involves the Lost Colonists. At the behest of Governor William Berkeley of Virginia, he has plunged into the trackless sea of timber lapping at the southern edge of Jamestown and her satellite communities to make contact with certain mysterious Englishmen rumored to be alive among a nation known as the Tuscarora. Their territory, one in which Europeans have never yet set foot, lies to the southwest of the Secotan country.[3] Bland's instructions are to locate the Tuscarora *to speak with an Englishman amongst them, and to inquire for an English woman cast away long since,* who was *amongst those nations.*

But the next night, the forest dripping with mist, a Nottoway king named Chounterounte enters Bland's quarters *frowning, and with a countenance noting much discontent,* urges him *to go no farther, alleging there was no English there, that the way was long,* and the passage *very bad by reason of much rain that had lately fallen and many rotten marshes and swamps there was to pass over; in fine, we found him, and all his men, very unwilling we should go any farther.* Bland resolves to push forward, regardless, prompting Chounterounte to show *a fear in his countenance.*

By the following morning, as Bland's company prepares to depart, Chounterounte edges closer to the truth of the matter. He again *came privately unto us,* said Bland, *in a most serious manner,* confiding that *he lively apprehended our danger and that our safety concerned him . . . for that he certainly knew that the nations we were to go through would make us away by treachery.* Bland ignores him and pursues his course.

The Meherrin

The long, tiring day progresses without mishap. At night, with gloom again pervading the forest, the path underfoot grows so intensely dark that only with difficulty can the travelers pick their way forward. The deathly silence that has accompanied them undisturbed for many miles is suddenly shattered as they catch the sound of voices and discern a muted light flickering ahead. The party passes through a dark copse of trees with trunks *five feet* wide and *a hundred foot* tall, and enters a town called *Maharineck.* Who these people are, or what their connection to the neighboring nations is, is never disclosed. Bland only reports that its leader is *a youth.*

The Englishmen are not the only visitors to this town. Soon after their arrival, as the horses are watered, a Tuscarora man presents himself and *told us that the Englishman* we were searching for *was a great way off at the further Tuskarood Town.* Far to the south. Bland immediately hires him to convey certain letters to this stranger, hastily written in English, Latin, Spanish, French, and Dutch. It is arranged that the Englishman will be brought to them at a place called *Hocomowananck,* where they agree to rendezvous.[4]

There would seem to be a great parade of foreigners among the Meherrin. They were nothing, apparently, if not rich in guests, for Bland is next accosted by a man introduced as the *werrowance of Hocomawananck River* himself which, by any standard, was undeniably convenient. What this leader has to say, however, is of primary importance. There is a tremendously powerful nation nearby, he tells Bland, known as the *Wainoakes.* The Tuscarora, many thousands strong, can attest to this: the Wainoke block their passage north to Jamestown, preventing trade. It is difficult to imagine anyone inhibiting the movement of a nation as numerous as the Tuscarora. We begin to suspect that it is the Wainoke who created such terror in Chounterounte that he urged Bland to abort his mission. This is the nation whose territory he would have to cross should he try to contact the Englishmen directly.

The following day, intent on keeping his appointment at Hocomawananck, Bland pushes southwest to the swollen Roanoke River. And here something strange occurs, for notwithstanding his friendly conversation the day before with the Hocomawananck leader, both Bland's Appomattoc and Nottoway guides immediately grow nervous and wary, asserting that *the Hocomawananck Indians were very treacherous.* Only at this juncture do they tell Bland what they knew all along: that the Hocomawananck chief was an impostor. He was, in fact, Meherrin.

What on earth is going on? It would seem that both the Meherrin and the Wainoke — whoever they are — are intent on impeding Bland's progress. The Appomattoc and Nottoway guides, with increasing agitation, exhibit great uneasiness at the party's perilous position, which is now somewhere north of the Roanoke River. Hocomawananck territory. Their immediate response is to get out, informing Bland that if he follows the river upstream as he intends, he will encounter two nations — the *Occonacheans and the Nessoneicks* — whose towns are built on islands in the river. At their urging, Bland proceeds no farther, merely noting something that strikes him as an oddity. The people *of this region,* he says, *have beards.* And, he adds, *we saw among them copper.*

Double Dealing

September 2. The bizarre events continue. At dawn Bland is jarred awake by yet another remarkable visitor. This time, a man calling himself Occonosquay and claiming to be the *son to the Tuscarora King,* arrives to inform the party that the Englishman they are supposed to meet at Hocomawananck is now at his house *a long way off.* He requests that they follow him there instead.

Bland refuses, hurriedly retracing his steps to what he inexplicably assumes to be the safety of the Meherrin town. To his surprise, the people this time greet him as though *they were angry at us,* owing to *Wainoake spies* who had been there in his absence. Bland now belatedly realizes that his first "Tuscarora" visitor was also an impostor. Rather than carry his letters to the Englishman as directed, the imposter delivered them into the hands of the Wainoke, *and we had information that at that time there were other English among the Indians.* Bland's party, at last considering itself in grave danger, beats a retreat to Jamestown by the swiftest route possible. They are trailed all the way by *Wainoake spies, set out there to prevent our journeyings.*

What's in a Name?

When we look at John White's map, it is clear that much of Bland's route lay within the area delineated "Mandoag." So where was this nation? Why did Bland never encounter them? The various countries far and near were carefully pointed out by his guides, yet none at all went by the name of Mandoag. Could Hariot, Lane, and White — independently — have got the location wrong? Or had the Mandoag and their Lost Colony captives moved away? Not likely, for Bland heard a great deal about the presence of Englishmen in the area. So how could they remain invisible? How could a people, so well known in Lane's time for their ferocity, independence, and wealth, now be so wholly out of the picture? Or were they?

The truth is that the Mandoag were present, but were not what they seemed. Indeed, Bland was among them, and never even knew it. To understand what happened, we must examine the written reports from other regions. We must translate a word. We know that Lane and Hariot learned about the Mandoag through conversations with Secotan and Chowanoc informants, both of whom spoke Algonquian. The word "Mandoag" is documented among this language family the entire length of the eastern seaboard, from the Carolinas to Canada and far interior, with dialectical variations: Mangoak, Mangoage, Manató, Mengwe, Mingo, Doeg, Toag. The forms are slightly different. The meanings are all the same. Mandoag, the *stealthy* and the *treacherous,* means *enemy.* Distrusted; *snakes.*[5]

Bland has seen them. Or heard of them. The problem is, of the nations he encountered, which were the Mandoag?

Copper

In order to find the Mandoag, we need evidence — something, anything — to go on. Without it, we are hunting for a needle in a haystack. The region is large, the nations many. And yet we do know something. A single, tangible piece of information has been within our grasp all along. A clue, imprinted in the journals, to guide us. It is repeated incessantly. The writing insists upon it. The formula is simple: *the Mandoag use copper.* This connection appears again and again — the Mandoag ornament their homes with it. The Mandoag hire out as mercenaries for it. The Mandoag control access to the mines of Chaunis Temoatan. The Lost Colonists are last reported at the *rich copper mines of Ritanoc.* Like the Spaniards, the Mandoag are formidable because of their wealth. The Monocan, too, have copper. Jamestown repeatedly tries to locate the source, vaguely described as lying somewhere to the southwest.

Until recently it was assumed that all native copper in the region was imported via trade from Indian mines on Lake Superior. This is now known to be false. Copper occurs in sheets within rock at various localities in the Southeast. Scientific analysis of metal artifacts recovered demonstrates that the majority of southeastern copper was obtained and worked locally.[6]

Lake Superior, then, can only serve as an analogy. Mines there were often merely surface quarries in which copper sheeting was extracted from folds sandwiched between rock. Newport was told of a similar excavation process used west of the Powhatan. However, Lake Superior metalworkers also culled copper from extensive subsurface pits. Of those documented, many were more than twenty feet deep. In Minnesota, at the bottom of a twenty-six-foot abandoned shaft, a six-ton mass of copper was discovered, along with more than ten cartloads of hammers.[7] Mauls, shovels, chisels, bowls, and ladders were the tools of the copper trade.

Extracted ore was annealed by cold hammering. That is, the copper was heated by fire to very high temperatures, from 900° to 1,500° Fahrenheit, then hammered and heated again until sheet metal was formed. Heat prevented brittleness. They *dig a hole in the ground in which they put the ore,* reported a Jamestown colonist, duly impressed, *and make thereon a great fire, which causeth it to run into a mass, and become malleable.* English copper only became pliable after it *passeth eleven fires.*[8]

Conversion of copper into sheets for trade, then, was a time-consuming operation, involving the mining of raw material, the stoking of fires, and the melting and hammering of ore into sheets before delivery to artisans. The activity was labor-intensive, which is why Strachey — in the midst of reporting the Lost Colony murder — recorded something truly astonishing. At *Ritanoc,* he said, *the Weroance Eyanoco preserved 7 of the English alive, four men, two boys, and one young maid (who escaped and fled up the River of Chaonoke) to beat his copper, of which he hath certain mines at the said Ritanoc.*[9] Ritanoc has never been translated. Yet a clue to its meaning may lie in the Delaware word *liteu,* relating to fire, meaning literally "it burns."[10] *Oc* is a locative ending. *Ritanoc,* then, may be rendered as a "Place of Fire," a "Burned Place." The Lost Colonists were at a center of copper manufacture. Ore was annealed over fire into malleable sheets.

But where was Ritanoc? Jamestown investors learned from Hariot that *Southwest of our old fort in Virginia, the Indians often informed him that there was a great melting of red metal. . . . Besides, our own Indians have lately revealed either this or another rich mine of copper or gold in a town called Ritanoe near certain mountains lying west of Roanoac.*[11] Ritanoc was either the same place as Chaunis Temoatan, or familiar to it.

Yet here we encounter another problem, for the location of Chaunis Temoatan was never determined. As far as we know, no Europeans ever went there. To find the Mandoag, then, we must discover what neither Lane nor Newport nor Virginia Company officials ever did. We must find the copper. We must find the mines of Chaunis Temoatan.

Chaunis Temoatan

Copper ornaments worn by the Secotan were made, *as we understood,* said Hariot, *by the inhabitants that dwell farther into the country where, as they say, are mountains and rivers.*[12] Because of this description, past investigations of Chaunis Temoatan have focused on the Blue Ridge Mountains of the Appalachian chain and the gold-producing region of northern Georgia.[13] And have found nothing.

It is *a thing most notorious to all the country,* Lane enthused, *that there is a province to the which the said Mangoaks have recourse and traffic up that River of Moratico, which hath a marvellous and most strange mineral. This mine is so notorious among them, as not only to the savages dwelling up the said river, and also to the savages of Choanoke, and all them to the westward, but also to all them of the main: the country's name is of fame, and is called Chaunis Temoatan.*[14]

Here is a stumbling block, for the River Moratico — so designated on early maps for the Roanoke — flows from the northwest. Yet Hariot reported the mines to be located southwest of the fort on Roanoke Island. Neither man had ever been there. Hariot, at least, could speak the language and was confident of what he had heard. In fact, both may have been correct: Chaunis Temoatan lay to the southwest, but the normal route to it — or, more properly, to the province that retailed its product — lay northwest via the Roanoke River.

Skiko, who had been a prisoner of the Mandoag but had never been to Chaunis Temoatan, declared it to be *twenty days' journey overland from the Mangoaks to the said mineral country, and that they passed through certain other territories between them and the Mangoaks* before they arrived.[15]

How far was a day's travel? Strachey said that an Indian march is *some fourteen or sixteen miles a day,* while Smith reported six days' travel from Jamestown to the village of Powhatan, approximately fifty miles.[16] Menatonon directed Lane to the Chesapeake Bay, a journey up the Chowan River, followed by a four-day descent overland.[17] Supposing the foot portion to begin near the current Carolina/Virginia border, the four days would correspond to about forty miles. We might conclude, therefore, that a day's travel was anywhere from ten to fifteen miles — presumably less in swampy areas, more on higher and drier ground.

Here we have, then, a reasonably accurate measurement. Chaunis Temoatan lay twenty days away, or roughly two to three hundred miles deep in the interior, in a direction angling southwest from Roanoke Island. On a modern map, this would place us somewhere between the Haw River west of Chapel Hill as the lesser distance, and a point east of the Catawba River at, say, Mooresville, as the greater.

But was there copper here? There certainly was! The exact area we have delineated as the probable position of Chaunis Temoatan lies within a geological formation known as the Carolina Slate Belt.[18] A zone of volcanic and faulted rock consisting of rhyolitic to basaltic flows and tufts, it contains deposits of gold, copper, lead, and zinc. Copper occurs in mineralized veins three to five feet wide, tending to the northeast, with deep pockets and dips.

When we examine the Slate Belt more closely, however, we discover a curious pattern. The formation stretches in a southwesterly band from Granville County in the northeast to Union County in the southwest. Its width varies from twenty-five to seventy miles. The thickest portion of the belt, where the heaviest concentration of metallic deposits is located, occurs roughly in its middle, in present-day Randolph County. Just to the west lie faults of gold and silver, giving rise to a rash of modern town names such as Gold Hill, Eldorado, Richfield, Silver Hill, and Goldston. Lane observed that some of the copper of Chaunis Temoatan was soft and pale, like gold. Tests conducted by his mineralogist on samples of Secotan copper revealed trace amounts of silver. The copper mine we are looking for, then, should optimally be near all three mineral deposits. Is

Randolph County our target area? Distance from Roanoke Island: approximately 250 miles.

The Intriguing Zúñiga Map

If we are right that Randolph Country is the location of Chaunis Temoatan, then we have defined the east/west coordinates within which the Mandoag operated. We must now find the boundaries to the north and south. As a result of John Smith's investigations of the Lost Colonists, he had a map drawn on which he pinpointed their known locations. A copy of this map, as we have seen, fell into the hands of Spanish agent Pedro de Zúñiga and has been preserved.[19]

When we examine the Zúñiga map, we find that south of the James River, four additional rivers are depicted, which we will label A, B, C, and D. Against the southernmost, D, is a notation that appears to read: *Pakerakanick. Here remaineth 4 men clothed that came from roonock to okanahowan.* River C bears the label *Morattico* toward its mouth, and *Machemenchecock* along its higher reaches. Beside River B is the marking: *Panawiock. here the king of paspahegh reported our men to be and went to se.* Finally, A is a river divided into three branches: *Chawwone, Ocanahowan,* and a third, rather unintelligible, word that appears to be *Nottawmusawone.*

The translation of this map is difficult. The words are very likely skewed. What foreign sounds, for example, did Smith actually hear and try to record? Did Zúñiga copy the letters correctly? The handwriting is small and hard to read. Have we ourselves accurately deciphered each letter? Is an *a* really an *a* and not an *e*? What about the letters *n, m, w,* and *u,* which often look the same? And, finally, what connection is there between this map and the Mandoag or the copper mines?

1890. The first person to attempt to decipher the Zúñiga map is Alexander Brown.[20] He identifies the rivers D, C, and A as the Neuse, Tar, and Roanoke, speculating — from the wording on River D — that Ocanahowan is located on the Neuse. He places River B in present-day Sampson County, and reads the text as: *Here the King of Paspahege reported our men to be and wants to go.*

1908. Historian Samuel A'Court Ashe includes a rough sketch of Brown's tracing of Zúñiga's map in his study of North Carolina.[21] In doing so, he transcribes the foreign words on Rivers D and A as *Pakrakwick, Ocanahonan,* and *Chawwan.* Pages later, he spells them differently — demonstrating how orthographic errors can result from the hand of a single copyist. Ashe locates *Ochanahonan* on the Nottoway River, *Panawicke* between the Chowan and the Roanoke, and *Peccarecamek* on the Tar.

1969. Philip Barbour reproduces Zúñiga's map from a photograph of the original.[22] He interprets the words on River D as *Pakerakanick* and *Oconohowan.* For B, the location of Panawiock, he reads: *Here the king of paspahegh reported our men to be and went to se[e].* He places Pekerakanick on the Neuse River, Panawiock between the Roanoke and Pamlico Rivers, and Ocanahowan on the south side of the Roanoke.

1985. David Beers Quinn reprints Barbour's reproduction and identifies the following: River D — *Pakeranik, roonock,* and *ihanowan* — on either the Neuse or the Pamlico.[23] River C — *morottico.* River B — *Panawick. here the king of paspageh reported one man to be.* Quinn equates this with the Secotan town of Pomeioc on Wysocking Bay. River A — *Chawanoac* and *Ocanahowan* — on Albemarle Sound. He places Ocanahowan on the Roanoke River.

A summary of the confusion is as follows: *Pakerakanick* (D): on the Neuse or Tar or Pamlico; *Morattico* (C): the Pamlico, Tar, or Roanoke; *Panawiock* (B): between the Roanoke and the Chowan, or on Wysocking Bay at the site of Pomeioc; *Ocanahowan* (A): on the Neuse or Roanoke or Albemarle Sound or Nottoway River. So much for the experts. The problem, however, does not at all lie with them. It lies with Smith. There is something wrong with the map.

Let us begin with River C, labeled Morattico. This is certainly the Roanoke, for early maps equate the two names. Moratoc, we remember, was the abandoned town Lane visited on the Roanoke River. If C is the Roanoke, then D is very likely the next river to the south, the Tar. Zúñiga's map depicts this river branching to the right. The Tar also has this feature: Fishing Creek north of the modern town of Tarboro.[24]

If we are correct that C is the Roanoke, then B, a small waterway, might well be Cashie Creek. However, it is precisely here that we encounter a problem. *This portion of the map is incorrectly oriented.* The section covering Virginia, comprising the Chesapeake Bay drainage area, was drawn according to the standard orientation used by European mapmakers, north/south. Rivers B, C, and D were similarly aligned. However, River A is twisted in the wrong direction by ninety degrees. River A, the Chowan, is oriented east/west.

It is this peculiarity of the Zúñiga map that has confused previous investigators, who mistook the Chowan for the Chowan and Roanoke combined, which meant that the locations of Lost Colony survivors were never clearly identified. Once corrected, and compared to the map John White made, the four prongs of the Chowan River are clearly distinguishable: Bennett's Creek, Wiccacon River, the Meherrin, and the Nottoway — the split with the Blackwater River farther north is not portrayed. According to the Zúñiga map, Ocanahowan appears to be located on, or south of, a branch of the Chowan.[25]

Such a positioning mistake also occurred on John White's map of North America.[26] He composed it by fusing together three separate charts. The northernmost, oriented north/south, depicted the Outer Banks and was drawn from onsite surveys by Raleigh's men. The southern portion was copied from LeMoyne's map of Florida. It also was oriented north/south. The middle section, however, was taken from Ayllon's Spanish map of 1520. It was inserted incorrectly. It is oriented east/west.

The Zúñiga map supplies us with the missing coordinates for our search. We now know that we are looking for the Lost Colonists in an area bounded by Randolph County to the west, the Chowan River to the east, the Tar River to the south, and the Meherrin River — a branch of the Chowan — to the north. But if the Mandoag were here, so was something else whose impact on the Lost Colony would be devastating.

The Great Trading Path

If we return to the Carolina Slate Belt and observe it more closely, we begin to see an interesting pattern. Like a game of connect-the-dots, the copper deposits form a northeast arc within the same overall pattern of the belt.[27] Curiously, Interstate 85 — a modern highway — follows this configuration most of its way, shadowing the Southern Railway, whose lines were constructed in the same general arc many years before. But why? What prompted modern railroad and highway engineers to follow this route? For it is evident that these transportation lines were not built at random, but follow a very definite course.

What this course was is revealed in the reports of the earliest Europeans to enter the interior in the wake of Edward Bland: John Lederer (1670), James Needham and Gabriel Arthur (1673), John Lawson (1701), and William Byrd (1728). What they described is astonishing. There was a great highway, they said, stretching more than five hundred miles into the interior, known as the Great Trading Path. Beginning in Granville County, North Carolina, it ran in a southwesterly course, crossing the

Tar, Flat, Little, Eno, Haw, Alamance, and Deep Rivers. At the Yadkin, it passed over luxurious banks of grass *and prodigiously large trees,* and here the traders rested. Six miles farther on, it crossed Crane Creek, so named for the *rendezvous of great armies of cranes.*[28] After that, it reached the Catawba and there, at a distance of 250 miles from the Roanoke River, the trail was half complete. Snaking to the east and west were secondary arteries, linking the Appalachian Mountains to the Carolina coastal plain. The Great Trading Path itself ended at present-day Augusta, Georgia.

But this highway was also called by another name, after the nation who controlled its northern terminus: the Occaneechi. Bland was the first Englishman to have heard of these people and of their fortified town on an island in the middle of the Roanoke River. Four miles long, covered with timber and peach trees, the island lay at the confluence of the Staunton and the Dan, providing the only easy access across the Roanoke. Flanking it on the east and west were swift, churning rapids. The Occaneechi, Lederer said, are *fixed here in great security, being naturally fortified with fastnesses of mountains and water on every side.*[29]

South of this, the Occaneechi Trading Path disappeared into the Carraway Mountains — a land of *swift currents* and *very high mountains.*[30] This was Randolph County, the copper- and gold-producing region of Chaunis Temoatan. The Occaneechi territory, at the northern edge of the Carolina Slate Belt, also contained deposits of copper. *There are so many appearances of copper in these parts,* Byrd marveled, that the English *inhabitants seem to be all mine-mad.*[31]

In the colonial period, both Virginia and North Carolina will seize on the potential of the Great Trading Path. Fur traders will coax one-hundred-horse caravans along the highway, exchanging hides for guns, powder, hatchets, kettles, red and blue duffels, rum, and brass rings. But the trade does not start here, at this late date.[32] The route existed long before. Nor do colonial traders create Occaneechi Island, with its famous trade mart, a warehouse for the brisk exchange of copper, salt, shells, and mica. The Occaneechi are middlemen, and foreign visitors flock to the town. When Lederer arrives there, he finds four ambassadors of an original delegation of fifty, *whose bodies were painted in various colours with figures of animals.* They have come from the northwest, all but four dying *en route* from *famine and hard weather, after a two-month's travel by land and water in quest of this island of Akenatzy.*[33] *Occaneechi,* an Algonquian term, similar to the Cree word *Woconichi* — the place *Where People Gather.*[34]

They *have a sort of general language,* reported an amazed Robert Beverly, *which is understood by the chief men of many nations as Latin is in most parts of Europe. . . . The general language here used is said to be that of the Occaneechees, though they have been but a small nation, ever since those parts were known to the English.* Occaneechi is also used by priests in ceremonies throughout Virginia, *as the Catholics of all nations do their mass in Latin.*[35] Years later the remnant of this language, recorded at the military camp of Fort Christanna, is found to contain fragments of Siouan, Algonquian, and Iroquoian words, suggesting a language used in business transactions. Occaneechi, a trade jargon spoken for five hundred miles.[36]

Border Patrol

Strategically located on their island fortress, the powerful but numerically small Occaneechi control access to the Great Trading Path. As such, they determine who shall and shall not enter. John Lederer is forced to obtain permission from the neighboring Saponi even to pass into Occaneechi territory. At *Sapon, a village of the Nahyssans . . . situated upon a branch of Shawan,* the people *examined me strictly whence I came, whither I went, and what my business was.* Satisfying them, I *got my passport, having given my word to return to them within six months. The Saponi,* in contrast to the Powhatan, *were people of a high stature, warlike and rich.* A subtribe of the Monocan, they were friends of the Occaneechi. Significantly, Lederer observed a *great store of pearl* in their temple, *which they had won, amongst other spoils,* from a coastal people.[37] Which people did they mean?

If Lederer thought the Saponi kept the trail well guarded, he was wholly unprepared for the severity of the Occaneechi. A Rickohockan ambassador and five attendants, their faces daubed with gold pigment, *in which mineral these parts do much abound,* arrive — and are murdered in the night. *Every nation gives his particular ensign or arms,* said Lederer. The Occaneechi's is *a serpent. A serpent,* he added, expresses *wrath.*[38]

When James Needham and Gabriel Arthur neared the Occaneechi, their eight Powhatan guides turned back, showing great *unwillingness* to enter the country. The expedition was aborted. Although they tried again with eight new guides, all but one Appomattoc man turned around at Occaneechi Island, and *no more durst to go along with them* beyond. Needham himself approached the island, but *was stopped there by ye Occhenchees from going any farther.* He finally persuaded them to let him pass, only to be killed later by his Occaneechi guide. Gabriel Arthur, who had crossed the barrier with permission the year before in the company of fifty-one Tomahitan traders, was ambushed in the dead of night by the Occaneechi upon his return. The *Occhenee began to work their plot and made an alarm,* calling all to arms. The Tomahitan flee, leaving their trade goods scattered. Hidden behind trees, the *moon shining bright,* Arthur escapes *and runs for it all night.* Occaneechi Island is *strongly fortified by nature,* he said, *and that makes them so insolent, for they are but a handful of people, besides what vagabonds repair to them, it being a receptacle for rogues.*[39]

Hunting Apes in the Mountains

It is a known fact that North Carolina does not have, nor ever has had, monkeys. This being the case, we might suppose that William Strachey had that rare sense of humor that finds levity in the most obtuse subjects, for we see him relaying a rather strange tale from a Powhatan informant named Machumps, involving primates and the Lost Colonists. At *Peccarecamek and Ochanahoen,* said Machumps, *the people have houses built with stone walls, and one story above another, so taught them by those English who escaped the slaughter at Roanoak . . . the people breed up tame turkeys about their houses, and take Apes into the mountains.*[40]

A helpful synopsis reads: *Houses of stone, tame turkeys, and monkeys, supposed at Peccartcanick.*[41]

Historians, not surprisingly, have dismissed Strachey's statement out of hand. In so doing, they have discarded a very important clue. Nor is it the only word amiss in Strachey's narrative. We read elsewhere that Powhatan gardens are planted with fruits and apoke. Apoke, from Powhatan *uhpooc,* means "tobacco."[42] Strachey recorded the word in Algonquian, not English. There is no reason to assume that he did not do the same with *Apes.*

At *Peccarecamicke,* Sir Thomas Gates was told, *you shall find four of the English alive, left by Sir Walter Raleigh. . . . They live under the protection of a wiroans called Gepanocon.* And *were worth much labour.* At *Peccarecanick,* added Strachey, they have English-style houses and hunt *apes* in the mountains. The Cree would understand this as *apisk,* the Pequot as *apess,* and the Wicocomoco as *tapisco.*[43] The word is Algonquian: it is a noun and denotes "metal." Strachey was telling us that in Gepanocon's town, Lost Colonists were used for the gathering of ore.

This interpretation is supported by the names of the surrounding people themselves. 1898: Linguist William Tooker translates the Powhatan names for nations within the enemy Monocan Confederacy. The Monocan capital, Strachey said, was Rassawek, *unto whom the Mowhemenchuges, the Massinnacacks, the Monohassanughs, and other nations pay tribute.*[44]

Rassauwek, from *wassau* "it is bright, it glistens," conjoined to *wek,* "house or home." *Monocan,* from *Mona-ack'añough. Mona,* "to dig" + *ack,* "land or earth" + *añough,* "nation or people." Meaning: "People Who Dig the Earth." Freely translated: "Miners." Smith's *Monanacah Rahowacah [Mona-ack-añough-wassau-wek],* therefore, meant *the home of the people who dig the earth for something bright. Massinnacack,* "The Stone Place." *Monahassanughs,* "People Who Dig the Rock," synonymous with a nation called Tutelo.[45] Their last known king was Kolstáhagu, meaning "Dwelling in Stone."[46]

Closing in on the Mandoag

Our investigation, then, has come to this: we believe that the majority of the Lost Colonists relocated to the Chowan River, where they, along with their much-weakened Chowanoc hosts, were attacked and defeated by the Mandoag. We know that the Mandoag were powerful and greatly feared, that they controlled access to the copper-producing region of Chaunis Temoatan, and that these mines were located in a mountainous, river-laced region twenty days' journey — or approximately 250 miles — away from the Mandoag country. We have identified a place within the Carolina Slate Belt, modern Randolph County, that physically fits this description, both in terms of ore content and in the Deep River and Carraway Mountains that characterize it. We know that the vast highway, known as the Great Trading Path, ran through this location approximately ninety miles south of Occaneechi Island, a vital trading center and distribution terminus for products moving up from the south. We know that the Occaneechi rigorously monitored entry onto the Trading Path, and thus controlled northern (as well as eastern and western) access to the mines. We also know that the Occaneechi were small in number and that other nations, allied to them, performed similar policing functions. We know that the Mandoag were mercenaries and that they hired themselves out for copper. The Occaneechi likely welcomed such assistance. The question remains, who are the Mandoag? And where are the Lost Colonists?

Which Nation?

The North Carolina Piedmont is a highly complex region, made all the more difficult because it is imperfectly known. From John White's map, as well as Lane's description, the Mandoag bordered the Chowanoc/Secotan frontier, a hilly country penetrated by the Roanoke River. We now know their characteristics and the coordinates of their sphere of influence. By a process of elimination, we should be able to identify them.

Recent historians have favored the theory that the Mandoag are Tuscarora.[47] Yet this assumption rests upon faulty evidence. The Secotan-Chowanoc-Weapemeoc were Algonquian, therefore their enemies probably were not; on this, everyone agrees. *Mandoag* is a name commonly applied by Algonquians to enemy nations. Before 1870 the only other known linguistic group in North Carolina was Iroquoian; therefore the Mandoag were proclaimed to be an Iroquoian-speaking people. This classification held despite later evidence that revealed that most of the nations of the Piedmont spoke Siouan, a very different language. Nevertheless, since the Tuscarora were Iroquoian — so went the theory — they must be Mandoag. Three other pieces of evidence were also offered to support this claim: (1) Population: the Mandoag were powerful and strong. In sheer numbers, the Tuscarora were supreme. (2) Pakerakanick was located on the Tar, so were the Tuscarora. (3) Bland's mysterious Englishmen were in a Tuscarora town.

The Tuscarora theory can be rejected on the following grounds: (1) It does not necessarily follow that numerical strength equals power. The Occaneechi were reputedly the most powerful nation for a distance of five hundred miles because of their strategic position and copper monopoly. Furthermore, a small nation does not at all preclude the possibility of confederacies and alliances, which could render them very strong indeed. (2) Pakerakanick was located on the Tar River, but not necessarily within Tuscarora territory. Other nations lived west of the Tuscarora, and Pakerakanick could have belonged to them. (3) The fact that two of the Lost Colonists were among the Tuscarora means nothing more than that the Tuscarora may have obtained them through trade, intermarriage, or adoption from another nation. Their presence does not prove that the Tuscarora are Mandoag. (4) The Tuscarora were Iroquoian and may indeed have been antagonistic to the Secotan. This does not guarantee, however, that they were the Mandoag. They may merely have been the nation to the west that Barlowe reported to be at war with the

Secotan. Or maybe not. In 1654 Francis Yeardley's traders visited Roanoke Island and were taken by its *great Commander* on a friendly visit to the neighboring Tuscarora.[48] In 1711, in response to colonial abuses, the Secotan and Tuscarora formed a powerful alliance and jointly declared war on North Carolina.[49] In point of fact, the only direct evidence we have indicates that they were friends! (5) The Tuscarora were located west-southwest of the Secotan. We would expect the Mandoag, by all accounts, to be farther north.

The Nottoway are more problematic.[50] For years, it was assumed that they were Algonquian, despite the fact that they were called Nottoway by the Powhatan, a derogatory term applied to enemies. This meant little, for the Powhatan were antagonistic to many Algonquian nations not part of their confederacy. Bland himself was told that the Nottoway were allied to the Chowanoc, their near neighbors. The Nottoway carefully preserved a memorial over the dead body of a Chowanoc king slain by the Powhatan. Nevertheless, in 1820, the Nottoway were judged to be Iroquoian, based on a word list supplied by Edie Turner, one of their last surviving speakers.[51] Therefore: (1) Because the Mandoag were already considered Iroquoian, the hypothesis was advanced that the Nottoway were Mandoag. (2) The word *Nottoway* is Algonquian, meaning "snake" or "adder."[52] They, like the Mandoag, were clearly enemies to somebody; hence their name. (3) The Nottoway were in a location roughly consistent with Mandoag territory, though slightly too far north.

The Nottoway theory may be contested for these reasons: (1) There is no proof that the Mandoag were Iroquoian, therefore identification with the Nottoway on this basis alone is untenable. (2) The Nottoway were not enemies of the Chowanoc, but allied to them. They took the Chowanoc side against the Powhatan in the dispute over the slain Chowanoc king. (3) There is no evidence that the Nottoway were regionally powerful or strong like the Mandoag. Bland reported that their leaders were fearful of both the Wainoke and the residents of Hocomawananck; nor did they seem very much at ease among the Meherrin. (4) There is no evidence that the Nottoway dealt in copper, controlled access to the mines of Chaunis Temoatan, or hired themselves out as mercenaries.

By far the most enigmatic candidate are the Meherrin.[53] (1) Their location was immediately south of the Nottoway, therefore conceivably within Mandoag territory, though perhaps still a little too far north. (2) Their behavior toward Bland and their evident alliance with Wainoke spies make them suspect, to say the least. (3) The Meherrin are regarded as Iroquoian, and therefore presumably hostile to both the Secotan and Chowanoc.

The most serious problem with the Meherrin theory hinges on language and identity. Who exactly were these people? 1650. Edward Bland is the first European to encounter them; he called them *Maharineck*, tacking on an Algonquian *oc* ending denoting "place." 1701. Surveyor John Lawson lists them as *Meherring.* 1788. Thomas Jefferson writes of *the Meherrins and Tuteloes* living on Meherrin River.[54] Could these two nations have had some connection? 1836. Albert Gallatin thinks so. He undertakes the classification of southeastern languages and concludes that the Meherrin and Tutelo are one and the same. So does Henry Schoolcraft in 1850.[55] Yet the Tutelo (a Monocan subtribe) speak Siouan. How, then, did the Meherrin later come to be confused with Iroquoian speakers?

The mistake was made by Gallatin himself. Since no Siouan nations were thought to exist in North Carolina, and the Meherrin and Tutelo were not Algonquian, then it was assumed that they were Iroquoian. Later, vocabularies taken from Tutelo refugees in Canada prove that they are indeed Siouan.[56] But by this time the Meherrin language is extinct, no reclassification is made, and Gallatin's original pronouncement of Iroquoian remains unchanged. The Meherrin themselves (and perhaps the Nottoway too, which might well skew their own classification) apparently received into their midst a large influx of Iroquoian-speaking Susquehannock from Maryland. Colonial records, confounding the two, went so far as to state that the Meherrin *were* Susquehannock.[57]

The single word recorded of their language is the name *Meherrin* itself. Linguists have been unable to produce an Iroquoian translation, though it is said to mean "People of the Muddy Water." In Onondaga *o'dae'ge* means "muddy water." In Mohawk it is *o'nawatsta: keri. Meherrin,* is something different. It is Siouan, and the original name must have been closer to *Meheree. Here* means "banks." We see the name in Catawba as *Yeíswa here,* "People of the River Banks." In Wateree as *Waterá here,* "banks washed away." In Sugaree as *sigrí here,* "spoiled (rotten) banks." In Congaree as *iswá kerá here,* "deep river banks." The word *ma* occurs in Biloxi. Its meaning is "mud." *Meherrin* or *Ye(íswa) Mahere,* "People of the muddy (river) banks."[58]

Yet the Meherrin were not the Mandoag. They were not for the simple reason that there was another nation in this region that fits the description much better. It is a nation we have not yet considered, but now it is time that we do.

Solving the Mandoag Riddle

The Meherrin knew the Mandoag. They were neither the Iroquoian Tuscarora; nor the Nottoway, allies of the Chowanoc. They were a people related to the powerful Occaneechi and to the Siouans of the Piedmont. They were a people who sent out spies. They were a people whom the Meherrin assisted in diverting Bland. They were the Wainoke.

The Secotan and Chowanoc call them the Mandoag: *the stealthy, the treacherous.* To their fellow Siouans, they are the Eno. The *Yeínari,* the "people disliked," the "mean" or "contemptible."[59] This in recognition, perhaps, of their general reputation.

At Ritanoc, the leader Eyanoco (Eno) holds seven Lost Colonists. At Anoeg (Eno), Strachey is informed by Wahunsonacock's servant Weinock that the *houses are built like ours.* Its location is ten days' march from the Powhatan, or about one hundred miles through swampy terrain. There is *a country called Anone* (Eno), Wahunsonacock tells Smith, *where they have abundance of brass, and houses walled as ours.*[60] Machumps reports much brass at Pakerakanick and Ocanahowan also, along with storied houses that the English taught them to build. They hunt for ore — *apess* — in the mountains.

The Eno are in constant association with a people called Shakori. Edward Bland, beating a retreat away from their spies, crosses over *Schockoores old fields.*[61] The Tuscarora, Francis Yeardley reports in 1654, are at war with *a great nation called the Cacores, a very little people in stature, not exceeding youths of thirteen or fourteen years, but extremely valiant and fierce in fight and, above belief, swift in retirement and flight.* Amazingly, the Tuscarora are unable to beat them. The Shakori easily *resist the puissance of this potent, rich, and numerous people.* Allied to the Shakori *is another great nation* called the *Haynokes* [Eno]. They are even more intrepid: it is the Eno *who valiantly resist the Spaniards' further northern attempts* into North Carolina.[62]

1701. Surveyor John Lawson hires *Enoe Will,* whose town of Adshusheer lies on the upper Neuse and Tar Rivers, to conduct him from the Great Trading Path to Roanoke Island. Enoe Will is leader of a mixed nation of *Enoe* and *Shoccorie.* His former home was at the mouth of the Neuse, at Enoe Bay, *by which,* said Lawson, *I perceived he was one of the Corees by birth.* The Coree and Secotan *had been a long time at war.* They are *a bloody and barbarous people,* John Archdale flung at the Coree. That they are the Shakori, or a branch of the same people, is likely.[63]

The profile matches. The Eno are the Mandoag. *They are of mean stature and courage.* They are *covetous and thievish.* The Mandoag were mercenaries. They are ever *industrious to earn a penny, and therefore hire themselves out to their neighbours.* The Shakori are joined with them. They *agree with the Oenocks in customs and manners.*[64] They control access to the mines of Chaunis Temoatan. They prevent the Tuscarora from trading with Jamestown. The Tuscarora *were afraid, for the Wainoakes had told them that the English would kill them.*[65] Their *name and multitude besides their valour is terrible to all the rest of the provinces.*[66] They are the Mandoag. Their *very names were terrible unto them.* They would fight Lane's men for hire. Firing on them, they *wooded themselves we know not where.*[67] They are *extremely valiant and fierce in fight and, above belief, swift in retirement and flight.* They are the Mandoag. Gates's instructions to find the colonists who escaped from the *Powhatan of Roanoke* were pointing not to Roanoke Island but to Roanoke River.

The *Tacci, alias Dogi, formerly possessed* the Piedmont, Lederer said. But *they are extinct, and the Indians now seated here are distinguished into the several nations of Mahoc [Manahoac] . . . Nahyssan [Tutelo], Sapon [Saponi], Managog [Eno], Mangoack [Eno], Akenatzy [Occaneechi], and Monakin [Monacan], etc. One language is common to them although they differ in dialects.*[68] The language of the Mandoag is Siouan.

Thirty years after Lawson met Enoe Will, we hear of him again, now an old man. 1733. William Byrd, crossing the Nottoway River, *sent for an old Indian called Shacco-Will, living about 7 miles off, who reckoned himself 78 years old. This fellow pretended he could conduct us to a silver mine, that lies either upon Eno River, or a Creek of it, not far from where the Tuscaruros once lived.* "Not far from where the Tuscarora once lived" was Eno country. Times have changed. *All the nations round about,* Byrd said, *bearing in mind the havoc these Indians used formerly to make among their ancestors in the insolence of their power, did at length avenge it home upon them.* William Byrd rejects the offer of an old man that would have taken him into the old Mandoag territory. Enoe Will is no longer needed. Instead, to *comfort his heart, I gave him a bottle of rum.*[69]

The Great Dispersal

Our search is over. The Eno are the Mandoag. But when we look for the Lost Colonists among them, we make a disconcerting discovery. Something is wrong, for there is no Lost Colony here. Europeans who have penetrated into the interior report no such community.

Sightings of individuals, however, are rife: Arrohattoc (Powhatan Confederacy): one boy. Tuscarora: two Englishmen, a man and a woman. The Eno: town of Ritanoc, four men, two boys, one girl. In addition, Bland reports *other English among the Indians,* number undisclosed. From the Zúñiga map: Pakerakanick — four men reported, who came from Ocanahowan. Panawiock — housing *many* Lost Colonists, number undisclosed. Ocanahowan — *Certain men* reported, number unknown.

From the lower Tar, a strange story emerges from the territory of the Pamlico nation. 1669. The Reverend Morgan Jones, a Welsh cleric, is taken prisoner by the Tuscarora. He and his five companions are informed that they will die. Bemoaning his fate aloud in Welsh, *an Indian* — a visiting *Doeg* war captain — immediately *came to me* and spoke in the same language. Jones gapes, amazed, as the man assures him in the ancient *British tongue I should not die, and thereupon went to the Emperor of the Tuscaroras, and agreed for my ransom and the men who were with me.* Jones follows them home and remains in their town for four months, preaching in Welsh. *They are settled,* he said, *upon Pontigo River* — the Pamlico, or lower Tar.[70]

The story is picked up by a Turkish spy living in Paris, and translated into English. *There is a region* in North America, it claims, *inhabited by a people whom they call Tuscorards and Doegs. Their language is the same as is spoken by the Welsh. They are thought to descend from them.* Part of White's company was Welsh.[71]

At first sight the evidence is completely baffling. How could individuals from White's company be reported in so many places at the same time? Why are the Lost Colonists not together? What have the Mandoag done with them?

In 1670 and again in 1701 the Eno and Shakori were visited along the upper Tar and Neuse Rivers near present-day Durham and Hillsborough. Their location was then near the Great Trading Path, south of the Occaneechi, and they were heavily involved with the English trading caravans that were working up and down it. Enoe Will was renowned as a guide. He readily offered his services to Lawson, as he did later to William Byrd. Lederer said that they were eager to earn a penny.

In 1587, however, the most lucrative income from trade for the Eno did not course down the Great Trading Path from Jamestown, but ran east/west to the coast. The Powhatan possessed a rich pearl fishery and, according to the Tuscarora, a salt corridor existed. We also know that there was a vigorous trade in copper, and that the Mandoag controlled coastal access to it so thoroughly that Secotan informants told Hariot that they had never seen the mines from whence the copper came.

In 1587, then, the Eno — the Mandoag, according to White's map — were located farther east, poised midway between the coastal nations and the Occaneechi trade mart. The Chowanoc reported their towns to be only a day away. This was the region in which Bland crossed Shakori old fields, an area so close to the Tuscarora that Lawson mistakenly listed Eno as a Tuscarora town.[72] As we have seen, the Eno were middlemen, exchanging copper for salt and pearls from the coast . . . and something more. *The Eno traded slaves.*

This was not uncommon in the Southeast. The presence of slaves was reported again and again.[73] Taken as war captives, what befell them depended on the needs of the nation. They were employed to till fields, to cut wood, to hunt, and to work in mines. Others were adopted as full members of the nations into which they were taken. Still others were dispersed through trade.

At last we understand the situation. Powell and Todkill, dispatched by John Smith to the Mandoag, were denied access to the Lost Colonists. There would be no repatriation — because they were slaves. They were used at Ritanoc, said Strachey, *to beat copper.* Others were detained at Pakerakanick where Gepanocon would not release them, for *one of these were worth much labour.*

If we are right that the Eno/Mandoag took Lost Colony captives, those who were not distributed among their towns would have been conducted to the Occaneechi trade mart. From there, they would have been separated and disseminated into the interior. But did this happen? The evidence is in the Zúñiga map.

Smith reported Lost Colony survivors at Panawioc, Pakerakanick, and Ocanahowan. Those at Pakerakanick had originated at Ocanahowan. We know that Ocanahowan was located in the north, probably along the Roanoke River, although the Zúñiga map placed it south of the Meherrin River, above Occaneechi Island. Bland met a "Tuscarora" among the Meherrin who agreed to conduct Lost Colonists from the lower Tuscarora town to a place called Hocomawananck, on a river. Is there a connection between this location and Ocanahowan, where so many of the colonists were reported? Could either, or both, have been Occaneechi Island? The names on the Zúñiga map have never been translated. We must try to do so now.

Ocanahowan. Recorded by Smith, and later by Strachey. It has not been decipherable in Algonquian. This is because the word is Siouan. Its construction is derived from the Tutelo *yu:xkañ,* "man," "person" + *ohon,* "many" + *hi wa,* "come," "gather." Its meaning: "many people gather here."[74] We have seen the exact word before in Algonquian: Occaneechi, the place *where people gather.* The Lost Colonists were there. At Ocanahowan — the Occaneechi trade mart.

Hocomawananck. A place name recorded by Bland. It is Algonquian, and appears to be a combination of *accomac, ogkomé,* "the other side place," or "beyond" + *Ma-wig-nack,* "the place where two streams meet," thus *accomawignack,* "beyond the place where the two streams meet."[75] In 1650 Bland traveled south from Jamestown with the intention of entering the Tuscarora villages. At Meherrin, he changed plans and agreed to meet the Lost Colonists at *Hocomawananck* somewhere to the west, a rendezvous obviously of some renown, easily accessible, a logical selection. What better site to choose than Occaneechi Island? It is indeed "beyond the place where two streams meet," lying in the midst of the Roanoke River at the junction of the Staunton and the Dan. Bland was instructed to open up trade; Occaneechi Island was the gateway to the Great Trading Path.

If the Lost Colonists were dispersed from Occaneechi Island, they would logically reappear throughout the Piedmont, among the Occaneechi's trading partners and among the Eno towns themselves. Pakerakanick. Never translated, yet compare to Abenaki *kara,* "scraped," *kon,* "pines, forest" + Passamaquoddy *pe,* "extensive, extended" + *oc,* locative ending. *Pekarakonoc,* "Extensive place of scraped trees."[76] If correct, it is a haunting reminder: in the deep woods, Powell and Todkill discovered *crosses & letters, the characters and assured testimonies of Christians newly cut in the barks of trees.*

On the Zúñiga map, Pakerakanick appears on the Tar, located substantially west of a fork in the river. Whether this was Tranters Creek or Fishing Creek to its northwest is unknown, but the nation within whose territory it lay was the same. This was an area in the vicinity of modern Rocky Mount. This was Eno country. The town's leader was Gepanocon. His name is untranslated, though a clue to its meaning may be found in a Siouan chief's title, recorded among the Tutelo as *Gá pogá tadyi.*[77]

Panawioc. Smith was told that many Lost Colonists were here. The word is Algonquian. Its meaning: *Place of Foreigners,* an apt name for a site where they *reported our men to be.*[78] It appears on the Zúñiga map on Cashie Creek, Bertie County. This, too, was likely Eno territory, or perhaps associated with the tribal town of Moratuc. At Panawioc, Strachey reported, *are said to be store of salt stones.* Two substantial salt deposits have been discovered on the Carolina coast. One is located far south near present-day Wilmington; the other occurs at the confluence of the Roanoke and Chowan Rivers in the vicinity of Cashie Creek.

If the Zúñiga map were our only source for Lost Colony sightings, we might still be in doubt. It is not. The reports of Smith and Strachey also confirm the dispersal, as does a peculiar finding in the Blue Ridge Mountains. 1671. Thomas Batts and Robert Fallam are sent on a government-sponsored expedition into Tutelo territory. They will be the first Englishmen to reach the Blue Ridge Mountains. As they pass along a trail at the base of the first range, they notice several letters burned into the brow of a tree, *marked in the past.* Peering closer, they observe them to be the initials *MA. NI.* Five days later, still marching west, they spot two more marked trees: the first is again inscribed *MA. NI.* (or *NJ.*, since *J* and *I* were written the same); the second is cut with the initials *MA. and several other scratchments.*[79] Is it coincidence? Among the Lost Colonists were Morris Allen and Nicholas Johnson.

The China Box

The Trading Path was a debris field. Wahunsonacock himself showed the English a musket barrel, a brass mortar, and pieces of iron from the diaspora that marked the end of White's colony.[80] A road ran directly from the Powhatan to the Trading Path at Occaneechi Island. In fact, the Powhatan were so rich in copper from this trade that Jamestown initially believed that the mines must exist at their very own back door.

1621. Edward Waterhouse records the expedition of Marmaduke Parkinson, who traveled north from Jamestown to the Potomac River. The nations here, though autonomous, are within the Powhatan sphere of influence. At *one of the King's houses where they were,* Waterhouse spies *a China box.* Being *demanded where he had it,* the King *made answer, that it was sent him from a King that dwelt in the West, over the great hills, some ten day's journey away, he having that box from a people, as he said, that came thither in ships, that wear clothes, crooked swords and, somewhat like our men, dwelt in houses, and were called Acanack-China.*[81] It is tempting to see in this word Lederer's *Akenatsy* — the Occaneechi and their trading mart, away across the hills.

The China box is perhaps our final image of the Lost Colonists, more poignant than any words. A delicate enameled keepsake, a personal luxury, brought from England by one of eleven women who sailed with White to find a new home.

26 EPILOGUE

As in a country strange without companion,
I only wail the wrong of death's delays,
Whose sweet spring spent, whose summer well nie done
Of all which past, the sorrow only stays.

Sir Walter Raleigh[1]

Farewell

With a sense of utter desolation, White's colonists stand alone on the shore on an August afternoon and watch White's boat slowly recede from view. Leaving them forever. Birds pass quietly overhead, adrift on the breeze, as a cold horror descends on those who wait — cut off, as they are, without the means of rescue. Eleanor stands in the surf, her legs heavy as lead, water rushing around her dress as the shadows lengthen across the quiet fringe of trees. They are, each of them — every man, woman, and child — consumed by dread. John White's chances of success are slim.

Far away, thousands upon thousands of miles away, beyond the horizon, lies a country never to be seen again. Lies London, with its bustling trades and market fairs and multitudes who have long forgotten about Roanoke Island and the colonists huddled on its shore. Who never knew they even existed. Far away lies a world as in a dream.

Power lurks in the corridors of Whitehall amid weighty affairs of state. Power hides in secret machinations and decrees, in jealousies and deceit. There is power in ambition, power in a churning European caldron of alliances and gain. It is this power that destroys the hopes and dreams of Raleigh; of 116 men, women, and children; of John White; and of the Secotan. Someone orders a sabotage and the innocent are ground down in the maw of power and corruption. On Roanoke, a cry fades into despair.

The colonists raise a rough palisade for protection, while the houses on Roanoke Island are disassembled. Lumber is stacked aboard the pinnace, along with bricks and tiles and furnishings. Even the nails are taken away. A trench is dug in the soft sand, and White's trunk — his maps and drawings — are carefully laid inside and covered over. On the palisade post someone carves the word "Croatoan," a message for John White, should he ever return. With fearful eyes, they pass George Howe's grave and step into the boat that will carry them inland — away from the threat of Spain on this unprotected coast, away from Roanoke, where so much wrong was done. Lane's rage here has doomed them all. The Secotan, too, are reeling from horror. And yet they are very like the colonists: the innocent, struck down without discretion, victims of an overarching power in which human life is insignificant.

The pinnace disappears into the interior and someone on the island — Eleanor, perhaps — urgently carves another message for her father. "CRO," in the bark of a tree. He must, he will see it! The colony separates and a much smaller party finds its way to Croatoan. Neither group imagines that they will never see each other again.

In a lonely house in Kilmore, before a flickering fire, John White dips a quill into ink and pens a letter to Richard Hakluyt. February 1593: *To the Worshipful and my very friend Master Richard Hakluyt, much happiness in the Lord.*[2] But what can the letter say? Six years have passed since he last saw his colony; he can but detail the sad events of his fruitless search for them, and that is all. What can he write of pain? He does not even attempt it.

John White posts his letter. It is finished. He can never tell Eleanor that he had tried to come back, that he had struggled so hard to reach her. The forces against him were simply too great. White stands alone on the cliffs overlooking the sea and imagines Roanoke. He is never heard from again.

Deep in the woods, far in the interior of a country called Mandoag, where the tall trees close in the darkness, melted copper runs in rivulets. Ralph Lane should be here, Ralph Lane who wreaked misery in this land in his quest to find it. Cut off from any communication, dispersed one from the other, four men, two boys, and a young girl work the copper. Men have come looking for them. Englishmen, stumbling through the interior, from faraway Jamestown. Steam rising up from the fires of the melting copper reflects a sudden spark of hope in eyes dulled from drudgery — if only they can speak to the search party, if only they can cry out, "We are here! We are here!" But the Mandoag won't allow it. Through stinging tears, a man carves a cross on a tree, and another. And another. A forest etched with crosses.

Power and politics are in Jamestown. No one understands the message. The search for White's colonists is called off and a story fabricated. All hope is gone.

1701. Surveyor John Lawson travels to Croatoan and is greeted there by the *Hatteras Indians, who either then lived on Roanoke Island, or much frequented it.* Observing him jotting down notations, they tell him that *several of their ancestors were white people, and could talk in a book as we do.* Astonished, Lawson scrutinizes them and is stunned: *the truth of which is confirmed by grey eyes being found frequently amongst these Indians, and no others. They value themselves extremely for their affinity to the English, and are ready to do them all friendly offices.*[3] Lawson believes they are descendants of White's Lost Colonists.

The Croatoan people, he says, relate *a pleasant story that passes for an uncontested truth among them all.* On certain clear days, *the ship which brought the first colonies does often appear amongst them under sail, in a gallant posture, which they call Sir Walter Raleigh's ship.*[4] Ghost ships. The rescue parties sent out by Raleigh have become the stuff of legend.

> *Thus may you plainly perceive the success of my fifth & last voyage to Virginia, which was no less unfortunately ended than forwardly begun, and as luckless to many, as sinister to myself. But I would to God it had been as prosperous to all, as noisome to the planters, & as joyfull to me, as discomfortable to them. Yet, seeing it is not my first crossed voyage, I remain contented. And wanting my wishes, I leave off from prosecuting that whereunto I would to God my wealth were answerable to my will. Thus committing the relief of my discomfortable company the planters in Virginia to the merciful help of the Almighty, whom I most humbly beseech to help & comfort them, according to his most holy will and their good desire.*
>
> *Your Most Well Wishing Friend,*
>
> *John White*[5]

APPENDIX A: WINGINA AND THE SECOTAN

William Gerard (Hodge, *Handbook,* II, pp. 392–3) was the first to advance the theory of a separate Roanoke tribe centered on Roanoke Island with Wingina at its head, as distinct from the Secotan. Few of his contemporaries agreed. James Mooney, the preeminent southeastern ethnologist, dismissed Gerard's claim (ibid., pp. 494–5), identifying the Secotan as a nation embracing present-day Albemarle Peninsula (Washington, Tyrrell, Dare, Hyde, and Beaufort Counties) and adjacent islands, an area synonymous with Barlowe's "Wingandacoa." Frank Speck ("Ethnic Position," p. 188) and Maurice Mook (*Algonkian Ethnohistory,* pp. 213–17, and map, p. 183), both distinguished southeastern scholars, concurred that the Secotan territory encompassed Roanoke Island. Both identified Wingina as the Secotan leader. Swanton (*Indian Tribes,* p. 81) focused on the nation's later identity as Machapunga, and placed it in the same location as Mooney's Secotan, that is, in Hyde, Washington, Tyrrell, Dare, and Beaufort Counties.

In recent years, Quinn (*Roanoke Voyages,* I, pp. 99, n. 2, 100, n. 1; II, p. 862) has followed Gerard in rejecting Wingina as the leader of the Secotan and in postulating the existence of a separate "Roanoke Tribe" encompassing the villages of Roanoke Island and Dasamonquepeuc (on the mainland in Dare County). Although he asserts that "the bulk of the evidence" supports this claim, he offers none, other than "Lane's experience," and concludes that "the extent of Wingina's dominion must therefore be ascribed to Indian boasting." Even more remarkable is his contention (*Set Fair,* p. 44) that the Secotan were actually hostile to Wingina and that it was they who had shot him before Barlowe's 1584 arrival (see below). It is clear, however, that the primary accounts support the conclusion of Mooney, Speck, and Mook that Wingina was the head of the Secotan nation and that the existence of a separate "Roanoke Tribe" is not warranted by the available evidence.

Arthur Barlowe was the first to document the people of the Outer Banks in 1584 (Hakluyt, *Principall Navigations,* 1589, pp. 728–33). The King's name, he said, was Wingina and the country called Wingandacoa.

Wingina had been wounded in a fight "with the King of the next country" and was recovering "at the chief town of the country," which was "six day's journey off," or roughly sixty miles from Barlowe's landing at Wococon. Later, he tells us that Secotan (Secota) was the westernmost town of Wingandacoa and that a country called Ponouike (Pomouik) adjoined it to the west, whose King maintained "mortal war with Wingina, King of Wingandacoa." We might conclude, therefore, that Wingina was wounded by the Pomouik and was recovering at his own capital of Secota. Barlowe next tells us that the three kings of Wingandacoa, Chowanoc, and Weapemeoc were "in league" together. The King's brother was called Granganimeo. He resided in a village of nine cedar houses on Roanoke Island and, given Barlowe's account of the commands his wife issued there, it is logical to assume that Granganimeo was a Roanoke *weroance,* or leader.

Barlowe composed a narrative of his expedition for publication. While describing the political geography, he wrote, "adjoining unto this town aforesaid called Sequotan. . . ." Significantly, this wording was amended in the next addition of the work (1600, III, p. 250) to read, "adjoining unto this *country* aforesaid called Sequotan. . . ." His statement that the King of Wingandacoa was Wingina, however, was not changed. This is significant, for Barlowe lived with Wanchese and Manteo in Raleigh's house, and presumably they had every opportunity to correct him had he been wrong, just as the second edition of his narrative was corrected.

When we turn to the second Roanoke expedition, additional information is provided. On John White's map the entire area now known as the Albemarle Peninsula (Washington, Tyrrell, Hyde, Dare, and part of Beaufort County) is labeled "Secotan," implying that White and Hariot understood Wingina's country to encompass the area including, at the very least, the towns of Secota, Aquascogoc, Pomeioc, Dasamonquepeuc, and Roanoke. This was the conclusion reached by Mooney, Speck, Mook, and Swanton.

Hariot *(A Briefe and True Report)* wrote, "in some places of the country, one only town belonged to the government of a Wiroans or chief Lord; in other some two or three, in some six, eight, & more; the greatest Wiroans that yet we had dealing with had but eighteen towns in his government, and able to make not above seven or eight hundred fighting men at the most."* According to Lane (Hakluyt, *Principall Navigations,*

*Additional proof, by the way, that Lane's men did not reach the Chesapeake Bay, where the Powhatan Empire comprised more than thirty national towns.

1589, pp. 737–47), the Weapemeoc possessed six towns. Chowanoc, he said, "was the greatest 'province' on the river. Its capital could muster 700 fighting men." From this, we might infer that Chowanoc was the nation Hariot mentioned as having eighteen towns. Secotan territory, then, was not as large as this, but it is not difficult to believe that six or eight towns might have been theirs. Quinn's argument for a separate Roanoke tribe on the sole basis of "Indian boasting" is therefore unreasonable. Once Quinn based his argument upon this foundation, however, he had no choice but to assume that since Wingina (as leader of the Roanoke tribe) was at war with the adjoining king, he must have been at war with the Secotan. This, however, must suppose that the primary source material is faulty: Barlowe would have to be wrong, as would White's map. We would have to assume that Hariot, who annotated White's map and drawings for De Bry, would not have caught the error, nor would subsequent editions of Hakluyt's *Principall Navigations,* and that the Secotan disappeared from view by the time trouble erupted with Lane — for Lane doesn't mention them in his list of Wingina's allies — only to reappear a year later in close alliance with the "Roanoke" town of Dasamonquepeuc avenging Wingina's death.

Barlowe had said that Wingina was recuperating at the "chief town" six days' travel from Wococon. Combining this with Hariot's information that the tombs of "their kings and princes" were located at Secota, we might postulate that Secota was the "chief town" of Wingina's country. Nevertheless, six days after Grenville's arrival at Wococon, he sent words of greeting to Wingina at Roanoke. This has been taken to mean that Wingina's capital was on Roanoke Island after all, and "proof" that the Secotan were another nation entirely. However, ample evidence to the contrary is furnished by the related Powhatan to the north.

By the time the Jamestown chroniclers met the Powhatan, they were an "empire" of more than thirty independent nations (consisting of one, or more than one, town each) ruled over by a paramount chief named Wahunsonacock. According to Smith (*Map of Virginia,* p. 173) his authority extended "over many kings and governors." Many of these were high-ranking kinsmen placed in positions of authority at key towns in the territory. For example, Opechancanough, Opitchapam, and Kekataugh — Wahunsonacock's brothers — were introduced as "kings" of the Pamunkey, the most powerful member nation in the empire. Parahunt, Tatahcoope, and Pochins — his sons — held leadership positions over Powhatan, Quiyoughquohanock, and Kecoughtan, respectively. Furthermore, leaders of nations within the Powhatan confederacy in turn appointed relatives over smaller towns, as Strachey noted in 1612. Opussoquionuske was "Queen" of a small Appamatuck village, while her brother Coquonasum ruled over the Appamatuck proper. The "great king" of the Patawomeck placed his brother Iopassous over the allied town of Pastanze (*Historie,* ch. 2 and 4).

Evidence that Granganimeo's brother was *weroance* of Roanoke is consistent with this pattern. We know nothing of Wingina's other arrangements, except that his sister's husband, Eracano, was sent with Lane to the Chowanoc. Osocan was another individual mentioned as a *weroance* close to Wingina, but the nature of the relationship was not recorded. Although we have no proof, it is likely that the leaders of the intermediate towns of Pomeioc and Aquascogoc may have been related as well. It is interesting, in this connection, that Wahunsonacock initially sent his brother Opechancanough, as proxy, to deal with the English at Jamestown, just as Wingina sent his brother Granganimeo to treat with the first Roanoke expedition of 1584.

However, if Wingina were the head of the Secotan nation, living in 1584 at his "chief seat" of Secota, why was he at Roanoke six days after Grenville's arrival on the Outer Banks? Again, the Powhatan supply the answer. In 1607 John Smith was received by the Powhatan leader Wahunsonacock at his capital at Werowocomoco on the York River. Two years later, he moved his capital to Orapax on the Chickahominy River (*Map of Virginia,* pp. 34–5). In 1614 the capital was shifted again to Matchot on the Pamunkey River (*General Historie,* p. 115). Some of the movement was due, as Smith thought, to the English presence and Wahunsonacock's desire to be closer to them, or farther away, as occasion demanded. However, Wahunsonacock was traditionally in the habit of traveling from town to town throughout his territory (much as Elizabeth I embarked on summer progresses). According to Smith (ibid., p. 34), statehouses were maintained for Wahunsonacock's use in six of the principal towns, and Strachey (*Historie,* ch. 3) said that he moved "from house to house" during his "visitation of his several houses."

When we return to Roanoke, we see that a month after Grenville's arrival, Lane met Granganimeo — presumably the *weroance* of Roanoke — to work out the conditions incumbent upon his troops' residence on the island. It is clear that Wingina himself moved to Roanoke Island to buffer the English presence for reasons both positive (trade) and negative (for example, the burning of Aquascogoc). In effect, he wanted to keep an eye on them. Hariot's remark that Wingina accompanied the survey team to villages around the country might have been expected from the leader of those villages who, like Wahunsonacock, probably had dwellings in each one. Later, when relations deteriorated and Pemisapan (Wingina) conscripted his allies to eradicate the English, whom did he summon? The Chowanoc and Weapemeoc (the very allies Barlowe mentioned), along with hired Mandoag and Chesepioc mercenaries. Where were the Secotan? If enemies, they might have helped the English. If allies, and separate from the "Roanoke Tribe" as Quinn proposes, then why were they absent when Wingina needed help? The answer is they *weren't* absent. They were there, precisely because Wingina himself was their leader.

Evidence for this comes from the third Roanoke expedition of 1587, when White was told that Grenville's fort had been "set upon by 30 of the men of Secota, Aquascogoc and Dasamongueponke." These towns were certainly in alliance. Later, White waited for peace overtures to be accepted by the "Wiroances of Pomeiok, Aquascoquos, Secota and Dasamonguepeuke," the village on Roanoke having, by that time, been abandoned.

This is the sum of the primary evidence. Taken together, it presents a convincing picture of Wingina as paramount leader of the Secotan, whose territory included Secota (the chief town), Aquascogoc, Pomeioc, and the towns of Dasamonquepeuc and Roanoke at the very least, and portions of the Outer Banks and Washington and Tyrrell Counties as well. The evidence does not sustain a picture of a Roanoke tribe separate from the Secotan and, for this reason, I have chosen to treat Wingina, Roanoke, and the Secotan as part of the same political entity.

APPENDIX B: THE MEANING OF MANDOAG AND NOTTOWAY

Mandoag and *Nottoway* are both epithets traditionally employed by Algonquian speakers to designate foreign, generally enemy, nations. In proto-Algonquian, they appear as: *menkwew* (and its derivatives: *maquas, mingo, mangoge, mandoag*) and *natowewa* (from which: *nottoway, natowewok, nadowe,* etc.). Because of geography, the recipients of these names were often neighboring Iroquoian speakers, although this was not always the case. For example, the word *Sioux,* applied to Siouan-speaking Lakota and Dakota, is a corruption of the Chippewa word *nadouessi* (cf. *nottoway*).

The picture is complicated by the fact that neither word, *Nottoway* nor *Mandoag,* has been translated to the satisfaction of linguists, though, roughly speaking, both mean "enemy." *Natowewa* appears to be related to the word *atowe,* "to speak a foreign language" (Fenton, "Northern Iroquoian Culture Patterns," p. 320), though Morgan ("Indian Migrations," p. 52) defines the term as "marauders"; Gerard ("Tapehanek Dialect," p. 326) as "he goes to seek flesh to eat," i.e., a cannibal; and Schoolcraft (*Indian Tribes,* 5, pp. 36–7) as a compound composed of *nado,* or "adder, snake" + *awasie,* a "beast." Mooney (Hodge, *Handbook,* II, p. 87) agrees with Schoolcraft, as does Siebert ("Proto-Algonquian na:tawe:wa," pp. 635–42), who derives the word from *na:t,* "to close [in] upon" + *awe,* a "state of warmth," rendering "seeker of warmth" as applied to the mississauga pit viper.

Problematic as the word *Nottoway* is, *Mandoag* is even more so. Linguists assert that it is unanalyzable (Fenton, ibid., p. 320). Interestingly, *manató, manetó* also means "snake" in Shawnee, making it comparable to *nottoway* (Pearson, *Shawnee Language,* p. 25; Morgan, *Ancient Society,* p. 168). *Manató* and *Mandoag* sound very similar (t's and d's, and k's and g's, are often interchangeable depending on dialect and on European perceptions and orthography) and, on this basis, at least, one might propose that *manató* and *Mandoag, Mangoag, Menkwew,* and *Mengwew* are all derived from the same root.

Morgan (ibid.) relates the word *nottoway* to the Ojibway *nayadowa,* "one who comes stealthily and takes," i.e., "a marauder," which is similar to *nadink,* "the act of getting." It is interesting, then, to compare this with the Natick words *manado,* "to buy"; *magu,* "he gives or sells"; *maugoke,* "give you"; and *noh maguk,* "a giver, a seller" (Trumbull, *Natick Dictionary,* p. 266). Is there, in fact, a connection between the words *Mandoag/Mangoag* and *manado, maugoke, nayadowa,* etc.? The Eno Mandoag were the enemies, but they were also those who were aggressive at trade. The Eno bought and sold.

Whatever the derivation, the conclusions that may be reached concerning both words are three: (1) The terms *mandoag* and *nottoway* were applied to enemy nations by Algonquian speakers. These enemy nations were non-Algonquian, but not necessarily Iroquoian, for the terms were applied to Siouans as well. In the case of Virginia/North Carolina, Siouans dominated the Piedmont, so we should not be surprised to discover them referred to by these terms. (2) There is no inherent relationship (though one is not precluded) between the Mandoag/Mangoag of North Carolina and the Nottoway of Virginia on the basis of name alone, except that neither were Algonquian. The Chippewa, for example, referred to the Iroquois (the Seneca, in particular) as *natowe,* to the Wyandot as *natowe,* and to the Lakota as *nadouessi.* All are variants of the word Nottoway, yet the Wyandot, the Seneca, and the Lakota are entirely distinct nations. (3) A clue to the meaning of the name Mandoag may be found in words relating to buying and selling; enemy nations in control of trade might indeed be equated with snakes.

Finally, given the identification of the Eno (the *Yeínari,* "the disliked") as advanced in this book, their role as aggressive middlemen who controlled coastal Algonquian access to the Occaneechi trade would indeed make them "Mandoag."

NOTES AND REFERENCES

1 THE DISAPPEARANCE

1 The Roanoke Island settlement has not yet been found. Therefore little is known of the houses themselves (Harrington, "Archeological Explorations"). Darby Glande, at Roanoke in 1585, said that bricks were made for use in their construction (ch. 9, n. 13). Since Ananias Dare was a bricklayer and tiler (Hulton, *America, 1585*, p. 7), it is likely that his skills were utilized in 1587. According to Hentzner in 1598 (*Travels*, p. 110), common homes in England were built of wood, but "those of the richer sort with bricks."

2 For an account of the 1587 voyage, see Hakluyt, *Principall Navigations* (1589), pp. 764–71.

3 See Chapters 21–4; also McMillan, *Raleigh's Lost Colony;* Cotten, *The White Doe;* Amer, *The Lost Colony in Literature;* Howe, *Solving the Riddle of the Lost Colony.*

4 The events in this chapter and all quotes contained therein, unless otherwise noted, are taken from John White's February 4, 1593, letter and account printed in Hakluyt, *Principall Navigations* (1600), III, pp. 287–95.

5 According to Pedro Diaz, a Canary Island pilot who visited Roanoke in 1586, the sound was so shallow that a person could walk across it to the mainland (Quinn, *Roanoke Voyages*, II, p. 789).

6 An estimated two thousand shipwrecks lie off the Outer Banks (Neil Morgan, "Home to North Carolina," *National Geographic Magazine*, 157 [3], March 1980, p. 341).

7 Brown, *Genesis*, I, p. 99.

8 Wright, *Further English Voyages*, doc. 69, p. 244.

9 The original text reads "Gwathanelo," a place as yet unidentified. Sams (*Conquest of Virginia*, p. 293, n. 4) took this to mean Guatemala. Quinn (*Roanoke Voyages*, II, p. 601, n. 6) proposes Point Guanjibo, Hispaniola. A more likely suggestion, however, is Guantanamo, Cuba. An aspirated *h* (of which there are numerous Elizabethan examples: *hithe* for *height, Wathling* for *Wattling, lanthorn* for *lantern* in Stow, *Survey*, I, pp. 26, 250; II, pp. 352, 357–8) would render Guatanelo and Guantanamo a close match.

10 Wright, *Further English Voyages*, doc. 68, p. 244.

11 Oré, *Relación de los Mártires* (1936), p. 48.

12 Wright, *Further English Voyages,* doc. 70, p. 246; doc. 73, p. 257. For the attack, see ibid., pp. 245–57.
13 Ibid., 71, enclosure 2, pp. 253, 256.
14 The hurricane season lasts from August to October, peaking in early September. Many of the violent storms reported off the Outer Banks by the Roanoke expeditions were almost certainly hurricanes or lesser tropical depressions.
15 Wave action has since changed the barrier island configuration. From John White's map (De Bry, *America,* I, pl. I), Croatoan Island appears to have been a fusion of modern-day Ocracoke Island with the southern portion of Hatteras Island. Roanoke Island lay to the north of Croatoan and inland from the banks, some forty-five miles away.
16 Modern Pea Island/Hatteras Island extending south perhaps to the vicinity of Rodanthe.
17 The fires may have been no more than conflagrations induced by lightning from the recent storms, yet signal fires are well documented for the central Atlantic coastal region. In Maryland: Father Andrew White's account of Piscataway fires on the Potomac River, 1634 (White, *A Briefe Relation,* in Hall, *Narratives of Early Maryland,* p. 40). Virginia: Percy's *Observations* (1907), pp. 10–11. North Carolina: Ecija's 1609 report of smoke signals set two to three leagues apart and stretching inland along the entire North Carolina coast, some for the purpose of hailing ships. (Quinn, *New American World,* V, pp. 145–7). Georgia: Oré, *Relación* (1936), p. 36.
18 Kenricks, or Kindrickers, Mounts is no longer a physical feature of the Outer Banks. Quinn (*Roanoke Voyages,* II, p. 864) locates it on Hatteras Island, near the present-day town of Rodanthe.
19 Thirty men left the *Hopewell* with Spicer and White, with fifteen men per shallop.
20 Hakluyt, *Principall Navigations* (1589), pp. 770–1. See also Chapter 7 for the colonists' roster.
21 The *Hopewell* was already close, lying just off the north end of Croatoan Island.
22 The treasure fleet — filled with gold, silver, and other American commodities — departed from Havana for Spain twice each summer, and returned to the West Indies each January and August (Lowery, *Spanish Settlements,* II, pp. 11–12).
23 Hakluyt, *Principall Navigations* (1600), III, p. 294; Wright, *Further English Voyages,* doc. 89, p. 283.

2 A CASE OF MISSING PERSONS

1 Camden, *The History* (1688), pp. 380–1.
2 Hakluyt, *Principall Navigations* (1589), pp. 768–9.

3 Ibid., p. 769.
4 Sir Edward Norreys to Essex, Salisbury Mss., VI, p. 5.
5 Anonymous, *Willobie His Avisa,* Harl. Mss. 6849, cant. LIIII, fol. 48a.
6 Quinn, in particular, finds John White meek and ineffective as an expedition commander (*Roanoke Voyages,* II, p. 503). The same sentiment is repeated elsewhere by Hulton and Quinn (*American Drawings,* p. 17). This, of course, was the conclusion that White's enemies hoped would be reached; see Chapter 19.

3 JOHN WHITE: GOVERNOR

1 Nichols, *The Progresses,* II, p. 228.
2 In his 1593 letter to Hakluyt, White said that he had been to Virginia five times. There were five known voyages to Roanoke: 1584, 1585, 1586, 1587, 1590.
3 Hakluyt, *Principall Navigations* (1589), p. 735.
4 White's drawings are reproduced in Hulton, *America, 1585;* Hulton and Quinn, *American Drawings.* The originals are in the Prints and Drawings Division of the British Museum, 1906–5–9–1.
5 Hulton, *America, 1585,* p. 8.
6 Accounts of Frobisher's expedition are found in Hakluyt, *Principall Navigations* (1589); Collinson, *Martin Frobisher,* pp. 117–206; Deacon, *John Dee,* pp. 85–9.
7 Deacon, *John Dee,* pp. 85, 87.
8 For the capture of the Nugumiut prisoners and the Bloody Massacre, see Collinson, *Martin Frobisher,* pp. 130–43. Calichoughe was not seized at Bloody Point with the woman and child but was taken on the coast a month earlier. The prisoners' names were recorded on the postmortem report and burial register; see ibid., p. 191; Quinn, *New American World,* IV, pp. 216–18. Platter copied the words "Ginoct Nutioc"— the names of mother and daughter — written above Ketel's Nugumiut portrait on display at Hampton Court; *Travels* (1937), p. 201.
9 For Calichoughe's injuries, see n. 12, below.
10 Quinn, *New American World,* II, p. 44; Platter, *Travels* (1937), p. 201.
11 For John White's painting style described here and throughout this chapter, see Hulton and Quinn, *American Drawings,* I, esp. pp. 9–11; Hulton, *America, 1585,* pp. 35–8; Quinn, *New American World,* II, p. 30; Binyon, *English Water-colors,* pp. 2–3. Binyon credits White as the founder of the English school of watercolor.
12 For Frobisher's disaster, see Collinson, *Martin Frobisher,* pp. 359–62; Quinn, *New American World,* IV, pp. 180–1, 225; for Michael Lok, the financier, see *Dictionary of National Biography,* XII, p. 92; Rowse, *Expansion,* p. 194; for Calichoughe's death and Dr. Dodding feeling "bitterly grieved," see Collinson, ibid., pp. 189–91 (in Latin); State Papers Domestic, Elizabeth,

Nov. 25, 1577, cxviii, 40 i (Latin); Quinn, *New American World,* IV, 216–18 (translated).

13 Suggested by Hulton, *America, 1585,* pp. 7, 35.

14 For White's painting technique, see n. 11 above.

15 Wirtemberg, *True and Faithful Narrative* (1865), p. 44.

16 Hulton (*America, 1585,* p. 20) and Hulton and Quinn (*American Drawings,* I, p. 9) suggest that White did not draw these figures from life, but copied them from a costume book.

17 Lee, *Huguenots in France and America,* I, p. 134.

18 Hakluyt, *Principall Navigations* (1600), III, p. 301.

19 Hulton, *America, 1585,* p. 36; Hulton and Quinn, *American Drawings,* I, p. 9; II, plates 60–1; LeMoyne's drawings are found in De Bry, *America,* II.

20 Title page to De Bry, *America,* I. White was the official artist on the 1585 expedition. Since he also accompanied the first expedition of 1584, it is not unreasonable to assume that he might also have been commissioned then to make a pictorial record for Raleigh to distribute to the Queen and potential investors.

21 Hakluyt (the elder), *Inducements* (1602), item 31.

22 White's annotated drawing of an alligator, British Museum, P & D, 1906–5–9–1 (72); Hulton, *America, 1585,* plate 10, p. 46.

23 In Latin, author's translation, Moffett, *Insectorum* . . . ; Hulton and Quinn, *American Drawings,* I, pp. 24, 48–9, 71–2, 134–5.

24 Gerard, *Herball,* pp. 709–10.

25 Title page to De Bry, *America,* I.

26 A point also made by Adams, "An Effort to Identify John White," p. 89; Hulton, *America, 1585,* p. 19.

27 Virginia Dare was born on August 18, 1587. Assuming that Eleanor's term was normal, her pregnancy would have been almost into its sixth month when the ships left England on May 8.

28 In 1560 the average age for marriage was twenty-one or twenty-two; Stone, *Crisis of the Aristocracy,* pp. 652–4.

29 Hakluyt, *Principall Navigations* (1589), p. 769. For Cutbert White, see ibid., pp. 770–1. For Butlers, see White's coat of arms in Quinn, *Roanoke Voyages,* II, p. 509; College of Arms, Ms. Vincent Old Grants, 157, fol. 397. For Thomas Payne, see Hulton, *America, 1585,* pp. 20–6.

30 College of Arms, ibid.

31 Hulton, *America, 1585,* p. 7.

32 "master," Hakluyt, *Principall Navigations,* III (1600), p. 288; "gentleman," College of Arms, Ms. Vincent Old Grants, 157, fol. 397; Hulton and Quinn, *American Drawings,* p. 13; Adams, "An Effort to Identify John White."

4 OF LONDON

1 Wirtemberg, *True and Faithful Narrative* (1865), p. 7.
2 Stow, *Survey* (1908), I, pp. 11–18, 160, 168–70, 333, 345.
3 Hentzner, *Travels* (1865), p. 111.
4 Williams, *Elizabeth*, pp. 221–4.
5 Stow, *Survey* (1908), II, p. 212.
6 Ibid., II, pp. 211–12.
7 For descriptions of London, see Rye, *England as Seen by Foreigners;* Stow, *Survey;* Norden, *Notes on London and Westminster;* Smith, *Brief Description;* Platter, *Travels;* Dekker, *Seven Deadly Sins.*
8 Smith, *Brief Description.*
9 *Harrison,* Description of England (1807), p. 395.
10 Platter, *Travels* (1937), p. 153.
11 Stow, *Survey* (1908), I, p. 84.
12 Platter, *Travels* (1937), pp. 154; 153–4.
13 Dekker, *Dead Tearme,* p. D4.
14 Dekker, *Guls Horn Booke,* Chapter IV.
15 Platter, *Travels* (1937), p. 226.
16 Stow, *Survey* (1908), I, p. 26.
17 Wirtemberg, *True and Faithful Narrative* (1865), p. 9; for the camel see Platter, *Travels* (1937), p. 173.
18 Moryson, *Itinerary,* pt. 3, p. 53.
19 Stubbes, *Anatomie,* pp. Hviii-l.
20 Harrison, *Description of England* (1807), p. 317.
21 Fuller, *Worthies* (1840), II, p. 342. Webster's dictionary (*9th New Collegiate Dictionary,* p. 255), however, derives Cockney from the Middle English word *cocken* [cock] + *ey* [egg], thus cock's egg. Not so, according to Fuller.
22 Fuller, *Worthies* (1840), p. 343.
23 Harrison, *Description of England* (1807), p. 387.
24 Ibid., p. 387.
25 Camden, *Remains* (1674), p. 327. Or Luke Hutton's version, "Love me, and hang my dog!" from *The Black Dog of Newgate* [1596].
26 Camden, *Remains* (1674), p. 541.
27 Ibid., p. 536.
28 Ibid., p. 393.
29 Harrison, *Description of England* (1968, Georges Edelen's translation of Harrison's Latin), pp. 132–3, n. 17.
30 Smyth, *Hundred of Berkeley* (1883–5), III, p. 27.
31 Camden, *Remains* (1674), p. 299.
32 Stubbes, *Anatomie,* pp. I, Iii.
33 Ibid., p. Lii.
34 Walker, *Manifest Detection* (1850), p. 41.

35 Stubbes, *Anatomie,* pp. Nii, N.
36 Ibid., pp. Gvii–viii.
37 More, *Utopia* (1906), Book 2, p. 113; for pregnancies and venereal disease, Stubbes, *Anatomie,* pp. Niv–v; Greene, *A Disputation,* pp. 206, 224–5; Dekker, *Lanthorne and Candlelight,* p. 364.
38 Stubbes, *Anatomie,* pp. Liii–iv.
39 Harrison, *Description of England* (1807), p. 340.
40 For the thieves' school at Smart's Quay, see Judges, *Elizabethan Underworld,* xxxix; Rye, *England as Seen by Foreigners,* p. 268, n. 123; Walker, *Manifest Detection* (1850), p. 103; "the pitiful cries . . . ," Stubbes, *Anatomie,* p. Kviii.
41 Bacon, "Of Seditions and Troubles," *Essays* (1887), p. 143.
42 Stubbes, *Anatomie,* Lviii.
43 Ibid., p. Lviii.
44 For a description of bear baiting, see Platter, *Travels* (1937), pp. 168–70; Stubbes, *Anatomie,* section P; Wirtemberg, *True and Faithful Narrative* (1865), pp. 45–6.
45 Farley, *St. Paules-Church, the bill for the Parliament* (1865), pp. 188–9, n. 16.
46 "general contempt . . ." Harrison, *Description of England* (1807), p. 235; "from the highest . . ." Stubbes, *Anatomie,* p. Jvii.
47 Harrison, *Description of England* (1807), pp. 308–9; see also Harman, *Caveat or Warning;* Dekker, *O per se O.*
48 Harrison, *Description of England* (1807), p. 276.
49 Ibid., p. 329.
50 Camden, *Remains* (1674), p. 386.
51 Stubbes, *Anatomie,* p. K.
52 Camden, *Remains* (1674), p. 401.
53 Harrison, *Description of England* (1807), p. 392.

5 OF POPULATION

1 Wirtemberg, *True and Faithful Narrative* (1865), p. 7.
2 Quinn, *Set Fair for Roanoke,* p. 17. Dekker, *Seven Deadly Sins* (1879), p. 31, speaks of thundering crowds moving in such a "shoal that posts are set up of purpose to strengthen the houses lest with jostling one another they should shoulder them down."
3 Stow, *Survey of London* (1908), I, p. 252.
4 Harrison, *Description of England* (1807), p. 308.
5 Ibid., p. 344.
6 Stow, *Survey of London* (1908), II, p. 72.
7 Ibid., II, p. 60.
8 Ibid., I, p. 171.
9 Quinn and Cheshire, *Parmenius,* p. 101.
10 For the changes in the countryside, see Harrison, *Description of England;*

Stone, *Crisis;* Tawney, *Agrarian Problem;* "encroaching and joining . . ." Harrison, *Description of England* (1807), p. 325.

11 Stone, *Crisis of the Aristocracy,* p. 165. The wool crisis of 1586 was precipitated by a Spanish embargo on English shipping. Inflation was worsened by the tremendous influx of Spanish gold and silver subsequently captured by English privateers (Byrne, *Elizabethan Life,* p. 308). For vagrancy, see the Vagabond Act of 1572, 14 Eliz., c.5, s.5; also 18 Eliz., c.6; and 39 Eliz., c.4; Judges, *Elizabethan Underworld,* pp. xix-xlvii; Webb, *English Poor Law History.*

12 Norden, *Surveyor's Dialogue;* Harrison, *Description of England* (1807), pp. 314–15, 317, 356–7.

13 Harrison, *Description of England* (1807), pp. 355, 358.

14 Ibid., p. 358.

15 Harrison, *Description of Britaine* (1807), pp. 80–1.

16 Harrison, *Description of England* (1807), p. 371.

6 OF RELIGION

1 Cooper, *An Admonition* (1882), p. 70.

2 For the Anglican Church, see Frere and Douglas, *Puritan Manifestoes;* Knappen, *Tudor Puritanism,* pp. 168–86; Turner, *Second Course;* Platter, *Travels* (1937), pp. 176, 209; Strype, *Annals,* I; Byrne, *Elizabethan Life,* pp. 176–94; Williams, *Elizabeth,* pp. 64–77.

3 Thomas Savile to Camden in Quinn and Cheshire, *Parmenius,* p. 15; for the three hundred Cambridge protesters who threw off their surplices, see Strype, *Annals,* I, pt. 2, pp. 153–4; Knappen, *Tudor Puritanism,* pp. 195–6.

4 Marprelate, *Epistle* (1911), p. 86. Turner's dog, Marprelate said, was "full of good qualities."

5 Usher, *Presbyterian Movement,* p. 3. For Separatists, see also Cooper, *An Admonition;* Waddington, *Congregational History;* Knappen, *Tudor Puritanism;* Byrne, *Elizabethan Life.*

6 Parker, *Correspondence,* p. 61.

7 Knappen, *Tudor Puritanism,* p. 497; see also Bancroft, *Dangerous Positions;* Strype, *Annals,* III, pt. 1, pp. 22–4, 513; Bilson, *The True Difference.*

8 Cooper, *An Admonition* (1882), pp. 43, 48. John Penry and Job Throckmorton are generally regarded as the authors of the Marprelate tracts.

9 Marprelate, *Epistle* (1911), pp. 24, 26.

10 Cooper, *An Admonition* (1882), pp. 30–1.

11 Marprelate, *Epistle* (1911), pp. 90–1.

12 Cooper, *An Admonition* (1882), p. 27.

13 "ignorant rash . . ." George Gifford in Knappen, *Tudor Puritanism,* p. 311; "new-found equality," Cooper, *An Admonition* (1882), p. 54.

14 Whitgift, *Works,* I, p. 372.

15 John Field to D. Chapman, November 19, 1583, in Usher, *Presbyterian Movement,* p. 96; for the Cambridge protest, see Knappen, *Tudor Puritanism,* p. 239.

16 Knappen, *Tudor Puritanism,* p. 310.

17 "tyranny, dangerous days," W. Teye to Richard Parker, December 22, 1587, in Usher, *Presbyterian Movement,* p. 82; "I see a miserable desolation . . ." Parker to Teye, February 1587, in ibid., p. 83. For Burghley's condemnation, see Strype, *Whitgift,* I, p. 338; Pierce, *Historical Introduction,* p. 86. Puritans claimed that Whitgift pursued them with "deadly hatred and extreme rage," inflicting beatings, imprisonment, and even in-prison murder; Harleian Mss. 6848, fol. 7. See also Arber, *Introductory Sketch,* pp. 35–6; Pierce, *Historical Introduction,* pp. 92–8.

18 Knappen, *Tudor Puritanism,* pp. 265–82, 310–13; Byrne, *Elizabethan Life,* p. 192. For the manhunt, see Marprelate, *The Epitome,* pp. 117–18, *Hay Any Work,* p. 220, *Just Censure,* pp. 351–9, all in Pierce, *Tracts;* Strype, *Whitgift,* I, pp. 551–5, 601–2; "like furious . . ." Marprelate, *The Epitome* (1911), p. 151.

19 Imprisoned Brownists themselves later petitioned to be removed to the Magdalen Islands in Canada (State Papers Domestic, Elizabeth, ccxlvi, no. 56; Quinn, *New American World,* IV, p. 67). For Raleigh's opposition, see Edwards, *Sir Walter Raleigh,* I, p. 271. His shipping captain, Charles Leigh, was a Brownist (Quinn, *Raleigh and the British Empire,* p. 346). A further interesting connection was Raleigh's 1592 marriage to Bess Throckmorton, cousin to Job Throckmorton — the anonymous writer of the Marprelate tracts (Pierce, *Historical Introduction,* p. 218). Lodge said that "the Queen reasoned" with Raleigh on the subject of religion, "and censured his opinions with sharpness." Raleigh "defended the learned Puritan Udal" — John Penry's friend — "who had libelled the hierarchy with the most virulent bitterness and, when that minister was therefore condemned for high treason, interfered successfully to save his life" (Lodge, *Portraits,* II).

20 Knappen, *Tudor Puritanism,* pp. 312–13; Bancroft, *Dangerous Positions.*

7 THE COLONISTS

1 Nichols, *The Progresses,* II, p. 231.

2 College of Arms, Ms. Vincent Old Grants, 157, f. 397.

3 The seal is pictured without citation in Oakeshott, *Queen and the Poet,* plate II, facing p. 28. The inscription translates as "Knight; Guardian of the Stannaries of Cornwall and Devon; Captain of the Queen's Guard; Governor of the Island of Jersey."

4 Hariot, *A Briefe and True Report* (1589), p. 763.

5 Information about the colonists here and below is drawn from Powell, *Roanoke Colonists and Explorers: An Attempt at Identification.* Among the

colonists who went to Jamestown in 1606–7 were a number whose surnames were identical to White's Lost Colonists. Were they related? Interestingly, they seem to have been rather well-to-do: John Taverner, William Bayley, John Nickols, Nathaniell Powell, Thomas Wotton (a surgeon), and Captain John Martin were all gentlemen; William Johnson was a goldsmith; and John Powell and Bishop Wyles were tailors. Nathaniell Powell headed a team to search for the Lost Colonists in 1609. Smith, *Proceedings,* pp. 6–7, 26.

6 Hakluyt, *Principall Navigations* (1589), p. 769.

7 Gerard, *Herball,* pp. 709–10.

8 A point also raised by Hawks, *History,* I, p. 253: "The affluent and the possessors of moderate comfort, in the home of their youth, are not likely to sever all ties and cross an ocean to people a wilderness. There must ordinarily be some strong moral influence to prompt such men to remove."

9 For a roster of the Lost Colonists, see n. 28 below.

10 Hakluyt, *Principall Navigations* (1589), p. 769.

11 College of Arms, Ms. Vincent, 157, ff. 397–8.

12 Hakluyt, *Principall Navigations* (1600), III, p. 292. Interestingly, Spaniards carved crosses on trees to show Spanish occupancy, Lowery, *Spanish Settlements,* I, p. 156.

13 Deacon, *John Dee,* p. 107.

14 Banishment of Separatists to Scotland was first proposed by Archbishop Edmund Grindal, Knappen, *Tudor Puritanism,* p. 215; see also Byrne, *Elizabethan Life,* p. 192. "Our land . . ." Hall, *A Common Apologie* (1625), p. 576.

15 Hakluyt, *Principall Navigations* (1600), III, p. 301.

16 For the charges of atheism, see Chapter 19. Edwards noted that within Raleigh "there lay a longing for greater freedom, in civil matters as well as religious, than England had enjoyed," *Raleigh,* I, p. 346.

17 Hentzner, *Travels* (1865), p. 111.

18 Hakluyt, *Principall Navigations* (1589), p. 768.

19 Ibid. (1589), pp. 768–9. Whitgift complained that Separatists "sought to overthrow commonwealths and states of government. They gave honour and reverence to none. And they used to speak to such as were in authority without any signification of honour. Neither would they call men by their titles"; Strype, *Whitgift,* I, p. 72. John Smith complained of the "continual inundations" of "libertines" into America, who "could not endure the name of a Bishop, others not the sight of a cross nor surpless, others by no means the Book of Common Prayer"; *Advertisements,* pp. 29, 33. See also Quinn, *England and the Discovery of America,* pp. 340–4.

20 Hakluyt, *Discourse,* chapter 1.

21 Hakluyt, *Principall Navigations* (1589), p. 767.

22 Lane to Walsingham, September 8, 1585. State Papers Colonial, 1/1, 6.

23 Hakluyt, *Principall Navigations* (1600), III, p. 301.

24 Quinn and Cheshire, *Parmenius,* p. 14.
25 Examination of David Ingram, State Papers Domestic, Elizabeth, clxxv, 95. Ingram had been a member of Hawkins's expedition attacked by Spain at San Juan de Ulloa, Mexico, in 1568. Set ashore, he and two companions walked on foot to an area southwest of Cape Breton (Canada), where they were picked up by a French ship.
26 Ingram, *Relation* (1589), pp. 561–2.
27 "dead victual" and food lists, see Hakluyt, *Discourse,* chapter 21.
28 Hakluyt, *Principall Navigations* (1589), pp. 770–1. The colonists originally numbered 117. White returned to England and George Howe was later killed, leaving 115 people on Roanoke Island.

8 IN CERTAIN DANGER

1 Camden, *The History* (1688), p. 364.
2 For the members of Lane's 1585–1586 expedition, see Hakluyt, *Principall Navigations* (1589), pp. 736–7.
3 Ibid. (1589), p. 769.
4 This and all other quotes in this chapter are taken from ibid., pp. 766–9.

9 SABOTAGE

1 Raleigh, "Ocean to Scinthia," 11th book, lines 88–92.
2 Brown, *Genesis,* I, p. 219; II, p. 1061.
3 For Glande's story, see n. 13 below.
4 The details of the 1587 voyage and the quotes contained in this chapter, unless otherwise noted, are taken from Hakluyt, *Principall Navigations* (1589), pp. 764–70.
5 Virginia Company, *Records,* III, pp. 178–89; also Anon., *For the Colony in Virginea Britannia.*
6 Marmalade and butter were given to Maurice Browne at his departure for Newfoundland with Raleigh's brother Gilbert in 1583; Quinn and Cheshire, *Parmenius,* Appendix 1, p. 208.
7 Manteo first went to England in September 1584 with the return of Raleigh's first Roanoke expedition. He came home to North America in the spring of 1585 with Raleigh's second Roanoke expedition, and returned to England again with either Lane or Grenville in 1586.
8 Diaz, *Examination of the Masters and Pilots* (1600), pp. 866–8.
9 Ibid.
10 Ibid.
11 Modern Tallaboa Bay, Puerto Rico.
12 "Darby Glande," Hakluyt, *Principall Navigations* (1589), p. 737; "Darbie

Glaven," ibid., p. 765; "David Glavin," Gonçalo Mendez de Canço, *Report;* "David Glavid," Oré, *Relación* (1936), p. 49.

13 Canço, *Report,* p. 155. Glande's deposition was taken in February 1599 by Canço and forwarded to Philip III on February 8, 1600. He located Jacan at 36 degrees and said it was the place where Grenville made his fort. Roanoke, by modern measurements, is located at 35 degrees, 54 minutes, 29 seconds north latitude.

14 Oré, *Relación* (1936), p. 49, says that Glande served as a galley slave until he was brought from Havana to St. Augustine, or from July 1587 to possibly sometime in the year 1594 or 1595, for in 1600 Canço reported (*Report,* p. 155) that Glande had been in St. Augustine for more than five years.

15 Canço, *Report,* p. 156; in Spanish, author's translation. The phrase in question is *tubo orden de huyrse.*

16 The original text reads "pines."

17 Original text reads "plantanos."

18 Captain John Smith hit the nail on the head when he wrote, "it seems Simon Ferdinando did what he could to bring this voyage to confusion . . ." *General History,* p. 13. Hulton and Quinn (*American Drawings,* I, p. 17), on the other hand, question White's claim that Fernandez was deliberately sabotaging the expedition. They suggest that because no piratical attacks had been made on Spanish shipping on the way out due to the presence of the colonists, an unhappy Fernandez took revenge on White. They suggest alternatively that Fernandez may have been protecting the company from "hostile" Indian nations on the Chesapeake Bay. Yet thanks to Ralph Lane, there was assured hostility on Roanoke Island, and Fernandez certainly knew through Stafford that the local Indian leaders had failed to respond to White's peace overtures.

19 "Our water did smell so vividly," wrote Jamestown colonist George Percy upon reaching the Caribbean, "that none of our men were able to endure it," *Observations* (1907), p. 8. The Jamestown ships, however, were able to take on fresh supplies, whereas White's were not.

20 Edwards, *Raleigh,* II, pp. lxii-iii.

21 Nichols, *The Progresses,* ii, p. 231.

22 Fernandez made the round-trip reconnaissance for Gilbert in three months, or roughly half the sailing time of Raleigh's Roanoke voyages; State Papers Colonial, 1/1, 2; "not without almost . . ." Taylor, *Two Richard Hakluyts,* II, p. 367.

23 White steadfastly calls this entry Hatorask, rejecting the English name of Port Ferdinando.

24 The anonymous gentleman acted at the instigation of Simon Fernandez.

25 If White's colonists were Separatists, they may have known that there was little chance of being admitted back into the realm. The Jamestown colonists, even without this stigma, were refused readmission in 1614. Their

petition to return was refused by King James I, "with the suggestion," reported Spanish agent Gondomar, "that it was well to preserve that place, altho' it be good for nothing more than to kill people"; Brown, *Genesis,* II, p. 681. Overpopulation was reaching epidemic proportions.

26 White lists a Thomas Smith among the dead. One of his colonists bore the same name, though they were probably different men, since White mentions only himself as returning to England.

27 Hakluyt, *Principall Navigations* (1600), III, p. 301. Despite the May 1587 date on Hakluyt's document, the material was not published until at least October 1587, after Stafford's return; Quinn, *Roanoke Voyages,* II, p. 552, n. 6.

28 Quinn (*Set Fair,* p. 279) notes that even Stafford did not protest about Fernandez's actions and suggests that White may have been secretly pleased with the arrangement to remain on Roanoke Island, since it had been "a happy place for him."

10 THE SECOND ROANOKE EXPEDITION: GRENVILLE AND THE SECOTAN (1585)

1 Hakluyt, *Discourse,* chapter 7.

2 Manteo was from Croatoan Island; Wanchese's hometown was unknown, although since he later served as an adviser to Wingina and was numbered among the Dasamonquepeuc survivors, it may be safe to assume that he was from Roanoke Island or the adjacent mainland. For their dress, see the testimony of Lupold von Wedel in Quinn, *Roanoke Voyages,* I, p. 116, n. 6.

3 State Papers Domestic, Elizabeth, CCXV, 89, [August?] 1588.

4 Camden, *The History* (1688), p. 312.

5 Hakluyt, *Discourse,* chapter 7.

6 Hakluyt, *The Honourable Voyage unto Cadiz* (1600), III.

7 The Spaniards feared a North American English settlement for precisely this reason. Drake's 1586 raid on St. Augustine and his carrying away of so many supplies led to Spanish fears that Drake himself would establish a base on the coast from which to attack the fleets; Quinn, *New American World,* V, 44. In 1581 Walsingham, Leicester, and Burghley drew up plans for a fortress on Terceira to intercept the returning Spanish plate fleet; Taylor, *Troublesome Voyage,* p. xxxix. That Raleigh's intention was to establish a similar military base on Roanoke, see Andrews, *Elizabethan Privateering,* pp. 191, 193. Hakluyt recommended such a plan in his *Discourse,* chapter 5. Spain also recognized the significance of the Outer Banks, positioned so close to Bermuda, as a base for attack; Wright, *Further English Voyages,* xxii, n. 3; 44, p. 185. This was still uppermost in their mind when Jamestown was settled in 1607. Pirates will be sent to Virginia, Pedro de Zúñiga warned the King, and the "thing is so perfect — according to what they say . . . that Y. M. will not be able to get the silver from the Indies . . ." Brown, *Genesis,* I, p. 244.

8 Hakluyt, *Discourse,* chapter 11.

9 Ibid., chapter 7.
10 Raleigh, "Ocean to Scinthia," 11th Book, line 61.
11 Hakluyt, *Discourse,* chapter 7.
12 Calendar of State Papers, Spain, 1580–6, p. 536. Bernardino de Mendoza, the ousted Spanish ambassador who was reporting from Paris via agents still in England, believed that the ships were headed for Norumbega on the American North Atlantic coast.
13 Quinn, *Roanoke Voyages,* I, pp. 119–20, 130–9, 173, n. 5; see Wright, *Further English Voyages,* p. 15, for the deposition of Enrique Lopez, who said that three hundred Englishmen were landed in North America to build Lane's fort. Hakluyt recommended utilizing soldiers returned from the wars who were "idle" and "hurtful" to the realm (*Discourse,* chapter 20, item 21, and *Principall Navigations* [1600], III, p. 303). A number of Lane's men were Irish, and at least one, Edward Nugent, had served under him in Kerry (ibid. [1589], p. 746; Quinn, *Roanoke Voyages,* I, p. 195, n. 3).
14 Lane's mother was a cousin to Catherine Parr, the sixth wife of Henry VIII; Brown, *Genesis,* II, p. 936.
15 Holinshed, *Chronicles* (1807), IV, p. 598.
16 For Grenville's officers and specialists, see Quinn, *Roanoke Voyages,* I, pp. 158–9, 196, n. 1. For the total complement of men involved, see State Papers Colonial, 1/1, 3; Rowse, *Grenville,* p. 204.
17 Andrews, *Elizabethan Privateering,* p. 3.
18 Calendar of State Papers, Spain, 1580–6, p. 651.
19 Andrews, *Elizabethan Privateering,* pp. 3, 32–3; Strype, *Annals,* III, part 1, pp. 422–4.
20 Hentzner, *Travels* (1865), p. 110.
21 For the ships' names listed here and below, see index in Andrews, *Elizabethan Privateering,* pp. 289–94; for the London merchants, see ibid., pp. 34, 75, 118–19.
22 Rowse, *Expansion,* p. 297; see also Andrews, *Elizabethan Privateering,* pp. 14, 129, who estimates (p. 133) that in the two-year period between 1589 and 1591, £100,000 of sugar was taken by English privateers from Spanish vessels.
23 State Papers Domestic, James, xcix, 77, September 28, 1618.
24 Hakluyt, *Principall Navigations* (1589), p. 733. For details of Grenville's expedition, see ibid., pp. 733–6.
25 Holinshed, *Chronicles* (1807), IV, p. 599.
26 For Hernando de Altamirano, see Quinn, *Roanoke Voyages,* II, pp. 740–3; for White's paintings, see Hulton, *America, 1585;* Hulton and Quinn, *American Drawings.*
27 Wright, *Further English Voyages,* doc. 9, p. 12.
28 Lane to Burghley, January 7, 1591/2, Lansdowne Mss. 69, fol. 29–29v, British Museum.
29 Hakluyt, *Principall Navigations* (1589), p. 734.

30 Lane to Walsingham, September 8, 1585, State Papers Colonial, 1/1, 6.

31 Committee decision making, of course, was the old way of doing things aboard ship. Drake was the first to break with this tradition during his circumnavigation of the world. Times had changed; sea battles with Spain made split-second decisions necessary, and the councils of war increasingly assumed a more advisory role; Williamson, *Age of Drake,* pp. 180–1.

32 Lane to Walsingham, September 8, 1585, State Papers Colonial, 1/1, 6.

33 Lane to Walsingham, August 12, 1585, State Papers Colonial, 1/1, 3.

34 Ibid.

35 Ibid.

36 Holinshed, *Chronicles* (1807), IV, p. 599.

37 Lane to Walsingham, August 12, 1585, State Papers Colonial, 1/1, 3.

38 For Butler's very confused account, see Quinn, *New American World,* III, pp. 329–31. Thirty men from the missing *Lion* had already been retrieved from Croatoan Island, where they had been living for three weeks. This can only have been a great burden on the people of Croatoan, since their own population probably did not exceed one hundred; Haag, *Archeology,* p. 15.

39 "sent word . . ." Hakluyt, *Principall Navigations* (1589), p. 735; "the King," ibid., p. 729.

40 Wanchese clearly did not look favorably upon England. Lane later accused him of inciting Wingina against his soldiers, ibid. (1589), p. 744.

41 Ibid. (1589), p. 736.

42 Lane to Walsingham, August 12, 1585, State Papers Colonial, 1/1, 3. This region was later known as the Little Dismal Swamp, or the Alligator Dismal. Tragically, most of the swamp is now drained and the magnificent trees have been cut down.

43 "They are a people . . ." Hariot, *Briefe and True Report* (1589), p. 759; "and to confess . . ." De Bry, *America,* I, p. xxiii.

44 Hakluyt, *Principall Navigations* (1589), p. 793.

45 De Bry, *America,* I, plate xix.

46 Ibid., plate ii. "Babies" were baby dolls.

47 "multitude . . . ample vent . . ." Hakluyt, *Inducements* (1602), p. 25 (D). For Mr. Ashley, see Rowse, *Expansion,* p. 187; Quinn, *Gilbert,* p. 243; "Looking glasses. . ." Peckham, *True Report* (1589), p. 706.

48 "of the age of 8 or 10," White's annotation of a woman and child of Pomeioc, British Museum, P & D, 1906–5–9–1 (13); "They are greatly delighted . . ." De Bry, *America,* I, plates viii, ii.

49 Hakluyt, *Principall Navigations* (1589), p. 735. In 1605 Englishmen referred to North Carolina ("Wingandecoia") as the "land of parrots," Hall, *Mundus.* Jamestown colonist Francis Perkins described the country as full of "the prettiest parrots there are"; Barbour, *Jamestown,* I, p. 161. According to Lawson (*History of North Carolina* [1903], p. 83), they were gorgeous, with a

brilliant green plumage and a splattering of orange on the head. The Carolina parrot has been hunted to extinction.

50 De Bry, *America,* I, plates viii, ix.

51 Strachey, *Historie of Travaile* (1849), p. 78.

52 De Bry, *America,* I, plate xix.

53 "most courteous . . . " Hakluyt, *Principall Navigations* (1589), p. 793; "esteem our trifles . . ." Hariot, *Briefe and True Report* (1589), p. 759.

54 Smith, *Map of Virginia,* p. 17. Strachey gives the word as *appones,* while corn bread boiled in water was *ponepopi; Historie* (1849), p. 74. Other familiar loan words have come into the English language from Powhatan, for example, *chum,* which Smith defines as "friend," ibid., Powhatan vocab., p. 3v. The word may derive from a canoe partner, one who is trusted, cf. Shawnee *choom,* "paddle," Pearson, *Shawnee Language,* p. 23.

55 De Bry, *America,* I, plate xix. For examples of woven house mats throughout the Southeast, see Swanton, *Indians of the Southeastern United States,* pp. 244, 247, 414–15; 602–3, 606.

56 Hariot, *Briefe and True Report* (1589), p. 761. That the missing silver cup was a communion chalice is likely. According to Harrap (Byrne, *Elizabethan Life,* p. 184) the Anglican service utilized common loaf bread and wine served in a silver cup.

57 "fairer," De Bry, *America,* I, plate xx; "well entertained," Hakluyt, *Principall Navigations* (1589), p. 736.

58 White's annotation of the village of "Secoton," British Museum, P & D, 1906–5–9–1 (7).

59 De Bry, *America,* I, plate xx.

60 "Six or seven foot . . ." Hariot, *Briefe and True Report* (1589), p. 753; "In their corn fields . . ." De Bry *America,* I, plate xx.

61 Ibid., plate iv.

62 Ibid., plates xiii, vi.

63 Ibid., plate xviii. The original text read "certain markes on the backs."

64 Ibid., plate xiv.

65 Ibid., plate xv. The original text read "boil together like a galliemaufrye" (a stew). The menu suggested here and below was generated by comparing accounts of foodstuffs grown and gathered, as reported by Raleigh's men and the Jamestown colonists, to American Indian cuisine extant in North Carolina and Virginia. For an excellent summary of food items, see Swanton, *Indians of the Southeastern United States,* pp. 244–95, 351–68; also various cookbooks available, such as Mary Ulmer and Samuel E. Beck (ed.), *Cherokee Cooklore,* Cherokee, N.C.: Museum of the Cherokee Indian, 1951.

66 De Bry, *America,* I, plate xv. Grenville's men were almost certainly witnessing the Green Corn Celebration held just before the cobs of flour corn reached maturity, generally in July or August. The ceremony occurred

throughout the agricultural Southeast and was (and is) the greatest ceremony of the year, marked by a sense of tranquillity and the absence of discord, which was exactly the mood that Hariot reported at Secota.

67 "void of all . . ." De Bry, *America,* I, plate XX; "trifles," Hariot, *Briefe and True Report,* p. 759.

68 Hakluyt, *Principall Navigations* (1589), p. 736.

69 Ibid.

70 British Museum, P & D, 199.a.3.

71 Hariot, *Briefe and True Report* (1589), p. 759.

72 Holinshed, *Chronicles* (1807), IV, p. 598. We could wish for a far more detailed account of this episode. However, the three-day delay off Wococon, coupled with Lane's zealousness to remain in the country, his vehement letters to the government condemning Grenville, Grenville's instructions to occupy the coast, and the disastrous inadequacy of supplies with which to do so lend credibility to this sequence of events, which must remain conjectural until further evidence is found to clarify it.

73 "bold letter . . ." Lane to Walsingham, August 12, 1585, State Papers Colonial, 1/1, 4; "intendeth to accuse . . ." Lane to Walsingham, ibid., 1/1, 3.

74 Lane to Walsingham, September 8, 1585, State Papers Colonial, 1/1, 6.

75 Ibid.

76 Hakluyt, *Principall Navigations* (1589), p. 737; for the military complement, see State Papers Domestic, Elizabeth, CLXXXV, 36; Wright, *Further English Voyages,* p. 15.

77 Lane to Walsingham, September 8, 1585, State Papers Colonial, 1/1, 6.

78 Ibid.

11 THE SECOND ROANOKE EXPEDITION: LANE'S COMMAND (1585–1586)

1 Bacon, "Of Plantations," *Essays* (1887), p. 353.

2 Hakluyt, *Principall Navigations* (1589), p. 736. No document has yet been discovered that explains the nature of the agreement reached between Lane and Granganimeo. However, it is clear that since Lane was proposing a settlement within his territory, Granganimeo was brought aboard the *Admiral* with Manteo as interpreter for some form of negotiation. Given that Lane's company doubled Roanoke's population, and that an agricultural crisis was unfolding whose severity had yet to be determined (see n. 17 below), I think it not unlikely that part of the negotiation concerned the food supply, with Granganimeo refusing to commit himself to any provisioning arrangement for the fort beyond the sale of surpluses. Excess corn from the previous year had been reduced by the first Roanoke expedition of 1584.

3 Hariot claimed that Lane had only enough provision to last twenty days! *Briefe and True Report* (1589), p. 763.

4 For Vaughan's identification, see Quinn, *Roanoke Voyages,* vol. 1, p. 194, n. 7; also Corbett, *Spanish War,* p. 293.
5 Hakluyt, *Discourse,* chapter 20, #21.
6 Lane to Sidney, August 12, 1585, State Papers Colonial, 1/1, 5.
7 Lane to Walsingham, August 12, 1585, State Papers Colonial, 1/1, 3. In 1574, Lane proposed leading a crusade of two thousand Englishmen, under Spain's Christian banner, against the Turks — on condition that he retain disciplinary authority within his own regiment. Lane claimed that the Queen initially favored the project as recompense for his past ill fortune (Strype, *Annals,* II, i, p. 518), which may have been caused by the Earl of Leicester; see Chapter 16, n. 13.
8 "we discharged any piece . . ." Hakluyt, *Principall Navigations* (1589), p. 732; "were amazed . . ." De Bry, *America,* I, plate ii.
9 Haag, *Archeology,* pp. 62–4.
10 Hakluyt, *Principall Navigations* (1589), p. 730.
11 Ibid., p. 729; for the identification of Wingina as head of the Secotan, as well as the practice of shifting residence, see Appendix A.
12 Ibid., p. 736.
13 Lane to Walsingham, September 8, 1585, State Papers Colonial, 1/1, 6. The holy day in question was the Green Corn Ceremony, or Busk.
14 Hariot, *Briefe and True Report* (1589), p. 749.
15 "pagatowr . . ." ibid., p. 753; "have found here. . . ," Hakluyt, *Principall Navigations* (1589), p. 793; "sweet juice," Strachey, *Historie* (1849), p. 117.
16 Hariot, *Briefe and True Report* (1589), p. 753.
17 Lane to Walsingham, August 12, 1585, State Papers Colonial, 1/1, 3.
18 Stahle et al., "Lost Colony and Jamestown Droughts," p. 565. Stahle places the start of the drought at 1587. In the absence of correlating historical data, his conclusion that it caused the death of the Lost Colonists is reasonable. However, there are several factors that can prevent the occurrence of a late-season drought from being recorded in tree rings (Cook and Kariutskis, *Methods of Dendrochronology,* pp. 43, 45, 68–70; Stokes and Smiley, *Tree-Ring Dating,* pp. 48–9, 53). Stokes and Smiley stress the need for correlating tree ring dating with other available information (p. 61). The historical data, the absence of skeletal remains on Roanoke, and the message left by the colonists themselves provide that information. Stahle's work shows the presence of an intense drought in the vicinity of 1587, while Hariot's record dated it to 1585 or 1586. Very little attention has been paid to Hariot's statements about the drought, and thus the severity of Lane's food demands upon the Secotan have been drastically underestimated.
19 Hariot, *Briefe and True Report* (1589), p. 761.
20 Ibid., p. 761.
21 Ibid., pp. 760–1.
22 Ibid.

23 Lane to Walsingham, August 12, 1585, State Papers Colonial, 1/1, 3.

24 "daily discovery . . ." Lane to Walsingham, September 8, 1585, State Papers Colonial, 1/1, 6; "Cedar, a very sweet wood . . ." Hariot, *Briefe and True Report* (1589), p. 751.

25 Ibid.

26 Hariot reported dugout canoes carrying "20 men at once . . . their timber being great, tall, straight . . ." ibid., p. 758. In the Powhatan country, Captain John Smith marveled at the great open spaces underneath the massive trunks, such "that a man may gallop a horse amongst these woods any way, but where the creeks or rivers shall hinder," Smith, *Map of Virginia,* p. 21. Smith then destroyed what he admired, for he ordered timbering crews to hack down the woods — it was a "delight," he said, "to hear the trees thunder as they fell"; *Proceedings,* p. 48.

27 Hakluyt, *Principall Navigations* (1589), p. 793.

28 There were four comets that might have appeared to the naked eye over Roanoke that summer, but the largest and by far the closest to earth was c/1585 TI. Unfortunately, although the dating of the comet is crucial in determining the sequence of events during Lane's tenure on Roanoke Island, Hariot does not do so. Since he stated that it appeared "but a few days before the beginning" of an epidemic that struck the Secotan (*Briefe and True Report,* p. 762), and given that they blamed the Englishmen for the illness, the event, in all probability, occurred after Lane had moved into the fort in September and there was sustained contact between them. On September 27 c/1585 TI appeared in the sky almost directly south of the island at 13 degrees, 3 minutes (presumably the minimum height to be seen above the tree line), at its closest position to earth thus far at .197356 at 9 P.M. On October 17 it reached its brightest and most visible at 34 degrees, 42 minutes, having achieved its maximum proximity to earth at .135492, before receding. This was spectacularly close — by comparison, Hale-Bopp appeared over Roanoke on July 27, 1996, at a distance of 2.744585. Based on the position of c/1585 TI, therefore, we might suppose that the disease struck the Outer Banks sometime toward the later half of September; data supplied by RedShift computer software program.

29 "rare and strange accident . . ." Hariot, *Briefe and True Report* (1589), p. 761; "sundry that came sick . . ." Lane to Walsingham, August 12, 1585, State Papers Colonial, 1/1, 3.

30 Ibid., p. 761.

31 Ibid.

32 Ibid., pp. 758, 760.

33 Ibid., pp. 761–2.

34 Ibid., p. 761.

35 Hakluyt, *Principall Navigations* (1589), p. 738.

36 Quinn, *Set Fair,* p. 75.

37 Adamson and Folland, *Shepherd of the Ocean*, pp. 100–3.

38 Hakluyt, *Principall Navigations* (1589), p. 736.

39 For Grenville's assessment of the cargo: Andrews, *Elizabethan Privateering*, p. 192; Rowse, *Grenville*, p. 222. For Grenville's enemies' claim: Quinn, *Roanoke Voyages*, I, pp. 218–21. Portuguese/Spanish claims: ibid., I, p. 169; Rowse, *Grenville*, p. 218. Anonymous account: Quinn, *Roanoke Voyages*, I, pp. 225–6. The anonymous writer appears to have been none other than William Herllie, an agent employed by Burghley and, in 1585, by Walsingham.

40 Lane to Burghley, January 7, 1592, Lansdowne Mss. 69, folios 29–29v., British Museum; Quinn, *Roanoke Voyages*, I, p. 229.

41 Grenville to Walsingham, October 29, 1585, State Papers Colonial, 1/1, 7.

42 Lane to Walsingham, August 12, 1585, State Papers Colonial, 1/1, 3.

43 "oyssan . . ." Quinn, *New American World*, V, p. 115; "as common there . . ." Hakluyt, *Principall Navigations* (1589), p. 793; "piece of silk . . ." Hariot, *Briefe and True Report* (1589), p. 750. The "silk" grosgrain was presented to Queen Elizabeth (Va. Co. *A Note of Shipping* [1906–35], III, p. 642). The word *oyssan* was possibly a corruption of *wighsacan* or *wysauke* (*wisak-an-wi* "it is bitter"). John White's drawing of a milkweed "wisakon" was utilized by Gerard, who called it "wisanck" and described it as having pods "stuffed full of most pure silk" (*Herball*, p. 752; Barbour, *Complete Works*, I, p. 154, n. 6; Quinn, *Roanoke Voyages*, II, p. 900).

44 Platter, *Travels* (1937), pp. 171–3.

45 Taylor, *Two Richard Hakluyts*, I, p. 45, n. 4; "It is a world also to see . . ." Harrison, *Description of England* (1807), p. 351.

46 "very large diamonds . . ." Wirtemberg, *True and Faithful Narrative* (1865), p. 18; the unicorn horn, ibid., p. 17; "that horn of Windsor," Peacham, *Sights and Exhibitions in England*.

47 Weelkes, *Ayeres or Phantasticke Spirites;* Rye, *England as Seen by Foreigners*, p. 202, n. 37.

48 Hakluyt, *Inducements* (1602), p. 30 (D3).

49 See Chapter 19, n. 3.

50 Hariot, *Briefe and True Report* (1589), p. 760. Although Quinn (*Roanoke Voyages*, I, p. 374, n. 1) states that this story is without precise parallels, there are, in fact, many. Johnson (*Ojibway Ceremonies*, pp. 134–50) records almost exactly the same story among the Ojibway. There is a numerous literature on messianic, millenarian, and revitalization movements following extreme social disruption, in which individuals receive divine instruction. Often this involves death, a journey to the afterlife, a return to the living, a rejection of foreign influences, and a revival of the old traditions according to the instructions given in the other world. That a revival of this nature occurred among the Secotan has, to my knowledge, never before been proposed, but seems quite clear given Hariot's statements.

51 Hariot, *Briefe and True Report* (1589), pp. 755–6. See Quinn, *Roanoke Voyages,* I, pp. 347–50, for identification of the wild plants and roots consumed.

52 Hariot, *Briefe and True Report* (1589), pp. 763, 755, 750. As relations worsened with Lane's men and the drought increased, Wingina commanded that his people "should not, for any copper, sell us any victuals whatsoever"; Hakluyt, *Principall Navigations* (1589), p. 744.

53 Hariot, *Briefe and True Report* (1589), pp. 749, 757.

54 Stone, *Crisis of the Aristocracy,* p. 572.

55 "very miserable . . ." Thomas Harvey to the Chancery Court, February 4, 1591, Public Record Office, C.2, Elizabeth S. 16/48 (2/13/314); "Some want also . . ." Hariot, *Briefe and True Report* (1589), p. 763.

56 "misdemeanour and ill dealing . . ." Hariot, *Briefe and True Report* (1589), p. 749. Grenville's 1586 relief expedition reached Roanoke less than a month after Lane's men had been evacuated by Drake. Pedro Diaz, present on the expedition, reported that Roanoke Island was deserted except for two bodies found hanged there — one English, one Indian (Quinn, *Roanoke Voyages,* II, p. 790); "any woman," Notes for Master Rauleys Viage, Essex County Record Office, County Hall, Chelmsford, MS D/DRh, M 1, f. 2v; Quinn, *Roanoke Voyages,* I, pp. 126–39.

57 De Bry, *America,* I, plate viii.

58 Hakluyt, *Principall Navigations* (1589), p. 732.

59 Hariot, *Briefe and True Report* (1589), p. 752.

60 Hakluyt, *Principall Navigations* (1589), p. 730.

61 Ibid., p. 793.

62 "plate of copper," De Bry, *America,* I, plate vii; "and other noblemen," Hakluyt, *Principall Navigations* (1589), p. 730; "of good parentage," De Bry, *America,* I, plates vi, iv; "esteem more . . ." ibid., plate xxi.

12 CHAUNIS TEMOATAN AND A MURDER (1586)

1 British Museum, Additional Ms. 6788, f. 490.

2 Lane to Sidney, August 12, 1585, State Papers Colonial, 1/1, 5.

3 Lane to Walsingham, September 8, 1585, State Papers Colonial, 1/1, 6.

4 Hariot, *Briefe and True Report* (1589), p. 763. The supposition has been made by historians that Lane's winter camp was located on the Chesapeake Bay. However, Lane's own statement (n. 19 below) clearly refutes this. He said that he planned to send them to the west, to the country Amadas had visited. It is possible that the party encamped in the region of Moratoc on the Roanoke River, or within the Chowanoc country, since Lane appeared to have a familiarity with both nations before his trip there in the spring. Where the winter camp went hinges not only on the correct identification of the Chesepiocs, among whom Lane said they resided (see n. 13), but on the

three neighboring nations who visited them there: the Mandoag, Tripanick, and Oppossian.

5 Hariot, *Briefe and True Report* (1589), p. 763. Lane seldom gave dates for his activities on the island, and the return of the winter camp was no exception. Presumably it came back to Roanoke in time to provide Lane with information for his March expedition against the Chowanoc. A second Secotan epidemic probably occurred at about this time — late February — which claimed Granganimeo's life. At his brother's death, Wingina changed his name to Pemisapan. We know that both events took place before Lane's March expedition.

6 Hariot, *Briefe and True Report* (1589), pp. 751–2.

7 For White's map, see De Bry, *America,* I; also British Museum, P & D, 1906–5–9–1 (3); "Mangoaks . . ." Hakluyt, *Principall Navigations* (1589), pp. 740, 743. *Mangoak* and *Mandoag* were used interchangeably by Lane.

8 Ibid., p. 740. Such name changing was not uncommon, particularly among the Powhatan; Wahunsonacock's brother Opitchapam changed his name twice: to Itoyatin and Sasawpen, while another brother, Opechancanough, changed his name to Mangopeesomon (Rountree, *Pocahontas's People,* p. 73). It occurred elsewhere too, as when Liliwathika of the Shawnee changed his name to Tenskwatawa. Among the Pokanoket there was Woosamequin (alias Massasoit) and Tatamumaque (alias Cashewashed); and the Narragansett leader Nawnawnoantonnew was also Canonchet. Many more examples are known. Strachey said that the Powhatan were ruled "by a great king, by them called by sundry names . . . and so commonly they of greatest merit amongst them aspire to many names"; *Historie,* Book 1, chapter 3.

9 The remainder of the events in this chapter and all quotes contained therein, unless otherwise noted, are from Lane's account, published in Hakluyt, *Principall Navigations* (1589), pp. 737–47.

10 Ensinore clearly was not motivated by regard for Lane, but by dread. The English soldiers, he said, could not be destroyed, but were dead men who had come there to kill. This belief was very likely the Secotan equivalent to the North Algonquian man-shaped cannibal monster known as Windigo. If Gerard was correct that the Powhatan word *Wintuc,* recorded by Strachey as "fool," should really be "ghoul" ("Virginia Indian Words," p. 248. Gerard postulated a copyist's error), then we have confirmation of the existence of the idea among the Powhatan. Ensinore's attitude toward the English was clear: he believed, in effect, that Lane's men were *Windigo.*

11 Pemisapan supplied three guides: his brother-in-law Eracano, Tetepano, and Cossine.

12 Taken literally, 150 river miles would place Lane in the vicinity of Halifax, some distance east of Roanoke Rapids.

13 Identification of the Chesepians is extremely problematic. The general consensus by historians has been that they were a nation living along the

southern edge of the Chesapeake Bay. Yet in 1895, the Algonquian linguist Tooker ("Chesapeake," p. 87) demonstrated that the word *Chesepioc* translated to "country on a great river," a name that had nothing at all to do with the bay, but might — Tooker proposed — have referred to the Elizabeth River. Since the Nansemond were living in this location when Jamestown was settled, the equation of this nation with the Chesepioc is clearly a question that must be determined. On the other hand, it is equally possible that a completely different river other than the Elizabeth was intended. Was White's placement of Chesepioc on his map based on verbal report? Was there more than one "country on a great river"? Since the word *Chesepioc* denotes a location (*k'tchi,* "great" + *sipi,* "river" + *aki,* "land, country"), rather than a people themselves, it is worth considering other nations living on large waterways who would likely be allied to the Mandoag and within the Secotan sphere of influence.

14 Is the implication here that Lane had Pemisapan's man killed? If so, why? Had he perhaps tried to rescue Skiko? Since Lane regarded the Secotan as subject to the laws of Queen Elizabeth, they were also subject to death for the crime of treason. Is there any proof that Lane ordered an execution? Someone certainly did. Immediately after Lane's evacuation from Roanoke, Raleigh's relief ships put in to the abandoned fort and made the grisly discovery of two hanged bodies, one of which was Indian (see Chapter 11, n. 56). A hypothetical sequence of events may have been that Pemisapan's man was forced to confess the plans, after which he was killed. Lane next applied to the terrorized Skiko for confirmation, threatening the boy with decapitation.

15 In London, the decapitated heads of executed nobles were hung from London Bridge. Did Lane hang Pemisapan's head from the fort? If so, the horror this would produce among the Secotan can scarcely be imagined.

16 *Primrose* log, printed in Corbett, *Spanish War,* p. 27.

17 Hakluyt, *Principall Navigations* (1589), p. 748.

18 Lane said that the vessel "was seen to be free" from the shore and "to put clear to sea." Since this boat had "all my provisions," its failure to return — from Lane's standpoint — was a reprehensible action.

19 This is the clearest evidence that Lane had not reached the Chesapeake Bay. Early historians such as Beverly, writing in 1705, believed that Lane had not yet located it; *Present State of Virginia,* chapter 1, C5.

13 THE LOST COLONISTS (1587)

1 Jeremiah 5:26.

2 Hakluyt, *Principall Navigations* (1589), p. 748.

3 Testimony of Pedro Diaz in Quinn, *Roanoke Voyages,* II, p. 788.

4 Hakluyt, *Principall Navigations* (1589), p. 748; Quinn, *Roanoke Voyages,* II,

p. 791. Pedro Diaz claimed that Grenville left eighteen men on Roanoke. This may be an error, yet the discrepancy may also have an explanation in Lane, who had departed from Roanoke in such a hurry that he left behind three men who had been sent into the interior. If so, they made their reappearance at the fort before Grenville sailed away and were conscripted to make up the number of the holding party.

5 Hakluyt, *Principall Navigations* (1589), pp. 766–7. The events described in this chapter and the quotes contained therein, unless otherwise noted, are taken from John White's account in ibid., pp. 764–71.

6 Ibid., p. 728.

7 Ibid., p. 729.

8 Ibid.

9 This is a completely irrational episode in every way: Why did only twenty-four men accompany Stafford when there were more than three times as many male colonists available to him? Were the men who agreed to fight with him colonists at all? Might Raleigh have sent over a small corps of soldiers to reinforce the holding party at the Roanoke fort, who were at Stafford's disposal? See n. 11 below.

10 Hakluyt's dedicatory preface to Raleigh of Laudonnière in Hakluyt, *Principall Navigations* (1600), III, p. 301.

11 It is possible that Stafford was sent to Roanoke with military authority independent of White's colonists. Hakluyt (*Principall Navigations,* 1589, table of contents) described the expedition as "The voyage of Edward Stafford, and John White, set out by . . . Sir Walter Raleigh." If such a division existed, it might explain why, when White's colonists left Roanoke Island, they went a very specific distance inland — fifty miles — to ensure that they were clear of the Roanoke fort's jurisdiction.

12 Supply ships did bypass Roanoke. According to the testimony of Alonso Ruiz, Sir George Carey (whom White called upon in 1587 as the colonists were departing) sent three ships to the Chesapeake Bay under Captain William Irish. They returned to England, having encountered no one. Wright, *Further English Voyages,* pp. 233–5; Quinn, *Roanoke Voyages,* II, pp. 499, 543, 782–4; also Andrews, *Elizabethan Privateering,* pp. 97, 193–4.

13 For Fernandez, see Chapter 16, n. 47. Spanish authorities referred to him as "a thorough-paced soundrel," Calendar of State Papers, Spain, 1568–79, nos. 496, 503.

14 In 1605 the Spaniards were still searching for the Roanoke colony. An expedition sent out under Ferdinand de Écija that year tried, but failed, to reach the Outer Banks. In 1609 he was dispatched again and succeeded in locating the English who, by then, were established at Jamestown; Quinn, *New American World,* V, pp. 141–50. It is clear from his report, however, that before this discovery Spain had no idea where the colony was.

14 RALEIGH'S RISE TO POWER

1 Raleigh's commendatory verses to Gascoigne's *The Steele Glas;* Hawks, *History of North Carolina,* I, p. 19.
2 Raleigh's mother was Catherine Champernoun, who married, first, Otho Gilbert, which union produced three sons and a daughter: John, Humphrey, Adrian, and Mary; and second, Walter Raleigh, to whom she bore Carew, Walter, and Margaret. Although biographers consistently refer to John, Humphrey, and Adrian Gilbert as Raleigh's half-brothers, Raleigh himself did not make such distinctions nor, apparently, did anyone within the family. This book has adopted their usage.
3 Hakluyt, *Principall Navigations* (1600), III, pp. 135–7. Letters Patent were issued by Queen Elizabeth under the Great Seal and conveyed authority to the recipient to pursue actions or partake of privileges and liberties encompassed within its terms. In Gilbert's case, the Queen's royal grant included license to discover and occupy foreign lands not possessed by any Christian prince or people, along with the right to profits from the land, giving him full authority and power over any cities or towns within it, and reserving to the Queen the fifth part of all gold and silver ore discovered and extracted there. Gilbert's patent, however, bore the stipulation that such lands must be settled in six years or the patent would revert to the Queen.
4 Nichols, *The Progresses,* II, pp. 228–30.
5 Ibid., p. 229.
6 For Raleigh's criticism of Grey, see Edwards, *Raleigh,* II, pp. 3–5, 12–18; "had much the better . . ." Naunton, *Fragmenta Regalia* (1810), p. 145.
7 Lemnius, *Touchstone* (1865), pp. 78–9.
8 Norden, *Notes* (1865), p. 99.
9 "very clear," Harrison, *Description of England* (1807), pp. 80, 82; "tennis courts . . ." Norden, *Notes,* p. 99; see also Nichols, *The Progresses;* Strype, *Annals,* II, i, pp. 580–5; Williams, *Elizabeth,* pp. 231–44.
10 Aubrey, *Brief Lives* (1898), II, p. 182; the average height for Elizabethan males was five-foot-three, Adamson and Folland, *Shepherd of the Ocean,* p. 26.
11 Naunton, *Fragmenta Regalia* (1810), p. 145.
12 For a discussion of the social changes occurring in England, see Stone, *Crisis of the Aristocracy;* Stubbes, *Anatomie of Abuses;* Harrison, *Description of England* (1807).
13 Harrison, *Description of England* (1807), p. 273.
14 More, *Utopia,* Second Book (1906), pp. 110–11.
15 Camden, *Remains* (1674), p. 391.
16 Bacon, "Of Nobility," *Essays* (1887), p. 135.
17 Sumptuary laws were repeatedly enacted: in 1565, 1577, and 1579 the Queen issued proclamations reinforcing the statutes (Strype, *Annals,* II, pt. 2, pp. 297–8); "fine and costly . . ." Harrison, *Description of England* (1807), p. 290.

18 Ibid., p. 280.
19 Ibid., p. 281.
20 Stubbes, *Anatomie of Abuses*, p. Bvii.
21 Camden, *Remains* (1674), p. 387.
22 Ibid., p. 382.
23 Stow, *Survey of London* (1908), II, p. 212. According to Walker (*Manifest Detection*, p. 30), London residences are "not like your large country houses. Rooms . . . in London be straight, but yet the furniture of them be costly enough; and victuals be here at such high prices, that much money is soon consumed." See also Stone, *Crisis of the Aristocracy*, pp. 449–50.
24 Camden, *Remains* (1674), p. 389; for the interest rate, see Stone, *Crisis of the Aristocracy*, p. 539.
25 Naunton, *Fragmenta Regalia* (1810), p. 145.
26 Fuller, *Worthies* (1840), I, p. 419.
27 Camden, *Remains* (1674), p. 388.
28 Bacon, "Of Great Place," *Essays* (1887), p. 104.
29 Harrison, *Description of England* (1807), p. 289.
30 Stubbes, *Anatomie of Abuses*, p. Dvii.
31 For Elizabeth's dress, see Williams, *Elizabeth*, pp. 226–7; "such is our mutability . . ." Harrison, *Description of England* (1807), p. 289.
32 Harrison, *Description of England* (1807), p. 289. Englishmen, Harrison says, are laughed at for bestowing "most cost upon our arses" merely "to bear out their bums and make their attire to fit plum round"; "no less monstrous . . ." Stubbes, *Anatomie of Abuses*, p. Eii.
33 Harrison, *Description of England* (1807), p. 330.
34 Aubrey, *Brief Lives* (1898), II, pp. 183, 190.
35 Shirley, *Sir Walter Raleigh*, p. 242.
36 Edwards, *Raleigh*, I, p. 52.
37 Aubrey, *Brief Lives* (1898), II, p. 182.
38 "Shepherd of the Ocean," Adamson and Folland, *Shepherd of the Ocean*, p. 91; Oakeshott, *Queen and the Poet*, p. 82, n. 3.
39 Quinn and Cheshire, *Parmenius*, Appendix 1, p. 205.
40 For Raleigh's rooms and his good conduct, see ibid.; "He was such a person (every way) . . ." Aubrey, *Brief Lives* (1898), II, p. 186.
41 Edwards, *Raleigh*, I, p. 67.
42 Lodge, *Portraits*, II, p. 10.
43 The anonymous *Leycesters Common-Wealth* [1584] was published in France and distributed — illegally — throughout England.
44 "when Jacks went up . . ." Bacon, *Works*, p. 475; "Jack of an upstart," Wood, *Athenae Oxonienses* (1813–20), II, p. 235.
45 Elizabeth was famous for playing factions; see Edwards, *Raleigh*, I, p. 62; Stone, *Crisis of the Aristocracy*, pp. 256–7, 482; Read, *Mr Secretary Cecil*, pp. 331–2; "The principal note . . ." Naunton, *Fragmenta Regalia* (1810), p. 124.

46 Anon, *Leycesters Common-Wealth* (1641), p. 71; Lodge, *Portraits,* II, p. 17.
47 Ibid., pp. 21–8, 34–5; Lodge, *Portraits,* II, p. 17.
48 Williams, *Elizabeth,* p. 211.
49 "men seeking to please . . ." Nicolas, *Hatton,* pp. 389–90; for false imprisonment, murder, see Naunton, *Fragmenta Regalia* (1810), p. 141; Morris, *The Troubles,* II, pp. 108–9, III, p. 175; Haynes, *Invisible Power,* xiii.
50 State Papers Domestic, Elizabeth, xcviii, August 2, 3, 1574.
51 Sir Anthony Bagot in Adamson and Folland, *Shepherd of the Ocean,* p. 104.

15 POLITICAL TURMOIL

1 Hakluyt, *Discourse,* chapter 6.
2 Hawkins, *Third and Troublesome Voyage,* pp. 521–5; Camden, *The History* (1688), p. 108.
3 Hawkins, *Third and Troublesome Voyage.*
4 Camden, *The History* (1688), p. 108.
5 Spain controlled — directly or indirectly — most of western Europe including the Netherlands, Sicily, Naples, Sardinia, the Duchy of Milan, and provinces in Belgium and Germany. Both the Holy Roman Empire and the Vatican were under its sway. Philip was titular King of England, France, and Jerusalem, Portugal (after 1580), half of America — and all of the Americas after 1580 — along with the East Indies and Portuguese Africa. Read, *Walsingham,* III, p. 227; Wright, *Further English Voyages,* xvii; Motley, *Dutch Republic,* I, p. 101.
6 Hakluyt, *Discourse,* chapter 6. By 1595 2,000 million ducats of gold and silver had been brought into Spain from the Americas; Lowery, *Spanish Settlements,* II, p. 5.
7 "proud, hateful Spaniards," Hakluyt, *Discourse,* chapter 7; "servitude . . ." Lane to Walsingham, August 12, 1585, State Papers Colonial, 1/1, 3. England perceived Philip's Spain and the machinery of the Inquisition in much the same way as the twentieth century regarded its totalitarian regimes. Hakluyt spoke in horror of their "monstrous . . . cruelties," and of the multitudes "done to death" in Europe and the Indies, where "there are dead more than fifteen millions of souls"; *Discourse,* chapter 11.
8 Ibid., chapter 6.
9 State Papers Colonial, 1/1, 3.
10 Schiller, *History of the Revolt,* p. 200.
11 Camden, *The History* (1688), p. 120.
12 Schiller, *History of the Revolt,* pp. 285–311.
13 Ibid., p. 290. Motley, *Dutch Republic,* II, p. 129, states that 3 million people in the Netherlands were sentenced to be hanged. For a particularly vivid — and gory — eyewitness account, see Strype, *Annals,* II, pt. 2, pp. 1–6.

14 Schiller, *History of the Revolt*, p. 294.
15 Ibid., p. 150.
16 Ibid., p. 295. Motley, *Dutch Republic*, II, p. 118, puts the number of dead at eighty-four.
17 Guzman de Silva to Philip, January 3, 1568. Calendar of State Papers, Spain, 1568–79, I, p. 1.
18 Camden, *The History* (1688), p. 331.
19 Calendar of State Papers, Spain, 1568–79, 88, p. 133.
20 Camden, *The History* (1688), p. 121.
21 Ibid., p. 121.
22 Ibid., pp. 121, 123.
23 For Ireland, see Canny, *Elizabethan Conquest;* Rowse, *Expansion of Elizabethan England.*
24 For Scotland, see Camden, *The History* (1688), pp. 108–32; Fraser, *Mary, Queen of Scots;* Calendar of State Papers, Scotland, 1547–1603.
25 Camden, *The History* (1688), pp. 133–6; Strype, *Annals*, I, pt. 2, pp. 312–28; Dixon, *Her Majesty's Tower*, p. 179.
26 Deacon, *John Dee*, p. 73; for Dee being a spy, see ibid., pp. 64, 259; Fell-Smith, *John Dee*, p. 168. The idea was first suggested in the seventeenth century by Elias Ashmole, and reported by Robert Hooke in "An Ingenious Cryptographical System," Gwydir Papers, Manuscript Collection, Ashmolean Museum. See also Dee, *A True and faithful relation of what passed for many years between Dr. J. Dee & some spirits: tending, had it succeeded, to a general alteration of most states & kingdoms in the world*, 1659.
27 Camden, *The History* (1688), p. 134.
28 Antonio de Guaras to Zayas, August 1, 1570, Calendar of State Papers, Spain, 1568–79, 199, p. 263.
29 For nationalism as a result, see Meyer, *England and the Catholic Church*, p. 84; "the great Bull and certain calves . . ." Daye, *A Disclosing of the Great Bull.*
30 For details of the plot, see Dixon, *Her Majesty's Tower*, pp. 181–8.
31 Ibid., p. 184.
32 Ibid., pp. 193–4; Williams, *Elizabeth*, p. 175; Read, *Burghley*, p. 44; Camden, *The History* (1688), pp. 134–6.
33 Guerau de Spes to Philip, Calendar of State Papers, Spain, 1568–79, 301, p. 364.
34 Adamson and Folland, *Shepherd of the Ocean*, p. 29.
35 Harrison, *Description of England* (1807), p. 333.
36 The slaughter began on Sunday night and continued for two days, not even sparing babies in cradles. The streets were "paved with bodies cut and hewed in pieces," and the River Seine was awash with blood; Strype, *Annals*, II, pt. 1, pp. 235–6. See Chapter 3, n. 17, above.
37 Lodge, *Portraits*, III; Welwood, *Material Transactions*, p. 12.

38 Hakluyt, *Principall Navigations* (1589), p. 595.
39 Rowse, *Grenville*, p. 81.
40 Knappen, *Tudor Puritanism*, p. 243; Strype, *Annals*, II, i, pp. 426–7, asserted that Hawkins was killed in the fray; Lansdowne Mss. 17, art. 88.
41 Gascoigne's introduction to Gilbert, *Discourse of a Discoverie.*
42 "Quid non?" Frontispiece of ibid.; "is not worthy to live at all . . ." ibid., chapter 10.
43 For Frobisher, see Collinson, *The Three Voyages of Martin Frobisher.*
44 Gascoigne's introduction to Gilbert, *Discourse of a Discoverie.*
45 For Hariot, see Morley, "Thomas Hariot"; Aubrey, *Brief Lives*, I.
46 Johnson, *Astronomical Thought*, p. 135.
47 Deacon, *John Dee*, pp. 80–1.
48 Ibid., pp. 38–9; for the mechanical devices, see ibid., p. 43.
49 For Dee's library, see Johnson, *Astronomical Thought*, pp. 138–9; "gotten as in a manner . . ." Fell-Smith, *John Dee*, pp. 30, 240, 253.
50 Taylor, *Two Richard Hakluyts*, II, p. 365.
51 Andrews, *Elizabethan Privateering*, p. 161; Lowery, *Spanish Settlements*, II, p. 12.
52 Gilbert, *A Discourse How Hir Majesty* . . . no. 12 (ii).
53 Ibid., no. 12 (i). Shakespeare, using Gilbert's own words, later parodies Raleigh's failed Roanoke venture and rupture with the Queen as *Love's Labours Lost.*
54 Fell-Smith, *John Dee*, p. 19; Deacon, *John Dee*, p. 97.
55 Hakluyt, *Principall Navigations* (1589), pp. 677–9.
56 Mendoza to Philip, June 3, 1578, Calendar of State Papers, Spain, 1568–79, no. 503.
57 Hakluyt, *Principall Navigations* (1589), p. 674.
58 Edwards, *Raleigh*, II, p. 6. According to the report, Pope Gregory XIII himself was raising troops to be sent into Ireland. The force didn't arrive until the autumn of 1580, consisting of only six hundred soldiers — mostly Italian — who landed on the Irish coast at Smerwick.
59 Camden, *The History* (1688), pp. 236–7.
60 Hakluyt, *Discourse*, chapter 19.
61 For the hold ballasted with silver, see Rowse, *Grenville*, p. 155; for the Queen's 4,700 percent return, netting a £160,000 profit, see Williams, *Elizabeth*, p. 207.
62 Brown, *Genesis*, I, pp. 9–10.
63 Wedgwood, *William the Silent*, pp. 268–70; Strype, *Annals*, III, i, p. 131. The would-be assassin was twenty-year-old Juan Jauréguy.
64 Stow, *Survey* (1908), I, p. 266. The statue was finally repaired in 1595–6. Five years later, "our Lady was again defaced," wrote Stow, "by plucking off her crown and almost her head, taking from her her naked child, and stabbing her in the breast, etc."

65 Tarbox, *Sir Walter Raleigh,* p. 29; Adamson and Folland, *Shepherd of the Ocean,* p. 78.
66 "Your true brother . . ." letter of March 17, 1583 (Edwards, *Raleigh,* II, p. 19); for the token, see Quinn and Cheshire, *Parmenius,* Appendix 1, p. 205.
67 Hakluyt, *Principall Navigations* (1589), p. 695; for the voyage, see Edward Haies [Hayes], *A True Report.*
68 Hakluyt, *Principall Navigations* (1589), p. 695.
69 Quinn and Cheshire, *Parmenius,* p. 79.
70 For Throckmorton, see Williams, *Elizabeth,* pp. 263–4; for Dee, Deacon, *John Dee,* p. 7.
71 Camden, *The History* (1688), p. 296.
72 Hakluyt, *Principall Navigations* (1589), pp. 725–8. That Raleigh's intent was to establish a privateering base on Roanoke seems clear given his preparations, which included consulting a military expert, hiring Ralph Lane, a fortifications expert, and raising a large complement of soldiers to serve under Sir Richard Grenville. See also Chapter 10, n. 7; Quinn, *Roanoke Voyages,* I, p. 78.
73 For the first Roanoke expedition of 1584, see Hakluyt, *Principall Navigations* (1589), pp. 728–33; "well furnished . . ." ibid., p. 728; for the Secotan, see Appendix A. The surrender of Antwerp took place on August 7, 1585.
74 Camden, *The History* (1688), p. 304.
75 Hakluyt, *Discourse,* chapter 15.
76 Camden, *The History* (1688), p. 300.
77 Deacon, *John Dee,* pp. 9–10.
78 Lodge, *Portraits,* II, p. 18; Camden, *The History* (1688), p. 346.
79 Nichols, *The Progresses,* II, p. 468.
80 Deacon, *John Dee,* p. 75; for the effects of lead poisoning, see Handler, Aufderheide, et al., "Lead Contact and Poisoning."
81 Hakluyt, *Discourse,* chapter 19; for refugees pouring into London, see Platter, *Travels* (1937), p. 156, who reported the city swelled by "many thousands of families" from France and the Netherlands; Strype, *Annals,* I, pt. 2, pp. 269, 290.
82 Nichols, *The Progresses,* II, pp. 478–9.
83 Quinn (*Raleigh and the British Empire,* p. 99) suggests that Raleigh participated in Drake's venture as an investor, and yet, interestingly, one of Drake's original objectives had been to seize a base in the Indies, where Sir Philip Sidney was to command the land forces. The plan had originated in 1584 with Sidney, who had projected a scheme similar to Raleigh's, to settle a colony there as a base. Lane knew of it (see his August 12, 1585, letter to Sidney, State Papers Colonial, 1/1, 5). Sidney, however, was double-crossed by Drake, who informed the Queen of Sidney's plan to join the expedition, which, until that moment, had been kept secret (though Wilson, *Sir Philip Sidney,* p. 231, suggested that Walsingham may have known about it). The

Queen forbade Sidney to go, and Walsingham's stepson Christopher Carleill replaced him as Lieutenant General of the land forces; Quinn, *Roanoke,* I, p. 204, n. 5. In the end, plans for the projected base fell through and Drake arrived in the Indies only to remove Raleigh's troops from the American base that already was established! For reports of Drake's depredations, see Wright, *Further English Voyages,* pp. 16–30, 161–74; for Raleigh's diversion to Newfoundland, see Quinn, *Roanoke,* I, p. 172.

84 See Chapter 19, n. 3.

85 Williams, *Elizabeth,* p. 299; for Drake's boasting, Quinn, *New American World,* III, p. 309. According to him, Santo Domingo was equal in size to the cities of London, Trevolentum, and Augusta combined. Yet, despite Drake's reception, there is evidence that the Queen was angry at him for evacuating Lane's post. A deposition by Darby Glande, recorded by Canço, stated that Drake "fell into disfavor with the Queen for having taken the people from Jacan"; Canço, *Report,* p. 155, in Spanish, translated by the author.

86 Quinn, *New American World,* III, pp. 309–10.

87 Bacon, "Of Prophecies," *Essays* (1887), p. 378.

16 THE PLAYERS

1 Hakluyt, *Principall Navigations* (1589), p. 674.

2 For the following information on Leicester, see Camden, *The History* (1688), pp. 418–19; Lodge, *Portraits,* II, pp. 15–21; Naunton, *Fragmenta Regalia* (1810), pp. 130–2; Lloyd, *Worthies,* pp. 518–21; Nichols, *The Progresses,* II; Winstanley, *England's Worthies,* pp. 227–36.

3 Anon., *Leycesters Common-Wealth* (1641), pp. 45, 59.

4 Camden, *The History* (1688), p. 419.

5 Anon., *Leycesters Common-Wealth* (1641), p. 45; for Queen's love of, see Adamson and Folland, *Shepherd of the Ocean,* p. 87; Williams, *Elizabeth,* pp. 108–16.

6 Leicester "was always beforehand with his designs," said Lloyd, "being a declared enemy to after-games"; *Worthies,* p. 520.

7 For the Antwerp delegation, see Edwards, *Raleigh,* I, p. 60; for Maurice Browne, see Quinn and Cheshire, *Parmenius,* Appendix I, p. 207.

8 Naunton, *Fragmenta Regalia* (1810), p. 144.

9 Anon., *Leycesters Common-Wealth* (1641), p. 85; for his wealth, see ibid., p. 59.

10 Walsingham to Leicester, March 1586, Mss. Cotton, Galba, C.ix fol. 157; Edwards, *Raleigh,* I, pp. 61–2.

11 Raleigh to Leicester, March 29, 1586, in Edwards, *Raleigh,* II, p. 33.

12 Ibid., I, p. 62; II, p. 33.

13 Anon., *Leycesters Common-Wealth* (1641), pp. 56–7. Leicester's ill-feelings stemmed from Lane's suggestion to the Earl of Huntington about how he could deprive Leicester of Killingworth Castle.

14 For the following information on Hatton, see Lodge, *Portraits,* II, pp. 29–32; Nicolas, *Hatton;* Lloyd, *Worthies,* pp. 521–5; Naunton, *Fragmenta Regalia* (1810).
15 Lloyd, *Worthies,* pp. 521–3; Camden, *The History* (1688), p. 401.
16 Nicolas, *Hatton,* pp. 17–19.
17 Ibid., pp. 297–8; see also pp. 275–7.
18 Camden, *The History* (1688), p. 311; Dixon, *Her Majesty's Tower,* p. 199.
19 Lodge, *Portraits,* II, p. 30.
20 Camden, *The History* (1688), p. 401.
21 Naunton, *Fragmenta Regalia* (1810), p. 142.
22 For the following information on Burghley, see Lodge, *Portraits,* II, pp. 48–51; Lloyd, *Worthies,* pp. 473–85; Naunton, *Fragmentalia Regalia* (1810), pp. 133–5; Winstanley, *England's Worthies,* pp. 236–46; Read, *Burghley.*
23 Jenkins, *Elizabeth,* p. 63.
24 Read, *Burghley,* p. 168.
25 Camden, *The History* (1688), p. 154. Burghley once informed a friend that he loved "heartily the honest virtues" and, though "tormented with the blasts of the world" by way of slander, he trusted to his armor, which was forged by "confidence in God by a clear conscience," Strype, *Annals,* II, pt. I, p. 33.
26 State Papers Domestic, Elizabeth, clxxx, 45, July 24, 1585; Strype, *Annals,* III, ii, p. 380.
27 Elizabeth was furious at Leicester for his involvement in the proposed match between Mary Queen of Scots and the Duke of Norfolk in 1569. Burghley did not press his advantage against Leicester but, instead, did his best to placate the Queen's anger; Read, *Mr Secretary Cecil,* p. 451. For other instances of the same, see ibid., p. 332.
28 So went the story according to Robert Parsons; Hicks, "Father Robert Persons," pp. 98–9.
29 Read, *Mr Secretary Cecil,* p. 83.
30 Williams, *Elizabeth,* p. 237.
31 Wirtemberg, *True and Faithful Narrative* (1865), p. 45.
32 For the flowers that were likely to be planted there, see Bacon, "Of Gardens," *Essays* (1887), pp. 442–4. Bacon was Burghley's nephew and presumably drew his material from his uncle's world-famous gardens; for Gerard, see Hulton, *The Work of Jacques Le Moyne,* I, p. 56.
33 Hawks, *History of North Carolina,* I, p. 24.
34 Ibid., p. 40; Irwin, *That Great Lucifer,* pp. 91–2. As late as 1597 Burghley enjoined Raleigh to act as a mediator to mend the differences between his son, Robert Cecil, and the Earl of Essex; Read, *Burghley,* p. 533. It is also interesting to note, in connection with Raleigh's 1593 opposition to banishing Brownists, that the sect's leader, Robert Browne, was Burghley's relative; Knappen, *Tudor Puritanism,* p. 305.

35 However, it was Burghley who convinced Elizabeth to confiscate Spanish ships in 1569, following their attack on Hawkins, and to pocket the Genoese loan (Fraser, *Mary Queen of Scots,* p. 480). There is also evidence that he supported Gilbert's and Frobisher's voyages (Irwin, *That Great Lucifer,* p. 95; Read, *Burghley,* p. 411; Quinn, *Gilbert,* I, p. 31); some or all of Drake's ventures (Williamson, *Age of Drake,* p. 171; Strype *Annals,* III, pt. 2, pp. 168–72); the establishing of a fortress on Terceira to intercept the returning Spanish plate fleet (Taylor, *Troublesome Voyage,* p. xxxix); and Raleigh's 1595 Guiana scheme. Burghley was also a great proponent of the new geography of his kinsman Dr. Dee (Rowse, *Grenville,* p. 84). Records from the Roanoke expeditions are missing — Burghley may well have been an investor.

36 Lodge, *Portraits,* II, pp. 48–9. "He had rather tire out opposition by his moderation," said Lloyd, "than improve by his impatience. Others were raised to balance factions; he to support the kingdom: fickle favour tossed them, constant interest secured him"; *Worthies,* p. 476.

37 The information on Walsingham that follows is taken from Read, *Walsingham;* Naunton, *Fragmenta Regalia* (1810), pp. 136–7; Lodge, *Portraits,* II, pp. 25–8; Lloyd, *Worthies,* pp. 513–17; Winstanley, *England's Worthies,* pp. 257–61.

38 Fuller, *Worthies* (1840), II, p. 143; see also Read, *Walsingham,* I, pp. 24–5.

39 Evidence for the "decay of Popery" was readily available; Strype, *Annals,* I, pt. 2, p. 65. Francis Bacon observed that by the time of Pope Gregory XIII (1572–85), the Vatican was no longer an aggressive power but had been put on the defensive. The Pope, he said, "is not so much carried with the desire to suppress our religion, as drawn with fear of the downfall of his own, if in time it be not upheld and restored"; *State of Christendom* (1862), p. 18.

40 "extremely self-seeking . . ." Mendoza to Philip, March 31, 1578, Calendar of State Papers, Spain, 1568–79, p. 486; "notwithstanding that outward profession . . ." Harleian Mss. 290, f. 84. "They tax him," said Fuller of Walsingham, for "oft-times borrowing a point of conscience, with full intent never to pay it again . . ." *Worthies* (1840), II, p. 143.

41 Naunton, *Fragmenta Regalia* (1810), p. 136.

42 Winstanley, *Worthies,* p. 258.

43 Haynes, *Invisible Power,* p. 13.

44 Camden, *The History* (1688), p. 444.

45 For the spy system and how it operated, see Haynes, *Invisible Power;* Meyer, *England and the Catholic Church,* pp. 170–1; Camden, *The History* (1688), pp. 294–5; State Papers Domestic, Elizabeth, ccxxxii, 12, May [7], 1590. For evidence that Walsingham planted spies on Leicester and Burghley, see nn. 72–73 and Chapter 18, n. 31.

46 For Radcliffe, Strype, *Annals,* II, pt. 2, p. 130; Camden, *The History* (1688), pp. 225–6; Read, *Walsingham,* I, p. 409, n. 1. For Gifford, Read, ibid., III, pp. 1–2. For Mawde, Pollen, *Mary Queen of Scots,* p. lxxxv. For Fernandez,

Quinn, *England and the Discovery,* p. 249. For other examples, see Read, *Walsingham,* II, p. 321.

47 For Fernandez, see Quinn, "A Portuguese Pilot," *England and the Discovery,* pp. 246–63.

48 Ibid., p. 249.

49 "Walsingham's man," according to Rev. Richard Madox, Taylor, *Troublesome Voyage,* p. xxxiii; also State Papers Colonial, 1/1, 2. For Spanish restrictions on the sharing of navigational information of American waters and the banning of foreigners from Spanish vessels, see Lowery, *Spanish Settlements,* II, pp. 7–8.

50 November 7, 1574, Calendar of State Papers, Spain, 1568–79, II, no. 404, p. 487; Read, *Walsingham,* I, p. 312. Walsingham, said Lodge, was "practiced and even hackneyed in a sort of treachery legalised by the fatal necessity of states," *Portraits,* II.

51 Winstanley, *Worthies,* p. 258.

52 Welwood, *Material Transactions,* pp. 10–11.

53 Ibid., p. 9.

54 Read, *Walsingham,* I, pp. 319, 322–5, 334–5, 370–1; II, 141–2, 144–7.

55 January 15, 1574/5, State Papers, Scotland, xxxvi, 66.

56 Welwood, *Material Transactions,* p. 12.

57 Read, *Walsingham,* II, pp. 290, n. 1, 340–1, contends that Walsingham's accusers were wrong, and that there is "practically no evidence" that he plotted against Elizabeth's life. Haynes (*Invisible Power,* p. 35) notes that plots were often imagined or contrived by the government to bring about desired ends.

58 Robert Parsons (aka Andrea Philopatrus), *Response to the Unjust and Bloody Edict of Elizabeth against the Catholics* (1592); Read, *Walsingham,* II, pp. 267–8, n. 4.

59 Read, *Walsingham,* I, p. 324.

60 Ibid., p. 335.

61 Calendar of State Papers, Foreign, 1578–9: 473, 510, 519, 538. Naunton reported that in June 1583 the Earl of Sussex's last words on his deathbed were to Hatton, "Beware of the Gypsy [meaning Leicester] for he will be too hard on you all, you know not the Beast so well as I do"; *Fragmenta Regalia* (1810), p. 132. Yet could Naunton, reporting years after the fact, have misunderstood this cryptic message? Sussex disliked Leicester, but he also had every reason to dislike Walsingham as well. Sussex's brother was none other than Egremont Radcliffe, who was executed for attempting to murder Don John of Austria under Walsingham's orders — Walsingham denying all involvement in the affair. Walsingham's nickname was "the Moor" (Jenkins, *Elizabeth,* p. 224), and the terms *Moor, gypsy,* and *Egyptian* were then synonymous. Walsingham himself, in a letter to Burghley, referred to Ethiopia as "my native soil," Digges, *Compleat Ambassador,*

p. 426. See also n. 74. Sussex might well warn Hatton to beware of his friendship with Walsingham, who, in 1583, was beginning to surpass even Burghley in power.

62 Winstanley, *Worthies*, p. 259.

63 Naunton, *Fragmenta Regalia* (1810), p. 137.

64 Nicolas, *Hatton*, pp. 75–6; Read, *Walsingham*, I, pp. 418, 422.

65 Read, *Walsingham*, II, pp. 85–6; Calendar of State Papers, Foreign, 1581–2: 314; 1583: 715.

66 Jenkins, *Elizabeth*, p. 258. In 1578 Mendoza informed Philip II that Walsingham and Leicester were scheming on a project in which only the Queen was privy — although other members of the Privy Council believed that they were deceiving Elizabeth herself; Kendall, *Robert Dudley*, p. 173.

67 Taylor, *Troublesome Voyage*, p. 197.

68 Williams, *Elizabeth*, p. 200. On the proposed match with Alençon, see ibid., pp. 185, 189, 193–213; Camden, *The History* (1688), pp. 131–6.

69 Read, *Walsingham*, II, pp. 20, 22, 27. As a result of Walsingham's interest in the affair, he was banished from Court and remained in disgrace for two months.

70 January 30, 1585, State Papers Domestic, Elizabeth, clxxvi, 19.

71 Read, *Walsingham*, III, pp. 116–19; Strype, *Annals*, III, i, pp. 502–3; II, pp. 379–83. Burghley, greatly upset, told a friend that if his "conscience did not ascertain me of God's favour and protection against these satanical and fanatical spirits, I should think myself in a most wretched state"; Strype, *Annals*. Significantly, in 1587, the year of the Roanoke sabotage, further libels came out against Burghley, weakening his position and — possibly — distracting him from helping Raleigh; ibid., III, i, p. 725.

72 State Papers Domestic, Elizabeth, clxxvi, 19.

73 January 30, 1585, State Papers, ibid., 20; for Herllie, see Read, *Walsingham*, III, p. 117; Read, *Burghley*, pp. 315–16; Strype, *Annals*, III, ii, pp. 379–82. If Herllie were acting as Walsingham's agent here, might Walsingham have been his employer that same year, when Herllie's "anonymous" note was sent to the Queen regarding Grenville's cheating Roanoke investors of profits? (see Chapter 11, n. 39).

74 For the particulars of the Babington plot, see Calendar of State Papers, Scotland; Camden, *The History* (1688), pp. 336–45; Fraser, *Mary Queen of Scots;* Pollen, *Mary Queen of Scots;* Morris, *Troubles*, ii; Read, *Walsingham*, III. Lodge remarked that Walsingham's "designs to entrap" Mary "savoured more of a natural taste for deception than of zeal for the public service"; *Portraits*, II. Did Walsingham merely uncover Babington's conspiracy, or did he orchestrate it from start to finish? Walsingham's secretary, Thomas Harrison, said it was Walsingham's creation. In a 1587 confession he admitted "that the plot and conspiracy . . . was drawn, plotted and done by Sir Francis Walsingham," with the assistance of people employed by him; Calendar

of State Papers, Scotland, ix, 429, p. 530. That it was conceived as early as 1583 is suggested by an entry in the diary of Dr. Dee. Dee's assistant had received a vision of a woman's hand being chopped off by a tall, black man. During a séance, Dee learned that the dream signified the death of the Queen of Scots by beheading; Fell-Smith, *John Dee,* p. 95; Deacon, *John Dee,* p. 172. The tall black man may have been a euphemism for Walsingham: Elizabeth called him her Moor, and he referred to himself as Ethiopian.

75 Camden, *The History* (1688), p. 337.
76 Ibid., p. 340.
77 Read, *Walsingham,* III, p. 30; Morris, *Sir Amias Poulet,* pp. 209–12.
78 Camden, *The History* (1688), p. 342.
79 Weston's memoirs in Morris, *Troubles,* II, p. 184. Ballard was arrested on August 4, 1586.
80 Camden, *The History* (1688), pp. 342–3.
81 "city testifying their public joy . . ." ibid., p. 343; "for joy of the taking . . ." Nichols, *The Progresses,* II, p. 481.
82 Camden, *The History* (1688), p. 343.
83 Ibid., p. 371.
84 Ibid., p. 362. On September 10, 1586, four days after his confession, Nau wrote to Elizabeth, denying all charges against Mary; State Papers, Scotland, xix, no. 98. In 1605 Nau wrote an Apology to King James, testifying that he had proclaimed Mary innocent and claiming that he had been threatened by Walsingham; ibid., p. 362; Read, *Walsingham,* III, p. 55, n. 3. For the pressure Walsingham put on Curle, see Camden, *The History* (1688), p. 345. Both secretaries had been threatened; Read, *Walsingham,* III, p. 37 and n. 2; Fraser, *Mary Queen of Scots,* p. 593.
85 Camden, *The History* (1688), p. 355.
86 Ibid., p. 355. Among those things that Babington confessed was a conversation broached by Robert Poley, Walsingham's agent, about the possibility of killing Leicester and Burghley! Pollen, *Mary Queen of Scots,* p. 69.
87 Camden, *The History* (1688), p. 341; see Walsingham's letter to Phelippes regarding the forged postscript, dated August 3, 1586, British Museum, Cotton Mss. Appendix L, f. 144.
88 Camden, *The History* (1688), pp. 355–6.
89 Ibid., pp. 362, 364, 370–1.
90 Ibid., pp. 371, 386.
91 Ibid., p. 379; Nicolas, *Life of William Davison,* p. 79.
92 For the Stafford Conspiracy and Walsingham's role in it, see Haynes, *Invisible Power,* pp. 80–2; Read, *Walsingham,* III, pp. 62–3.
93 Calendar of State Papers, Spain, 1580–1586, no. 505, p. 656.
94 Calendar of State Papers, Scotland, ix, no. 429, p. 530. The executioner was contacted by Walsingham's servant, Anthony Hall, while another of

Walsingham's employees — named Digby — escorted him to Fotheringhay disguised as a serving man; Fraser, *Mary Queen of Scots,* pp. 612–13.

95 B.M., Additional Mss. 32091, f. 262; Read, *Walsingham,* II, p. 124.

17 THE MOTIVE

1 Camden, *The History* (1688), p. 91.

2 Welwood, *Material Transactions,* p. 14; Read, *Walsingham,* III, p. 173.

3 Walsingham's statement in Digges, *Compleat Ambassador,* p. 426.

4 Walsingham's dislike of Raleigh may have been similar to the antipathy expressed by Lord Cobham for the youthful Essex; "I have disliked some of your ambitious courses, which could not but breed danger to the state, in which respect I sought to hinder their growth." Jardine, *Criminal Trials,* p. 350. See Read, *Walsingham,* III, p. 406, n. 3, for instances in which Raleigh's agenda thwarted Walsingham's plans in Scotland and in the Netherlands. Ironically, Babington himself — aware of Raleigh's influence with the Queen — offered him a bribe to obtain his pardon; Edwards, *Raleigh,* I, pp. 68–9. Although Raleigh did not accept it, Walsingham nevertheless must have felt the potential of his power. According to Aubrey, Raleigh was opposed to putting Mary Queen of Scots to death; *Brief Lives* (1898), II, p. 186.

5 Read, *Walsingham,* III, p. 1. "Machiavel's two marks to shoot at," said Raleigh, are "riches and glory," *History of the World,* Book 1, chapter 1. Babington netted Walsingham neither.

6 Haynes, *Invisible Power,* p. 48. As early as 1570, while still ambassador to France, Walsingham ran so deeply into debt on account of his intelligence efforts that an appeal was made to Leicester for assistance; Strype, *Annals,* II, i, p. 34.

7 Morris, *Troubles,* II, p. 169. According to the imprisoned Jesuit Father Weston (ibid.), Walsingham paid agents in gold and silver; Read, *Walsingham,* II, p. 320. Lodge, quoting Camden, said that Walsingham employed spies "with so great an expense that he lessened his estate by that means, and brought himself . . . far in debt." Walsingham's own will confessed to the "greatness of my debts"; Lodge, *Portraits,* II.

8 Read, *Walsingham,* I, p. 394.

9 Nicolas, *Hatton,* p. 179.

10 Haynes, *Invisible Power,* p. 48; Read, *Walsingham,* II, p. 371; III, p. 419. Walsingham's salary was supplemented by various sources, such as the farm of the customs, in which — in return for a lease paid to the Queen — he was allowed the income from customs duties levied at ports in western and northern England. Despite this, Walsingham's finances were poor. He died, bankrupt, in 1590.

11 Nichols, *The Progresses,* III, p. 28.

12 For a description of events relating to Sidney, see Lloyd, *Worthies,* p. 501; Naunton, *Fragmenta Regalia* (1810), pp. 135–6; Lodge, *Portraits,* II, pp. 5–12.

13 Nicolas, *Hatton,* p. 211. A large part of Sidney's fortune was apparently sunk into a failed project to establish a base in America from which to attack Spain (see Chapter 15, n. 83). From the Netherlands, Sidney wrote a cryptic letter to his father-in-law, noting that Walsingham seemed troubled and "full of discomfort which I see . . . you daily meet with at home," acknowledging that "my part of the trouble is something that troubles you"; Lodge, *Portraits,* p. 9.

14 Read, *Walsingham,* III, p. 168.

15 November 2, 1586, State Papers Domestic, Elizabeth, cxcv, 1; Read, *Walsingham,* III, p. 167.

16 Bruce, *Correspondence of Robert Dudley,* p. 457. For a description of Sidney's extremely elaborate funeral, see Nichols, *The Progresses,* II, pp. 484–5.

17 Letter of Dr. William Gifford, Lansdowne Mss. 96, f. 69.

18 Ibid.

19 December 6, 1586, State Papers Domestic, Elizabeth, cxcv, 64.

20 Edwards, *Raleigh,* I, p. 70

21 Ibid., p. 71.

22 Ibid., p. 70–1.

23 Virginia doubled England's dominion. Walsingham, meanwhile, slid into bankruptcy. He died in 1590 "at his house in Seething Lane, so poor, it is said, that his friends were obliged to bury him late at night, in the most private manner, in St. Paul's Cathedral"; Nichols, *The Progresses,* III, p. 28.

18 THE GAME

1 Raleigh, *The History of the World,* preface.

2 For Rastell and the sabotage of his voyage, see Reed, "John Rastell's Voyage"; Records of the Court of Requests, 3/192; Williamson, *The Voyages of the Cabots,* pp. 85–8, 244–8; Quinn, *England and the Discovery of America,* pp. 164–7.

3 The Earl of Surrey was Lord Thomas Howard. Henry VIII was, of course, Queen Elizabeth's father.

4 Reed, "John Rastell's Voyage," pp. 143, 145; for Rastell's condemnation by historians, see Quinn, *England and the Discovery of America,* p. 166. Quinn labels White "amateurish" and "weak," whose portrayal of Fernandez as a "sabotaging villain" is "somewhat hard to accept"; *Raleigh and the British Empire,* pp. 73, 110; *Set Fair,* p. 276. White's suspicion of Fernandez — an Assistant — is an example of his "paranoia." Regarding Fernandez: "The strangest thing is that he should have involved himself so deeply in the enterprise, become one of the Assistants . . . and so had, one would imagine,

every incentive to keep the colony on the track that had been agreed upon"; Quinn, *Set Fair,* pp. 277, 282. Yet the Rastell episode demonstrates that Fernandez's intimate position within the company was perfect for sabotage.

5 Records of the Court of Requests, 3/192; Reed, "John Rastell's Voyage," p. 143.

6 Bacon, "Of Cunning," *Essays* (1887), p. 225. Walsingham himself was an investor and Assistant in the Muscovy Company since 1569, which would imply interest in its welfare. Yet it was rumored that both he and Sir Jerome Horsey were involved in a private trade deal to Russia in violation of the Muscovy Company's monopoly; Read, *Walsingham,* III, p. 371. For an example of Walsingham employing delaying tactics — in this case, with the French ambassador to Scotland — see ibid., II, p. 183.

7 Rowse, *Grenville,* pp. 89–110; Williamson, *Age of Drake,* p. 170. According to Rowse, Walsingham was Drake's protector and friend; *Expansion,* p. 285.

8 For Gilbert's patent, see Chapter 14, n. 3.

9 Read, *Walsingham,* II, pp. 51, 81–2; Rowse, *Grenville,* p. 158; Taylor, *Troublesome Voyage,* pp. xxviii-xxix. Drake's project may have been behind the 1581 Privy Council order for Gilbert to surrender his North American patent. The order, however, was later rescinded; *Acts of the Privy Council,* 1581–2, p. 240.

10 Quinn, *Gilbert,* I, p. 73; II, pp. 255–6.

11 Ibid., pp. 74–6; II, pp. 278–9. Investors' fears may have been the reason why Gilbert's departure plans for July 1582 suddenly collapsed for that year; ibid., I, pp. 62, 75; II, pp. 364–5. Peckham, in association with Sir Philip Sidney (Walsingham's son-in-law), is the only Catholic investor who appears to have maintained interest in North America despite Spanish threats. His *True Report of the Late Discoveries,* dedicated to Walsingham, was published in November 1583.

12 Taylor, *Two Richard Hakluyts,* I, pp. 26–7.

13 For the suggestion to relinquish Gilbert's patent, see Quinn, *Gilbert,* I, p. 82; II, pp. 339–41; "especially seeing I have . . ." Gilbert to Walsingham, February 7, 1583, State Papers Domestic, Elizabeth, clviii, 59; for Gilbert selling his own estate, Quinn, *Gilbert,* I, p. 26. 1583 was the second time Gilbert's patent was almost taken from him: in 1581, he was ordered to turn it in after the Privy Council was tipped off that he was using his privileges to export food to Europe. Significantly, he was also ordered to give Walsingham the names of his associates; ibid., II, p. 242. Gilbert exonerated himself, and the patent was kept.

14 Hakluyt, *Principall Navigations* (1600), III, p. 182. That this was preposterously short notice for the Bristol ships to prepare is a point made by Quinn in *Gilbert,* I, p. 76.

15 Hakluyt, *Principall Navigations* (1600), III, p. 182.

16 Lansdowne Mss. 37, no. 72; Taylor, *Two Richard Hakluyts,* I, pp. 26–7.

17 Brown, *Genesis,* I, p. 12. Quinn noted that Carleill's proposed colony, largely

financed by the Muscovy Company, who insisted on a royal patent of their own, could not have been granted while Gilbert's patent was active and that both Walsingham and Carleill appeared to be double-crossing Gilbert; *Gilbert,* I, pp. 78–9, 81.

18 For Hakluyt, see Taylor, *Two Richard Hakluyts,* I, p. 27. Dee, claiming enemies at Court, fled to Cracow; Deacon, *John Dee,* pp. 184–7; "a dream of being naked . . ." and his dream of Walsingham, see Fell-Smith, *John Dee,* p. 64.

19 See Chapter 15, n. 26.

20 Fell-Smith, *John Dee,* pp. 107–9.

21 Quinn, *Gilbert,* I, p. 94; II, pp. 438–9.

22 For Raleigh's patent, see Hakluyt, *Principall Navigations* (1589), pp. 725–8; "levelled your line . . ." Holinshed, *Chronicles,* II (1587), sig. A33–3v. In 1584 merchant adventurers violated Raleigh's license to export cloth. When the Queen arrested their ships, Walsingham defended them, accusing the Queen of damaging the trade to the ruin of the company; State Papers Domestic, Elizabeth, clxxi, 35.

23 Read, *Walsingham,* III, p. 102.

24 Andrews, *Elizabethan Privateering,* p. 92.

25 "will stomach . . ." Lemnius, *Touchstone* (1865), p. 80; "cherish a plot . . ." Lodge, *Portraits,* II, p. 26.

26 While Walsingham's fortune plummets, Raleigh's successes in 1586 mount. He is granted eighty thousand acres of land in Munster, more than six times the usual allotment, along with Lismore Castle and the College of Youghal. His prosperity continues into the next year: he is awarded Babington's estates; made Captain of the Queen's Guard — regarded as a stepping stone to higher public office; and John White's colony departs for the Chesapeake Bay, a move predicted to make Raleigh both powerful and tremendously rich.

27 Calendar of State Papers, Spain, 1587–1603, 23, p. 24; Read, *Walsingham,* III, p. 231.

28 Ibid., pp. 166, 172–3.

29 Lodge, *Portraits,* II, pp. 52–9. The marriage is assumed to have occurred in 1591, since April of that year saw the birth of the couple's first child. However, a letter written by William Gifford to a friend in the spring of 1587 dates the marriage to sometime before May 1587. If so, it was kept secret from Queen Elizabeth for four years, until the pregnancy made concealment impossible; Read, *Walsingham,* III, p. 170.

30 Walsingham, "A Memorial for Needham," Harleian Ms. 1582, f. 53. Naunton stated that Essex was introduced to Court by Leicester, *Fragmenta Regalia* (1810), p. 146. Lodge, following Naunton (*Portraits,* II, p. 53), dated the event to 1584 as Leicester's means of lessening public suspicion that he poisoned Essex's father. Yet, he added, "it has been said that Essex was inclined to reject his proffered friendship." However this may be, it is evident that the agent responsible for promoting Essex's interests at Court was not

Leicester, but Walsingham. In September 1587 Herllie adroitly informed Leicester, who was away in the Netherlands, that Raleigh was jealous of Essex, who was effecting "good offices" at Court on Leicester's behalf; Cotton Ms., Galba Dii, f. 27. Walsingham must have smiled when he noted that Raleigh thought Essex had been "brought in as he supposed" by Leicester. It was at this time, in 1587, that Essex married Walsingham's only daughter.

31 Walsingham's agent was Francis Needham, Leicester's own secretary; Harleian Ms. 287, f. 41; "I find there is some dealing . . ." August 2, 1587. Cotton Mss. Galba Di, f. 230. Read, *Walsingham,* III, p. 250, n. 1, also believes that this reference was to Raleigh.

32 September 21, 1587. Cotton Mss. Galba Dii, f. 27.

33 Nicolas, *Hatton,* p. 296.

34 Calendar Rutland Papers, I, 234.

35 Hakluyt's dedicatory preface to Raleigh of Peter Martyr's Decades, translated from Latin by Taylor, *Two Richard Hakluyts,* II, p. 367. White, of course, threw Walsingham for a loop. His company was independent of investor interests. Willing to finance their own voyage to America, they thus preserved Raleigh's patent.

36 Hakluyt, translated from Latin by Taylor, ibid., II, p. 368.

37 Read (*Walsingham,* III, p. 336, n. 3) notes the unusual bond forming between Walsingham and Essex, while at the same time, Walsingham "distrusted and opposed" Raleigh. In July 1587 Essex staged a scene before the Queen in which he violently slandered Raleigh. When it was over, he sent an account of the incident to a friend, eagerly requesting that it be shown to his mother and to Walsingham; Devereux, *Lives and Letters,* I, p. 189. Raleigh spoke sadly of corruption in which mankind has learned to "provide for ourselves by another man's destruction" and "to destroy those whom we fear"; *History of the World,* Book II, chapter IV, pt. 6. Raleigh, said Fuller, had "many enemies"; *Worthies,* I, p. 420.

38 Adamson and Folland, *Shepherd of the Ocean,* p. 104.

39 "the whole court doth follow" and "best-hated man . . ." see Chapter 14, nn. 39, 51.

40 Lloyd, *Worthies,* p. 515.

19 THE FALL

1 Edwards, *Raleigh,* I, p. 686.

2 Hakluyt, *Principall Navigations* (1589), pp. 771–2.

3 From 1585 onward, England was in constant fear of attack by Spain; Rowse, *Grenville,* p. 245; Read, *Walsingham,* II, p. 299. In June 1585 Sir George Carey informed Walsingham of reports coming into the Isle of Wight that Spain was planning an offensive against England; Corbett, *Spanish War,*

p. 34. In December word reached Dartmouth that an Armada was preparing and 62,000 troops were gathering in Lisbon for the campaign, the first target being the Isle of Wight; ibid., p. 52. For the stay of shipping since October 9, see *Acts of the Privy Council,* 1587–8, p. 254.

4 Rowse, *Expansion,* p. 245; State Papers Domestic, Elizabeth, cc, 46, April 27, 1587. Drake sailed against Spain in April 1587, the same month that White's colonists were allowed to leave for Roanoke. Surely the crisis was vastly more acute then! Could there really have been greater danger in October with the Spanish fleet destroyed? Furthermore, negotiations were still under way: peace overtures were initiated with Spain in November 1587, with such effect that Walsingham complained to Leicester that the Queen was lulled into a "dangerous security" and all warnings of "perils and dangers are neglected"; November 12, 1587, Cotton Mss. Galba Dii, f. 178. In December, Elizabeth commanded Walsingham and Burghley to negotiate a peace treaty with Spain on any terms; December 27, 1587, Calendar of State Papers, Spain, 1587–1603, p. 184. In April 1588 Walsingham was again instructed to make peace overtures; Read, *Walsingham,* III, p. 276.

5 Hakluyt, *Principall Navigations* (1589), p. 772.

6 State Papers Supplementary, 9/55 (ii); Quinn, *Roanoke Voyages,* II, pp. 559–60. I agree with Quinn's suggestion that Raleigh's instructions to John to let certain ships "steal away" referred to Gilbert's squadron; p. 560, n. 3.

7 "seven or eight . . ." and for word leaking out, see *Acts of the Privy Council,* 1588, pp. 7–8.

8 Hakluyt, *Principall Navigations* (1589), p. 772.

9 Ibid., p. 772; "Ancient prophecies . . ." Van Meteren, *Miraculous Victory* (1600), I, p. 412; for the earthquake and the Glastonbury Abbey tablets, see Deacon, *John Dee,* pp. 242–3. The book refuting the prophecies was Tymme's *A Preparation Against the Prognosticated Dangers of 1588.* Deacon (*John Dee,* p. 243) suggests that Dee himself may have been spreading rumors of disaster as part of a counterespionage plan.

10 *Acts of the Privy Council,* 1588, p. 8. It was Walsingham's job to prepare the business agenda for Privy Council discussions and report back to the Queen; Read, *Walsingham,* II, pp. 267–8, n. 4, p. 300.

11 Watts got two ships out in April, the *Drake* and the *Examiner.* These sailed in company with two other ships. One of these, the *Chance,* was probably Sir George Carey's vessel; Andrews, *Elizabethan Privateering,* p. 194; Quinn, *Roanoke Voyages,* II, p. 556. These may or may not have been the four ships Spaniards sighted in the West Indies in July; Wright, *Further English Voyages,* doc. 63, p. 235. Raleigh's brother, Sir John Gilbert, also got a ship out, though he was in trouble for it from the Privy Council; Rowse, *Grenville,* p. 258. Other vessels may have left as well — the *Black Dog* certainly did; Quinn, *Roanoke Voyages,* II, p. 557.

12 "straightly charged . . ." *Acts of the Privy Council,* 1588, p. 8; "their Lordships . . ." ibid., p. 27.
13 Ibid., p. 27.
14 Hakluyt, *Principall Navigations* (1589), p. 772.
15 *Acts of the Privy Council,* 1588, p. 27.
16 Rowse, *Grenville,* p. 264.
17 Hakluyt, *Principall Navigations* (1589), p. 772. The following account of the *Brave,* along with all the quotes contained therein, is found in White's account in Hakluyt, pp. 771–3. White's subsequent bitterness toward the crew of the *Brave* was owing to the ship's having chased vessels during the entire voyage out, with the intention of making a privateering attack. Their consort, the *Roe,* became permanently separated from them giving chase to a foreign ship.
18 Camden, *The History* (1688), p. 404; for the Mendicant monks, see Sams, *Conquest of Virginia,* p. 276.
19 Raleigh, *The History of the World,* Book V, chapter 1, part 6; Adamson and Folland, *Shepherd of the Ocean,* p. 115; Platter, *Travels* (1937), p. 152.
20 Platter, *Travels* (1937), p. 151.
21 Deacon, *John Dee,* p. 241.
22 Camden, *The History* (1688), p. 411.
23 Ibid., p. 410.
24 Ibid., pp. 411, 413.
25 Van Meteren, *Miraculous Victory* (1600), I, p. 604.
26 Camden, *The History* (1688), p. 417.
27 Deloney, *Of the Strange and Most Cruell Whippes . . .*
28 Van Meteren, *Miraculous Victory* (1600), I, p. 606.
29 It was received in June 1587; Read, *Walsingham,* III, p. 416.
30 Camden, *The History* (1688), p. 131.
31 Leicester died on September 4, 1588.
32 "errors," Raleigh, "Ocean to Scinthia," 11th book, line 367; "great treasons," Edwards, *Raleigh,* II, p. 53. Raleigh was flying too high. We know from Birch (*Memoirs,* II, p. 45) that Raleigh and the Queen disagreed on the plan of attack before the Armada, Raleigh preferring to disable Spanish ships within their own ports before they could set sail, but Elizabeth would not listen to him. Perhaps she was also made aware of Raleigh's view that all men were equal before God, and that the power of kings was beholden to the will of the people (*History of the World,* Book I, ch. IX, pt. 3), an idea treasonously opposed to the monarchy's notion of divine kingship and absolute obedience to princes. Were Raleigh's enemies whispering in the Queen's ear that his wings needed clipping? Four years later their efforts were given a boost when Elizabeth's inability to stop the pillaging of a carrack in the West Country was due to her imprisonment of Raleigh. It was only Raleigh — released from prison and brought forward under guard —

who was able to stop the rioting. The question must be asked: If the Lost Colonists were Separatists who operated according to democratic principles, were they singled out as a symbol of Raleigh's recalcitrance? It is noteworthy that the Armada attack itself was blamed on Puritan turmoil in the land; Marprelate, *Mineral* (1911), p. 187.

33 Naunton, *Fragmenta Regalia* (1810), p. 145. The argument that lay behind Essex's challenge to Raleigh is unknown.

34 Bacon, "Of Envy," *Essays* (1887), p. 94.

35 Sir Francis Allen to Anthony Bacon, in Birch, *Memoirs*, I, p. 56. "There was never in court," Allen added, "such emulation, such envy, such back-biting, as is now at this time," p. 57.

36 Raleigh, "Ocean to Scinthia," 11th book, lines 467, 267–8. According to Spenser, Raleigh composed this poem in 1589.

37 Bradbrook, *School of Night*, pp. 3, 5.

38 Raleigh, "Ocean to Scinthia," 11th book, line 156.

39 Raleigh, "Who list to hear the sum of sorrow's state." Raleigh, in an earlier line, says that he was born "to lose his labour still." For Shakespeare's use of this phrase, see Chapter 15, n. 53.

40 Spenser, *Faerie Queen*, introduction, Book II. Raleigh appeared in the *Faerie Queen* as Timias, who — significantly — is beset by the malicious Blatant Beast (jealousy) whose weapon of destruction is slander and scandal. Timias is waylaid in the forest by three men who shoot him with barbs. The Queen revives him with plants from Virginia, but she herself inadvertently wounds him with a dart from her eye.

41 Anon., *Willobie His Avisa*, preface.

42 "all alone . . ." Raleigh, "As You Came from the Holy Land"; Latham, *Poems*, pp. 22–3. Latham (p. xxvii) described this as Raleigh's "most naked poem." Oakeshott (*Queen and the Poet*, pp. 173, 59) called this the most moving of all of Raleigh's poems, adding that he did not seem to be writing about himself but about something more far-reaching. The difficulty has always been that although the poem seems to date to 1588, no one has been able to identify problems between Raleigh and the Court at this early date (everyone assuming that Raleigh's marriage of 1592 was the source of the upset). Edwards (*Raleigh*, I, p. 119), indeed, noted a "passing cloud" in 1589, but admitted that "we are nowhere told what it was that caused it." Accusations regarding the failed Lost Colony and its sabotage, however, supply the necessary context for very acrid disagreements that must have begun in early 1588 when John White's story was confirmed.

43 "Complaints . . ." Raleigh, "Ocean to Scinthia," 11th book, lines 476–7; "A secret murder . . ." Raleigh, "Secret Murder"; "if I complain . . ." Raleigh, "Wounded I am."

44 Raleigh, "Ocean to Scinthia," 11th book, lines 145, 159.

45 Raleigh, "Farewell to the Court." The slander, Raleigh said, had even

reached Ireland, so that he was scornfully treated there by the Lord Deputy, Sir William Fitzwilliam; Edwards, *Raleigh,* II, p. 51.

46 Raleigh's poetry has been analyzed to discover its hidden meanings, just as the works of Spenser and Shakespeare have been. See Latham, *Poems;* Oakeshott, *Queen and the Poet;* Bradbrook, *School of Night.*

47 Edwards, *Raleigh,* II, p. 42.

48 Hakluyt, *Principall Navigations* (1589), p. 815; Sanderson was married to Margaret Snedale, daughter of Raleigh's sister, Mary; Brown, *Genesis,* II, p. 991.

49 Shirley, *Sir Walter Raleigh,* p. 149; for the Queen's annual budget, see Stone, *Crisis of the Aristocracy,* p. 419; "I have consumed . . ." April 29, 1586, letter in Edwards, *Raleigh,* II, p. 33; Bruce (*Correspondence,* p. 193) dates it to March 29, 1586.

50 Hariot, *Briefe and True Report* (1589), p. 749. Hakluyt calls it treachery; see his 1587 dedicatory preface to Raleigh in Martyr, *Decades of the New World,* translated from Latin by Taylor, *Two Richard Hakluyts,* II, p. 368.

51 Raleigh, *History of the World,* preface.

52 Walsingham died on April 16, 1590. He was active in affairs of state up to the very end; Read, *Walsingham,* III, p. 448.

53 For the 1590 rescue attempt and the quotes contained therein, unless otherwise noted, see Chapter 1, n. 4.

54 For Watts, see Andrews, *Elizabethan Privateering,* pp. 105–9; Brown, *Genesis,* I, p. 99; for the love messages to Havana's governor Juan de Texeda, see Andrews, *Elizabethan Privateering,* p. 166.

55 White was presumably in London, since the ships belonging to Watts were outfitted on the Thames. He may have boarded there or even in Portsmouth, although I think Plymouth a far more likely choice. The ships left London toward February's end and docked at Plymouth until March 20, giving White a great deal of time to gather colonists and supplies, but very little time — once the captains' decision had been made to depart — to contact Raleigh, especially if Raleigh were in London.

56 For the sum recalled by William Sanderson, Raleigh's man of business, see Quinn, *Roanoke Voyages,* II, p. 580.

57 Indeed, Chief Justice Popham, one of the founders of the Jamestown colony, informed Spanish agent Zúñiga that the sending of Englishmen to America was done "in order to drive out from here thieves and traitors to be drowned in the sea"; Brown, *Genesis,* I, p. 46. Nonconformists, and certainly Separatists, were considered "traitors . . . more troublesome" than Papists; Pierce, *Historical Introduction,* p. 96. Walsingham ranked them second among the "inward diseases" facing the realm; Read, *Walsingham,* II, p. 14.

58 Aubrey, *Brief Lives* (1898), II, p. 188. "It is certain," Bacon admitted, "that heresies and schisms are, of all others, the greatest scandals"; "Of Unity in Religion," *Essays* (1887), p. 20. "He was scandalized with Atheism," said

Aubrey, "but he was a bold man, and would venture at discourse which was unpleasant to the Church-men"; Mss. Aubrey 6, fol. 77. In 1592 Raleigh was investigated following a charge of atheism made against him in Dorset; Harleian Mss. 6849, ff. 183–90. He was kept under surveillance, his house searched, and Hariot himself came under suspicion; Morley "Hariot," p. 61. Is it possible that the charge of atheism was leveled at Raleigh to prevent an investigation of the events relating to Roanoke? Such an accusation prevented an investigation into the death of Christopher Marlowe at this same time; Haynes, *Invisible Power,* p. 102. Slanderers consistently linked Raleigh to Marlowe. For Parsons, see Philopatrus, *Response to the Unjust and Bloody Edict;* Strathmann, *Sir Walter Raleigh,* pp. 25–6. Interestingly, Parsons was friendly with Essex, dedicating a 1594 book to him about Arabella Stewart.

59 Verstegan, *A Declaration of the True Causes of the Great Troubles . . .*

60 Philopatrus, *Response to the Unjust and Bloody Edict;* Strathmann, *Sir Walter Raleigh,* p. 26. For the loss of life of men, see Verstegan, *A Declaration,* pp. 56–7; Strathmann, *Sir Walter Raleigh,* pp. 25–35.

61 Elizabeth was the daughter of Sir Nicholas Throckmorton. Curiously, Raleigh's own family remembered the marriage to have taken place much earlier, in 1588; Oakeshott, *Queen and the Poet,* p. 45. Was it then, or were they merely confusing the unpleasant events of that year with the later upset involving Raleigh's marriage? In any case, if he were married in 1588, it would go far toward explaining the Queen's anger, which kept him long in disgrace — following, as it did, on the heels of the slander against him.

62 Mss. Aubrey 6, fol. 77. The child, a boy named D'amerie Raleigh, was born on March 29, 1592, but died in infancy; Adamson and Folland, *Shepherd of the Ocean,* p. 202.

63 Edwards, *Raleigh,* II, pp. 50–1. Significantly, Anthony Bacon wrote to Anthony Standen in February, saying that Raleigh had "been almost a year in disgrace for *several occasions,* as I think you have heard" (ital. added); Birch, *Memoirs,* I, p. 93. Standen was a Walsingham agent who operated under the name of Pompeo Pellegrini. Bacon's letter implies that Raleigh's imprisonment, and the lengthy banishment to follow, was not owing simply to his marriage, as historians have supposed, but to several causes. Raleigh spoke of "errors made" (in 1588) and of "disgraces" (in 1592); Edwards, *Raleigh,* II, p. 50. "I am tumbled down the hill," he said, "by every practice," ibid., p. 79.

64 Raleigh, "The Lie"; Hawks, *History,* I, pp. 57–8; Latham, *Poems,* pp. 45–7.

65 Hakluyt, *Principall Navigations* (1600), III, pp. 287–8.

66 Raleigh, quoting Seneca, in *The History of the World,* Book V, chapter 1, pt. 6. Latin translation by Hadow, *Sir Walter Raleigh,* p. 205. Why did White settle in Ireland? Did he have family there? One interesting possibility is that since 1585 Ireland had become a refuge for religious dissidents of all

kinds: Catholics, Brownists, Separatists, and Puritans; Quinn, *England and the Discovery of America,* p. 339.

67 Powell, "Roanoke Colonists," p. 226.

20 RALEIGH'S SEARCH

1 Raleigh, *The History of the World,* preface.
2 Canço, *Report,* p. 156.
3 Richard Hawkins and fourteen of his crew in the *Dainty* were captured off the Peruvian coast in 1594. In 1597 they were shipped to Spain. Glande, however, said that he met them on a visit to Havana in 1599 — presumably during their transport. Quinn (*Roanoke Voyages,* II, p. 386, n. 5) believes that Glande was mistaken in the date and that he saw them when they came through Havana in 1597.
4 Brereton, *A Briefe and True Relation,* p. 14.
5 Ibid.
6 British Museum, Additional Mss. 6788, fol. 417.
7 Brereton, *A Briefe and True Relation,* p. 14. See Quinn, *England and the Discovery of America,* p. 408, for an identification of the botanical products laded.
8 For details of the two voyages, see Brereton, *A Briefe and True Relation.*
9 Camden, *Remains* (1674), p. 524.
10 Irwin, *Great Lucifer,* p. 160. Elizabeth "was but ill-attended in her last sickness," James Welwood said, "and near her death, forsaken by all but three or four persons, everybody making haste to adore the Rising Sun"; *Material Transactions,* p. 18. Raleigh was among those who remained loyal; Robert Cecil, Burghley's son and Walsingham's successor as Secretary of State, was among the first to rush to King James.
11 From the diary of John Manningham of the Middle Temple, Mss. Harleian 5333, f. 83; Aubrey, *Brief Lives* (1898), II, p. 182.
12 Ibid., p. 186.
13 Attributed to Essex. Chetham Mss. 8012, p. 107.
14 Dixon, *Her Majesty's Tower,* pp. 224–5.
15 Hawks, *History,* I, pp. 36–7; Philip Raleigh, *A Relation of the Cadiz Action.*
16 Raleigh, *History of the World,* preface.
17 For the trial account, see Shirley, *Raleigh;* Hawks, *History,* I; Jardine, *Criminal Trials.*
18 Hawks, *History,* I, pp. 47–9; Shirley, *Raleigh,* pp. 87, 132, 153; Jardine, *Criminal Trials,* I, pp. 407, 410, 444.
19 Jardine, *Criminal Trials,* I, pp. 450–1; Shirley, *Raleigh,* pp. 164–5. The jury deliberated for only fifteen minutes; ibid., p. 162.
20 Hawks, *History,* I, p. 50.
21 Ibid.

22 Jardine, *Criminal Trials,* I, p. 466.
23 Lansdowne Mss. 142, f. 396. It was said that the Scots themselves cried out against King James's injustice; Shirley, *Sir Walter Raleigh,* p. 173.
24 *Eastward Hoe,* Act II, Scene 1; Act III, Scene 2; Brown, *Genesis,* I, pp. 29, 30. The original text reads "bred of those that were left there in '79." The date has been corrected to 1587. No voyages were made to Virginia before 1584.

21 JAMESTOWN

1 Raleigh, "Petition to the Queen," lines 7–9.
2 Barbour (*Jamestown,* I, p. 14) speculates that John Popham and Robert Cecil were aided in their draft of the Virginia Company charter by Sir Edward Coke and John Doddridge, Solicitor General.
3 Virginia Company, *Records,* III, p. 34.
4 "but the town . . ." Brown, *Genesis,* I, pp. 113–14; for Jacobopolis and James-Fort, ibid.; "murmured at our planting . . ." Percy, *Observations* (1907), p. 18.
5 Ibid., p. 17.
6 Ibid., pp. 20, 22; Smith, *General Historie,* p. 163.
7 Smith, *True Relation,* B4v. This version of Smith's book, now in the British Museum, was annotated in a hand that has not been identified, but has been dated with relative certainty to the latter part of Smith's life. The notes may have been made by Samuel Purchas, though whether his information was accurate is unknown, Barbour, *The Complete Works,* I, pp. 6–7. In any case, above Smith's line stating that men were clothed at a place called Ocanahonan, are written the words: "6 days' journey beyond Ocanahonan."
8 Smith, *True Relation,* C2r.
9 Ibid., C4r.
10 The original is in the Archivo General de Simancas, M.P.D., IV-66, XIX-153; reproduced in Brown, *Genesis,* I, Map LVII, facing p. 184; Barbour, *Jamestown,* I, facing p. 238.
11 Smith, *General Historie,* p. 66.
12 Ibid., pp. 70–1.
13 Ibid., p. 71.
14 Ibid.
15 Smith, *Advertisements,* pp. 4–5, 21.
16 Ibid., p. 21.
17 Smith's account does not mention the Werraskoyack leader by name. However, Strachey's 1610 roster of Powhatan leaders records Tackonekintaco as "an old Weroance of Warraskoyack"; *Historie of Travaile,* Book I, chapter 4. Presumably, then, he was the leader in 1608.
18 Smith, *Proceedings,* p. 57.
19 Brown, *Genesis,* I, p. 78; see also Smith, *Proceedings,* p. 45.

20 Smith, *General Historie,* p. 87; *Proceedings,* p. 90.
21 Smith, *Proceedings,* p. 90.
22 Smith, *A Map of Virginia,* p. 9.
23 Smith, *Proceedings,* p. 90.

22 WAR ON THE POWHATAN

1 Bacon, "Of Plantations," *Essays* (1887), p. 356.
2 Aubrey, *Brief Lives* (1898), I, p. 285; for evidence of the meeting, see Hakluyt's dedicatory epistle to *Virginia Richly Valued* (1846).
3 Virginia Company, *Records,* III, p. 17.
4 Brown, *Genesis,* I, p. 324.
5 "The allowance . . ." Johnson, *Tragical Relation* (1907), pp. 422–3; "unnaturally . . ." Vaughan, *American Genesis,* p. 66.
6 "looked like anatomies . . ." Percy, *A Trewe Relacyon* (1921–2), p. 269; "so lamentable . . ." Johnson, *Tragical Relation,* p. 423.
7 Virginia Company, *Records,* III, p. 18.
8 Archer, *A Relatyon* (1910), p. xliv.
9 Virginia Company, *Records,* III, pp. 19, 14–15.
10 Brown, *Genesis,* I, p. 247. War was declared by then Virginia governor, Lord De la Warr; Rountree, *Pocahontas's People,* pp. 54–5.
11 "throwing them overboard . . ." Percy, *A Trewe Relacyon* (1921–2), p. 272; for the attack on the Namsemond, see ibid., p. 263. For an excellent overview of this first Jamestown war, see Fauz, "Abundance of Bloodshed."
12 "cunning and coloured . . ." William Crashaw in Brown, *Genesis,* II, p. 613; "our invasion . . ." Johnson, *Nova Britannia.*
13 Virginia Company, *Records,* III, p. 22.
14 Johnson, *Nova Britannia.*
15 "Many good religious . . ." Smith, *Advertisements,* p. 10; "vulgar opinion . . ." Virginia Company, *A True Declaration.*
16 Johnson, *Nova Britannia.*
17 Smith, *Advertisements,* p. 10.
18 Virginia Company, *A True Declaration.*
19 For Strachey's biography, see Barbour, *Complete Works,* II, p. 27. Strachey's *Historie of Travaile* was essentially a promotional tract and apology for colonization.

23 REQUIEM

1 Strachey, *Historie of Travaile* (1849), p. 50.
2 Ibid., pp. 85–6.
3 Purchas, *Pilgrimes* (1905–7), XVIII, p. 527. Smith, however, declared that he was the "first Christian" that Wahunsonacock or his attendants had ever

seen; *General Historie,* p. 121. Nor was there evidence of miscegenation. The anonymous 1607 *Brief Description of the People* noted that the hair of the Powhatan people was black and "I found not a grey eye among them all."

4 Smith, *General Historie,* p. 49. When Pocahontas visited England in 1616, Smith wrote on her behalf to Queen Anne, asserting that he had received "exceeding great courtesie" from her father. (This letter was later published and inserted within Smith's story of his near-execution at their hands! *General Historie,* p. 121.) For its apocryphal nature, see Rountree, *Pocahontas's People,* pp. 38–9. Smith, even in his own day, was accused of lying by Edward Maria Wingfield, President of Jamestown in 1607; Barbour, *Jamestown,* I, p. 220.

5 Anon., *For the Colony in Virginea Britannia.*

6 Smith, *True Travels,* p. 42.

7 Shirley, *Sir Walter Raleigh,* p. 234.

8 State Papers Domestic, James I, xcix, 77, September 28, 1618.

9 Cayley, *Life of Ralegh,* II, pp. 161–3.

10 Shirley, *Sir Walter Raleigh,* p. 240. It was Spain that demanded, and secured, Raleigh's execution from James; ibid., p. 222; Edwards, *Raleigh,* I, pp. 246–7. Raleigh, said Aubrey, fell a sacrifice to Spanish politics; he was "the great scourge and hate of the Spaniard"; *Brief Lives* (1898), II, p. 189. According to Hawks (quoting Monson, *Naval Tracts*), Raleigh's spectacular 1596 raid on Cadiz forever remained Spain's most embarrassing blow; *History,* I, p. 37. Carew Raleigh agreed. Raleigh "lost his life," he said, "for being their enemy"; Irwin, *Great Lucifer,* p. 290. Hariot outlived Raleigh by only two years, dying on July 2, 1620, reputedly of mouth cancer; Morley, "Hariot," p. 62. However, it was probably skin cancer — contracted, perhaps, from sun exposure on the Outer Banks — for Aubrey said "on the top of his nose came a little red speck (exceedingly small) which grew bigger and bigger, and at last killed him"; *Brief Lives* (1898), I, p. 286.

11 Harlow, *Last Voyage,* p. 315.

12 Fuller, *Worthies* (1840), III, p. 176; for White's coat of arms, see Chapter 3, n. 29.

13 Personal communication from Tecumseh Cook, Chief, Pamunkey Nation, 1992.

14 For Pory's history, see Powell, *John Pory.*

15 Copland, *Virginia's God Be Thanked.*

16 Virginia Company, *Note of the Shipping* (1906–35), III, p. 641.

17 Anon., *A Perfect Description,* p. 10.

18 For the fighting at Jamestown, see Waterhouse, *A Declaration; The Barbarous Massacre* printed in Purchas, *Pilgrimes* (1905–7), XIX, pp. 157–64; Virginia Company, *Records,* III, pp. 551–5; for Nathaniel Powell among the dead, see Purchas, *Pilgrimes,* pp. 162–3.

19 Powell, *Roanoke Colonists,* p. 225; Powell, *John Pory,* p. 124. See also ibid.,

p. 100, n. 75, which suggests that Lost Colonists Alice and John Chapman may also have been related to Pory.

20 Smith, *General Historie,* p. 16.

24 DEEP IN THE INTERIOR

1 Bacon, "Of Simulation and Dissimulation," *Essays* (1887), p. 72.

2 Hakluyt, *Principall Navigations* (1600), III, p. 293.

3 Ibid., p. 769.

4 Ibid., p. 767.

5 The theory that White's colony divided was cogently proposed by Quinn in *England and the Discovery of America,* pp. 441–2. However, I propose that a much smaller number of colonists remained at Croatoan, composed especially of those women who had recently given birth and those with infants too young to travel. Although the majority of White's company moved inland, there is absolutely no evidence that they ever reached Virginia or the Chesapeake Bay. Any theory that proposes to account for their disappearance must explain how they were reduced and dispersed in such a way that survivors subsequently appeared at multiple locations, and in such small numbers that miscegenation was not noticeable to later European travelers. Quinn's theory (*Set Fair,* p. 350) that the "inland" party maintained themselves intact for twenty years but lost contact with those remaining at Croatoan due to time and distance is not as tenable an explanation as that the inland group was in trouble from the very beginning and was dispersed soon after their settling, so that they could not make contact with Croatoan. The distance was not great.

6 Barbour, *Jamestown,* I, p. 26.

7 Hariot, *Briefe and True Report* (1589), pp. 756, 762.

8 Lane to Walsingham, September 8, 1585, State Papers Colonial, 1/1, 6.

9 Smith, *General Historie,* p. 87; Smith, *Proceedings,* p. 90.

10 Hakluyt, *Principall Navigations* (1589), p. 738.

11 Hariot, *Briefe and True Report* (1589), p. 761.

12 For pandemics, see Brasser, "Early Contacts," p. 83; Salwen, "Southern New England," pp. 171–2; for Luna see Hudson et al., "Tristan de Luna Expedition"; for an account of a sick servant left by de Soto among the Coosa, see Garcilaso de la Vega, *Florida of the Inca,* p. 347; "pleased Almighty . . ." Archdale, *Description* (1911), p. 285.

13 Smith, *Proceedings,* p. 60.

14 Anon., *Brief Description of the People.*

15 The Powhatan directed Smith's search for the Lost Colonists to the Chowanoc first, indicating that this was either where they thought members of White's company would be, or where information about them could be obtained. Later instructions issued to Thomas Gates in 1609 stated that

members of White's company were thought to be at "Chonahorn Ohonahorn" on "the River Choanocki." In the margin someone wrote, "Ohonahoen, chief seate"; Virginia Company, *Records,* III, p. 17. Lane listed "Ohanoak" as a Chowanoc town, otherwise known as the "blind town." It appears on White's map as Ohaunoock — possibly a printer's error for Chaunoock [Chowanoc].

16 Hakluyt, *Principall Navigations* (1589), p. 729.
17 Ibid., pp. 730, 732.
18 Salwen, "Indians of Southern New England," pp. 171–2.
19 Archdale, *Description* (1911), pp. 285–6, 289.
20 For repercussions attending the collapse of the southern chiefdoms, see Smith, "Indian Responses," pp. 143–9.
21 Hakluyt, *Principall Navigations* (1589), p. 767.
22 Ibid., p. 732.
23 Ibid., p. 743.
24 Smith, *Map of Virginia,* p. 25.
25 Archer, *A Relatyon* (1910), p. xlvi. Nauiraus was the name of the Arrohattoc guide.
26 Jefferson, *Notes on the State* (1801), p. 137.
27 See Chapter 10, n. 38.
28 Hariot, *Briefe and True Report* (1589), p. 761.
29 Virginia Company, *Records,* III, p. 17.
30 Barbour, "Earliest Reconnaissance," p. 297, though Gerard (cited by Swanton, *Indian Tribes,* p. 66) proposes its meaning to be "falls in a current." Tooker gives Powh-atan, "the falls town," "Meaning of the Name Anacostia," p. 392. If so, "the falls town on the Roanoke" — Mandoag territory — is a very interesting definition indeed.
31 Strachey, *Historie* (1849), p. 86. Bushnell, "Virginia Before Jamestown," p. 131, also speculated that Strachey was referring to a leader on Roanoke Island.
32 Hakluyt, *Principall Navigations* (1589), p. 732.
33 Virginia Company, *Records,* III, p. 228.
34 Smith, *General Historie,* p. 33. For the treatment of captives, see Lauber, *Indian Slavery;* for adoption, see Speck, "Tutelo Rituals," p. 3.
35 Strachey, *Historie* (1849), p. 36.
36 Smith, *Map of Virginia,* p. 27.
37 Despite the bizarre attack on Dasamonquepeuc, it is by no means certain that the colonists did fight back. They were settlers, unused to frontier warfare, and many may have surrendered. They might not, in fact, have had a great deal of ammunition available to them. If so, the number of survivors may have been appreciably higher than 30 percent. That this was possible is evidenced by the 1578 discovery by Florida governor Pedro Menendez Marqués of more than a hundred Frenchmen from the destroyed Huguenot

settlement of Santa Elena on the South Carolina coast alive in the interior and dispersed among the local chiefs. The principal leader himself was reported to have been harboring forty; Quinn, *New American World*, v, p. 26.

38 Virginia Company, *Records*, III, p. 17; Ashmolean Mss. 1147, f. 175–90. In the margin of the document, beside "Ohonahorn," is written the word "Ohonahoen." Bushnell reads "Gepanocon" as "Sepanocon," and theorizes that the name was Siouan; "Virginia Before Jamestown," p. 131.

39 Virginia Company, *A True and Sincere Declaration.*

40 Barbour, *Jamestown*, II, p. 279.

25 WHO ARE THE MANDOAG?

1 Hakluyt, *Principall Navigations* (1589), p. 743.

2 Bland's journey and the quotes contained in this section, unless otherwise noted, are taken from Bland, *Discovery of New Brittaine.*

3 The Tuscarora nation consisted of some twenty-two towns located between the Neuse and Tar Rivers, in an area roughly bounded by modern-day Kinston and Greenville; Swanton, *Indian Tribes*, pp. 85–6; Library of Congress, Captain John Evans Mss. submitted for publication.

4 For the identification of Hocomowananck, see n. 75.

5 For the etymology of the word *Mandoag*, see Appendix B.

6 Rickard, "Use of Native Copper," pp. 268–70; Feder, *Copper and the Indian*, p. 98; Hurst and Larson, "On the Source of Copper," pp. 177–81; Reynolds, "Algonkin Metal-Smiths," p. 345; Goad, "Exchange Networks," pp. 46–88, 210–14.

7 Reynolds, "Algonkin Metal-Smiths," p. 348; Rickard, "Use of Native Copper," p. 275.

8 Purchas, *Pilgrimes* (1905–7), XIX, pp. 153–4; Reynolds, "Algonkin Metal-Smiths," p. 348.

9 Strachey, *Historie* (1849), p. 36.

10 *Liteu*, "it burns," Brinton and Anthony, *A Lenapé-English Dictionary*, p. 67, in which *l* replaces *r* in North Carolina dialects. Compare to the word for "fire," in Quiripi *rout* and Natick *nootau* (Trumbull, *Natick Dictionary*, p. 143, *n* replacing *r*). Ives Goddard supplied the word *lu:t:e:hoki* in Unami, with the caveat that it is unattested (personal communication). Its meaning is roughly "fire land," or "burned land," in which case the ending is *aki*, "land." Since Ritanoc was recorded as a specific location, I am inclined to think that the ending is the locative *oc* (*unk* in Delaware) as recorded for this region by Hariot (see Tooker, *The Names Chickahominy*, p. 87). The *n* in Ritanoc may be the result of scribal error for an intended *h*.

11 Hakluyt's dedicatory epistle to *Virginia Richly Valued.* Strachey, writing from Jamestown, said that "the Indians talk of . . . copper to the Southward," *Historie* (1849), p. 33. "Ritanoe" is a copyist error for "Ritanoc."

Ritanoc appears in other versions, cf. Gates's instructions in Virginia Company, *Records*, III, p. 17.

12 Hakluyt, *Principall Navigations* (1589), p. 751.

13 Reynolds, "Algonkin Metal-Smiths," p. 347. Tooker ("Discovery," p. 9) would appear to be unique in locating Chaunis Temoatan beyond the Blue Ridge and Cumberland Mountains entirely. The route, he suggested, was "by tortuous paths" across Kentucky, to a locale in Gallatin County, Illinois. Both failed to consider that the Appalachians are not the only mountains in North Carolina. To the seventeenth-century residents of Jamestown, the Piedmont was consistently described as mountainous; Strachey, *Historie*, p. 25. See n. 30.

14 Hakluyt, *Principall Navigations* (1589), pp. 740–1.

15 Ibid., p. 741.

16 Strachey, *Historie* (1849), p. 34; Smith, *General Historie*, p. 42.

17 Hakluyt, *Principall Navigations* (1589), p. 738.

18 Carpenter, *Metallic Mineral Deposits of the Carolina Slate Belt*. In 1857 Hawks identified this same general region as Chaunis Temoatan, *History*, I, p. 123.

19 In the General Archives of Simancas, Legajo E2386, f. 145.

20 Brown, *Genesis*, I, p. 185.

21 Ashe, *History of North Carolina*, I, pp. 43, 48–9.

22 Barbour, *Jamestown Voyages*, I, p. 240; Barbour, "Ocanahowan," p. 4.

23 Quinn, *Set Fair for Roanoke*, pp. 371–3; Quinn, *England and the Discovery*, pp. 460–2.

24 In addition to Fishing Creek, the smaller Tranters Creek flows into the river closer to its mouth, west of the modern town of Washington.

25 See n. 75 for the suggested location of Ocanahowan on the Roanoke River.

26 White's map of Eastern North America, British Museum, P & D 1906–5–9–1 (2). Quinn also pointed out the composite nature of White's map, portions of which are incorrectly oriented; *New American World*, II, p. 55.

27 Carpenter, *Metallic Mineral Deposits of the Carolina Slate Belt*.

28 "prodigiously large trees . . ." Byrd, *Dividing Line* (1866), p. 181; for the Great Trading Path, see also Myer, "Indian Trails"; Rights, "Trading Path."

29 Lederer, *Discoveries* (1912), p. 154; see also Fallam, *Journal;* Tisdale, *Story of the Occoneechees;* Rights, "Trading Path"; Alexander, "Indian Vocabulary."

30 Lawson, *History of North Carolina* (1903), p. 26. The printed editions of Lawson's *History* differ, reading both "small currents" and "small swift currents." Rights ("Trading Path," p. 13) calls the Carraways the "forgotten mountain range."

31 Byrd, *Journey to Eden* (1866), p. 9.

32 Byrd, *Dividing Line* (1866), p. 180. Myer ("Indian Trails," p. 775) concedes that the Great Trading Path was prehistoric, but believes that its apex wasn't reached until the advent of European trade. Although the latter certainly

had a tremendous impact, the wealth and influence of the Occaneechi were already well established by the time the first English traders/explorers reached them and identified their language as the lingua franca for a vast region. For a more accurate understanding of what its pre-European configuration may have been, see the regional redistributive model IV proposed by Goad ("Exchange Networks," pp. 42–3, 219), though her reading of Strachey places the copper center in northwestern North Carolina.

33 Lederer, *Discoveries* (1912), p. 154. Goad ("Exchange Networks," p. 197), working with Middle Woodland material from Georgia, lists indigenous southeastern exchange items of copper, mica, galena, hematite, ochre, and shell. Smith (*General Historie,* pp. 87–8) said that the Piedmont people southwest of Jamestown traded skins for dried fish and corn from the nations on the coast. Barlowe (*Principall Navigations* [1589], pp. 728–33) obtained buffalo skins from the Secotan, which likely came via the Occaneechi from interior herds. Lederer (*Discoveries,* p. 170) noted shells (roanoke and peak), pearl, vermilion, and quartz among Carolina trade items, while Evans mentioned the Tuscarora obtaining salt; Library of Congress, Captain John Evans Mss. Lawson encountered Tuscarora traders bound for Occaneechi Island "to sell their wooden bowls and ladles for raw skins"; I (1903), p. 31. Yeardley (*Narrative* [1911], p. 28) was informed by the Tuscarora in 1654 that "the way to the sea was a plain road, much travelled for salt and copper."

34 According to Swanton, the meaning of Occaneechi is "unknown." Speck suggested a derivation from the Tutelo word for man, *yuhkañ;* Swanton, *Indians of the Southeastern U.S.,* p. 218. That Occaneechi is an Algonquian word, however, and not Siouan, is attested by the presence of the Woconichi River in northeastern Quebec. Danielle Sioui, Adario Sioui Masty, and Anne (Samson) Masty of Whapmagoostui, Hudson Bay, suggest "Place where people gather." Compare to Natick *wokonóus,* "fence, palisade, fort," Trumbull, *Natick Dictionary,* p. 196; Abenaki *oua'kanroúzen,* meaning "fort," Rasles, *Dictionary of the Abnaki Language,* p. 457, similar to Lederer's Akenatzy. Perhaps Cree *ichi,* "to go from one place to another," implies going to, or congregating at, such a fort or location, if such a construction is possible in Algonquian.

35 Beverly, *History of Virginia* (1855), pp. 161, 171.

36 John Fontaine visited Fort Christanna in 1716 and recorded a "Saponi" vocabulary, the then generic name for the Siouan nations grouped at the fort, which included the Saponi, Tutelo, Occaneechi, Stuckanox, and Meipontski; Alexander, "Indian Vocabulary." Alexander was the first to propose that Fontaine's vocabulary was the famous Occaneechi trade jargon described by Beverly. Ives Goddard noted that either it indeed represented the Occaneechi trade jargon, or the words were obtained from various individuals at the fort who spoke different languages; Goddard, "[Review of] An

Indian Vocabulary from Ft. Christanna," p. 220. Although there may have been non-Siouan-speaking individuals present at Fort Christanna, neither Iroquoian nor Algonquian nations were lodged there, so the former explanation appears the most likely.

37 Lederer, *Discoveries* (1912), pp. 152–3. The coastal people from whom the Saponi had taken the pearl were said to dwell in "Florida," yet "Florida" was the term by which the Spaniards called the coast from Florida to the Chesapeake Bay. The island of Wococon on the Outer Banks was, according to Spain, in central Florida; Quinn, *England and the Discovery of America,* p. 255. The Saponi, therefore, might have got the pearls from anywhere along the coast, though more likely from North Carolina rather than farther south; proof that interior Siouan nations did raid those along the coast. What effect, if any, the fall of the Secotan-Chowanoc-Weapemeoc alliance had on regional politics has yet to be determined.

38 Lederer, *Discoveries* (1912), pp. 155–6, 143.

39 Locke, *Memorandum* (1912), pp. 211, 215, 224–5.

40 Strachey, *Historie* (1849), p. 26. Editors of the 1973 Princeton University edition (from the Percy mss.) of Strachey read the word as *Peccarecanick.* The difference may be due to variations in the three manuscript copies of Strachey, or to more powerful magnification tools available in 1973 with which to read it.

41 Ibid., p. 26.

42 Ibid., pp. 55, 195.

43 "Peccarecamicke you shall find . . ." Virginia Company, *Records,* III, p. 17; "Peccarecamek (*Paccarecanick* in Percy Mss., Princeton) . . ." Strachey, *Historie* (1849), p. 36. Cree *apisk,* Anderson, *Plains Cree Dictionary,* p. 2, a noun, denoting metal or iron (a suffix); Pequot *apess,* perpetuated in the name of the famous William Apess (formerly spelled Apes until the same pronunciation mistake regarding simians forced an orthographic change. Apess himself changed the spelling to Apess); Wicocomoco *tapisco,* Oré, *Relación,* p. 51. Although the exact Chesapeake Bay nation was not named in the original, the description of its location makes Wicocomoco the most likely choice. The word *tapisco* was understood by the Spaniards to mean gold. See also *apsk* in Penobscot, Bond, *Native Names of New England,* p. 61, and *ompsk* in Natick, Trumbull, *Natick Dictionary,* p. 106.

44 Strachey, *Historie* (1849), p. 102.

45 Tooker, *Algonquian Names of the Siouan Tribes,* pp. 22–6, 32, 49.

46 Speck, *Tutelo Rituals,* p. 2.

47 People who think the Mandoag were the Tuscarora: Ashe, *History of North Carolina,* I, p. 86; Paschal, *The Tuscarora Indians.* Quinn (*Lost Colonists,* p. 47; *Set Fair,* pp. 108, 111, 371, 373), Painter ("Last of the Nottoway," p. 36), and Binford ("Ethnohistory," pp. 122–3) proposed that there were actually

two sets of Mandoag. Quinn suggested that the Mandoag who visited Lane's winter camp were Meherrin, while the Mangoaks who had copper and lived beyond the Moratuc were the Tuscarora. Elsewhere (*Roanoke Voyages,* II, p. 857), he grouped the Mangoak, Mandoag, Mandoak, Mandoage, and Mongoack together as variant names for the same people. Painter and Binford supposed that all of Lane's accounts of the Mandoag were Tuscarora, but identified the Mangoage of 1607 as the Nottoway. Quinn also suggested (ibid., I, pp. 257, n. 6, 265) that the Mandoag may have been the Nottoway, though he locates them west of the Moratuc and Chowanoc, between the Roanoke and Chowan Rivers, which was outside recorded Nottoway territory. Gepanocon and the Eyanoco he assigned to the Chowanoc, which then led him to believe that the Chowanoc had acquired copper. Durant (*Ralegh's Lost Colony,* p. 69) equates the Mandoag with a generalized "Iroquoi" [*sic*], and postulates that they were part of an alliance (along with the Tripanicks and Oppossians) that later formed the basis of the Powhatan Confederacy.

48 Yeardley, *Narrative* (1911), pp. 25, 27.

49 Swanton, *Indians of the Southeastern U.S.,* p. 148; Swanton, *Indian Tribes,* p. 81.

50 Those who think the Nottoway were the Mandoag: Mooney, "Siouan Tribes," p. 7; Binford ("Ethnohistory," p. 123) postulated an "early" Mandoag who were Tuscarora and a later Mangoak who were Nottoway; Swanton, *Indians of the Southeastern U.S.,* p. 163; Swanton, *Indian Tribes,* p. 65; Mook, "Algonquian Ethnohistory"; Tooker ("Discovery," p. 9) believed that the Mandoag were both Nottoway and Tutelo and that the main portion of the tribe lived at the foot of the Blue Ridge Mountains; Rountree, *Pocahontas's People,* p. 21; Barbour ("Ocanahowan," pp. 10, 12) suggested that the Mangoak were Iroquoian Nottoway, while the Mandoag — an entirely separate nation — were Algonquian.

51 The Nottoway vocabulary was collected by J. Wood in 1820, when it was reported that there were only twenty-seven Nottoway left. As early as 1788, Thomas Jefferson stated that no male Nottoway were alive and that only "a few women" remained; *Notes,* p. 141; Gallatin, *Synopsis,* p. 81. That the Nottoway were associated with the Susquehannock, see Swanton, *Indian Tribes,* p. 65.

52 See Appendix B.

53 People who think Meherrin were the Mandoag: Speck, *Chapters on the Ethnology* (map); Rountree, *Pocahontas's People,* p. 21; Feder, *Virginia Indian Tribes,* p. 28. Ashe (*History of North Carolina,* I, p. 86) muddied the water by suggesting that the Meherrin were actually Chowanoc. Binford (*An Ethnohistory,* p. 105) expressed everyone's frustration by noting that systematic investigation of both the Meherrin and the Nottoway had been sorely neglected, and that attempts to classify them linguistically had been prone to generalization without adequate citation.

54 Bland, *Discovery,* p. 6; Lawson, *History of North Carolina* (1903), p. 140; Jef-

ferson, *Notes* (1801), p. 139. For other variations, see Hodge, *Handbook,* I, p. 839.

55 Gallatin, *Synopsis,* p. 81; Schoolcraft, *Indian Tribes,* V, p. 36, n. 2.

56 Hale, "Tutelo Tribe and Language"; Sapir, "A Tutelo Vocabulary"; Frachtenberg, "A Tutelo Vocabulary."

57 Hodge, *Handbook,* I, p. 839; Swanton, *Indians of the Southeastern U.S.,* p. 149; Saunders, *Colonial Records,* II, pt. 2, p. 643. The fact that the Iroquoian-speaking Susquehannock merged with the Meherrin is no proof that the latter were Iroquoian, for the Susquehannock also sought refuge among the Siouan Occaneechi and were incorporated for a time with a Siouan town of refugee Monocan (Egerton Mss., pp. 1–3).

58 According to the Meherrin, their name means "Muddy Water." Yet I have been unable to find a word meaning "muddy water" that is similar to *Meherrin* in any Iroquoian language. The Onondaga word for muddy water was supplied by Audrey Shenandoah of the Onondaga Nation; the Mowhawk word for the same was furnished by the Akwesasne Freedom School, Mohawk Nation. The multilingual Iroquoian translators at the Freedom School did not recognize the word *Meherrin* as belonging to their language or meaning "muddy water." Linguist Blair Rudes said that the Tuscarora word for this nation was "dirty water," or *Awę'nęhra'r* (personal communication). He added that *Meherrin* could have been derived from the Tuscarora word for "dirt," or *yu'nęhrer.* The Siouan derivation outlined here is much more likely and is more consistent with the nation's own usage and with early English spellings. For Biloxi, see Dorsey and Swanton, *Dictionary of Biloxi and Ofo,* p. 307. For the Siouan words *here; Yeíswa, Waterá here, Sigrí here,* etc., see Speck, "Siouan Tribes," pp. 204, 218–21. The conclusion that the word *Meherrin* is Siouan, supported by other research in progress by the author, suggests that there may need to be a reclassification of the Meherrin as a Siouan nation.

59 Ibid., p. 215.

60 "houses are built like ours," Strachey, *Historie* (1849), p. 48; "a country called Anone . . ." Smith, *True Relation,* p. C2r.

61 Bland, *Discovery,* p. 15. Bland located the Shakori fields between Nottoway Creek and Penna Mount River, both branches of the Chowan. This argues for a more easterly location for the Shakori and the Eno than that traditionally given by historians. Swanton placed the Eno farther west at the headwater of the Tar and Neuse, along the Eno River in present Orange and Durham Counties, and in the locale of Enno in Wake County; *Indian Tribes,* pp. 79, 83; *Indians of the Southeastern U.S.,* p. 131. He located the Shakori to the east in Franklin, Vance, and Warren Counties along Shocco and Big Shocco Creeks. The Shakori, he admitted, moved so frequently that it was difficult to give their location, noting that they usually kept company with the Eno who, "in marked distinction of their neighbors . . . had taken to a

trading life." In 1670 Lederer found the Eno living east of the Shakori, and in 1701 Lawson placed their territory so far east that he mistakenly included the Eno in his list of Tuscarora towns. That they were near neighbors of the Tuscarora is evident from the fact that they were at war; Yeardley, *Narrative* (1911), pp. 27–8. As we have seen, Bland's account (1650), the earliest available, locates the Shakori old fields near the Nottoway and Meherrin Rivers. Their name in the east is perpetuated, perhaps, by Enfield in Halifax county (east of Shocco Creek). Occoneechee Neck and Occoneechee Creek in Northampton County northeast of Enfield, an area the Occaneechi were not known to inhabit, may possibly be related to the Eno as well. Wiccacon River, a branch of the Chowan, was called Weyanoke Creek as early as 1646. In 1710 John Beverly, for the Virginia government, located the former site of the Weyanoke town on *Wicocan Creek;* Saunders, *Colonial Records,* I, pp. 676, 740.

62 Yeardley, *Narrative* (1911), pp. 27–8.

63 Lawson, *History of North Carolina* (1903), pp. 30–1. It remains to be determined whether the Coree and the Shakori were related, or perhaps even one and the same. "I know some Indian nations," Lawson said, "that have changed their settlements many hundred miles. . . . I once met with a young Indian woman that had been brought from beyond the mountains. . . . She spoke the same language as the Coranine Indians that dwell near Cape Lookout"; ibid., p. 101. The woman, sold as a slave in Virginia, doubtless entered the colony via the Great Trading Path. "Beyond the mountains" may have been no farther away than the Piedmont.

64 Lederer, *Discoveries* (1912), pp. 156–7.

65 Bland, *Discovery,* p. 6.

66 Hakluyt, *Principall Navigations* (1589), p. 743.

67 Ibid., p. 741.

68 Lederer, *Discoveries* (1912), p. 141.

69 Byrd, *Dividing Line* (1866), p. 188; *Journey to Eden* (1866), pp. 2–3.

70 Bowen, *America Discovered,* pp. 48–9. Jones's narrative, originally published in the *Gentleman's Magazine of London,* 1740, has been discounted by the fact that a rash of other "Welsh-Indian" sightings have been claimed for North America, on the order of an urban legend. Be that as it may, word of Welsh-speaking Mandoags should at least excite our interest in light of the new evidence we have uncovered about the Lost Colony. Jones said that the nation that freed him was seated on the Pamlico River, not far from Cape Hatteras. Traditionally, this was Pamlico Nation territory. They were also enemies of the Secotan and might conceivably be called "Mandoag"— treacherous. Jones's choice of terminology for them, however, implies that an Algonquian speaker among the Tuscarora supplied the term. As it stands, there simply is not enough information available to make full sense of the statement.

71 Marana, *Letters Writ by a Turkish Spy;* Bowen, *America Discovered,* pp. 44–5. Quinn (*Roanoke Voyages,* II, p. 539, n. 1) proposes that there was a Welsh component among White's company. Certainly Jane, John, and Griffin Jones were Welsh, as perhaps were Wenefrid and Edward Powell. There may have been others.

72 As recorded by Lane. See Hakluyt, *Principall Navigations* (1589), pp. 737–47, for Lane's references to the Mandoag; Swanton, *Indians of the Southeastern U.S.*, p. 131.

73 For slavery, see Lauber, *Indian Slavery,* pp. 25–44; for Tutelo adoption, see Speck, "Tutelo Rituals." Skiko himself had been captured by the Mandoag, but escaped. Raleigh's first Roanoke expedition reported Pamlico slaves among the Secotan who had been captured in war; Hakluyt, *Principall Navigations* (1589), p. 732. See Chapter 24, n. 37, for the account of more than a hundred Frenchmen dispersed in the interior among local chiefs. A dispersal theory places the former Lumbee claim of Lost Colony ancestry in a very interesting new light (cf. Barton; McMillan; Weeks). If the Lost Colonists were disseminated along Siouan trade routes, survivors could be expected to be found throughout the interior, among various linguistic groups. The Occaneechi Path itself ran five hundred miles, and connected with other routes linking the coast to the Appalachian Mountains and beyond. This alone explains why later travelers into the interior found no Lost Colony aggregates, but why tales of anomalous individuals and artifacts were frequently reported. For accounts of the favorable treatment of adopted captives, see Demos, *Unredeemed Captive,* and Jemison, *Life of Mary Jemison.* European women adoptees, in particular, frequently reported leading very fulfilled lives. Zúñiga informed Philip III in 1612 that Jamestown women were living among the Powhatan and were "received and used kindly by them, and that they wounded a certain zealous minister of their sect for reprehending it"; Brown, *Genesis,* II, pp. 632–3. The lives of slaves, however, would have been much different.

74 My suggested etymology is drawn from words recorded by Hale, "The Tutelo Tribe and Language," pp. 25, 41, 38, and is supported by Speck's attempt to translate the first two syllables of *Occonichi* from the word for "man," *yuhkañ;* Swanton, *Indians of the Southeastern U.S.*, p. 218. Many thanks to John Koontz and Giulia Oliverio, who reviewed the syntax of my translation. The name would appear in Tutelo as *yu:xkan ohon: hi-wa* (man many come-wa), *wa* being an aspect clitic denoting something real to the speaker, including present tense. Although Smith stated that there were Lost Colonists at "Ocanahonan," the handwritten annotation amended this, saying that they were "6 days' journey beyond Ocanahonan," *True Relation,* B4v.

75 My suggested etymology is based on comparative analysis with other Algonquian languages: for *accomac* (Powhatan), *ogkomé* (Massachusett), see

Trumbull's analysis in Hodge, *Handbook,* I, p. 7; Beauchamp, *Indian Names,* p. 101. For *ma-wig-nack,* ibid., p. 93.

76 For *Pe,* compare to *Pejepscot; cara,* see *Caratunk;* and *con,* see *Taconic;* Bond, *Native Names of New England,* pp. 3, 17, 58, + *oc,* locative ending. Cree elders of Whapmagoostui verified that the syntax is in accordance with Algonquian grammatical rules.

77 Speck, *Tutelo Rituals,* p. 2.

78 Strachey calls it *Pannawaick* (Percy Mss.) and says that this was where stores of salt stones were located. Compare with Natick, in which *penowe, penoowe* is "foreign, strange, different," *penuwoht, penuwot* "foreigner"; Trumbull, *Natick Dictionary,* pp. 122, 262. A town called "Panauuaioc" is shown south of Secota on White's map as printed in De Bry, *America,* I, pl. i, but does not appear on the surviving copy of White's original, British Museum, P & D, 1906–5–8–1 (3). De Bry may have been wrong: salt deposits occur at the confluence of the Roanoke and Chowan Rivers in the region of Cashie Creek, but not south along the Pamlico or Neuse; Swanton, *Indians of the Southeastern U.S.,* map 13, facing p. 254.

79 Clayton, *A Journal* (1912), pp. 186, 188. The characters were burned into the bark with a live coal.

80 Francis Magnel reported that the Powhatan possessed knives and iron objects in trade from Indian nations to the west, in the direction of the mountains; Barbour, *Jamestown,* I, p. 156.

81 Waterhouse, *A Declaration* (1906–35), p. 547.

26 EPILOGUE

1 Raleigh, "Farewell to the Court," lines 9–12.
2 Hakluyt, *Principall Navigations* (1600), III, p. 287.
3 Lawson, *History of North Carolina* (1903), p. 34.
4 Ibid. For 114 years, they had even remembered Raleigh's name!
5 Hakluyt, *Principall Navigations* (1600), III, p. 288.

BIBLIOGRAPHY

PRIMARY MANUSCRIPTS

Bodleian Library, *Ashmolean Manuscripts,* 1147.
———, *Aubrey Manuscripts,* 6.
British Museum, *Additional Manuscripts* 6788; 32091.
———, *Cotton Manuscripts* Galba Cix; Di, Dii, Appendix L.
———, *Harleian Manuscripts* 290; 1582; 5333; 6848; 6849.
———, *Lansdowne Manuscripts* 17; 37; 69; 96; 142.
Chetham Library (Manchester), *Chetham Manuscripts* 8012.
College of Arms, *Vincent Old Grants,* manuscript 157.
Essex County Record Office (Chelmsford), *Notes for Master Rauleys Viage,* Round Manuscripts, D/DRh, M I. Reprinted in Quinn, *Roanoke Voyages,* I, pp. 126–39.
Hatfield House, Salisbury Manuscripts, VI.
Library of Congress, Captain John Evans Mss., *Diary of a Journey from Virginia to the Indian Country,* Manuscript Division, Acc. #4884 A.
Virginia State Library, Record Group 35, Office of the State Librarian. Transcripts of Records Concerning Colonial Virginia in the British Public Records Office, compiled by the Rev. Edward Eggleston, 1886, 1 volume. Bacon's Rebellion 1676, *Egerton Manuscript* 2395.

PRIMARY PRINTED SOURCES

Acts of the Privy Council of England, ed. John Roche Dasent, 32 vols., London, 1897–1900.
Alvord, Clarence, and Lee Bidgood (ed.), *First Explorations of the Trans-Allegheny Region by the Virginians, 1650–1674,* Cleveland: Arthur H. Clark, 1912.
Anonymous, *Brief Description of the People,* 1607, PRO, State Papers Colonial, C.O. 1/1, 15ii.
Anonymous, *For the Colony in Virginea Britannia: Lawes Divine, Morall and Martiall,* 1612, recorded by William Strachey. Reprinted in Peter Force, *Tracts and Other Papers Relating Principally to the Origin, Settlement, and Progress of the Colonies in North America,* III, Washington, D.C.: William Q. Force, 1846.

Anonymous, *Leycesters Common-Wealth; Conceived, spoken and published with most earnest protestation of dutifull goodwill and affection towards this realme,* 1584, reprinted 1641.

Anonymous, *The Passage of our most dread Soveraigne Lady Quene Elyzabeth through the Citie of London to Westminster, the daye before her Coronation, Anno 1558–1559,* 1559. Reprinted in John Nichols (ed.), *The Progresses and Public Processions of Queen Elizabeth,* vol. I, London: 1823.

Anonymous, *A Perfect Description of Virginia . . .* 1649.

Anonymous, *Willobie His Avisa; or, the true picture of a modest maid, and of a chaste and constant wife,* 1594. Also unpublished as Harl. Mss. 6849.

Archdale, John, *A New Description of that Fertile and Pleasant Province of Carolina,* 1707, reprinted in Alexander Salley (ed.), *Narratives of Early Carolina, 1650–1708,* New York: Scribner, 1911.

Archer, Gabriel, *A Relatyon of the Discovery of our River, from James Fort into the Maine . . .* 1607, reprinted in Edward Arber (ed.), *Travels and Works of Captain John Smith,* Edinburgh: John Grant, 1910.

Aubrey, John, *Brief Lives,* printed from Bodleian and Ashmolean mss., ed. Andrew Clark, 2 vols., Oxford: Clarendon Press, 1898.

Bacon, Francis, *Essays,* 1597, reprinted by Richard Whatley as *Bacon's Essays with Annotations,* Boston: Lee and Shepard, 1887.

———, *Notes on the Present State of Christendom,* 1582, reprinted in James Spedding, et al. (ed.), *The Works of Francis Bacon,* VIII, 1862.

Bancroft, Richard, *Dangerous Positions and Proceedings . . .* 1593, sections reprinted in R. G. Usher (ed.), *The Presbyterian Movement,* London: 1905.

Barbour, Philip (ed.), *The Complete Works of Captain John Smith (1580–1631),* 3 vols., Chapel Hill: University of North Carolina Press for the Institute of Early American History and Culture, Williamsburg, Va., 1986.

Beverly, Robert, *The History and Present State of Virginia,* 1705, reprinted ed. C. Campbell, Richmond, Va.: J. W. Randolph, 1855.

Bilson, Thomas, *The True Difference Between Christian Subjection and Unchristian Rebellion,* 1585.

Birch, Thomas, *Memoirs of the Reign of Queen Elizabeth from the Year 1581 till Her Death, in which the Secret Intrigues of her Court, and the Conduct of Her Favourite, Robert Earl of Essex, Both at Home and Abroad, Are Particularly Illustrated,* 2 vols., 1754.

Bland, Edward, *The Discovery of New Brittaine,* 1651.

Brereton, John, *A Briefe and True Relation of the Discoverie of the North Part of Virginia,* 1602.

Bry, Theodor De, *America,* pt. I, Frankfurt-am-Main, Germany: 1590.

Byrd, William, *History of the Dividing Line, and other tracts: from the papers of William Byrd, of Westover, in Virginia, Esquire,* Historical documents from the Old Dominion, nos. II–III, ed. Thomas H. Wynne, Richmond, 1866.

Includes in vol. I, *The History of the Dividing Line Between Virginia and North Carolina* [1728], in vol. II, *A Journey to the Land of Eden* [1733].
Calendar of Rutland mss., *The Manuscripts of His Grace the Duke of Rutland, G.C.B. Preserved at Belvoir Castle,* London: printed for HMSO by Eyre & Spottiswoode, 1888.
Camden, William, *The History of the Most Renowned and Victorious Princess Elizabeth, Late Queen of England,* 1688, orig. 1615.
———, *Remains Concerning Britain,* 1674, orig. 1586.
Canço, Gonçalo Mendez de, "Report of David Glavin, Irlandes, Soldado," recorded by Canço and forwarded to Philip III of Spain, February 1600, printed in *Documentos Históricos de la Florida y la Luisiana, siglos XVI al XVIII,* ed. Manuel Serrano y Sanz, Madrid: Librería General De Victoriano Suárez, 1913.
Collinson, Richard (ed.), *The Three Voyages of Martin Frobisher*... 1578, includes the account of George Best, London: Hakluyt Society, v, 38, 1867.
Cooper, Thomas, *An Admonition to the People of England,* 1589, reprinted ed. Edward Arber, Birmingham: N.P., 1882.
Copland, Patrick, *Virginia's God Be Thanked, or a Sermon of Thanksgiving for the Happie Successe of the Affayres in Virginia This Last Yeare,* 1622.
Daye, John, *A Disclosing of the Great Bull and Certain Calves that He Hath Gotten and Specially the Monster Bull that Roared at My Lord Bishop's Gate,* British Museum, c.37, d.36 (2).
Dee, John, *The Private Diary of Dr John Dee,* ed. James Orchard Halliwell, Cambridge: Camden Society, 1842.
Dekker, Thomas, *Dead Tearme,* 1608.
———, *Guls Horn Booke,* 1609.
———, *Lanthorne and Candlelight; or, the Bell-man's Second Nights Walk,* 1608, reprinted in Arthur Valentine Judges, *The Elizabethan Underworld,* London: Routledge, 1930.
———, *O Per Se O,* 1612, reprinted in Judges, ibid.
———, *Seven Deadly Sins of London,* 1606, reprinted by Edward Arber (ed.), London: English Scholar's Library, 1879.
Deloney, Thomas, *Of the Straunge and Most Cruell Whippes Which the Spanyards Had Prepared to Whippe and Torment English Men and Women,* British Museum, ballad.
Diaz, Pedro, *The Examination of the Masters and Pilots,* printed in Hakluyt, *Principall Navigations,* III (1600), pp. 866–8.
Digges, Dudley, *The Compleat Ambassador*... 1655.
Edwards, Edward (ed.), *The Life of Sir Walter Ralegh*... *Together with His Letters,* 2 vols., London: Macmillan, 1868.
Fallam, Robert, *A Journal from Virginia, beyond the Appalachian Mountains, in September 1671,* 1684–6, transcribed by Rev. John Clayton, reprinted in

Clarence Alvord and Lee Bidgood, *First Explorations of the Trans-Allegheny Region by the Virginians, 1650–1674,* Cleveland: Arthur H. Clark Co., 1912, pp. 183–205.

Farley, Henry, *St. Paules-Church, the bill for the Parliament,* 1621, British Museum (portion reprinted in Rye, *England as Seen by Foreigners*).

Field, John, and Wilcox, Thomas, *An Admonition to the Parliament,* 1572, reprinted in W. H. Frere and C. E. Douglas (ed.), *Puritan Manifestoes,* New York: E. S. Gorham, 1907.

Force, Peter (ed.), *Tracts and Other Papers Relating Principally to the Origin, Settlement and Progress of the Colonies in North Carolina from the Discovery of the Country to the Year 1776,* 4 vols., Washington, D.C.: printed by P. Force, 1836–46.

Fuller, Thomas, *The History of the Worthies of England,* 1662, reprinted ed. P. Austin Nuttall, 3 vols., London: printed for Thomas Tegg, 1840.

Garcilaso de la Vega, el Inca, *The Florida of the Inca,* ed. John and Jeanette Varner, Austin: University of Texas Press, 1988.

Gascoigne, George, *The Steele Glas: Complainte of Phylomenes,* 1576.

Gerard, John, *The Herball or Generall Historie of Plantes,* 1597.

Gilbert, Humphrey, *A Discourse How Hir Majestie May Annoy the King of Spayne,* State Papers Domestic, Elizabeth, 12/118, 12 (i), 1577. A second version appeared as: *A Discourse How Hir Majestie May Meete With And Annoy the King of Spayne,* State Papers Domestic, Elizabeth, 12/118, no. 12 (ii).

———, *Discourse of a Discoverie for a New Passage to Cataia,* 1576.

Gilby, Antony, *A Pleasaunte Dialogue, between a Souldior of Barwicke and an English Chaplaine,* 1581, sections reprinted in Edward Arber, *An Introductory Sketch to the Martin Marprelate Controversy,* London: English Scholar's Library, 1879.

Great Britain, Public Record Office, *Calendar of Letters and State Papers relating to English Affairs, preserved principally in the Archives of Simancas,* 1568–79, 1580–86, 1587–1603.

———, *Calendar of State Papers relating to Scotland and Mary, Queen of Scots,* 1547–1603.

———, *Chancery Proceedings, Elizabeth,* C.2/Eliz. s 16/48 (2/13/314).

———, *Court of Requests,* 3/192. November 15, 1519.

———, *State Papers Colonial,* C.O. 1/1.

———, *State Papers Domestic, Elizabeth,* 12/98; 118; 158; 175; 176; 180; 195; 200; 215; 232; 246.

———, *State Papers Domestic, James,* 14/99.

———, *State Papers Foreign, Elizabeth,* 1578–9: 473; 510; 519; 538. 1581–2: 314. 1583: 715.

———, *State Papers relating to Scotland and Mary, Queen of Scots,* S.P. 19.

———, *State Papers Supplementary,* 9/55.

Greene, Robert, *A Disputation Between a He-Cony-Catcher and a She-Cony-Catcher,* 1592, reprinted in Judges, *The Elizabethan Underworld.*

Hadow, Grace Eleanor (ed.), *Sir Walter Raleigh: Selections from his Historie of the World, his Letters, etc,* Oxford: Clarendon Press, 1917.

Hakluyt, Richard, *Principall Navigations, Voiages, Traffiques and Discoveries of the English Nation,* first edition, 1589; second edition, 1598–1600, 3 vols: includes Barlow, "The first voyage made to the coastes of America" (1589); "The voyage made by Sir Richard Grenville" (1589); Lane, "An account of the particularities of the imployments of the English men left in Virginia" (1589); *Tiger* journal of Grenville's voyage (1589); "The third voyage made by a ship" (1589); White, "The fourth voyage made to Virginia" (1589), and "The fifth voyage of Master John White" (1600); "Honourable Voyage to Cadiz, anno 1596" (1600).

———, *A Discourse on Western Planting,* 1584.

———, *Divers Voyages Touching the Discoverie of America,* 1582.

———, *Virginia Richly Valued,* 1609. Reprinted in Peter Force, *Tracts,* IV, no. 1.

Hakluyt, Richard (the elder), *Inducements to the Liking of the Voyage Intended Towards Virginia in 40 and 42 degrees,* 1585, reprinted in John Brereton, *A Briefe & True Relation* (1602).

Hall, Clayton (ed.), *Narratives of Early Maryland, 1633–1684,* New York: Charles Scribner's Sons, 1910.

Hall, Joseph, *A Common Apologie of the Church of England: Against the Unjust Challenges of the . . . Brownists,* 1610, reprinted in *The Works of Joseph Hall,* London: 1625.

———, *Mundus alter et Idem,* 1605, translated into English by John Healey, *The Discovery of a New World,* 1609.

Hamor, Ralph, *A True Discourse of the Present Estate of Virginia,* London: 1615.

Hariot, Thomas, *A Briefe and True Report of the New Found Land of Virginia . . .* 1588, printed in Hakluyt, *Principall Navigations,* 1589.

Harman, Thomas, *Caveat or Warning for Common Cursitors,* 1566.

Harrison, William, *The Description of the Iland of Britaine . . .* and *The Description of England,* 1587, printed together in vols. 1 and 2 of Raphael Holinshed, *Chronicles,* 1587, reprinted London: J. Johnson, et al., 1807, vol. 1. See also *The Description of England, Scotland and Ireland,* ed. Georges Edelen, Ithaca: Cornell University Press for the Folger Shakespeare Library, 1968.

Harryson, John, pseud. [John Bale], *Yet a Course at the Romyshe Fox,* 1543.

Hawkins, John, *The Third and Troublesome Voyage,* printed in Hakluyt, *Principall Navigations,* III, 1600.

Hayes, Edward, *A True Report,* 1583, printed in Hakluyt, ibid., 1589.

Hentzner, Paul, *Travels in England,* 1598, published in Latin as *Itinerary of Germany, France, &c.,* Nuremberg: 1612, reprinted by William Rye, *England as Seen by Foreigners,* London: J. R. Smith, 1865.

Holinshed, Raphael, *Chronicles of England, Scotland, and Ireland,* 3 vols., 1587, reprinted in 6 vols., London: J. Johnson, 1807–8.

Ingram, David, *Relation of David Ingram,* printed in Hakluyt, *Principall Navigations,* 1589.

Jefferson, Thomas, *Notes on the State of Virginia,* 1784, New York: M. L. & W. A. Davis, 1801.

Jemison, Mary, *A Narrative of the Life of Mrs. Mary Jemison,* ed. James E. Seaver, Canandaigua: J. D. Bemis, 1824.

Johnson, Robert, *Nova Britannia: offering most excellent fruites by planting in Virginia* . . . 1609, reprinted in Peter Force, *Tracts,* 1, no. 6.

———, *Tragical Relation of the Virginia Assembly,* 1624, reprinted in Lyon Gardiner Tyler (ed.), *Narratives of Early Virginia.*

Lawson, John, *A New Voyage to Carolina* . . . 1709, reprinted as *History of North Carolina,* ed. Fred A. Olds, Charlotte, N.C.: Observer Printing House, 1903.

Lederer, John, *The Discoveries of John Lederer in Three Several Marches from Virginia to the West of Carolina,* 1672, reprinted by Alvord and Bidgood, *First Explorations.*

Lemnius, Levinus, *Touchstone of Complexions,* 1576, reprinted in Rye, *England as Seen by Foreigners.*

Le Moyne de Morgues, Jacques, *Narrative of Le Moyne, an artist who accompanied the French expedition to Florida under Laudonnière, 1564,* Boston: J. R. Osgood, 1875.

Lloyd, David, *State-Worthies; or, the Statesmen and Favourites of England* . . . 1670.

Locke, John, *A Memorandum,* Calendar of State Papers Colonial, 1669–74, no. 1428, reprinted in Alvord and Bidgood, ed., *The First Explorations.*

Lodge, Edmund, *Portraits of Illustrious Personages of Great Britain,* London: London Printing and Publishing Company, 1854.

Marana, Giovanni Paolo, *Letters Writ by a Turkish Spy, Who Lived Five and Forty Years Undiscovered at Paris: Giving an Impartial Account to the Divan at Constantinople, of the Most Remarkable Transactions of Europe* . . . London: A. Wilde, 1770.

Marprelate, Martin, *The Epistle,* 1588, reprinted by William Pierce (ed.), *The Marprelate Tracts: 1588–89,* London: James Clarke, 1911.

———, *The Epitome,* 1588, ibid.

———, *Hay Any Work for Cooper,* 1589, ibid.

Marprelate, Martin (Senior), *The Just Censure and Reproofe,* 1589, ibid.

———, *Minerall and Metaphysicall Schoolpoints,* 1589, ibid.

Moffett, Thomas, *Insectorum Sive Minimorum Animalium Theatrum,* 1634, British Museum, Sloane Mss., 4014.

More, Sir Thomas, *Utopia,* 2d edition, 1556, reprinted by Edward Arber, London: Constable, 1906.

Moryson, Fynes, *An Itinerary* . . . *containing his ten yeeres travell through the twelve dominions of Germany, Bohmerland, Sweitzerland, Netherland, Den-*

marke, Poland, Italy, Turky, France, England, Scotland, and Ireland, London: John Bele, 1617.

Naunton, Robert, *Fragmenta Regalia; or, observations on Queen Elizabeth, Her Times & Favourites,* 2d edition, 1641, reprinted in *The Harleian Miscellany,* v, London: for Robert Dutton, 1810.

Nichols, John, *The Progresses and Public Processions of Queen Elizabeth,* 3 vols., new edition, 1823.

Norden, John, *Notes on London and Westminster,* 1592, from his *Description of Middlesex,* British Museum, Harl. Ms. 570. Reprinted in Rye, *England as Seen by Foreigners.*

———, *The Surveyor's Dialogue,* 1618.

Oré, Fray Luis Gerónimo De, *Relación de los Mártires que ha habido en las Provincias de la Florida,* 1617; reprinted and translated in Maynard Geiger, *The Martyrs of Florida, 1513–1616,* Franciscan Studies, 18, New York: Joseph Wagner, 1936.

Osborne, Francis, *A Miscellany of Sundry Essays, Paradoxes, and Problematical Discourses,* 1659.

Parker, Matthew, *Correspondence of Matthew Parker,* ed. John Bruce and Rev. Thomas T. Perowne, Cambridge: University Press for the Parker Society, 1853.

Parmenius, Stephen, *An Embarkation Poem for the voyage projected by the celebrated and noble Sir Humphrey Gilbert, Golden Knight, to take a colony to the New World,* 1582, reprinted in David Beers Quinn and Neil Cheshire, *The New Found Land of Stephen Parmenius,* Toronto: University of Toronto Press, 1972.

Peacham, Henry, "Sights and Exhibitions in England," printed in Thomas Coryat, *Three Crude Veines Are Presented in this Booke Following (Besides the Foresaid Crudities),* 1611.

Peckham, George, *True Report,* printed in Hakluyt, *Principall Navigations* (1589).

Percy, George, *Observations Gathered Out of a Discourse of the Plantation of the Southern Colonie in Virginia by the English, 1606,* reprinted in Tyler, *Narratives.*

———, *A Trewe Relacyon of the Proceedings and Occurences of momente which have happened in Virginia from 1609 until 1612,* 1612, reprinted in *Tyler's Quarterly Historical and Genealogical Magazine,* vol. 3, 1921–2, pp. 260–82.

Philopatrus, Andreas (aka Robert Parsons), *Elizabethae, Angliae Reginae Haeresim Calvinianam Propugnantis, Saevissimum in Catholicos sui Regni edictum . . . cum Responsione . . .* 1592.

Platter, Thomas, *Thomas Platter's Travels in England,* 1599, reprinted and translated from German by Clare Williams, London: Jonathan Cape, 1937.

Purchas, Samuel, *Purchas his Pilgrimage . . .* 1613, reprinted as *Hakluytus Posthumus, or Purchas His Pilgrimes,* 20 vols., Glasgow: James MacLehose, 1905–7.

Raleigh, Philip, *A Relation of the Cadiz Action in the year 1596,* 1700, reprinted as Appendix 1 in Walter Oakeshott, *The Queen and the Poet,* London: Faber & Faber, 1960.

Raleigh, Walter, "As you come from the Holy land of Walsingham," Ms. Rawlinson Poetry 85, Bodleian Library.

———, "Farewell to the Court," *The Phoenix Nest,* R. S., ed. 1593.

———, *The History of the World,* 1614. Portions reprinted in Hadow (ed.), *Sir Walter Raleigh, Selections from His Historie . . .*

———, "The Lie," 1592, reprinted in Francis Davison (ed.), *A Poetical Rhapsodie,* 1611, 3d edition.

———, "Ocean to Scinthia," Hatfield Ms., Cecil Papers, 144. Hatfield House.

———, "Petition to the Queen," Mss. Drummond (v.iii Drummond Miscellanies, ii, entitled "S. W. Raghlies Petition to the Queene, 1618"), Drummond Collection, Edinburgh University Library, printed in Latham, *The Poems of Sir Walter Ralegh,* p. 70.

———, "A Secret Murder . . . " *The Phoenix Nest.*

———, "Who list to hear the sum of sorrow's state," *The Phoenix Nest.*

———, "Wounded I am . . . " in William Byrd (ed.), *Songs of Sundrie Natures,* 1589.

Rasles, Sébastian, *A Dictionary of the Abnaki Language in North America,* ed. John Pickering, Cambridge: American Academy of Arts and Sciences, Memoir 1 (1833), pp. 375–565.

Shirley, John, *The Life of the Valiant and Learned Sir Walter Raleigh, Knight. With His Trial At Winchester,* 1677.

Smith, John, *A True Relation . . .* 1608, reprinted in Edward Arber (ed.), *Works,* 2 vols., Birmingham: 1884; Philip Barbour (ed.), *The Complete Works of Captain John Smith,* 3 vols., Chapel Hill: University of North Carolina Press, 1986.

———, *A Map of Virginia . . .* 1612.

———, *Proceedings of the English Colonie in Virginia . . .* 1612.

———, *The General Historie of Virginia, New England, and the Summer Isles . . .* 1624.

———, *True Travels, Adventures, and Observations . . . 1630.*

———, *Advertisements for the Unexperienced Planters of New England, or Any Where . . . 1631.*

Smith, William, *Brief Description of the Famous City of London,* Harl. Ms. 6363.

Smyth, John, *Lives of the Berkeleys,* reprinted in Sir John MacLean (ed.) as *The Berkeley Manuscripts,* 3 vols., Gloucester: John Bellows, 1883–5, vol. 3, *A Description of the Hundred of Berkeley in the County of Gloucester and of Its Inhabitants.*

Spenser, Edmund, *The Faerie Queene: disposed into XII bookes . . . 1590.*

Stow, John, *Survey of London,* 1598, 1603 edition, reprinted by Charles Kingsford (ed.), 2 vols., Oxford: Clarendon Press, 1908.

Strachey, William, *The Historie of Travaile into Virginia Britannia,* 1612, Sir Francis Bacon copy in the British Museum, R. H. Major (ed.), London: the Hakluyt Society, no. vi, 1849. See also the Earl of Northumberland edition, Percy Mss., Princeton University.

Stubbes, Philip, *The Anatomie of Abuses,* 1583.

Taylor, Eva G. R. (ed.), *The Original Writings and Correspondence of the Two Richard Hakluyts,* 2 vols., London: Hakluyt Society, 2d ser., LXXVI–LXXVII, 1935.

Turner, William, *The Seconde Course of the Hunter at the Romish Fox and Hys Advocate,* 1545.

Tyler, Lyon Gardiner (ed.), *Narratives of Early Virginia, 1606–1625,* New York: Charles Scribner's Sons, 1907.

Tymme, Thomas, *A Preparation Against the Prognosticated Dangers of 1588,* 1588.

Van Meteren, Emanuel, *The Miraculous Victory Atchieved by the English Fleete* . . . printed and translated by Hakluyt, *Principall Navigations,* I, 1600, from Van Meteren, *History of the Low Countries.*

Verstegan, Richard, *A Declaration of the True Causes of the Great Troubles, presupposed to be intended against the realm of England,* 1592.

Virginia Company, *A Note of the Shipping, Men and Provisions Sent and Provided for Virginia* . . . 1622, reprinted in Virginia Company, *Records.*

———, *The Records of the Virginia Company of London,* 4 vols., ed. Susan Myra Kingsbury, Washington, D.C.: Government Printing Office, 1906–35.

———, *A True and Sincere Declaration of the Purpose and Ends of the Plantation Begun in Virginia,* 1609, reprinted in Alexander Brown, *Genesis of the United States,* I, Boston: Houghton Mifflin, 1890.

———, *A True Declaration of the estate of the colonie in Virginia, with a confutation of such scandalous reports as have tended to the disgrace of so worthy an enterprise,* 1610, reprinted in Peter Force, *Tracts,* III, no. 1.

Walker, Gilbert, *Manifest Detection of the Most Vyle and Detestable Use of Dice Play,* 1552, reprinted ed. James O. Halliwell, London: for the Percy Society by Richards, 1850.

Waterhouse, Edward, *A Declaration of the State of the Colony and* . . . *a Relation of the Barbarous Massacre* . . . 1622, reprinted in Virginia Company, *Records,* III.

Weelkes, Thomas, *Ayeres or Phantasticke Spirites, for Three Voices,* 1608.

Welwood, James, *Of the Most Material Transactions in England for the Last Hundred Years, Preceding the Revolution in 1688,* 1700.

Whitgift, John, *The Works of John Whitgift,* 3 vols., ed. John Ayre, Cambridge: University Press for the Parker Society, 1851–3.

Winstanley, William, *England's Worthies: Select Lives of the Most Eminent Persons from Constantine the Great to This Present Time,* 1684.

Wirtemberg, Frederick, Duke of, *A True and Faithful Narrative of the Bathing Excursion Which His Serene Highness Frederick, Duke of Wirtemberg* . . . *Made a Few Years Ago to the Far-Famed Kingdom of England;* as recorded by his private secretary, Jacob Rathgeb, 1602, reprinted in Rye, *England as Seen by Foreigners.*

Wood, Abraham, "Letter to John Richards, August 22, 1674," reprinted in Alvord and Bidgood, *First Explorations.*

Wood, Anthony A., *Athenae Oxonienses,* 1721, reprinted by Philip Bliss, 2 vols., London: F. C. & J. Rivington, 1813–20.

Wright, Irene A. (ed.), *Further English Voyages to Spanish America, 1583–1594: Documents from the Archives of the Indies at Seville Illustrating English Voyages* . . . London: Hakluyt Society, 2d ser., no. 99, 1951.

Wynn, Peter, "November 26, 1608, letter to Sir John Egerton," Huntington Library, Jamestown Colony, EL, 1683.

Yeardley, Francis, *Narrative of Excursions into Carolina, 1654,* reprinted in Alexander Salley (ed.), *Narratives of Early Carolina, 1650–1708,* New York: Scribner, 1911.

ENGLAND — SECONDARY SOURCES

Adams, Randolph G., "An Effort to Identify John White," *American Historical Review,* XLI (1935–6), pp. 87–91.

Adamson, J. H., and Folland, H. F., *The Shepherd of the Ocean: An Account of Sir Walter Ralegh and His Times,* Boston: Gambit, 1969.

Andrews, Kenneth, *Elizabethan Privateering: English Privateering during the Spanish War, 1585–1603,* Cambridge: Cambridge University Press, 1964.

Arber, Edward (ed.), *An Introductory Sketch to the Martin Marprelate Controversy, 1588–1590,* London: English Scholar's Library, 1879.

Binyon, R. Laurence, *English Water-colours,* 2d edition, London: A. & C. Black, 1944.

———, "Governor John White, Painter and Virginia Pioneer," *Putnam's Magazine* (July 1907), pp. 400–11.

Bradbrook, M. C., *The School of Night: A Study in the Literary Relationships of Sir Walter Ralegh,* New York: Russell & Russell, 1965.

Bruce, John, *Correspondence of Robert Dudley, Earl of Leicester,* London: Camden Society, 1844.

Byrne, Muriel St. Clare, *Elizabethan Life in Town and Country,* London: Methuen, 1961.

Canny, Nicholas, *The Elizabethan Conquest of Ireland: A Pattern Established, 1565–76,* New York: Harper & Row, 1976.

Cayley, Arthur, *The Life of Sir Walter Ralegh, Knt,* 2 vols., London: Cadell & Davies, 1805.

Corbett, Julian, *Papers Relating to the Navy during the Spanish War, 1585–7,* London: for the Navy Records Society, 1898.

Cumming, William Patterson, "The Identity of John White Governor of Roanoke and John White the Artist," *N.C. Historical Review,* xv, no. 3 (1938), pp. 197–203.

Deacon, Richard, *John Dee: Scientist, Geographer, Astrologer and Secret Agent to Elizabeth I,* London: Frederick Muller, 1968.

Devereux, Walter, *Lives and Letters of the Devereux, Earls of Essex,* 2 vols., London: John Murray, 1853.

Dictionary of National Biography, ed. Sir Leslie Stephen and Sir Sidney Lee, 22 vols., London: Oxford University Press, H. Milford, 1921–2.

Dixon, William, *Her Majesty's Tower,* New York: Harper, 1869.

Fell-Smith, Charlotte, *John Dee,* London: Constable, 1909.

Fraser, Antonia, *Mary, Queen of Scots,* New York: Dell, 1971.

Frere, Walter Howard, and Douglas, C. E. (ed.), *Puritan Manifestoes: A Study of the Origin of the Puritan Revolt,* New York: E. S. Gorham, 1907.

Handler, Jerome, and Aufderheide, Arthur, et al., "Lead Contact and Poisoning in Barbados Slaves: Historical, Chemical, and Biological Evidence," *Social Science History,* 10, no. 4 (Winter 1986), pp. 399–425.

Harlow, Vincent T. (ed.), *Ralegh's Last Voyage,* London: Argonaut Press, 1932.

Haynes, Alan, *Invisible Power: The Elizabethan Secret Services, 1570–1603,* New York: St. Martin's Press, 1992.

Hicks, Leo, "The Growth of a Myth: Father Robert Persons, S. J and Leicester's Commonwealth," *Studies: an Irish Quarterly,* 46 (1957), pp. 91–105.

Hulton, Paul Hope, *America, 1585: The Complete Drawings of John White,* Chapel Hill: University of North Carolina Press; London: British Museum Publications, 1984.

———, *The Work of Jacques Le Moyne de Morgues: A Huguenot Artist in France, Florida and England,* 2 vols., London: British Museum Publications, 1977.

Hulton, Paul Hope, and Quinn, David Beers, *The American Drawings of John White, 1577–1590, with Drawings of European and Oriental Subjects,* London: Trustees of the British Museum; Chapel Hill: University of North Carolina Press, 1964.

Irwin, Margaret, *That Great Lucifer: A Portrait of Sir Walter Ralegh,* London: Chatto & Windus, 1960.

Jardine, David, *Criminal Trials,* 2 vols., London: C. Knight, 1832–5.

Jenkins, Elizabeth, *Elizabeth the Great,* New York: Coward-McCann, 1959.

Johnson, Francis R., *Astronomical Thought in Renaissance England: A Study in English Scientific Writings from 1500 to 1645,* New York: Octagon Books, 1968.

Kendall, Alan, *Robert Dudley, Earl of Leicester,* London: Cassell, 1980.

Knappen, Marshall M., *Tudor Puritanism: A Chapter in the History of Idealism,* Chicago: University of Chicago Press, 1939.

Latham, Agnes M. C. (ed.), *The Poems of Sir Walter Ralegh,* Cambridge, Mass.: Harvard University Press, 1951.

Lee, Hanna F., *The Huguenots in France and America,* 2 vols., Cambridge, Mass.: John Owen, 1843.

Meyer, Oscar, *England and the Catholic Church Under Queen Elizabeth,* London: Routledge & Kegan Paul, 1967.

Miller, Perry, *Errand into the Wilderness,* Cambridge, Mass.: Belknap Press of Harvard University Press, 1956.

Morley, Frank, "Thomas Hariot — 1560–1621," *Scientific Monthly*, 14 (January 1922), pp. 60–6.

Morris, John, *The Letter-books of Sir Amias Poulet, Keeper of Mary Queen of Scots*, London: Burns & Oates, 1874.

———, *The Troubles of Our Catholic Forefathers, Related by Themselves*, London: Burns & Oates, 1875, vol. 2, *The Memoires of Father William Weston*, from mss. at Stonyhurst College.

Motley, John Lothrop, *The Rise of the Dutch Republic: A History*, 3 vols., London: J. M. Dent; New York: E. P. Dutton, 1920.

Neale, John, *Elizabeth I and Her Parliaments, 1559–1601*, 2 vols., London: Jonathan Cape, 1953–7.

Nicolas, Nicholas Harris, *Life of William Davison, Secretary of State and Privy Counsellor to Queen Elizabeth*, London: J. Nichols, 1823.

———, *Memoirs of the Life and Times of Sir Christopher Hatton* . . . London: Richard Bentley, 1847.

Oakeshott, Walter, *The Queen and the Poet*, London: Faber & Faber, 1960.

Pierce, William, *An Historical Introduction to the Marprelate Tracts: A Chapter in the Evolution of Religious and Civil Liberty in England*, London: Constable, 1908.

Pollen, John Hungerford, *The English Catholics in the Reign of Queen Elizabeth*, New York: Burt Franklin, 1971.

———, *Mary Queen of Scots and the Babington Plot*, Edinburgh: University Press for the Scottish History Society, 1922.

Powell, William S., "Roanoke Colonists and Explorers: An Attempt at Identification," *N.C. Historical Review*, 34 (April 1957), pp. 202–26.

———, *Paradise Preserved*, Chapel Hill: University of North Carolina Press, 1965.

Quinn, David Beers, *England and the Discovery of America, 1481–1620* . . . New York: Knopf, 1974.

———, *The First Colonists: Documents on the Planting of the First English Settlements in North America, 1585–90*, ed. David Beers Quinn and Alison M. Quinn, Raleigh: N.C. Dept. of Cultural Resources, 1982.

———, *The Lost Colonists: Their Fortune and Probable Fate*, Raleigh: N.C. Dept. of Cultural Resources, 1984.

———, *New American World: A Documentary History of North America to 1612*, 5 vols, ed. David Beers Quinn, Alison M. Quinn, and Susan Hillier, New York: Arno Press and Hector Bye, 1979.

———, *Raleigh and the British Empire*, New York: Macmillan, 1949.

———, *The Voyages and Colonising Enterprises of Sir Humphrey Gilbert*, 2 vols., London: Hakluyt Society, 2d ser., LXXXIII-LXXXIV, 1940.

Quinn, David Beers, and Neil M. Cheshire, *The New Found Land of Stephen Parmenius* . . . Toronto: University of Toronto Press, 1972.

Read, Conyers, *Lord Burghley and Queen Elizabeth*, New York: Knopf, 1960.

———, *Mr Secretary Cecil and Queen Elizabeth*, London: Jonathan Cape, 1955.

———, *Mr Secretary Walsingham and the Policy of Queen Elizabeth,* 3 vols., Oxford: Clarendon Press, 1925.

Reed, Arthur, "John Rastell's Voyage in the Year 1517," *Mariner's Mirror,* IX (1923), pp. 137–47.

Rowse, A. L., *The Expansion of Elizabethan England,* London: Macmillan, 1955.

———, *Sir Richard Grenville of the* Revenge, London: Jonathan Cape, 1949.

Rye, William (ed.), *England as Seen by Foreigners: In the days of Elizabeth and James the First,* London: J. R. Smith, 1865.

Schiller, Friedrich, *The History of the Revolt of the Netherlands,* translated by E. B. Eastwick, Boston: F. A. Nicolls, 1901.

Stevens, Henry, *Thomas Hariot: The Mathematician, the Philosopher, and the Scholar* . . . London: private printing, 1900.

Stone, Lawrence, *The Crisis of the Aristocracy, 1558–1641,* Oxford: Clarendon Press, 1965.

Strathmann, Ernest, *Sir Walter Raleigh: A Study in Elizabethan Skepticism,* New York: Columbia University Press, 1951.

Strype, John, *Annals of the Reformation* . . . 4 vols., 1725–31.

———, *The Life and Acts of the Most Reverend Father in God, John Whitgift,* 2 vols., 1717–18, reprinted in 3 vols., Oxford: Clarendon Press, 1822.

Tarbox, Increase Niles, *Sir Walter Ralegh and His Colony in America,* vol. XV, Boston: Prince Society, 1884.

Tawney, Richard H., *The Agrarian Problem in the Sixteenth Century,* London: Longmans, Green, 1912.

Taylor, Eva G. R., *The Troublesome Voyage of Captain Edward Fenton, 1582–3,* Cambridge: for the Hakluyt Society at the University Press, 1959.

Usher, Roland, *The Presbyterian Movement in the Reign of Queen Elizabeth: As Illustrated by the Minute Book of the Dedham Classis, 1582–1589,* London: Offices of the Royal Historical Society, 1905.

Waddington, John, *Congregational History, 1567–1700,* London: Longmans, Green, 1874.

Webb, Sidney and Beatrice, *English Poor Law History,* London: Longmans, Green, 1910.

Wedgwood, C. V., *William the Silent, Prince of Orange,* London: Jonathan Cape; New Haven: Yale University Press, 1948.

Williams, Iolo A., *Early English Watercolours: and Some Cognate Drawings by Artists Born not Later than 1785,* London: The Connoisseur, 1952.

Williams, Neville, *Elizabeth: Queen of England,* London: Weidenfeld & Nicolson, 1967.

Williamson, James, *The Age of Drake,* London: A. & C. Black, 1960.

———, *The Voyages of the Cabots and the Discovery of North America,* New York: Da Capo Press, 1970.

Wilson, Mona, *Sir Philip Sidney,* London: Rupert Hart-Davis, 1950.

VIRGINIA — SECONDARY SOURCES

Alexander, Edward P., "An Indian Vocabulary from Fort Christanna, 1716," *Virginia Magazine of History and Biography,* vol. 79 (1971), pp. 303–13.

Amer, Robert, *The Lost Colony in Literature,* Raleigh: America's Four Hundredth Anniversary Committee, N.C. Dept. of Cultural Resources, 1985.

Anderson, Anne, *Plains Cree Dictionary in the "Y" Dialect,* Edmonton, Alberta: N.P., 1971.

Ashe, Samuel A'Court, *History of North Carolina,* 2 vols., Raleigh, N.C.: Edwards & Broughton, 1925.

Barbour, Philip, "The Earliest Reconnaissance of the Chesapeake Bay Area: Captain John Smith's map and Indian vocabulary," 2 parts, *Virginia Magazine of History and Biography,* vols. 79 and 80, 1971 and 1972.

———, "The Function of Comparative Linguistics in the Study of Early Transcriptions of Indian Words," *Studies in Linguistics,* vol. 23 (1973), pp. 3–11.

———, *The Jamestown Voyages Under the First Charter, 1606–1609* . . . 2 vols., Cambridge: for the Hakluyt Society at the University Press, 1969.

———, "Ocanahowan and Recently Discovered Linguistic Fragments of Southern Virginia, c. 1650," in *Papers of the Seventh Algonquian Conference, 1975,* ed. William Cowan, Ottawa: Carleton University, 1976, pp. 2–17.

Barton, Lew, *The Most Ironic Story in American History: An Authoritative, Documented History of the Lumbee Indians of North Carolina,* Pembroke, N.C.: Associated Printing Corp., 1967.

Baxter, James Phinney, "Raleigh's Lost Colony," *New England Magazine,* VII (January 1895), pp. 564–87.

Beauchamp, William M., *Indian Names in New York, with a Selection from Other States,* Fayetteville, N.Y.: Recorder Office, 1893.

Betts, R. E., "Raleigh's Lost Colony," *Cornhill Magazine,* CLVIII (1938), pp. 50–67.

Binford, Lewis, "Comments on the 'Siouan problem,'" *Ethnohistory,* vol. 6, no. 1 (1959), pp. 28–41.

———, "An Ethnohistory of the Nottoway, Meherrin and Weanock Indians of Southeastern Virginia," *Ethnohistory,* vol. 14, nos. 3–4 (1967), pp. 103–218.

Bond, C. Lawrence, *Native Names of New England Towns and Villages; Translating 199 Names* . . . Topsfield, Mass.: N.P., 2d edition, 1993.

Bowen, Benjamin F., *America Discovered by the Welsh in 1170 A.D.,* Philadelphia: J. B. Lippincott, 1876.

Boyce, Douglas, "Iroquoian Tribes of the Virginia–North Carolina Coastal Plain," in *Handbook of North American Indians,* vol. 15, ed. Bruce G. Trigger, Washington, D.C.: Smithsonian Institution, 1978, pp. 282–9.

Brasser, Ted J., "Early Indian-European Contacts," in *Handbook of North American Indians,* ed. Bruce G. Trigger, vol. 15, Washington, D.C.: Smithsonian Institution, 1978, pp. 78–88.

Brinton, Daniel G., and Albert S. Anthony, (ed.), *A Lenapé-English Dictionary,* from an anonymous manuscript in the Archives of the Moravian Church at Bethlehem, Pennsylvania, Philadelphia: Historical Society of Pennsylvania, 1888.

Brown, Alexander, *The Genesis of the United States,* 2 vols., Boston: Houghton Mifflin, 1890.

Bushnell, David, "Discoveries Beyond the Appalachian Mountains in September, 1671," *American Anthropologist,* vol. 9 (1907), pp. 45–56.

———, "The Five Monocan Towns in Virginia, 1607," *Smithsonian Miscellaneous Collections,* vol. 82, no. 12 (1930), pp. 1–38.

———, "Virginia Before Jamestown," *Smithsonian Miscellaneous Collections,* vol. 100 (1940), pp. 125–58.

———, "Virginia — From Early Records," *American Anthropologist,* vol. 9 (1907), pp. 31–44.

Carpenter, P. Albert, III, *Metallic Mineral Deposits of the Carolina Slate Belt,* Raleigh: N.C. Dept. of Environment, Health, and Natural Resources, Division of Land Resources, Geological Survey Section, Bulletin 84, 1993.

Cook, E. R., and K. Kariutskis, *Methods of Dendrochronology,* New York: Springer-Verlag, 1990.

Cotten, Sallie Southall, *The White Doe: The Fate of Virginia Dare: An Indian Legend,* Philadelphia: J. B. Lippincott, 1901.

Demos, John, *The Unredeemed Captive: A Family Story from Early America,* New York: Knopf, 1994.

De Vorsey, Louis, Jr., "Amerindian Contributions to the Mapping of North America: A Preliminary View," *Imago Mundi,* vol. 30 (1978), pp. 71–8.

———, "Silent Witnesses: Native American Maps," *Georgia Review,* vol. XLVI, no. 4 (1992), pp. 709–26.

Dial, Adolph, and David K. Eliades, *The Only Land I Know: A History of the Lumbee Indians,* San Francisco: Indian Historian Press, 1975.

Dorsey, James Owen, and John R. Swanton, *A Dictionary of the Biloxi and Ofo Languages,* BAE Bulletin 47, Washington: Government Printing Office, 1912.

Durant, David, *Ralegh's Lost Colony: The Story of the First English Settlement in America,* New York: Atheneum, 1981.

Faux, J. Frederick, "An 'Abundance of Blood Shed On Both Sides': England's First Indian War, 1609–14," *The Virginia Magazine of History and Biography,* vol. 98, no. 1 (1990), pp. 3–54.

Feder, Norman, *Copper and the Indian,* leaflet 75–6, Denver: Denver Art Museum, 1933.

———, *The Virginia Indian Tribes: 17th century names, locations and population,* Leaflet 57, Denver: Denver Art Museum, 1933.

Feest, Christian F., "North Carolina Algonquians," in *Handbook of North American Indians,* ed. Bruce G. Trigger, vol. 15, Washington, D.C.: Smithsonian Institution, 1978, pp. 271–81.

———, "Seventeenth Century Virginia Algonquian Population Estimates," *Archaeological Soc. of Va. Quarterly Bulletin,* 28–29, vol. 28, no. 2 (1973), pp. 66–79.

Fenton, William, "Northern Iroquoian Culture Patterns," in *Handbook of North American Indians,* ed. Bruce G. Trigger, vol. 15, Washington, D.C.: Smithsonian Institution, 1978, pp. 296–321.

Frachtenberg, Leo J., "Contributions to a Tutelo Vocabulary," *American Anthropologist,* vol. 15, no. 3 (1913), pp. 477–9.

Gallatin, Albert, "A Synopsis of the Indian Tribes . . ." *Archaeologia Americana: Transactions and Collections of the American Antiquarian Society,* vol. 2, 1836.

Gerard, William, "Some Virginia Indian Words," *American Anthropologist,* vol. 7 (1905), pp. 222–49.

———, "The Tapehanek Dialect of Virginia," *American Anthropologist,* vol. 6 (1904), pp. 313–30.

Gilliam, Charles, "Note on Monocan," *Names,* vol. 18 (1970), p. 324.

Goad, Sharon J., "Exchange Networks in the Prehistoric Southeastern United States," Ph.D. Dissertation, Dept. of Anthropology, University of Georgia (Athens), 1978.

Goddard, Ives, "[Review of] An Indian Vocabulary from Ft. Christanna," *International Journal of American Linguistics,* vol. 38 (1972), p. 220.

Greenwood, Isaac J., *The Reverend Morgan Jones and the Welsh Indians of Virginia,* Boston: David Clapp, 1898.

Haag, William G., *The Archaeology of Coastal North Carolina,* Baton Rouge: Louisiana State University Press, 1958.

Hale, Horatio, "The Tutelo Tribe and Language," *Proceedings of the American Philosophical Society,* vol. XXI, no. 114 (1883), pp. 1–47.

Harrington, John, "Archeological Explorations at Fort Raleigh National Historic Site," *North Carolina Historical Review,* vol. XXVI, no. 2 (April 1949).

———, "The Original Strachey Vocabulary of the Virginia Indian Language," *Anthropological Papers,* no. 46, Washington, D.C.: Government Printing Office, 1955.

Hawks, Francis L., *History of North Carolina,* 2 vols., Fayetteville, N.C.: E. J. Hale, 1857.

Hodge, Frederick Webb, *Handbook of American Indians North of Mexico,* 2 vols., BAE Bulletin no. 30, Washington, D.C.: Government Printing Office, 1907–10.

Howe, Charles K., *Solving the Riddle of the Lost Colony,* Beaufort, N.C.: M. P. Skarren, 1947.

Hudson, Charles, et al., "The Tristan de Luna Expedition, 1559–61," in *First Encounters: Spanish Explorations in the Caribbean and the United States, 1492–1570,* ed. Jerald T. Milanich and Susan Milbrath, Gainesville: University of Florida Press, 1991, pp. 119–34.

Hurst, Vernon J., and Lewis H. Larson, "On the Source of Copper at the Etowah Site, Georgia," *American Antiquity*, vol. 24, no. 2 (1958), pp. 177–81.

Johnson, Basil, *Ojibway Ceremonies*, Lincoln: University of Nebraska Press, 1990.

Kupperman, Karen Ordahl, *Roanoke: the Abandoned Colony*, Totowa, N.J.: Rowman & Allanheld, 1984.

Laland, Patricia, "John White and the Lost Colony," *Early American Life* (October 1997).

Lauber, Almon Wheeler, *Indian Slavery in Colonial Times Within the Present Limits of the United States*, New York: Columbia University, 1913.

Lefler, Hugh Talmage, and Albert Ray Newsome, *North Carolina: The History of a Southern State*, Chapel Hill: University of North Carolina Press, 1954.

Lewis, Clifford, and Albert Loomie, *The Spanish Jesuit Mission in Virginia, 1570–2*, Chapel Hill: University of North Carolina Press for the Virginia Historical Society, 1953.

Lowery, Woodbury, *The Spanish Settlements Within the Present Limits of the United States, 1513–1561*, 2 vols., New York: Russell & Russell, 1959.

McCary, Ben C., *Indians in Seventeenth-Century Virginia*, Charlottesville: University Press of Virginia for the Virginia 350th Anniversary Celebration Corp., 10th edition, 1990.

McMillan, Hamilton, *Sir Walter Raleigh's Lost Colony* . . . Wilson, N.C.: Advance Presses, 1888.

Martin, François Xavier, *History of North Carolina, from the Earliest Period*, 2 vols., New Orleans: A. T. Penniman, 1829.

Michelson, Truman, "The Linguistic Classification of Powhatan," *American Anthropologist*, vol. 35, no. 3 (1933), p. 549.

Miller, Carl F., "Revaluation of the Eastern Siouan Problem, with Particular Emphasis on the Virginia Branches — the Occaneechi, the Saponi and the Tutelo," BAE Bulletin 164, Washington, D.C.: Government Printing Office, 1957.

Mook, Maurice, "Algonkian Ethnohistory of the Carolina Sound," *Journal of Washington Academy of Sciences*, vol. 34, nos. 6 and 7 (1944), pp. 181–97, 213–28.

———, "The Anthropological Position of the Indian Tribes of Tidewater Virginia," *William and Mary Quarterly*, 2d ser., XXIII (1943), pp. 27–40.

———, "Virginia Ethnology from an Early Relation," *William and Mary Quarterly*, vol. 23, no. 2, 2d ser. (1943), pp. 101–29.

Mooney, James, "Siouan Tribes of the East," BAE Bulletin 22, Washington, D.C.: Government Printing Office (1894), pp. 5–100.

Morgan, Lewis Henry, "Indian Migrations," *North American Review*, CX, Boston, 1870.

———, *Ancient Society, or Researches in the Lines of Human Progress from Savagery through Barbarism to Civilization*, New York: Henry Holt, 1877.

Myer, William E., "Indian Trails of the Southeast," BAE Annual Report 42, 1924–5, Washington, D.C.: Government Printing Office (1928), pp. 727–857.

Nash, Thomas Palmer, Jr., "On the Trail of the Lost Colony: Discoveries Which Suggest that 'Croatoan' was Nag's Head," *North Carolina Review*, supplementary section of the Sunday edition of the *News and Observer*, Raleigh, North Carolina (November 5, 1911), p. 5.

Painter, Floyd E., "The Last of the Nottoway," *Archaeology Society of Virginia*, Quarterly Bulletin, vol. 15, no. 4 (1961), pp. 34–8.

Parramore, Thomas, and Barbara Parramore, *Looking for the "Lost Colony,"* Raleigh: Tanglewood Press, 1984.

Paschal, Herbert, *The Tuscarora Indians in North Carolina*, Chapel Hill: Master's Thesis, Dept. of History, University of North Carolina, 1953.

Pearson, Bruce L., *Shawnee Language Dictionary*, Columbia, S.C.: Yorkshire Press for the Absentee Shawnee Tribe of Oklahoma, 1995.

Phelps, David S., *Archeological Studies in the Northern Coastal Zone of North Carolina*, Raleigh, N.C.: Archeological Council Publication no. 6, 1978.

Powell, William S., *John Pory, 1572–1636: The Life and Letters of a Man of Many Parts*, Chapel Hill: University of North Carolina Press, 1977.

Quinn, David Beers, *The Lost Colonists, Their Fortune and Probable Fate*, Raleigh, N.C.: Dept. of Cultural Resources, 1984.

———, *The Roanoke Voyages, 1584–1590: Documents to Illustrate the English Voyages to North America Under the Patent Granted to Walter Raleigh in 1584*, 2 vols., New York: Dover Publications, Inc., 1991; orig. published London: Hakluyt Society, 2d ser., CIV, 1955.

———, *Set Fair for Roanoke: Voyages and Colonies, 1584–1606*, Chapel Hill: University of North Carolina Press, 1985.

Reynolds, Henry Lee, "Algonkin Metal-Smiths," *American Anthropologist*, vol. 1, October 1888.

Rickard, Thomas A., "The Use of Native Copper by the Indigenes of North America," *Journal of the Royal Anthropological Institute of Great Britain and Ireland*, LXIV (1934), pp. 265–87.

Rights, Douglas, *The American Indian in North Carolina*, Durham, N.C.: Duke University Press, 1947.

———, "The Lost Colony Legend," *Bulletin of the Archaeological Society of North Carolina*, vol. 1, no. 2 (September 1934), pp. 3–7.

———, "The Trading Path to the Indians," *Bulletin of the Archaeological Society of North Carolina*, vol. II, no. 2 (1935), pp. 8–24.

Robinson, Melvin, *Riddle of the Lost Colony*, New Bern, N.C.: Owen G. Dunn, 1946.

Rountree, Helen, *Pocahontas's People: The Powhatan Indians of Virginia through Four Centuries*, Norman: University of Oklahoma Press, 1990.

Salwen, Bert, "Indians of Southern New England and Long Island: Early Period," in *Handbook of North American Indians,* ed. Bruce G. Trigger, vol. 15, Washington, D.C.: Smithsonian Institution, 1978, pp. 160–76.

Sams, Conway, *The Conquest of Virginia: The First Attempt . . . Being an Account of Sir Walter Raleigh's Colony on Roanoke Island,* Norfolk, Va.: Keyser-Doherty Printing Corp., 1924.

Saunders, William (ed.), *The Colonial Records of North Carolina,* 10 vols., Raleigh: P. M. Hale, State Printer, 1886–90.

Sapir, Edward A., "A Tutelo Vocabulary," *American Anthropologist,* vol. 15, no. 2 (1913), pp. 295–7.

Schoolcraft, Henry Rowe, *Historical and Statistical Information Respecting the History, Condition, and Prospects of the Indian Tribes of the United States,* 6 vols., Philadelphia: Lippincott, Grambo, 1851–7.

Siebert, Frank T., Jr., "Resurrecting Virginia Algonquian from the Dead," in *Studies in Southeastern Indian Languages,* ed. J. M. Crawford, Athens: University of Georgia Press, 1975.

———, "Proto-Algonquian na:tawe:wa 'massasauga': Some False Etymologies and Alleged Iroquoian Loanwords," *Anthropological Linguistics,* vol. 38, no. 4 (1996), pp. 635–42.

Silver, Timothy, *A New Face on the Countryside: Indians, Colonists, and Slaves in South Atlantic Forests, 1500–1800,* Cambridge: Cambridge University Press, 1990.

Smith, Marvin, "Indian Responses to European Contact: the Coosa example," in *First Encounters: Spanish Explorations in the Caribbean and the United States, 1492–1570,* ed. Jerald T. Milanich and Susan Milbrath, Gainesville: University of Florida Press, 1991, pp. 135–49.

Speck, Frank, "The Ethnic Position of the Southeastern Algonkian," *American Anthropologist,* vol. 26 (1924), pp. 184–200.

———, *Chapters on the Ethnology of the Powhatan Tribes of Virginia,* Indian Notes and Monographs 1 (5), New York: Museum of the American Indian, Heye Foundation, 1928.

———, "Siouan Tribes of the Carolinas as Known from Catawba, Tutelo, and Documentary Sources," *American Anthropologist,* vol. 37, no. 2, pt. 1 (1935), pp. 201–25.

———, "Siouan Words," *Journal of the Washington Academy of Sciences,* vol. 14, no. 3 (1924), pp. 303–6.

———, "Tutelo Rituals: Aboriginal Carolina Cultural History Revealed in Canadian Research," *Archaeological Society of North Carolina,* vol. II, no. 2 (1935), pp. 1–7.

Speck, Frank, and C. E. Schaffer, "Catawba Kinship and Social Organization with a Resumé of Tutelo Kinship Terms," *American Anthropologist,* vol. 44 (1942), pp. 555–75.

Stahle, David W. et al., "The Lost Colony and Jamestown Droughts," *Science,* vol., 280 (April 24, 1998), pp. 564–7.

Stick, David, *Roanoke Island: The Beginnings of English America,* Chapel Hill: University of North Carolina Press for America's 400th Anniversary Committee, 1983.

Stith, William, *The History of the First Discovery and Settlement of Virginia . . .* Williamsburg, Va.: William Parks, 1747.

Stitt, Edward Walmsley, *The Lost Colony,* New Bern, N.C.: Owen G. Dunn, 1946.

Stokes, M. A., and T. L. Smiley, *Introduction to Tree-Ring Dating,* Tucson: University of Arizona Press, 1996.

Sturtevant, William, "Siouan Languages in the East," *American Anthropologist,* LX, no. 2 (1958), pp. 738–43.

Swanton, John, *The Indian Tribes of North America,* BAE Bulletin 145, Washington, D.C.: Government Printing Office, 1952.

———, *Indians of the Southeastern United States,* BAE Bulletin 137, Washington, D.C.: Government Printing Office, 1946.

Tisdale, John W., *The Story of the Occoneechees,* Richmond, Va.: Dietz Press, 1953.

Tooker, William, *The Algonquian Names of the Siouan Tribes of Virginia,* New York: Francis P. Harper, 1901.

———, "Discovery of Chaunis Temoatan," *American Antiquarian,* XVII, no. 1 (1895), pp. 2–15.

———, "Meaning of the Name Anacostia," *American Anthropologist,* VII (1894), p. 392.

———, *The Names Chickahominy, Pamunkey, and the Kuskarawaokes of Captain John Smith,* New York: Francis P. Harper, 1901.

———, "Origin of the Name Chesapeake," *Virginia Magazine of History and Biography,* no. 3 (1895), pp. 86–8.

———, *The Names Susquehanna and Chesapeake,* New York: Francis P. Harper, 1901.

Trumbull, James, *Natick Dictionary,* BAE Bulletin 25, Washington, D.C.: Government Printing Office, 1903.

Vaughan, Alden, *American Genesis: Captain John Smith and the Founding of Virginia,* Boston: Little, Brown, 1975.

Waselkov, Gregory A., "Indian Maps of the Colonial Southeast," in *Powhatan's Mantle: Indians in the Colonial Southeast,* ed. Peter Wood et al., Lincoln: University of Nebraska Press, 1989.

Weeks, Stephen Beauregard, *The Lost Colony of Roanoke: Its Fate and Survival,* New York: Knickerbocker Press, 1891.

Winston, Sanford, "Indian Slavery in the Carolina Region," *Bulletin of the Archaeological Society of North Carolina,* vol. III, no. 1 (April 1936), pp. 3–9.

INDEX

Alanson (French trader) 69–70
Albemarle Peninsula 266
Aldworth, Mayor Thomas 187
Alençon, Duke of *see* Anjou, Duke of
Alexander VI, Pope 145, 146
Algonquian language 241, 248, 249, 250, 252, 253, 258, 259, 270, 271
Allen, Sir Francis 199
Allen, Morris 260
Altamirano, Hernando de 84
Alva, Duke of 146, 147, 155
Amadas, Captain Philip ix, 15, 82, 93–4, 97, 98, 99, 108, 110, 128, 158
Anglican Church 43
Angulo, Governor Rengifo de 85
Anjou, François, Duke of (*formerly* Alençon, Duke of) 143, 156, 158, 174
Anne of Denmark, Queen of England 225
Antonio, Don, King of Portugal 33, 155, 158, 172, 189
Antwerp 146, 155–6, 158, 163, 172, 173
Appomattoc guides 237, 238, 240, 249
Aquascogoc 90–1, 93–5, 97, 130, 231, 266, 268, 269
Archdale, John 230, 232, 255
Archer, Gabriel 220, 245
Arthur, Gabriel 249–50
Arundel, Henry Fitzalan, 12th Earl of 143
Arundell, Sir John 103
Ashe, Samuel A'Court 245
Atkinson (a Walsingham spy) 85, 95, 96
Aubrey, John 137, 141, 203

Babington, Anthony 167, 175–7, 181, 183–4
Bacon, Sir Francis 97, 160, 198, 218, 227
Baffin Islanders 22–3
Bailiff, Thomas 165
Bailly, Charles 149–50
Ballard (plotter against Elizabeth I) 176
Bancroft, Richard 44
Barbour, Philip 246
Barlowe, Captain Arthur ix, 108, 128, 158, 229, 231, 234, 252, 265–6, 267
Batts, Thomas 260
Bennett, Mark 49
Berkeley, Governor William 238
Beverly, Robert 249
Bevis, Thomas 11
Bland, Edward 237, 238–41, 248, 253, 255, 257, 258, 259
Borgarucci, Julio 143
Brave 195–6
Brereton, John 207

Brown, Alexander 245
Browne, John/Brownists 46, 52, 215, *see* Separatists
Browne, Maurice 140, 156, 163
Browne, William 49
Brussels 146–7
Bry, Theodore de 26
Burchet, Peter 151
Burghley, William Cecil, Lord:
as Elizabeth's Lord Treasurer 143, 144, 151, 161, 166, 167
and Leicester 142–3, 166, 167
properties 24, 105, 167
and Ridolfi Plot (1571) 149, 150
as suspect in Roanoke sabotage 166–8
and Walsingham 143, 166, 168–70, 171, 172, 174–6, 188, 197
and Whitgift's treatment of Puritans 45
Butler, Richard 87, 233
Butler, Thomas 27
Byrd, William 247, 248, 256, 257

Cage, Anthony 49
Calichoughe 22–3
Cambridge University 45
St. John's College 43
Trinity College 43
Camden, William 139, 153, 165, 166, 170, 176
Carew, Sir George 200
Carey, Sir George 194
Carleill, Christopher 186, 187, 188
Carleton, Sir Dudley 210, 212
Carolina Slate Belt 244, 247, 251
Carrell, Denice 66
Cavendish, Thomas 81, 82, 84
Cecil, Sir Robert 168, 208, 209, 212
Challice, John 171
Champernowne, Henry 151
Chapman 125
Chapman, George
Eastward Hoe 210–11
Chapman, Master 127
Charnock, John 176
Chaunis Temoatan 114–15, 122, 123, 242, 243–5, 248, 253, 256
Chippewa, the 270, 271
Chounterounte, Nottoway king 237–40
Chowan River 230, 235, 245, 246, 247, 251
Chowanoc, the 112–14, 216, 226, 228, 229–32, 233–4, 235, 241, 251, 252, 253, 254, 255, 258, 267
Churchyard, Thomas: poems 21, 48, 70, 135–6
Cobham, Lord 149, 150
Cocke, Captain Abraham 5, 9, 10, 11, 14, 16, 18
Cockneys 33–4
Coffin, Master 127
Coke, Sir Edward 209–10, 212
Coleman, Robert 11
Coligny, Admiral Gaspard de 151
Colman, Thomas 11
Columbus, Christopher 110
Cooper, Christopher 53, 75
Cooper, Bishop John: *An Admonition* 43, 44, 45
Cope, Walter 105
Copland, Reverend Patrick 226
Coquonasum 268
Coree, the 232, 255
Cortés, Hernán 110
Croatoan 8, 14, 15, 16, 19, 63, 74, 119, 127–30, 132, 203, 228, 235, 263
Curle, Gilbert 177

Dare, Ananias 3, 5, 27, 74, 204
Dare, Eleanor (*née* White) 3, 5, 27, 70, 74, 77, 228, 261, 262
Dare, Virginia 3, 5, 9, 74

Dasamonquepeuc 15, 72, 73, 114, 119, 120, 130–1, 228, 229, 265, 266, 267, 269
Davison, William 178
Dee, Dr. John 21, 22, 24, 52, 148, 153, 154, 157, 158, 159, 188, 196
Dekker, Thomas 33
De la Warr, Governor 220
Digges, Thomas 153
Dodding, Dr. Edward 23
Dorothy 87
Drake, Sir Francis 67, 106, 122, 151, 155, 157, 159–60 186, 188, 189, 192, 194–5
Drexelius 141
Dyer, Edward 164

East India Company 61
Egnock 22–23
Elderton, Thomas: epitaph 34
Elizabeth 84
Elizabeth I, Queen 57 (quoted)
  and Burghley 161, 166, 167
  at Court 31, 139, 140, 142–4
  death 208
  and Dr. Dee 148, 153, 154
  and Drake 159, 160
  Hatton's passionate devotion 164–6
  and Leicester 158, 161 162, 163–4, 167
  marriage plans 143, 172
  and Mary Queen of Scots 146, 148–9, 157, 175–8
  popularity 30
  quells Northern Rebellion 148–9
  and Raleigh ix, 80–1, 136, 137, 139, 142–3, 160, 181, 184, 190–1, 197–200, 202, 209
  religious policies 43, 52, 169
  Ridolfi Plot 149–50
  and Spain 81–2, 145–7, 154, 155, 156, 159–60, 169, 171, 172–3, 196
  and Walsingham 171–2, 180–1, 182, 183–4, 197
Ellis, Anne (*née* Pory) 226
Ellis, Robert 226
Ellis, Thomas 226
Eno, the (Wainoke) 255–7, 258–9, 271
Ensinore 112, 117, 118
Eracano 268
Essex, Frances Devereux, Countess of (*née* Walsingham) 182, 189
Essex, Robert Devereux, 2nd Earl of 161, 189, 190, 191, 197, 198, 227
Essex, Walter Devereux, 1st Earl of 143
Eyanoco 242, 255

Facy, Captain Arthur 195
Fallam, Robert 260
Fernandez, Simon 54, 63–5, 66, 69–73, 75, 78–9, 82, 86, 131, 132–3, 135, 158, 163, 168, 171, 174, 185, 192, 193
Fleming, Abraham 86
Florida 6, 7, 24, 25, 52, 207
Fort Christianna 247
Frobisher, Sir Martin 22, 23, 152

Gage, Robert 176
Gallatin, Albert 254
Ganz, Joachim 81, 101, 111
Gascoigne, George 152
Gates, Sir Thomas 218, 219–20, 233, 236, 250, 256
Gawdy, Sir Francis 210
Gepanocon 236, 258, 259
Gerard, John 167
  Herball 26, 50
Gerard, William 265

Gifford, Gilbert 171–5, 176
Gilbert, Captain Bartholomew 208
Gilbert, Sir Humphrey 52, 71, 135–6, 148, 150, 152, 154–5, 156–7, 158, 186–8
Gilbert, Sir John 104, 152, 193
Giraldi, Francisco, Portuguese Ambassador 171
Glande, Darby 62, 66–8, 97, 132, 133, 207
Glastonbury Abbey 193
Golden Hind 155
Gonzalez, Captain Vicente 7, 67
Gosnold, Bartholomew 212
Granganimeo 97, 98, 108, 111, 129, 231, 266, 268
Great Trading Path 247–9, 251, 255, 257, 260
Gregory XIII, Pope 155, 157, 187
Gregory, Arthur 170
Grenville, Sir Richard ix, 62, 67, 82–8, 95–6, 103–4, 120, 127, 130, 159, 160, 186, 189, 193–9, 196, 234, 267
Grey of Wilton, Lord 136, 196
Guaras, Antonio de 149, 166, 171
Guise, Henry of Lorraine, 3rd Duke of 157, 178
Guise, House of 80, 148

Hakluyt, Richard 24, 79, 81, 97–8, 145, 146, 152, 153, 158, 187, 188, 190, 201
 Diverse voyages 54
 Principall Navigations 52, 53–4, 77, 121, 187, 267
 White's letter to 4–5, 18, 28, 77, 194, 204, 262, 263
Hakluyt, Richard ("the elder") 25, 106, 152, 154–5
Hall, Joseph: *A Common Apologie* 52
Hariot, Thomas 24, 71, 82, 87–93, 88, 99, 101, 110, 152, 207, 218, 241, 243, 258, 267
 Briefe and True Report of the New Founde Land of Virginia 26, 91, 94, 99, 100–3, 105, 107–8, 110, 111, 113, 117, 201, 229, 230, 233, 266–7, 268–9
Harris, Thomas 49
Harrison, Thomas 179
Harrison, William: *Description of England* 14, 140–1
Harvey, Thomas 108
Harvie, Dyonis 3
Harvie, Margery 3, 70, 226
Hatorask Island 8, 9, 10, 72, 73, 74, 87, 233
Hatton, Sir Christopher 143, 152, 161, 163, 164–6, 180, 182
Hawkins, Sir John 145, 146, 151–2, 188
Hawkins, Richard 207
Hay, Lord 210
Hayes, Captain 157
Heere, Lucas de 23, 24
Henry VIII 185
Henry of Navarre 173
Herllie, William 150, 175, 190
Hewet, Thomas 49
Hilliard, Nicholas 23
Hispaniola 69, 85
Hocomawananck 239–40, 253, 258–9
Hooker, John 188
Hopewell 5, 6, 7–12, 16–18, 20, 201, 202
Howard, Charles, 2nd Baron Howard of Effingham 195, 196, 197
Howe, George 3, 13, 55, 58, 73, 127, 130, 131
Howe, George, Jr. 74
Huguenots 24–5, 52, 147, 150, 151

Ingram, David "Davy" 54, 186, 187
Iopassous 268
Ireland 77–8, 82, 136, 148, 155, 199
Iroquoian language 249, 252, 254, 270

James I (VI) 148, 169–70, 208, 209, 210, 223, 225
Jamestown 212, 213, 214, 218, 219–20, 222, 223, 224, 225, 226, 229, 236
Jefferson, Thomas 233
John Evangelist 5, 6, 201, 202
Johnson, Nicholas 260
Johnson, Robert 219, 220–1
Jones, John 49
Jones, Reverend Morgan 256–7
Jonson, Ben 222
  Eastward Hoe 210–11

Kecoughtan 267
Kekataugh 267
Kelborne, Edward 11
Kelley, Edward (aka John Talbot) 11, 21
Ketel, Cornelis: portraits 22, 105
Knowles, Mayor Thomas 40
Kolstáhagu 251

Lakota, the 270, 271
la Mata, Antonio de 7
Lane, Ralph:
  as commander of Roanoke Fort 82, 95, 97*ff.*, 228
  and Grenville 84, 86, 95, 96, 104
  initial relations with Secotan 53, 90, 102–3
  and Leicester 164
  letters to Walsingham 86, 95, 96, 101
  obsession with copper mines and treatment of natives 108–9, 110–23, 232, 241, 242–3, 244, 268
  return to England 160, 189, 190
Lasie, James 57, 58, 61
Laski, Duke Albert, Prince of Poland 188
Laudonnière, René de 24, 25, 52, 54
Lawson, John 247, 255, 256, 257, 263
Lederer, John 247, 248, 249, 256, 257, 260
Leicester, Robert Dudley, Earl of:
  accused of poisoning opponents 142, 143
  and Burghley 143, 166, 167
  death 198
  and Elizabeth 141, 142, 153, 154, 158
  and Lane 164
  and Raleigh 190, 191
  as suspect in Raleigh's destruction 160–1, 162–4
  and Walsingham 168, 169, 170, 171–2, 182, 188–91
Lemnus, Levinus 136
LeMoyne de Morgues, Jacques 24–5, 28, 247
Lion 63–4, 67, 75, 76
Little John 5, 6, 18, 201, 202
London 30–9, 40–1, 42, 80, 159
London Company 212, 216, 218
Lopez, Blas 7
Lopez, Roderigo 143
Low Countries *see* Netherlands

Mace, Captain Samuel 207–8
Machumps 250, 255
Madox, Reverend Richard 174
Mandoag, the/Mandoak 111, 112, 113, 114–19, 215, 216, 219, 232, 234, 235–6, 237, 238, 241–2, 247, 251–60, 270–1

Manteo 3, 15, 63, 71, 72, 74, 80, 90, 108, 115, 117, 127–8, 234, 266
Marprelate, Martin 21
tracts 44–5, 46
Marston, John: *Eastward Hoe* 210–11
Mary I 168
Mary Queen of Scots 146, 148–9, 157, 159, 172, 175–8, 179
Mawde, Bernard 21, 171
Medici, Catherine de 151, 172, 174
Meherrin, the 239–40, 253–4
Menatonon, Chowanoc chief 112, 113, 114–15, 118, 120, 122, 230, 244
Mendez de Canço, Gonçalo 207
Mendoza, Bernardino de, Spanish Ambassador 154, 157, 186–7, 189
Mercator, Gerardus 156
Meteren, Emanuel van 153, 237
Minion 145
Monocan, the 213, 215, 232–3, 235, 242, 249, 251, 254
Mook, Maurice 265
Mooney, James 265
Moonlight 10–11, 18, 63–4, 73, 75–7
Moratico River 243, 245, 246
Muscovy Company 187

Narragansett, the 231
Nau, Chande 177
Naunton, Sir Robert 139, 142–3, 166, 170, 198
Needham, James 247, 249
Nelson, Captain Francis 214
Netherlands, the 80, 146–7, 150, 155–6, 158, 163, 172, 173, 174, 190
Neuse River 245, 246, 255, 257
Neusiok, the 232
Newport, Captain Christopher 5, 18, 212, 213, 214–15
Norfolk, Thomas Howard, 4th Duke of 148, 150
Northern Rebellion 148–9, 166
Northumberland, 8th Earl of 165
Northumberland, 9th Earl of 222
Nottoway, the 238–9, 240, 253, 270, 271
Nottoway River 245, 256
Nugent, Edward 96, 97, 121
Nugumiut, the 22–3
Nutioc 22–3

Ocanahowan 245, 246, 250, 255, 257, 258–9
Occaneechi, the 240, 249–50, 251, 252, 255, 259, 260
Occaneechi Island 249, 259, 260
Occonosquay 240
Ohanoac 113, 230
Ohonahorn 236
Okisko, Weapemeoc chief 99, 119
Opechancanough 214, 235, 267, 268
Opitchapam 267
Opussoquionuske 268
Ortelius, Abraham 152, 153
Osocon 121, 268
Oxford, Edward de Vere, Earl of 142, 165

Painter-Stainers' Company 22
Pakerakanick 246, 250, 252, 255, 257, 258, 259
Pamlico, the 231, 232, 235
Pamunkey, the 224, 267
Panawiock 245, 246, 258, 259
Paquype Lake 89
Parahunt 233, 267
Paris: St. Bartholomew's Day Massacre 24–5, 151

Parker, Matthew, Archbishop of Canterbury 44
Parker, Richard 45
Parkhurst, Sir Anthony 162
Parkinson, Marmaduke 260
Parmenius, Stephen 157
Parsons, Robert 173, 203
Paspahegh, the 212, 213, 214, 220, 224, 245, 246
Pasquotank, the 99
Patawomeck, the 268
Paulet, Sir Amyas 176
Payne, Henry 27
Payne, Thomas 27
Peckham, Sir George 186, 187
Pemisapan *see* Wingina
Penny, Dr. Thomas 26
Penry, John 21, 46
Percy, George 212, 213
Perquiman, the 99
Phelippes, Thomas 170, 176, 177, 179
Philip II, of Spain 79, 80, 145, 146, 150, 155, 156, 158, 159, 169, 172, 182, 209
Philip III, of Spain 209, 214, 218, 220
Piankatank, the 235
Pius V, Pope 146, 149
Pizarro, Francisco 110
Platter, Thomas 32, 196
Plymouth 63, 151
Pocahontas 224
Pochins 267
Poley, Robert 175, 176
Pomeioc 87–90, 130, 231, 246, 266, 268, 269
Popham, Sir John 210, 212
Port Ferdinando 8, 10, 16, 71
Portugal 145, 155; *see also* Antonio, Don
Pory, John 225–6
Poteskeet, the 99
Powell, Nathaniel 215–16, 226, 236–7, 258, 259
Powhatan Indians x, 212, 214, 219, 220, 221, 223–4, 226, 230, 232–7, 250, 253, 256, 267, 268
Puerto Rico 6, 66–9, 83–4
Purchas, Samuel 224
Pyancha 238

Quinn, David Beers 246, 265, 269
Quiyoughquohanock, the 216, 224, 267

Radcliffe, Egremont 171, 173
Raleigh (bark) 156
Raleigh, Carew 135
Raleigh, city of 27, 48–9, 66–8, 229
Raleigh, Sir Walter x, 24
- birth and early life 135–6, 150–1
- and Lord Burghley 161, 166, 167–8
- downfall 197–200, 203–4
- as Elizabeth's favorite 136, 137, 139, 141–2, 160–1, 181, 184, 190
- and Essex 161
- execution 225
- and Gilbert's expedition 156, 158
- and Hatton 161, 164–6
- *The History of the World* (quoted) 185
- in Ireland 198, 199
- knighted 80–1
- and Lane 95–6, 104, 160
- and Leicester 160–1, 162–4, 189–90
- opposes anti-Brownist bill 46, 52
- poetry 61, 199–200, 203–4, 212, 261
- rise to power 103

Raleigh, Sir Walter (*cont.*)
  and Roanoke expeditions ix, 3, 5, 25, 48, 49, 50, 73, 95–6, 103–5, 127, 133, 188, 200–202, 207–9, 218
  ships delivered to Drake 188–9, 194–5
  trial and imprisonment 208–13
  and Walsingham 161, 170, 178–9, 181, 182, 184, 188, 189–90, 227
  and war against Spain 81–82, 83, 106, 157, 158, 159, 196–7
  and White 21, 28, 58, 77, 192, 201–2
Randolph County 244–5, 248, 251
Rassawek 251
Rastell, John 185
Ravyn, John 185–6
Rickohockan 247
Ridolfi Plot 149–50
Ritanoc 236, 242–3, 255, 257, 258
Roanoke Island 5, 8–9, 12–16, 25–6, 72, 98, 99–100, 158, 256, 266, 267, 268, 269
Roanoke River 245, 246, 248, 252, 256
Robsart, Amy 143
Roe 195
Roebuck 87
Russell (a Walsingham spy) 84, 95, 96

St. Bartholomew's Day Massacre (Paris) 24–5, 151
Sanderson, William 200
Santa Cruz, Virgin Islands 64–5
Santa Maria de San Vicente 104, 189
Santo Domingo 160
  treasure fleet 7, 104
Saponi, the 249
Savannah, the 231
Savile, Thomas 54
Schoolcraft, Henry 254
Scotland 148
Secota 91–93, 130, 231, 234–5, 266, 269
Secotan, the 3, 58, 72, 74, 87–95, 97, 102–3, 111–12, 117–23, 207, 228, 232–3, 241–3, 252, 254, 255, 265–9
  agriculture and forest management 99–100, 101, 107
  cloth spinning 105
  deaths from disease 101–2, 111–12
  religious revival 106–7
Seneca, the 271
Separatists 43–6, 52
  colonists as 46–7, 49, 50–1, 52–3, 133, 202, 215
Shacco-Will 256, *see also,* Will, Enoe, 253
Shakori, the 255, 257
Sheffield, Lady Douglas 143
Shirley, John 225
Sicklemore, Michael 216–17, 229,–30, 231, 236
Sidney, Sir Philip 182–3, 189
Siouans, the 254, 255, 271
  language 249, 252, 254, 256, 258, 271
Sixtus V, Pope 193, 196
Skiko 115–16, 118, 120, 121, 244
Skinner, Ralph 11
Smerwick, Ireland 77
Smith, Captain John 213–17, 219, 221, 229, 230, 231, 232, 234, 235, 236, 245, 247, 255, 258, 267, 268
Somers, John 170
Spain/the Spanish 110, 145–6
  Armada 50, 106, 160, 192, 193, 194–5, 196–7
  and England x, 70, 81–3, 84–5, 105–6, 145, 146, 153–4, 155,

157–8, 159–60, 171–3, 186, 188, 201, *see also* Armada (*above*)
in Florida 24
Inquisition 50, 82, 145, 147, 197
invasion of Portugal 155
and the Netherlands 146–7, 150, 158
and the Roanoke settlement 6–7, 133
treasure fleets 7, 16, 104, 155
Speck, Frank 265
Spenser, Edmund 199
The Faerie Queene 199
Spicer, Captain Edward 9, 10–11, 63, 64, 73–4, 77–8
Stafford, Captain Edward 63, 66, 72, 78, 97, 119, 122, 127, 128, 130–2, 174, 228, 229
Stafford, Sir Edward 188
Stafford, William 178
Story, Dr. John 150
Strachey, William 222 223, 224, 233–4, 235, 242, 244, 250, 255, 258, 259, 268
Stubbes, Philip: *Anatomie of Abuses* 140
Surrey, Henry Howard, Earl of 185–6
Susquehannock, the 254

Tackonekintaco, Werraskoyack chief 216
Tar River 245, 246, 247, 252, 255, 256–7, 259
Tarleton, Richard 80, 191
Tatahcoope 267
Thames River 33, 42, 136
Theobalds (Burghley's estate) 24, 167
Throckmorton, Elizabeth 203
Throckmorton, Francis 157, 158
Throckmorton, Job 21
Throckmorton, Sir Nicholas 143
Thynne, John 163
Tiger 81–2, 83–7, 94, 95, 96, 97, 104
Timucua Indians 25
Todkill, Anas 216–17, 236–7, 258, 259
Tomahitan, the 251
Tooker, William 251
Tudor, Margaret 143
Turner, Edie 253
Turner, Reverend, of Wells 43
Tuscarora, the 232, 238, 239–40, 252, 255, 256–7
Tutelo, the 254 259, 260

United Provinces (Netherlands) 146–7

Valdés, Governor Diego Menendez de 6, 7, 67, 68
Valenciennes 147
Vaughan, Captain John 97
Verstegan, Richard: *A Declaration of the True Causes of the Great Troubles* 201
Virginia Company 221, 226, 227, 236–7
Virginia Council 218, 220

Wahunsonacock, Powhatan Emperor 214, 220, 222, 223–4, 225, 230, 233–4, 235, 255, 260, 267, 269
Wainoke, the 239–41, 253, 254–55, *see* Eno, the
Walsingham, Sir Francis:
birth 169
and Burghley 143, 166, 174
early career 169
and Elizabeth 170–1, 180–1, 182, 183–4, 197
and Fernandez 170, 185
and Gilbert's expedition 186–8
Grenville's letter to 104
and Huguenot uprising 150–1

Walsingham, Sir Francis (*cont.*)
interrogates Ingram 54, 186
Lane's letters to 86, 95, 96, 101
and Leicester 158, 163
and Mary Queen of Scots 157, 175–8
political agenda 169, 171–3, 180–2
and Raleigh 161, 163, 180–4, 189–90, 194, 198–200, 203
spy network 21, 153, 155, 166, 170–1, 182
Wampanoag, the 231
Wanchese 80, 87, 91, 108, 130, 234, 266
Waterhouse, Edward 260
Watts, John 5–6, 7, 194, 201–203
Weapemeoc, the 98, 110, 113, 114, 117, 119, 229, 231, 232, 233, 267, 269
Werowocomoco 214, 216
Werraskoyack, the 216, 224
Westo, the 231
Weston, Father 176
White, Cuthbert 27
White, John 21–2
as artist 22, 23–4, 25–6, 50, 53, 82, 84, 89, 93, 94
captured by French 195–6
disappearance 28, 204, 262
1584 expedition to Roanoke 128–9, 158
1585 expedition to Roanoke 82, 84, 88–94
1587 expedition to Roanoke ix, 26–7, 48, 57–8, 62–72, 127–32
letter to Hakluyt 4–5, 18, 194, 204, 262, 263
map 111, 241, 246, 247, 257, 266, 267
return to England (1587) 3–4, 19–20, 46–7, 50–1, 52–3, 75–9, 132, 192–3, 197, 198–9
return to Roanoke (1590) x, 4, 5–17, 200–203
Whitgift, John, Archbishop of Canterbury 45, 50, 51, 189
Wildye, Richard 49
Will, Enoe 255, 256, 257
William the Silent, Prince of Orange 146, 156, 158, 171, 172
Willobie His Avisa 99
Wingina (*later* Pemisapan) 86, 91, 97, 98, 102, 103, 111, 112, 113–14, 116, 118–19, 120, 121, 122, 130, 228, 231, 234, 265–9
Winstanley, William 170, 173
Wirtemberg, Frederick, Duke of 30, 33, 40
Wococon 86, 87, 95, 267
Wowinchopunk, King of the Paspahegh 214, 220
Wright, John 57, 58, 61
Wyandot, the 271
Wymark, Ned 225

Yeardley, Francis 253, 255
Yeopim, the 99

Zúñiga, Pedro de 214, 218, 220
map 214, 245–7, 258, 259